I0794539

LOVE AND LOSS AFTER WOUNDED KNEE

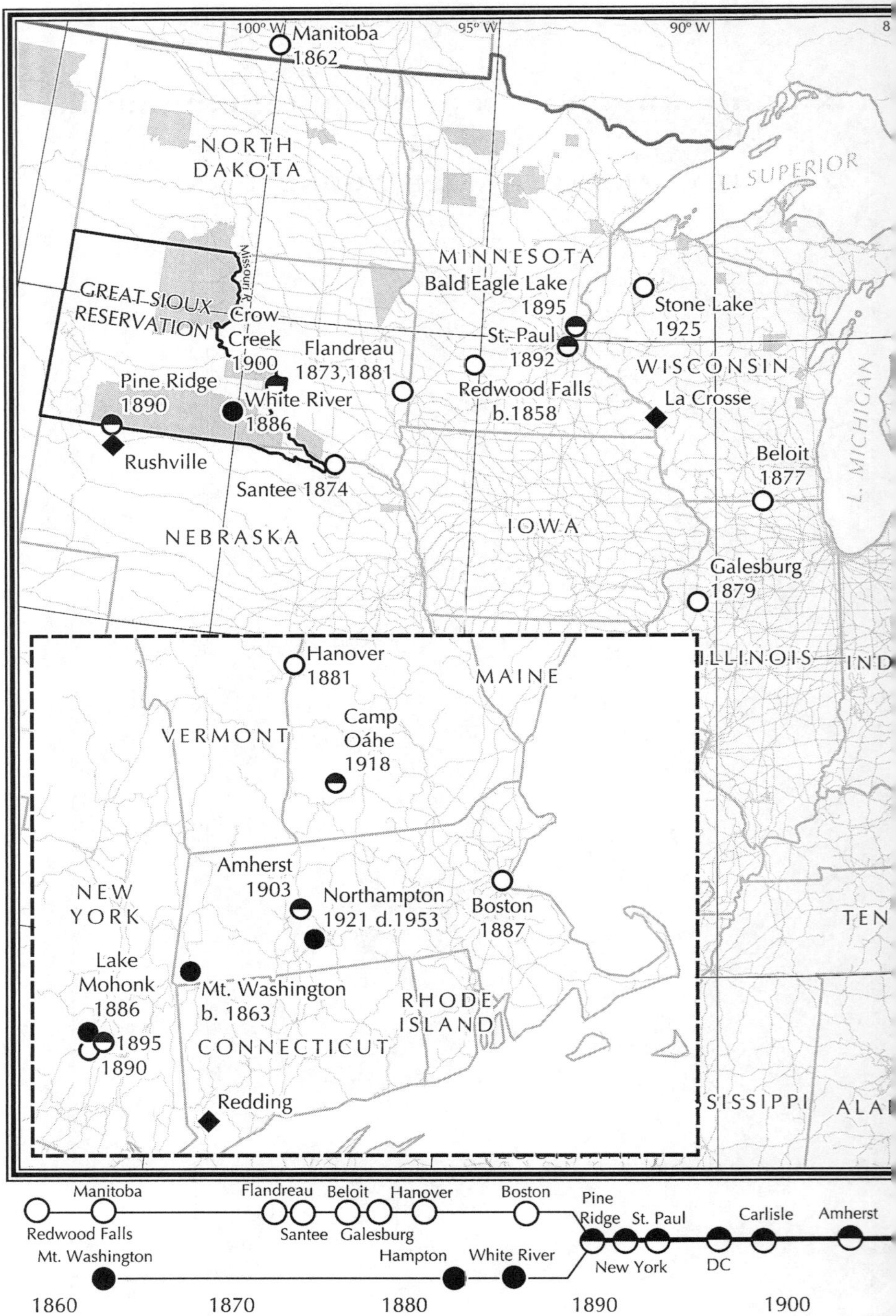

FIGURE M.1. Locations relevant to Elaine Goodale and Charles Eastman's lives. The timeline denotes places important to Charles, to Elaine, and to both of them. Based on data sets from Jeremy Atack, "Historical Geographic Information Systems (GIS) database of U.S. Railroads for 1900," Vanderbilt University; and "Historical Canadian Railroads." 2020, Cartography office, Geography Department, University of Toronto. Map annotations: Nick Allen.

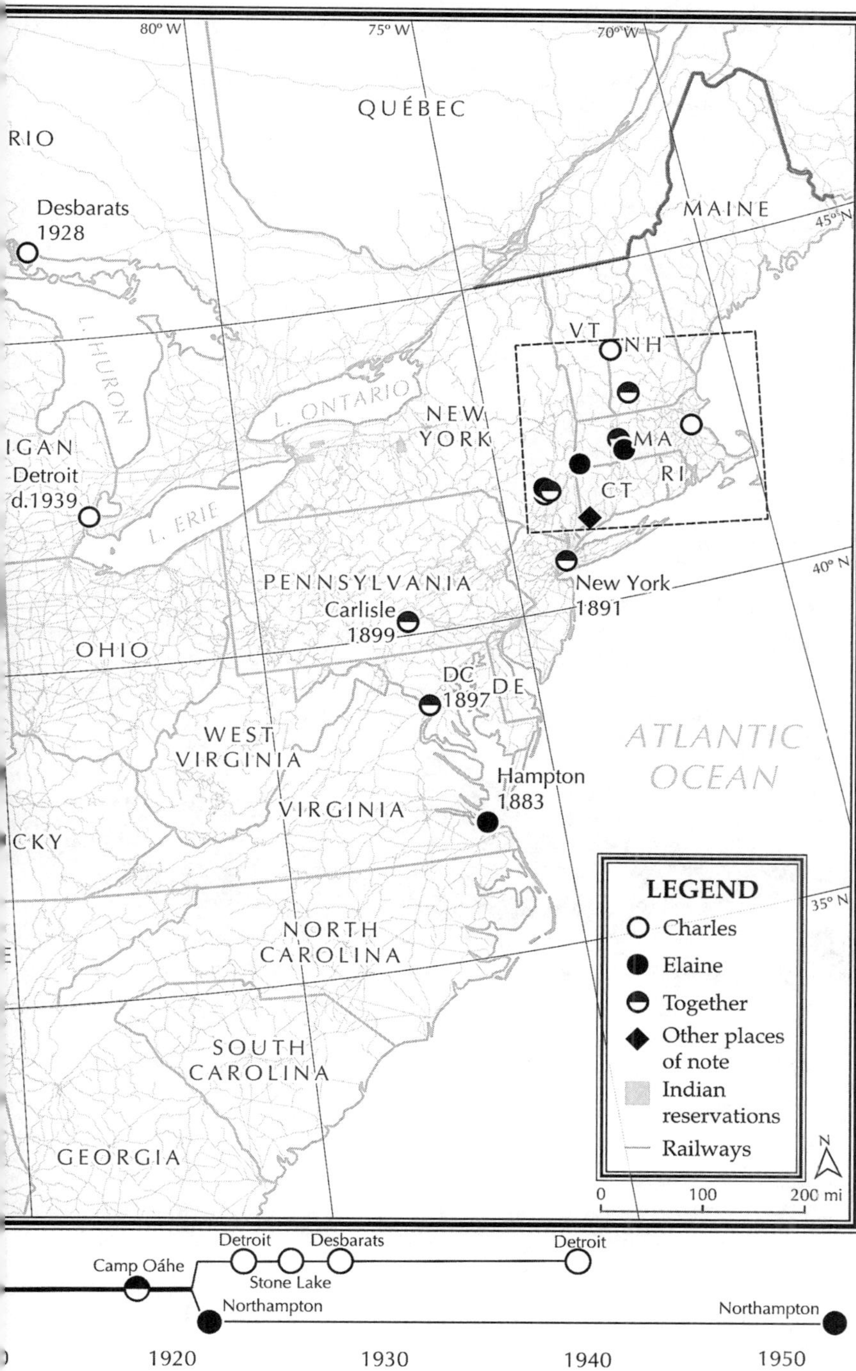

80° W
75° W
70° W
QUÉBEC
RIO
MAINE
45° N
Desbarats
1928
L. HURON
VT
NH
L. ONTARIO
NEW
YORK
MA
IGAN
Detroit
d.1939
RI
CT
L. ERIE
New York
1891
40° N
PENNSYLVANIA
Carlisle
1899
OHIO
DC
1897
DE
WEST
VIRGINIA
ATLANTIC
OCEAN
Hampton
1883
VIRGINIA
CKY
LEGEND
Charles
Elaine
Together
Other places of note
Indian reservations
Railways
35° N
NORTH
CAROLINA
SOUTH
CAROLINA
GEORGIA
N
0
100
200 mi
Detroit
Desbarats
Detroit
Camp Oáhe
Stone Lake
Northampton
Northampton
1920
1930
1940
1950

LOVE AND LOSS AFTER WOUNDED KNEE

A Biography of an Extraordinary Interracial Marriage

JULIE DOBROW

NEW YORK UNIVERSITY PRESS
New York

NEW YORK UNIVERSITY PRESS
New York
www.nyupress.org

© 2025 by New York University
All rights reserved

Please contact the Library of Congress for Cataloging-in-Publication data.

ISBN: 9781479837892 (hardback)
ISBN: 9781479837939 (library ebook)
ISBN: 9781479837915 (consumer ebook)

This book is printed on acid-free paper, and its binding materials are chosen for strength and durability. We strive to use environmentally responsible suppliers and materials to the greatest extent possible in publishing our books.

The manufacturer's authorized representative in the EU for product safety is Mare Nostrum Group B.V., Mauritskade 21D, 1091 GC Amsterdam, The Netherlands. Email: gpsr@mare-nostrum.co.uk.

Manufactured in the United States of America

Also available as an ebook

For my father, Dr. Alan Dobrow:

Avid reader, bibliophile, antiquarian,

western lore wrangler, incurable romantic—

who passed along his passions to me, and helped shape

this book in powerful ways

CONTENTS

PART III. SEPARATED BUT TIED TOGETHER

LIST OF FIGURES

FOREWORD

PHILIP J. DELORIA

In 1867, the Seneca military officer Ely S. Parker and the white Washington, DC, socialite Minnie Sackett fell in love and married, their cross-racial romance captivating and bewildering the national media. In 1930, my Dakota grandfather and my white, patrician grandmother fell in love. They married in New York City the following year and returned shortly after to South Dakota. In 1892, also in New York, the Dakota physician Charles Alexander Eastman married the white teacher and writer Elaine Goodale, a relationship that began with romantic love cast in a time of trauma and then solidified into a productive literary partnership with a social and cultural reach continuous to the present.

These marriages cannot have been easy. White Americans grudgingly admitted—while hesitating to accept—a long history in which white men married Indian women: in frontier situations, for instance, or to facilitate trade, or in communities already considered racially mixed. Those unions frequently proved expedient and temporary, for when white women arrived on the scene, Indian partners could be easily abandoned. Almost nowhere in this history was there room for the reverse situation, of Indian men marrying white women. Such a marriage was nearly unthinkable, for had not white men spent a great deal of energy justifying the killing of Indian men as necessary to the protection of white womanhood from racial contamination?

And yet. Ely S. Parker was a lieutenant colonel in the Union Army, military secretary to Ulysses Grant (with his outstanding handwriting, he recorded the terms of surrender at Appomattox), and the first Native American commissioner of Indian Affairs. My grandfather, Vine Deloria Sr., was an honorable mention All-American football player and an ordained Episcopal minister. Charles Eastman graduated from Dartmouth College and took his medical degree at Boston University. As Indian men marrying white women, they must have seemed relatively "safe": assimilated to American ways, embedded in American institutions, exemplars of genteel masculinity.

The three marriages unfolded in tellingly different historical moments. The Parker-Sackett union was generally seen as a freakish anomaly, a one-off that could be contained and explained; not in any way a model other couples might follow. My grandparents' marriage sixty-four years later might well have generated more unease, for theirs was one of several early twentieth-century unions between mixed-blood Indian men and white women, united by affection and thrown into ill-prepared social worlds as inclined to harden the boundaries defining miscegenation as to embrace tolerance.

The exceptional nuptials that opened the door to my grandparents' partnership? The union that made Americans think twice about the Parkers? The alliance that drew the concentrated attention of the entire nation? That extraordinary marriage was the one that joined together Charles Eastman and Elaine Goodale.

Eastman was one of the most interesting, unique, and accomplished Native people in American history, bar none. Medical doctor, writer, educator, organizer, and intellectual, Eastman lived through some of the most traumatic decades in Native American history. He experienced the consequences of the nineteenth-century Indian wars in their full horror. He survived within—and yet slipped the hold of—the American policy of assimilation. He devised strategies for Native survival and thriving within the confines of the modern United States. Though well-known in Indian Country, Eastman remains largely unrecognized within the broad frame of United States history. That ignorance is our loss.

Eastman did none of this work alone. Elaine Goodale Eastman was as formidable as her husband. A poetic child prodigy in an era when poetry mattered, with her sister she published her first book at age fifteen, with more to follow. A dedicated teacher at a moment when education offered one of the few possibilities for employment available to young women, she stepped boldly beyond the usual—a small local schoolhouse—to teach Native American students at Hampton Institute in Virginia. Unafraid to leave her Massachusetts home, she toured Dakota reservations and in 1886 began teaching at a reservation day school. By 1890, Goodale had been appointed superintendent of Indian education for the Dakotas. She continued a career in journalism and literary writing, working with Eastman on his many volumes, while crafting a range of articles and books of her own. In the late nineteenth century, both Eastman and Goodale had minor national reputations and separate lives. And then, against the backdrop of the devastating violence of the 1890 Wounded Knee massacre, they fell in love and married shortly after.

Their union ought to be considered a major cultural event of the era, a flashpoint through which later generations can grapple with the intricacies and challenges of American history writ large. This book, a joint biography of Eastman and Goodale, offers that opportunity, taking readers between the personal struggles of two individuals, the intimate triumph and disappointment they faced as a couple, and the tensions, constraints, and oppressions that pressed constantly upon them from all directions. In the end, Charles and Elaine Eastman could not keep their marriage alive, and its dissolution opens a window into these larger issues. Was Goodale truly open to Eastman's Indianness? Was Eastman as committed to the white world of America as he seemed? How much did her editorial skill shape his extensive writing? How much did his fame empower her?

Americans love to love-hate their Indians, and the occasion for doing so has too-often been limited to male leaders with compelling names: Sitting Bull, Crazy Horse, Geronimo, Chief Joseph, and Tecumseh, with Pocahontas and Sacagawea thrown in for good measure. Charles Eastman's name does not spring readily to that list. And yet, in their day, Americans could not look away from Charles and Elaine—in large part because of the proliferation of writing that sprang from their pens and typewriters: books and articles, but also speeches, youth education material, and even a summer camp for girls.

But the Eastman marriage also forced white Americans to face their own contradictions and hypocrisies. They had been pressing Indian people for decades to "civilize" and to "assimilate" to American society, devising policy after policy, and promising citizenship and maybe even something like equality. In 1819, Congress passed the first Civilization Act, and over the course of the next decades Indians were pushed to adopt plow-based agriculture on subsistence parcels, convert to Christianity, learn English, and adopt suits and dresses as their daily wear. In 1878, the first Native students arrived at the Hampton Normal and Agricultural Institute (where Elaine Goodale would teach), and the following year, the model of boarding school education was consolidated with the founding of the Carlisle Indian Industrial School, which in turn led to the creation of a host of other boarding schools across the country. In 1887, the General Allotment Act broke up collective landholding, forcing Native people to live on small 160-acre pieces of land—when those lands were not cheated from under them. Such policies—and there were many others—always based themselves on a promise to Indian people that there was a future for them in the United States, if only they would cease being Indian and join the American mainstream.

That vision had been articulated for Native people by Thomas Jefferson as early as 1803: "In truth, the ultimate point of rest and happiness for them is to let our settlements and theirs meet and blend together, to intermix, and become one people. Incorporating themselves with us as citizens of the United States, this is what the natural progress of things will, of course, bring on."[1] Surely there were few better ways for Native people to join in such incorporation than by becoming medical doctors and Christian ministers? In other words, Charles Eastman embodied a deep and powerful American challenge: As a Christian and a doctor, had he achieved a sufficiently "incorporated" status that he might transcend racial difference and participate in a vision of intermixing and equality . . . by marrying a white woman?

A different set of questions would be framed around Elaine Goodale: Explain yourself! Could a white woman have romantic desire for an Indian man? If so, was it something about her upbringing, isolated and largely homeschooled in western Massachusetts? Was it the pressure being exerted on gender and the "woman's sphere" by the suffrage and equality movements that had intensified following the Civil War? Was it a stubborn streak of transcendentalist thought or a language of racial equality that enjoyed a short moment before the violent downfall of Reconstruction? Or was it a personal quirk, a psychological question more than a social one?

We might well wonder how much the Eastmans were the products of their personal histories and the larger changes in American society in the late nineteenth and early twentieth centuries. But it is as important to see their relationship as a cause and to ask after its effects. In the early twentieth century, a small group of white Americans began to enact a curious reversal of their own past—or, if such a thing is possible, *two* reversals. The first of these inversions came out of the many and varied crises of modernity that set old familiar worlds spinning with anxiety. Rapid technological changes; influxes of immigrants; a draining of agrarian rural populations into the market worlds of the cities; weird expressive movements in art, literature, and music; new fields of study questioning the foundational premises of social and individual life; racial unrest: these challenges seemed to beg for a therapeutic sensibility looking for cures, restoratives, and alternate possibilities. That modernist group found such possibilities among Native Americans, and they worked to reverse more than a century of contempt, pity, and dehumanization, celebrating instead the exciting possibilities that Native life might have for the United States writ large—including a revitalized vision of Jeffersonian intermixing and amalgamation.

Americans had long understood Indian people through a triangle of key ideas: Indians were noble savages; they were destined by the "laws of nature" to vanish in the face of a superior society, even as the United States itself had a manifest destiny to overspread the entire continent. For over a century, Americans had mumbled the word "noble" and loudly screamed the epithet "savage"; now, they inverted those terms. In the years following the Eastmans' marriage, Native nobility became all the rage: Indian people had unmediated relations to a "nature" under threat; they had been spared the evils of the capitalist marketplace; they maintained authentic, visionary forms of spirituality. It was lovely to set up a corner of your house with baskets, pottery, and blankets, to remind yourself of these things. Savagery, too, was recast, signifying now the untouched purity of a people untainted by the modern world.

Charles Eastman found ways to position himself as a prominent voice, authoritative and appreciated, and it reminded him that there were virtues in being Dakota.

The non-Natives developing this belief system would become movers and shakers in the Progressive reforms that marked the twentieth century: future Indian commissioner John Collier, anthropologist Edgar Lee Hewett, literary muse Mabel Dodge Luhan, musicologist Mary Austin, youth advocate Ernest Thompson Seton, among many others. They wrote and inspired books, started museums, founded scouting organizations, and much more.

They would, in time, reverse something else: the decades of federal Indian policy based on assimilation and its legacies—Native cultures erased, religions and languages pushed toward extinction, tribal governance eliminated, Indian workers occupying the low rungs of the labor market. The people who originally devised those assimilation policies thought that *they* were being progressive and kind. They imagined that Native people could have no tribal life in the modern world, and that by transforming Indians, they were somehow saving them. One of those people—and one whose commitment to assimilation hardened over time—was Elaine Goodale Eastman.

If Charles and Elaine were formed in the cauldron of the 1860s and 1870s—the Minnesota Uprising, the Civil War, Reconstruction—and joined together in the violence of the last gasp of the Indian Wars and the assimilation era, they were reshaped yet again by the new world of modernist primitivism and new Indian policies and possibilities. That new world rejected a past to which the couple was tightly tied; their different responses to the changes would help unravel the knots and cords that bound together their union.

The story of Charles Alexander Eastman and Elaine Goodale Eastman must therefore be told across different registers. It is necessarily a biographical account of two individuals, each confronting their own subjectivities, the shaping of selves, the molding pressures of their world, and their unique responses to those pressures. At the same time, the story demands an intimate portrayal, a precisely anatomical treatment of a challenging marriage laid bare in its glory and pain. And how could it not be also a story of Native American history, of the trauma of war, flight, death, crushing repression, and resistant survivance? And, of course, it must also be a story of American history, in its broadest and most complex form. Julie Dobrow has told all these stories, melding together the biographer's sensitive vision with the historian's synthetic view. The result is both a portrait and a history, a psychological exploration and an argument, a tale with novelistic grace and revelatory conflict. It is, above all, a light shone on the collective ignorance of our American past, a restoration of something sadly lost: the story of two people whose lives illuminate our own, whose names deserve a place in our histories, whose courage and complexity might point to the possibilities of other futures.

PREFACE

The marriage of Elaine Goodale and Dr. Charles Alexander Eastman in 1891 was an event so unusual that more than two hundred newspapers from coast to coast ran articles about it. Newspapers abroad picked up the story as well. The *New York Herald* proclaimed the marriage "Poetry wedded to Science"; the *Boston Herald* stated simply, "The story of Dr. Eastman's fate . . . and of the romantic way in which he and Miss Goodale came to know and love each other, is interesting in the extreme."[1] Throughout their relationship the Eastmans would be subjects of countless other accounts in newspapers and magazines. The fascination with them came not only from the rare union of a white woman and a Native American man; not only because they both achieved early fame—she as a poet, and he as a Sioux, educated in Euro-American universities; and not only because the pair were writers, public speakers, and active in the Indian reform movements of the late nineteenth and early twentieth centuries. The fascination with the Eastmans was because they were part of a larger American story of change.

Between Charles Eastman's birth in 1858 and Elaine Goodale Eastman's death in 1953, the ensuing almost-century reflected tsunamic transformation in America. By the time of Charles's birth, the nation had become increasingly polarized and regionalized over opinions and policies about slavery; by the time Elaine was born, the Civil War tearing the nation apart still raged—that year an estimated fifty thousand Union and Confederate soldiers lost their lives at the Battle of Gettysburg alone. During the Eastmans' lifetimes, attitudes about race, influenced by theories of Social Darwinism and Euro-centrism, began to yield to attitudes tempered by cultural relativism, but tilted heavily toward a philosophy that Anglo-conformity and assimilation provided the optimal path forward for all people of color.

American policies toward Native Americans reflected these ideas. Indians were removed from their tribal lands, dislocated, placed on reservations, and forced to conform to ideas about land ownership that were anathematic to them. Christianization, education, and linguistic determinism attempted to get Indians to de-indigenize. Policies about food disbursement, health care, and governance enforced colonialist dominance and effectively made Native Americans wards of a state they never sought to be part of. Over the course of the Eastmans' lives, Indians were thought of as an inferior race needing to conform to Euro-American ways to survive; a race that would die out through conquest or intermarriage; as "noble savages"; as enemies; as obstacles to overcome; as quaint artifacts of an earlier era; as lost souls or heathens needing to be saved by Christianity; as icons whose distinctive practices could be copied as entertainment for Euro-American children in summer camps and scouting movements; as people whose cultures should be collected, commodified, and relegated to museums or sold to tourists; and as simple and childlike beings whose comity with nature was aspirational in an increasingly mechanized world.

As Ned Blackhawk asserts, such policies and ideas must be seen in the context of a mythology separating American history from Native American history.[2] The unending string of treaties made and broken, the notion that land could be owned and divided, and the displacement of thousands of Native children to boarding schools were policies underscoring the primacy of a Euro-American belief that they had *discovered* America rather than *encountered* it; that their cultures, religions, and languages were superior; and that only assimilation offered a path forward for those who were different. The America that changed so drastically during Charles and Elaine's lives was not, in fact, Native America—it was Euro-American America.

Ideas about gender, too, dramatically changed in the second half of the nineteenth century as growing numbers of American women received formal education. Dress reform and changing domestic expectations literally enabled women to do different kinds of things than they'd done before; expanding notions of the "woman's sphere" allowed women like Elaine Goodale to segue from poetry to journalism. A push for women's suffrage beginning in the late nineteenth century, paired with new opportunities for civic involvement, meant new possibilities for women's voices in reform movements of many kinds, and new forums for and definitions of women's agency.

America, itself, radically altered its identity over the course of the Eastmans' lives. There were three major wars, seventeen new states entered the union, twenty American presidents (Charles met five of them), and three times when the country roiled from presidential assassinations. The transcontinental railroad and discovery of gold in the West scattered the Euro-American population across three thousand miles and began to transform economies. By the time Elaine Goodale first traveled to the Dakota Territory in 1885, the frontier ideal was already fading; by 1893 Frederick Jackson Turner enshrined its significance in historical terms. Encoded in spectacles like Buffalo Bill Cody's Wild West Show and serialized novels, the idea of the West began to mythologize—and Indian Country's boundaries to dissolve.

Along with rapid industrialization following the Civil War, technological changes connecting dispersed spaces and disparate people transformed America. Time was standardized, different time zones created, watches and clocks made more affordable and their use more widespread, and workplaces governed by hours and marked by timecards—time, itself, meant something different by the mid-nineteenth century than it had previously. News disseminated more rapidly and widely; images became more easily captured so records of events, people, and places could be saved, transmitted, reproduced, and selectively altered to promote different ideologies. In the almost-century between Charles's birth and Elaine's death, the telegraph, telephone, film, radio, and television metamorphosed communication, information, and entertainment; the automobile and airplane radically altered getting from here to there; electricity brought light and heat to more American homes; penicillin modified medical practice; and the ballpoint pen altered writing. All these changes directly affected the course of Elaine and Charles's lives, and their own lives and work became symbols of how these changes, in turn, changed America.

After the Civil War, industrialization, the development of cities, and the influx of immigrants galvanized America. It became clear that people with discernible differences from one another—race, ethnicity, class—who had previously been geographically separated from Euro-Americans and whose distance was reinforced by policies keeping them largely separated, would begin to live in closer proximity, coming into increasing contact with each other. By the 1880s, intellectual theories and governmental policies, alike, reflected a view in which nonwhite peoples were considered inherently unequal but best dealt with by training them to become potential participants in American democracy through education. The union of Elaine Goodale and Charles Eastman was the epitome of this moment of Victorian optimism, the notion that virtue and devotion to duty could lay the foundation for a new society, bridging racial and social divides. Elaine and Charles believed, individually and collectively, they could integrate the past with the present, that their unusual marriage put them at the center of a struggle with prejudice and corruption and laid the groundwork for a new America.

Given these seismic shifts, it is not a surprise the marriage of a white woman poet-turned-teacher-turned-Indian-reformer, and an Indian doctor-turned-writer-turned-public-speaker of note, would garner so much press attention. Their unusual profiles and early achievements gave them some degree of celebrity before they walked down the aisle of the Church of the Ascension, and their writing and high-profile work ensured this focus continued as they strode forth in life. It's not shocking that Charles used his status as one of the most photographed Native Americans to selectively alter his image and messaging, or that Elaine optimized the bully pulpit of her writing to promote her ideas about reform. The Eastmans were savvy about the ways emerging media shaped image and opinion. They were the poster couple for change.

The story of the Eastmans' lives, their relationship, their marriage, and its dissolution, is in many ways a story set against and emblematic of a shifting American landscape. The stories of their lives embodied an America with morphing ideas about race and gender, an America with transmuting notions of what it meant to be an American citizen—who deserved to be one and how that would be expressed. The vision they shared early in their marriage of depicting Native American culture to a white Euro-American audience as a way of navigating their cultural differences and preserving Indigenous cultures in a changing world diverged as their relationship did. The beliefs they once thought shared about the best paths forward for Native Americans turned out not to be so mutual; Elaine's staunch assimilationist stance became more entrenched, and Charles's more acculturationist attitudes relaxed further as he leaned into his Dakhóta roots. Charles and Elaine's journeys into and out of Indian Country, as symbolic as they were actual, represented a vision of a Native America and of a United States of America familiar but unknown, entwined yet separated, inextricable yet never fully joined, just like Elaine and Charles themselves.

AUTHOR'S NOTE

Writing a book that is partially about race at a time of growing racial awareness has meant I've made some difficult decisions about the terminology I use. I have tried to be thoughtful and informed, while recognizing that words do matter and what is considered to be "correct" changes.

I use the words "Native American," "Indigenous," and "Indian." I have tried to use the term "Indian" only in its historical context. As Claudio Saunt points out, "Indian" often has "fanciful and specious associations" that distort our understandings of the peoples and roles this term identifies.[1] This word evokes a colonialist attitude and difficult, sometimes tragic polices. And yet because this term was used during the era in which my subjects lived, I have chosen to use it historically. I use the term "Euro-American" with recognition that during the late nineteenth century, many of the white people in America were European immigrants and American emigrants moving west, many of them taking over lands belonging to Native American tribes.

Although in 2025 the word "Sioux" can be considered a somewhat derogatory term, an abbreviation of *Anishinaabe Nadiwesioux,* at the time in which the Eastmans lived, "Sioux" was the umbrella term covering the linguistic groups of the Dakota, Lakota, and Nakota nations. Today the preferred generalizing term would be *Oceti Sakowin.* I use "Dakhóta" rather than "Dakota" when referring to contemporary times, since in many circles, this is the preferred spelling.

And regarding the spelling of Charles's Dakhóta name, in his own time he wrote it as "Ohiyesa," often relegating it to parentheses after his Euro-American name. I use the spelling Ohíye' S'a, believed to be an authentic transliteration of the Dakhóta, when referring to him as he would have been referred to as a boy. This would also be the preferred spelling today. I use "Ohiyesa" as Charles did in his own publications or the ways in which the press referred to him. Because he called himself a Santee Sioux, I have referred to him as such, although today it is likely a more precise designation would be made.

ABBREVIATIONS

ARCHIVES

Beloit: Beloit College Archives, Beloit, WI

Carlisle: Carlisle Indian School Digital Resource Center, Archives and Special Collections, Dickinson College, Carlisle, PA

Dartmouth: Charles Eastman Papers, MS-829, Rauner Special Collections Library, Dartmouth College, Hanover, NH

Jones: Jones Library Special Collections, Amherst, MA

Newberry: Edward E. Ayer Papers, Newberry Library, Chicago, IL

Smith: Eastman-Goodale-Dayton Family Papers, Sophia Smith Collection, Smith College, Northampton, MA

USC: USC Digital Archive, 2019, http://digitallibrary.usc.edu/digital/collection/p15799coll81.

Wisconsin: Katharine Martindale Family Papers, Wisconsin Historical Society Archives, La Crosse Area Research Center, La Crosse, WI

Wyoming: Grace Hebard Papers, Box 54, Folder 7, American Heritage Center, University of Wyoming, Laramie, WY

Yale: Mabel Loomis Todd Papers (MS 496C), Manuscripts and Archives, Yale University Library, New Haven, CT

PEOPLE

CAE: Charles Alexander Eastman; Ohiyesa

DRG: Dora Read Goodale

EG, EGE: Elaine Goodale Eastman

HSG: Henry Sterling Goodale

HM: Henrietta Martindale

KM: Katharine Martindale

RGD, RG: Rose Goodale Dayton

BOOKS AND THESES

America's Second Tongue: Ruth Spack, *America's Second Tongue: American Indian Education and the Ownership of English, 1860–1900* (Lincoln: University of Nebraska Press, 2002).

"Cultural Divide": Martha Viehmann, "Writing across the Cultural Divide: Images of Indians in the Lives and Works of Native and European Americans, 1890–1935" (PhD diss., Yale University, 1994).

Deep Woods: Charles Alexander Eastman, *From the Deep Woods to Civilization* (Boston: Little, Brown, 1916).

Final Promise: Frederick E. Hoxie, *A Final Promise: The Campaign to Assimilate the Indians, 1880–1920* (Lincoln: University of Nebraska Press, 1984).

Heartbreak: David Treuer, *The Heartbreak of Wounded Knee* (New York: Riverhead Books, 2019).

Indian Boyhood: Charles A. Eastman, *Indian Boyhood* (New York: McClure, Phillips & Co., 1902).

Indian Today: Charles A. Eastman, *The Indian Today* (New York: Doubleday, Page & Co., 1915).

Indigenous Intellectuals: Kiara Vigil, *Indigenous Intellectuals* (New York: Cambridge University Press, 2015).

"Journey": David Reed Miller, "Charles Alexander Eastman: One Man's Journey in Two Worlds" (MA thesis, University of North Dakota/Grand Forks, 1975).

Lakota America: Pekka Hämaläinen, *Lakota America* (New Haven, CT: Yale University Press, 2019).

Life: Theodore Sargent, *The Life of Elaine Goodale Eastman* (Lincoln: University of Nebraska Press, 2005).

Ohiyesa: Raymond Wilson, *Ohiyesa: Charles Eastman, Santee Sioux* (Urbana: University of Illinois Press, 1983).

Path: Stuart Reeve, *A Path from England to Lonetown: History of the Hill and Read Families of Redding, Connecticut* (Danbury, CT: Joseph Merritt, 2013).

Philosopher: David Martínez, *Dakota Philosopher: Charles Eastman and American Indian Thought* (St. Paul: Minnesota Historical Society Press, 2009).

Plains Indians: Jeffrey Ostler, *The Plains Indians and U.S. Colonialism from Lewis and Clark to Wounded Knee* (New York: Cambridge University Press, 2004).

Playing Indian: Philip J. Deloria, *Playing Indian* (New Haven, CT: Yale University Press, 1998).

Sister: Elaine Goodale Eastman, *Sister to the Sioux*, ed. Kay Graber (Lincoln: University of Nebraska Press, 1978).

They Met: Gretchen Cassel Eick, *They Met at Wounded Knee* (Reno: University of Nevada Press, 2020).

This Indian Country: Frederick E. Hoxie, *This Indian Country* (New York: Penguin, 2012).

Voice: Elaine Goodale Eastman, *The Voice at Eve* (Chicago: Bookfellows, 1930).

White Robe: Neil Schmitz, *White Robe's Dilemma: Tribal History in American Literature* (Amherst: University of Massachusetts Press, 2001).

Introduction

Wounded Knee (1890)

Who can pinpoint the moment two people fall in love? Sometimes love arrives unexpectedly, evanescent, like dust storms periodically filling the Western skies, sweeping in suddenly, darkening the sparse prairie landscape, gone almost as quickly, as unpredictably, as they arrive.

Elaine Goodale experienced plenty of dust storms in the four years she spent in the Dakota Territory. But she'd never experienced love until it suddenly enveloped her in December 1890.

Pine Ridge, South Dakota, was a long way from Elaine's birthplace, a farm outside Mount Washington, Massachusetts. She knew the journey that brought her to these lands white settlers were beginning to claim for themselves wasn't only geographic: she had crossed into Indian Country literally and symbolically. Despite her sheltered childhood, she knew the many untraditional personal and career choices that brought her to this place.

When Elaine arrived in Pine Ridge in her role as new supervisor of education in the Dakotas, she decided to accept the invitation from Reverend Charles Smith Cook and his wife to stay at their home. She immediately felt comfortable. Reverend Cook, an Episcopal missionary whose mother was a Yankton Sioux and father a white military officer, spoke both the Lakota language and English. Elaine, too, spoke the language of the Sioux, something she had considered necessary to better understand her students when she first came to the Dakotas as a teacher. Like Elaine, Reverend Cook was dedicated to his work with the Sioux. In the late days of 1890, Elaine wrote, he was "constantly busy—talking with police, army officers, press correspondents, going about the camps with food, medicines, partial help and religious consolation."[1] She understood why the minister felt so unsettled in the whirl of his many tasks. But knowing the language proved a mixed blessing these days: you couldn't help but hear Lakota people's anxiety as they discussed the tensions building all around Pine Ridge.

Despite the increasingly charged atmosphere, the Cooks decided to hold a tea to celebrate Reverend Cook's birthday. Mrs. Cook informed Elaine that she had invited the young ladies who taught in the school and mentioned that her husband had offered a special invitation to Dr. Charles Alexander Eastman, the young agency physician who had arrived in Pine Ridge a few weeks before Elaine. The newly minted MD was a Santee Sioux who'd graduated from an Ivy League college back East, spoke nearly flawless English, and had been hired by the Indian Bureau. Sioux people across Dakota Territory were talking about the handsome young doctor with his close-cropped dark hair, suit jackets, and ties.

Elaine listened to the conversations she heard with growing curiosity. "I had read of his college career in a chance newspaper clipping, had several times met his brother . . . and had looked forward with more than common interest to our meeting,"[2] she later wrote. The more she heard about Dr. Eastman, the more her interest piqued. Although Elaine's public facade was confident and assured, her personal dealings were anything but: Elaine usually avoided social gatherings whenever possible because they were trying for someone so reserved. She surprised herself, however, looking forward to the Cooks' tea party with a tingling anticipation she'd never known.

As soon as Dr. Eastman strode into the rectory Elaine became acutely aware of his presence. He walked up to her immediately, telling her by way of introduction he felt he already knew her from her work. Charles later recalled that Elaine "was not entirely a stranger, as I had read her *Apple Blossoms* in Boston, and some of her later articles on Indian education in the *Independent* and elsewhere."[3] To Elaine, whose writing had been an integral part of her

FIGURE I.1. Elaine Goodale and Charles Alexander Eastman before their marriage. Courtesy Newberry Library, Chicago.

identity since childhood, there could be no higher accolade. She blushed with pleasure.

The magnetism between Charles and Elaine was instant and undeniable. "It seemed that we were from the first mutually attracted," wrote Elaine. "Others have found me cold, distant in manner and unduly grave, but to him . . . it seemed as if I carried on my heart the sorrows of his people."[4] Charles later described himself as "caught up by the wind of destiny." He recorded of his first impressions of Elaine: "She was young for such a responsible position, but appeared equal to it in personality and experience. I thought her very dignified and reserved, but this first evening's acquaintance showed me that she was thoroughly in earnest. . . . Her personality impressed me deeply."[5]

In their conversations during the weeks that followed, the spark between them ignited. Improbably, these two people who had come from such different worlds had met. Implausibly, the young woman the influential magazine *Leslie's Weekly* later deemed "perhaps the shyest woman in America," who'd had so little exposure to romance, and the man who had been inducted into a social fraternity at Dartmouth and who Boston newspapers called "the hero of the Boston society girls, a Sioux brave," were drawn to each other in powerful ways.

They realized they had both grown up in isolated places and that their remove from "civilization" powerfully shaped their worldviews. Each found personal solace and professional direction from nature. Each believed, fervently, that education was the "master key" to a better life. Despite the vast differences between the situations in which they'd been raised, they found commonalities between their families: Charles had four siblings, and Elaine three. Both had grown up with a grandmother living with their families and playing an influential role in their lives. They learned they both felt more connection to their fathers than to their mothers.

As Elaine would discover, Charles, at thirty-three, already knew a lifetime's worth of tragedy and confusion. His early years were marked by familial death and separation, and more recent ones dominated by training at a series of boarding schools and colleges that gave him an impressive résumé but left him with many questions about how he could navigate between the Sioux world in which he'd been raised and the Euro-American world in which he'd been educated.

And as Charles realized, though Elaine's young life was filled with many accomplishments, she felt frustrated by what she considered her unrealized potential. Her success as a writer in different genres belied a belief that her writing had been limited by her inability to afford a college education. The streak of independence that encouraged her to leave her home in the rural Berkshire Hills to teach Native American students, undaunted by society's admonitions, left her frustrated by the Indian Bureau's bureaucracies, its male-dominated and Euro-American–centric ways.

But the intimacy of Elaine and Charles's developing connection was soon overshadowed by events that dominated their lives.

In the waning days of 1890, troubles fomenting on the Great Sioux Reservation seemed ready to burst. Tensions could not be higher. In an article published in *The Independent*, Elaine documented the escalating situation. "The unusual destitution of the [Indian] people, owing to a delay in the issue of clothing . . . the great amount of sickness, especially among the children . . . the vague terror and uneasiness everywhere existing among those who had taken no part in any rebellious action" all contributed to a growing sense of disquiet among the Sioux, she wrote. "The army was massing its forces in our neighborhood, the ghost dancers exciting one another to wilder frenzies, near at hand, the settlers fleeing from our borders in terror, and the newspaper correspondents filling the country with sensational alarms."[6]

And yet, it was almost Christmas. Elaine and others working at Pine Ridge felt perhaps their holiday preparations could help to ease some of the apprehensions they all felt and provide some measure of joy for the children suffering from chronic food shortages, poor health conditions, and the tensions all around them. Elaine and Charles spent evenings "fabricating candy bags and popping corn" and festooning the chapel with cedar boughs and ropes of evergreen. Their preparations would culminate in ornamenting a Christmas tree.

Before heading to the Christmas tree decorating party, Elaine paused. Never in her life had she given much thought to her appearance. Usually, she would forgo the popular hoop skirts and whalebone stays of the day for a simple calico dress and wear comfortable moccasins rather than lace-up boots. Tonight, perhaps, she wondered if she should depart from routine and wear something a bit fancier.

Elaine put on a new dress—brown, her favorite color, that she had sewn on a brief visit to Massachusetts the previous summer. She glanced briefly in the mirror, arranging her long, light-brown hair in a bun, with curly wisps she impatiently gave up trying to capture. They framed her delicate features.

As Elaine prepared to join the Cooks, Dr. Eastman, and others to finish decorating the rectory, she reflected on the magic of the past few weeks since she'd met Charles. She gazed out upon the falling snow. Winters on the Dakota prairies were harsher than the winters of her New England childhood.

But newly fallen snow always contained wonder. In one of her early poems to mark the arrival of the season's first snow, Elaine had written:

> Across the shadowy room I see,
> When, with the first awakening thrill,
> A message comes to me.
> Without, the cold grey hills stand fast
> Before the silver rim of heaven,
> Within, the shuddering night is past,
> And light and hope are newly given[7]

On this cold December day Elaine recalled her verse. Despite the growing tensions around Pine Ridge Agency, she saw newly given light and hope. She'd found that in Charles Eastman.

She pulled a shawl tightly around her and walked across the rectory to where the tree stood, undecorated. Elaine looked at the freshly cut pine and breathed in its strong scent, feeling all the possibility of the moment. Charles strode in and smiled. Somehow, they knew despite the differences in their background, despite the different worlds in which they had grown up, and despite the anxieties mounting all around them, they'd fallen in love.

* * *

On the morning of December 29, tensions that had been building around Pine Ridge Agency exploded as gunfire erupted. When it was over, 250–300 Lakota men, women, and children were killed or maimed, along with twenty-five U.S. soldiers, near Wounded Knee Creek. Beyond the carnage, this massacre was a turning point in U.S.-Indian relations. It marked a significant moment in the escalation of tensions between an American government bent on claiming Indigenous lands and Native groups struggling to retain them, an inflection point in the U.S. government's assimilationist efforts to curtail traditional Indian customs and Indian efforts to preserve their ways in a world that was rapidly forcing change. As historian David Martínez writes,

Wounded Knee "signaled the abrupt transformation of Indian nations from geopolitical powers . . . to symbols of conquest."[8]

The tragedy also marked a transformation in Elaine and Charles's relationship. They worked side by side, desperately—and often, futilely—to save the Sioux victims gunned down while fleeing for their lives. The massacre at Wounded Knee solidified their resolve to face the world as a couple, and to work together on behalf of Indian rights. "Events threw us together," Elaine wrote, but their connection was genuine.

The horrific events at Wounded Knee and its painful aftermath would have deep and long-lasting effects on U.S.-Indian relations. The massacre also had life-altering effects on Elaine, on Charles, and, ultimately, on their relationship. The tumult of Wounded Knee would prove to be a distressing metaphor for this union that started with such promise.

Over their years together the Eastmans navigated the complex boundaries of their individual and collective identities, crossing into and out of Indian Country geographically, personally, and professionally. During their lives they uneasily traversed the social and cultural issues surrounding their high-profile interracial relationship, one often documented by stories appearing in the press. They experienced career shifts and money problems, the joys and pains of parenthood, great achievement and significant failure. Charles steered an unsteady course between being widely known as an assimilated Indian and his own desires to reclaim and promote his Indigenous roots. Elaine never lost her passion for Indian rights work, but she also never lost the belief that assimilation provided the best path. Charles's progressive views on women's roles diverged from how he approached what women in his own family could do, while Elaine grappled with defining and retaining the agency of her own voice, torn between nineteenth-century gender norms and newly emerging roles for women in the twentieth century. The success Charles experienced in his career as a writer and public speaker contrasted with Elaine's more modest professional accomplishments, and her need to stay home and manage the lives of their growing family exacerbated the tensions in their relationship. The ideals they had seen in each other when they first met were tested by their lives, as well as by their individual and collective realizations about the constraints of the rapidly changing American society in which they lived.

Theirs is a story of two fascinating individuals, bound together by the same powerful cultural collision that would eventually tear them apart, swept up and propelled in their lives and their work by momentous historical events in U.S.–Indian relations. It is a story of deep love and deeper sorrow. The normal tensions in any marriage intensified in theirs with conflicts that went far beyond themselves, their personal lives acutely affected by the passing of broader national lifeways: with Native cultures challenged and suppressed, as debates raged about assimilation and acculturation, and as the world of the nineteenth century yielded to the twentieth. Two lives joined by one of the most iconic moments of the nineteenth century somehow split apart. And two people so well known in their own lifetimes all but disappeared from public sight, not unlike the dust storms they'd known in the Dakotas.

PART I

Coming Together

1

From Sky Farm to "Little Scotland" (1863–1883)

Below you warm and sheltering hill
A cottage nestles closer still;
And grandly would some castle rise
From heights like these to meet the skies;
Those be your thoughts, howe'er you come,
Who fails with land to make a home.[1]
—EG, "Land and Home" in *All Round the Year*

Tucked into a hillside, marked by a stone wall festooned with multihued nasturtiums, its walls, chimneys, and windows all but covered by flowering morning glories and trailing woodbine, the cottage in which Elaine Goodale was born and raised overlooked acres of plowed fields stretching beyond the front porch to the edge of the horizon, the trio of Mounts Darby, Sterling, and Whitbeck in the distance. The forest leading to Prospect Hill encroached right up to the house's far side. A visitor once wrote, "The whole aspect of the dwelling speaks of a home as much without as within, of a household at one with nature."[2] Nestled in a remote corner of the Massachusetts Berkshires, Sky Farm was aptly named: the morning mists hug the hills and fields, diminishing the boundary between earth and sky, creating an almost cosmic feeling of unity. Transcendentalist writers like Emerson and Thoreau traveled to nearby Bash Bish Falls and wrote ecstatically of the area's otherworldly, inspirational beauty. Sky Farm felt insulated from the rest of humanity, the nearest neighbor more than four miles away. Toward the end of her life Elaine recalled, "The hills were visible in a blue haze as far as Greylock but there were no signs of human occupation in sight. A lovely and cherished solitude!"[3]

FIGURE 1.1. Sky Farm's remains today. Photo: Larry Vale.

Elaine's father, Henry Sterling Goodale, sought solitude with nature when he set out on travels through the West and down the Mississippi River. Born in 1836, his health deemed too fragile to follow his older brother to Yale College and engage in a bookish life thought to lead to further illness, his parents sent him on a journey outdoors to strengthen his lungs. Upon his return to Massachusetts the young man hiked from the family home in Egremont in the southwestern corner of the state to the nearby tiny town of Mount Washington. As Elaine recounted the story many years later, on this walk Henry discovered a deserted Dutch farmhouse "facing a long slope of sunny meadow, at whose foot curled a singing brook. Beyond rose ample pastures, and a triangular gap in the mountain wall disclosed an eye-filled vista extending the full sweep of the county."[4] After his father purchased the ramshackle farmhouse and surrounding seven hundred acres for his youngest son in 1865, Henry named the property Sky Farm and began working the land depicted in the local *Berkshire Courier* newspaper as lying "high on the plateau of the Taconic hills, a full 2000 feet above tide level. Remote from the world . . . the hazy line of the Catskills makes the western horizon, with the shining ribbon of the Hudson at their feet."[5]

Elaine described her father's approach as "book-farmin'"—he read widely, took notes, made sketches, and devised his own methods of cultivation based on ideas about agriculture gleaned from diverse sources. His unique methods and experiments in breeding plants led to the development of several new hybrids. As his obituary in the *Springfield Republican* noted, Henry "worked with other scientific farmers in respect to problems of culture and reinforcement," and he became well known as "one of the most prominent farmers of the county and the state."[6] Henry garnered fame especially for his cultivation of potatoes; he had fourteen acres on which he grew 140 distinct varieties and kept meticulous notes about his experiments growing them. His efforts earned a silver medal at the New England Agricultural Fair in 1869, and the world record at the time for his yield of four hundred bushels per acre.[7]

Before becoming a farmer, Henry served as assistant principal of a school in upstate New York. During that time, he traveled to New York City in search of a wife. On the streets of Manhattan, he met Deborah Hill Read and, in true storybook fashion, fell in love at first sight, according to a letter he wrote to one of his nieces. Henry and Dora, as the attractive tall woman with piercing gray eyes was known, would marry in 1862. As countless young brides before her, Dora left behind the comfort of her family home and the world she'd known for the unknown, unfamiliar world of her new husband, on his isolated farm in western Massachusetts.

Dora was the youngest daughter in the Read family originally from Redding, Connecticut. The Reads descended from a long line of educated, thoughtful, and cultured people whose family fortunes waxed and waned.[8] As Elaine would write, "Though straitened in means, they were people of some pretensions and she [Dora] was a city-bred girl of fastidious tastes, unused to hard work and hardly born to fit so primitive a setting. She had a bright and active mind and a craving for the best things in life, both material and spiritual. . . . With her trousseau of hoop-skirted silks she was brought home to a rustic brown cottage, solitary, in the middle of something like a square mile of half-tamed field and forest."[9]

The disparities between Henry and Dora were perhaps unwittingly embodied in descriptions from an article published in 1887. "One sees in Mrs. Goodale the source of the striking perfection of . . . girlish features. . . . Her face is sweet and delicate, a woman of broad culture and education, her gray hair seems to have no quarrel with her youthfulness," the author wrote, when Dora was forty-eight. By contrast, "Mr. Goodale . . . has more of the traditional poetic appearance than any other member of the family. His brown hair falls in long locks over his neck, and is parted above in the middle. But for the half-farmerly shirt . . . he might pose effectively for Swinburne, or even the aesthetic Oscar Wilde."[10]

Looking back, Elaine reflected that the cupboard of "delicate French wedding china reserved for ceremonious occasions" dominating the small dining room of her childhood home no doubt symbolized for her mother the "elegance and distinction which she never ceased to crave in the midst of rustic simplicity, for there was in her nature none of the whimsical humor and gay adventurousness with which my father was endowed."[11]

Given Dora's city roots and social aspirations, and Henry's poetic soul and ties to his land, it is not surprising there would be dissonance in their marriage. In retrospect, this was evident to their children. In a letter to her sister Rose in 1931, Elaine noted their father endured their mother's "persistent belittling of him in every way—very sad, that was." She added, "She was a devoted mother to her young children, particularly, perhaps, Dora and me—but after I was really grown I hardly got any impression but of constant and (as it seemed and still seems to me) quite unfair demands for devotion, submission of my wishes and ideals and unlimited sacrifices."[12] And in another letter she reflected, "I always thought Mother ambitious for honors for herself, rather than for her husband. She never seemed to pour all her energies into building him up."[13]

Elaine, named for Alfred Lord Tennyson's "lovelorn Elaine" of Arthurian Astolat, came into the world on October 9, 1863. She was joined by sisters Dora (in 1866) and Rose (in 1870) and brother Robert (in 1878). Their maternal grandmother, Eleanor Lyon Read, came to live with the family in 1868. Elaine recalled her grandmother as "a dear invalid [who was] our household saint. She had seemingly risen above hardship and sorrow to a plane of all but unearthly sweetness"[14] and noted the formative influence of her presence. The Goodale family also had frequent contact with Henry's parents, Chester and Sophia, who lived in nearby Egremont. Chester, who came to western Massachusetts at the age of fourteen as apprentice to a tanner and shoemaker, learned the trade and set up his own shop, becoming so successful he built his own tannery, and earning him the capital for his next business venture. The Goodale White Marble Company also became successful, with five quarries in operation at its height, supplying marble for buildings including the Custom House in Boston, Girard College in Philadelphia, and the state capitol in Hartford.[15] Throughout her life Elaine retained images of her paternal grandfather driving his buggy up the mountain behind Sky Farm each week to oversee a quarry, then coming to visit. She noted, "Our little family circle formed a kind of private world to which only a few close friends were admitted."[16]

To Dora's despair, Henry had neither his father's business acumen nor his drive. Late in life Elaine recalled her father's "lack of practical wisdom" and "his choice of a vocation . . . dictated by a passion for country life, together with an innate shirking of the market-place."[17] Elaine came to believe her mother's extreme parsimony (extending once to her refusal to allow the Eastmans to cut firewood on the property of the house in which they lived but to which Dora held title) was a direct result of her dissent from Henry.

There were other sources of tension in the marriage as well. Dora's mother, Eleanor, frequently noted in her diary her daughter's incessant complaints, and of frequent times "Dora lies in bed until evening." As adults Elaine and her sisters would mention in letters to one another remembrances of their mother's emotional lability and depressive nature, Elaine concluding her mother had become "a nervous invalid" who couldn't take care of her younger two children as she had the older ones.

Elaine's complicated relationship with her mother was established early. On the one hand, she viewed her mother as "all but infallible," an

FIGURE 1.2. Henry Sterling Goodale, undated photo. Eastman-Goodale-Dayton Papers, Smith College Special Collections, Northampton, MA.

"accomplished woman for that era" who read widely, home-schooled her children in literature, Latin, and French, played the piano and sang; a woman who transmitted her belief in the value of service to others on a near-daily basis; a woman who, despite her own rarified upbringing, learned to navigate the "appalling primitive domestic" situation in which she found herself at Sky Farm and because of her "wish to excel in every undertaking" learned to make soap and cheese, can fruit, knit stockings, and sew clothes. Conversely, Elaine saw Dora retaining an entitled sensibility, never relinquishing aspirational ties to the Read family, whom she viewed as aristocratic, believing their lineage more distinctive than it was. Elaine drew sharp contrasts between her father, with whose sense of adventure and poetic bent she firmly identified, and her mother, "whose temperament was her greatest enemy." She concluded her mother "was at heart a disappointed woman."[18] Elaine came to believe her mother's failure to fully develop her writing abilities became a major source of Dora's discontent; Elaine would not view this issue so clearly in her own life.

Elaine would also fail to draw the obvious parallels between the dissolution of her parents' relationship and what would happen in her own marriage years later. While the tensions between Dora and Henry had no doubt simmered for years, they boiled over after two decades. The couple separated in 1882 though they never officially divorced.

* * *

"After all, say what they may about the farmer's life and labor, it is a pleasant, aye, and a profitable thing to be a farmer's daughter! . . . The opportunities offered to one who stands a little aside alike from the engrossing toil and every-day interests of the farm, with a realizing sense of its value as art, as life, are not to be lightly regarded," wrote Elaine in *Journal of a Farmer's Daughter*, published in 1881 after being previously serialized in the *Christian Union*.[19] At just eighteen years old this was her second solo-authored book, in addition to the two previous books of published poetry written by both Elaine and her younger sister Dora. She wasn't being flip: for her it *had* been both a pleasant and a profitable thing to be a farmer's daughter. With the aid of parents who encouraged and curated their young daughters' incipient poetic talent, who leveraged connections and carefully marketed their daughters' output, Elaine and her sister became widely known in late nineteenth-century America as "poetic childhood prodigies" or "the divine child poet geniuses." Yet, as Elaine stated, a lot of her early success derived from an ability to see the work at Sky Farm and the abundant natural beauty of her world as art, and to translate its simple but intricate splendor into words.

In an article Henry saved from an unknown newspaper entitled, "How I Became a Teacher: A Non-Professional Confession," Dora wrote that though she'd trained as a teacher in New York, once she moved to Mount Washington and became a mother she could "not willingly intrust [*sic*] my children" to the local school and therefore "began reviewing and rounding out my own studies" so she could better teach her daughters.[20] Elaine recalled her mother's early training bestowed on her "a genuine love of knowledge—a real gift for imparting it—and studied along with her pupils with the zest and fervor of a born intellectual."[21] Dora gave her children daily lessons, supplemented by "an artist friend" who taught the children botany and sketching, and a local clergyman who instructed them in Greek. Their education was "overwhelmingly literary and humanistic," focusing on classic literature. Elaine claimed to be a fluent reader by the age of three, to know and quote long Shakespearean soliloquies by age eleven. Because of Dora and Henry's interest in poetry, the girls began composing their own poems. "I used to make up verses and croon them to myself some time before it occurred to me to commit them to odd scraps of paper," Elaine later wrote.[22] When she was seven and her sister Dora was four, they began to write a magazine called "The Child's Monthly Gem," which transformed into "Sky Farm Life" when they were a bit older. The Goodales showed these hand-printed magazines to family friends. The positive reaction encouraged Henry to share his daughters' poetry more widely.

The poetry's dissemination led to Mary Mapes Dodge, editor of *St. Nicholas*, becoming aware of it. Dodge, a popular author and founder/editor of the successful children's magazine, which had a circulation of over seventy thousand in the late nineteenth century, would have been extremely taken by the Goodale family. She herself had been home-schooled and earned money for her family through writing, and her father, a professor of "scientific farming" like Henry, bridged the worlds of literature and agriculture. Dodge published six short poems by sisters Elaine and Dora in 1877, with an introduction that read in part, "Elaine and Dora Read Goodale . . . are children thirteen and ten years of age. Their home . . . is a large and isolated farm lying upon the broad slopes of the beautiful Berkshire Hills, and is quaintly called Sky Farm. Here, in a simple country life, divided between books and nature, they began almost as soon as they began to talk to express in verse what they saw and felt, rhyme and rhythm seeming to come by instinct."[23]

Perhaps as astonishing as the check for seventy-five dollars that arrived after the poems' publication were the letters that began coming to Sky Farm, praising the girls' precocious talents and seeking autographs. The Goodales also received letters from notable people in American literature, including Henry Wadsworth Longfellow.[24] Some friends suggested to the Goodales it would be advisable to collect the girls' poetry in a single published volume. Seeking to capitalize on the girls' early success and yet at the same time leery of it, Henry sought the counsel of several literary people. Charles Whiting, a family friend and an influential editor at the *Springfield Republican* newspaper, wrote Henry that while he understood the initial reticence the Goodales felt about wider publication, "lest the stimulus hurt minds so young . . . [I am] convinced that the common dangers do not exist in their case."[25]

Henry also solicited thoughts from Colonel Thomas Wentworth Higginson, a well-known Civil War commander of a Black regiment, Unitarian minister, author, and literary advocate. At the time of Henry's letter, Higginson was also advising and encouraging another poet from western Massachusetts, a reclusive young woman from Amherst named Emily Dickinson. In response to Henry's query, Higginson replied he had "already been told of your children, & had even heard the names of some of these poems. . . . They are certainly the most remarkable verses I have ever seen from writers so young." He suggested it was a "very serious responsibility" to have charge of children so gifted. He recommended exposing the girls to more of the world. Higginson believed they should be sent to school rather than educated at home, they should be introduced to more fiction because it gives "a sort of vicarious experience of life & enlarges our area of sympathy & knowledge," and submitted that rather than advocating the Goodale sisters only to pursue literary careers, they should be encouraged to take on an "active" vocation such as teaching. Higginson did not believe the girls' work was yet ready for further publication and dissemination.[26] In a subsequent letter to mother Dora, Higginson reemphasized his beliefs that "early publication . . . tends to limit people at that early standard," and the girls' education should not focus exclusively on literature but that "a *broad foundation* is needed."[27]

Henry and Dora's concerns about protecting their young daughters by restricting their exposure to the world and limiting the publication of their poetry were apparently overshadowed by the potential for the girls' poetry to bring in some much-needed income. Even with supplemental income from Henry's father, the Goodale family's finances remained precarious.[28]

Soon an offer came along that the Goodales couldn't refuse. G. P. Putnam, whose literary reputation emanated from introducing the works of Washington Irving, extended a generous contract to the Goodales for a collection of

Elaine and Dora's poetry. And in 1878, *Apple Blossoms: Verses of Two Children* came out, going through five editions in two years and selling ten thousand copies. The book garnered strong critical acclaim in many reviews. One in *The Watchman* mentioned Elaine and Dora's "remarkable poetic power"; the *New York Post* declared, "This little book . . . is one worthy of no trifling notice," and the *Berkshire Eagle* proudly claimed, "The Berkshire hills have again vindicated claim to title, not only of the home, but the mother of genius. . . . [The poems have] the highest quality of genius yet manifested by them, tender grace and delicious delicacy of poetic expression."[29]

Most of the 136 poems in *Apple Blossoms*, roughly equally divided between poems by Elaine and poems by Dora, are about nature, seasonal activities or animals around the farm, or poems marking holidays and family occasions. For Elaine, poetry was always a primary form of expression; poetry written across her life gives clues to her inner thoughts. Apart from the flowery language of nineteenth-century verse in this early collection are whispers that would become louder in Elaine's later life, hints about her relationships with her parents, her siblings, and suggestions about her own life's directions. For example, in "Papa's Birthday" she lauds "the anniversary of his auspicious birth, who singled out from all the world, this cherished spot on earth." In the sonnet "Mother," clearly written after the birth of Dora's youngest child, Robert, Elaine observed, "Upon her snowy couch she drooping lies, A languor on her limbs that seems a grace. . . . She knows who drew her strength and not rise."

Another early poem, "Jewels," gives hints of how Elaine would come to view herself and her life's missions:

> Some have souls like rubies, intense in a living glow,
> Strong to conquer and save, in a deep and fervid might;
> And some whose brilliant intellect has none of the heart's warm flow,
> Are like diamonds, clear and cold, flashing out a dazzling light.
> Some burn like the fiery opal, now kindling into a flame,
> Now dying down to the embers, yet quick with a changeful gleam;
> Full of artistic spirit, that spirit never the same,
> Living half in a sharp reality, and half in a vivid dream.[30]

Along with the fan mail arriving at Sky Farm and the glowing reviews from newspapers, which Henry pasted into a scrapbook, came requests for interviews with the child poets. In Elaine's memoir she recalled, "Metropolitan journalists, who persisted from time to time in making their way over the mountain" seeking to interview the girls, "were obliged to content themselves with meeting and interviewing my father."[31] This was either another example of Elaine's idolatry of Henry or a recollection glazed over by the years; in fact, there were numerous articles published in papers in which both Elaine and Dora clearly met with visiting journalists after her parents screened them. For example, a writer for the *Washington Evening Post* noted after he had passed muster with the parents of the poets, the girls he saw were "rosy cheeked and bright eyed"; Elaine reported history and languages as her favorite subjects and noted that "she had the power of reciting long passages after a single reading." An article in the *Boston Post* suggested, "Genuine prodigies, like poets, must [be] born and not made. . . . The best specimens of the latter are the Goodale sisters," who the journalist quoted at length, detailing both their "poetic precocity" and their "plain manner of speech." And an article in the local *Berkshire Courier* found, "There could be no more mistaken impression than that which many people seem to have, that Elaine and Dora are 'not like other children.' They are as much like other children as children of genius ever are. . . . In all that goes to make up a healthful, beautiful childhood, properly so called, there are no more perfectly natural children than they."[32] Henry and Dora Read were no doubt eager to dispel any suggestion their girls were peculiar and so cultivated an image of them as healthy, normal children who happened to have unusual facility with words.

The success of *Apple Blossoms* led to the publication of two other collections of poetry in short order: *In Berkshire with the Wild Flowers* (1879) and *All Round the Year: Verses from Sky Farm* (1881). Cleverly published to coincide with Christmas purchases, these volumes, too, garnered high praise. "The poems, of themselves, challenge admiration for their grace and force of expression," wrote a reviewer in the *National Journal of Education*. *In Berkshire with the Wild Flowers* was accompanied by plentiful illustrations by the well-known artist William Hamilton Gibson, and printed on "superb tinted paper and highly ornamental binding," making this reviewer conclude the volume would make an excellent holiday gift.[33] Among the many reviews of *All Round the Year*, a reviewer from the *Sacramento* (CA) *Daily Record-Union* noted the poems were "fresh, gentle, pure and sweet, and speak to the gifted natures of their youthful writers."[34]

However, the poems' publication and articles about them also laid the groundwork for what would become lifelong, if often unstated, resentment between the two sisters. As children they had been inseparable (Elaine mentioned they "slept, studied and played together," binding them to one other night and day); as adults, they rarely saw one another and frequently used their other siblings as intermediaries in their correspondence. The long-festering dissent might well have taken root in some of the early reviews that inadvertently instigated sibling rivalry, and differences in how their poetry appeared.

One of Elaine's poems originally published in *Apple Blossoms*, "The Coming of the Birds," was republished as a stand-alone volume in 1880 along with color illustrations. Dora had no book of her own for years to come.

In some of the published critiques of their poetry, it is clear the seeds for an incipient sisterly competition were sown. For example, an article in the *Chicago Daily Tribune* observed, "We are pained to see that Elaine . . . is growing cynical. The younger sister as yet seems wholly to have escaped this danger." "While resembling each other in general characteristic, the sisters are yet in many respects quite unalike," wrote Professor E. G. Giddings in the *Berkshire Courier*. "Elaine is becoming grave and thoughtful and will be the more reserved of the two. Dora is witty, sprightly and full of fun. Elaine sometimes reasons, Dora always sees as by intuition. Their differences will be yet more noticeable in maturity." And a critic for the *New York Times* singled out Dora's verses: "Especially does the younger child reflect in graceful words and even metres."[35]

And despite Henry and Dora Read's best, albeit naïve, efforts to protect their girls from unwanted scrutiny, close examination of one of Elaine's poems by press across America yielded controversy.

Originally published in *St. Nicholas Magazine* in 1877, "Ashes of Roses" became well known before its reprinting in *Apple Blossoms*. In November 1878,

Dora Read Goodale received a letter from Mary Mapes Dodge at *St. Nicholas*. "With sincere regret and reluctance," the editor wrote, "I feel myself compelled to send you the enclosed [article]. . . . Can you give any explanation of it?"[36] The article from the *Boston Daily Advertiser* suggested Elaine's "Ashes of Roses" was a plagiarized version of another poem, "Attar of Roses," by the British poet F. W. Bourdillon, published in the *Louisville Courier-Journal*. Given the amount of publicity the child poets received and the common custom of nineteenth-century newspapers to publish poetry, this small item got picked up by many papers. "One of the precocious poets who made a sensation in *St. Nicholas* last year turns out to be a precocious plagiarist," suggested an article in the *Charlotte* (NC) *Observer*,[37] a headline not unlike many appearing in newspapers across the country.

Eager to steer clear of any controversy for *St. Nicholas*, Dodge wrote again to the Goodales a couple of weeks later: "We are anxious to take some course which will clear Elaine to the readers of *St. Nicholas*," she stated. "I have not, from the first, believed that she had been guilty of plagiarism," adding she felt Elaine's poem the superior of the two. Dodge suggested some damage control by having Elaine quickly write something "explicitly replying to the charge" for the next edition of *St. Nicholas*. G. P. Putnam's Sons, too, was keen to protect the image of the pristine childhood poet whose poetry had already generated significant profits for the publisher. Henry Goodale received a note from Mr. Putnam suggesting the article in the *Boston Daily Advertiser* "calls we think for some word of reply. We should be glad to have a copy of any word that Miss Elaine may decide to send."[38]

But before Elaine was forced to defend herself, an editor for the *Louisville Courier-Journal* publicly admitted that "Attar of Roses" had been published *after* "the appearance of little Elaine Goodale's. . . . It was merely a bit of pleasantry which the heading explained"—in other words, this poem was a spoof of Elaine's poem. "We hope the Boston paper that accepted the accusation as truth, with a sniff at precocious poets, will be honest enough to confess its mistake," the editor concluded. And Henry Goodale received a letter from F. W. Bourdillon himself, from Oxford, in which the poet clearly stated, "I am not the author of the verses called 'Attar of Roses.'"[39] Bourdillon's name had been used fraudulently without his knowledge as part of the parody. Concluded the *Springfield Republican* newspaper, "The charge that Elaine Goodale plagiarized her poem . . . incredible on the fact of it, is now completely disproved." In a coda to the amazing amount of newspaper coverage this non-incident generated, Elaine wrote in a letter to the editor that the *Springfield Republican* had given the "final truth" regarding the unwarranted charge of plagiarism and thanked the *Louisville Courier-Journal* for "your able and generous defense of 'Ashes of Roses.'"[40]

This incident was a significant one in Elaine Goodale's life not because it caused her to cease writing poetry—indeed, she continued to write and publish poetry in newspapers periodically well into her seventies—but because when her writing turned primarily to journalism during her twenties, she was acutely aware that newspapers of the era did not fact-check. Much of what ended up in late nineteenth-century newspapers was incorrect; often, patently misleading. While the number of newspapers in America increased exponentially during the Civil War, by the 1880s there were so many papers the competition between them became cutthroat, leading to the rise of yellow journalism and an increase in sensationalized stories. Later in her life, when Elaine tried to use the press as a vehicle for disseminating information about Indian life and policy, she felt compelled to do so partially because she knew most of the stories about Indians in newspapers were the fake news of the day, designed more to sell papers than to factually inform.

As for "Ashes of Roses," it became Elaine's best-known poem and her most anthologized piece of poetry, set to music on four separate occasions. Today it remains readily available on poetry websites.

* * *

A childhood marked by relative isolation turned into an adolescence similarly devoid of peers and, as the girls passed into their late teens, provided few opportunities to develop romantic attachments. In her memoir Elaine mentioned "an unwise family friend [who] embarrassed me profoundly by a premature declaration of love" and that she "resented the advances of an occasional 'admirer' with disproportionate indignation,"[41] although she also recalled that two or three men had "offered marriage." In *The Voice at Eve,* Elaine recalled, "Throughout my girlhood I invariably preferred the society and conversation of my elders to that of boys and girls of my own age, even when the latter was attainable." (She would always prefer the company of older people, noting in a letter to Rose in 1927 that most women of her own age were "boring.") She also suggested that her mother, "an aristocrat by temperament and conviction," saw herself and her children as distinct from the those of their nearest neighbors and "chose to remain aloof from such society as offered and was doubtless termed 'stuck-up' and proud by our country neighbors."[42] Elaine described herself, too, as "aloof," "extremely naïve," and "socially abrupt and awkward."[43]

Part of Elaine's self-professed awkwardness may have come from her realization of her differences from anyone near her own age. She, like her father, was of "bookish habit" and poetic soul. The seclusion of Sky Farm and the isolation of home-schooling meant Elaine and her siblings had little exposure to anything considered fashionable in their day—not the literature, not the music, not the clothing. Elaine later wrote she was a "nonconformist, indifferent to fashion . . . an ardent votary of 'dress reform' long before that movement had any general support. I insisted upon loose frocks and low-heeled shoes. . . . I cared little what I wore, seldom thought about my looks."[44]

This disinclination to engage with people her own age and removal from any contemporary culture continued until Henry and Dora yielded to Colonel Higginson's suggestion that the girls needed greater exposure to the world to develop as writers and as people. Elaine, almost eighteen, and Dora, fifteen, were sent to a boarding school in New York in 1881. Elaine recalled this time as both brief—they were there only two terms—and difficult: "Our schoolmates were hardly congenial, the teachers wholesomely critical, and we unaffectedly homesick. Nevertheless, by the end of the year I had made the necessary adaptations and should have been glad to go on to college."[45] And though she won admission to the new "Harvard Annex" (later Radcliffe College), founded in 1879, Elaine's family couldn't put together sufficient funding for her to attend, even with the aid of some scholarship money. Rather than wandering Cambridge among peers, Elaine roamed the fields of Sky Farm with her siblings.

The Goodale children's physical isolation and mother Dora's snobbish attitudes contrasted with her insistence on the necessity and value of service to others. Elaine recalled, "Certain phrases were constantly on her [mother's] lips: 'the beauty of service'; 'plain living and high thinking'; 'our own duties and others' rights.'" Dora sought opportunities for herself and her children to help others in the tiny community of Mount Washington, with a population of roughly two hundred in 1870. In 1930 Elaine remembered her mother's "firm belief in 'women's rights,' and became what is now known as a feminist."[46] Dora's insistence on the importance of civic engagement, as well as her belief that women needed to be active participants in it, was part of a broader tradition of the Protestant ethic of the nineteenth century. Although the realms in which women could participate in service work were more limited than men's, women—especially women of the burgeoning middle class or those who aspired to be part of it—increasingly became involved with a variety of charitable organizations and endeavors. This sense of idealism and the value of service emanating from her youth is one Elaine carried throughout life. In 1940 she stated, "The only goals worthwhile [are] those of pure art, and of service to others. . . . And I *still* believe this, at the end of a long life."[47]

As Elaine looked back on her life, she recalled one specific incident that lit the fire of civic engagement for her; one moment, when viewed across a full lifetime, that stood out as a singular turning point.

On a "glowing midsummer day" in 1878, Elaine remembered a "gallant figure" who arrived unannounced at Sky Farm. General Samuel Chapman Armstrong, the forty-year-old former Civil War commander of a Black brigade, cut a dashing figure. Tall, with a high forehead and classically handsome face, Armstrong had light hair set off by his dark uniform and chestnut steed. As he would be remembered by fellow reformer Lyman Abbott, Armstrong had "broad shoulders, with no superfluous flesh, erect in pose, with keen eyes that looked not at you but into you, and an electric energy at once physical and moral."[48] Armstrong had grown up the son of missionaries in Hawaii and attended the school at which his father taught children of other missionaries and of Hawaiian tribal leaders. In a biography of her father, Edith Armstrong Talbot noted that his education at Punahou School gave Armstrong "dark-skinned" playmates including the pair who became king and queen.[49] This provided young Armstrong with both an indication that non-white people could productively be educated and a determination to carve out a career to do so.

After rising through the military ranks and surviving the Battle of Gettysburg, Armstrong joined the Freedmen's Bureau, a governmental agency formed in the wake of the Civil War to assist freed slaves and further their education. Inspired, Armstrong subsequently founded the Hampton Normal and Agricultural Institute (later called the Hampton Institute, now Hampton University) in 1868, a school designed to teach Black students and provide them with vocational skills. Armstrong's educational philosophy emphasized manual labor as the key to character development, with the goal of helping African Americans assimilate to white Euro-American norms and practices. Like many people in the nineteenth century—even those who might be thought of progressive—Armstrong firmly believed people of color would best be served by abandoning much of what made them different from mainstream white culture. Ten years later this philosophy extended when Hampton began accepting Native American students.

Elaine recalled, "Armstrong's dramatic personality instantly gripped our imaginations. His shining countenance and rapid speech, overflowing with enthusiasm for humanity and bubbling with wit, proved irresistible." Nor was this indelible first impression the only one the Goodales would have of the general: "Even from the hour of that first auspicious meeting under the lilacs, the famous champion of the red and black races was no stranger in our home."[50] He and Henry struck up a cordial correspondence, exchanging thoughts on books and images of their children; Armstrong once cautioned Henry he should not let his poet daughters become too "citified, but keep on telling as sailors of the human sea the lovely things they see."[51] Armstrong, who had graduated from Williams College in northwestern Massachusetts and whose first wife came from Stockbridge (only twenty-one miles from Sky Farm), had enough ties to the area to make numerous trips; he also used some of these visits to solicit funding for his educational endeavors and to recruit teachers for Hampton.

Though fifteen-year-old Elaine was no doubt transfixed by the romantic, charming, and inspirational figure, it wasn't until several years later, at a time marking the end of the first phase of Elaine's early life, that General Armstrong and his mission would become more central to her own.

* * *

By 1882 the problems building within Henry and Dora Goodale's marriage reached a crisis point. The financial pressures present from the start of their relationship were only exacerbated in 1879 when vagrants beat Chester Goodale to death, took his wallet, and ransacked his Egremont home. The Goodales, along with most residents of Berkshire County, were stunned and deeply saddened by the brutal crime. Chester's death also meant the end of a regular source of supplemental income for Henry and Dora.

Dora's depression deepened with her mother's death in 1878; it also seems she may have suffered from severe postpartum depression after the birth of her youngest child the same year. With no clear or appropriate suitors in sight and a college education financially out of reach, Elaine's path was uncertain, and the Goodales were looking at a similar fate for their other daughters. At this point Henry decided the best course of action would be to leave his beloved farm and his beloved children and try to provide for them elsewhere with a salaried position. Oddly, he left Sky Farm to become manager of the Windermere Hotel in Manhattan. (Even in midtown Manhattan, Henry appeared unwilling to completely leave behind his farming roots: an article in the *New York Times* described the "quaint combination of greenery and hennery on Fifty-seventh street," with Henry's chickens on the roof of the abode in which the self-proclaimed "attic philosopher" now lived.[52]) Unable and unwilling to run the farm herself, Dora proclaimed that her oldest daughter should either accept a tutoring position with a local family, or the offer of General Armstrong to join the teaching staff at Hampton; she would decamp to the Read family home in Connecticut with the three younger children.

Elaine wrote that her mother "decreed that I should accept the invitation of General Armstrong (whom we . . . greatly admired)." She added,

"Unwittingly, no doubt, she shaped my whole future by her decision to accept for me the tentative offer of a share in the Hampton experiment. The altruistic motive appealed to us both."[53]

It is easy to imagine the mixed feelings Elaine must have had as she departed from Sky Farm, riding by wagon to the train station in Great Barrington to begin the long journey south to Virginia, her family split, her world splintering. Despite her incipient sense of adventure and her ardent desire to serve, the financial pressures and the sense of leaving behind her childhood world must have weighed heavily on the young woman, about to turn twenty in fall 1883.

It is also easy to imagine how Elaine's heart must have pounded when she finally caught sight of the imposing Georgian-style house with large white pillars, flanked by towering trees, fronting the Hampton River, and arrived at the school built on the grounds of a former plantation. The dwelling in which General Armstrong lived couldn't have been more strikingly different from the modest farmhouse in which Elaine had grown up. "The Mansion House," as it is still known today, was built in 1828 by George Drummond, said to have been a relative of the infamous pirate Blackbeard.[54] It's not clear whether Elaine, upon learning that the Hampton Institute arose on grounds originally called Little Scotland, realized the irony of a place named for the colonialist origins of white Americans who subsequently enslaved African workers, or the further irony that this very site would be turned into a school devoted to teaching the young men and women freed from the bonds of this slavery. What she certainly knew upon her arrival at Hampton was she would now "try [her] unfledged wings" in untested and unanticipated ways.

2

From Hampton Institute to White River Camp (1883–1890)

Upon her arrival at Hampton, one of the first things Elaine Goodale would have seen was the enormous, sprawling live oak tree. Today, with a diameter of close to a hundred feet and limbs expanding both upward and outward like some kind of giant with arms akimbo, it's been designated as one of the world's Ten Great Trees by the National Geographic Society. Even in 1883, its size and location near the school's entrance made the tree stand out. The Emancipation Oak already had a storied history, as Elaine would learn. In 1861 a freed Black woman named Mary Peake held classes for other freed Blacks beneath its branches; in 1863 came the first reading of the Emancipation Proclamation in a Southern state under its shade. That same year, building on Peake's work, Union general Benjamin Butler founded a School for Negro Children nearby; five years later, General Samuel Armstrong would take over the site around the tree and build the Hampton Normal and Agricultural Institute.

In the ensuing fifteen years before Elaine arrived at Hampton, Armstrong expanded the school considerably. The first class at Hampton had only fifteen students; by 1883, the student population swelled to more than five hundred. Armstrong engaged in endless fundraising for his enterprise, adding new buildings (often built by the students themselves) and buying land to increase the campus's acreage. Though the school was initially funded by religious organizations and private donation, and later partially funded by government subsidies, Armstrong always pursued additional dollars.[1] When the U.S. government began investing more money in educating Indians, Armstrong quickly saw another avenue to add to his funding base.[2] Having Indian students also gave Armstrong other opportunities for his proselytizing.[3]

Once she had been at Hampton and amply demonstrated both her devotion to the Hampton cause and her unusual facility with words, Elaine, too, was called into the service of fundraising. In an adulatory piece published in the influential *Chautauquan Magazine*, Elaine concluded a lengthy article about Hampton's mission, writing, "The immense burden of supporting this great work . . . has rested for these twenty years almost wholly upon the shoulders of one man. . . . There is a general, a widely-supported, an imperative call for an endowment. Half a million dollars is asked of the people—a debt of honor to the Negro and to the Indian. . . . With all the earnestness which an intimate knowledge of its purposes, workings, and results can give, I add my personal appeal to the general voice."[4]

As the school grew, it continued to be guided by Armstrong's abiding educational philosophy. He firmly believed that giving African Americans vocational skills would be their best hope for succeeding as free people in American society. Based on his own upbringing and observations of Native Hawaiian pupils in missionary schools, Armstrong considered skilled labor and industrial education key to moral development. This education consisted of classroom learning in academic areas including English, math, and geography, supplemented by skills classes in sewing, cleaning, and cooking (for girls) and farming, blacksmithing, carpentry, and wheelwrighting (for boys). All students were required to work in the school's shops, kitchens, or farms two days a week. The Hampton curriculum was augmented by instruction in Christian morality, personal hygiene, and etiquette, a holistic approach encapsulated in the Hampton motto of "make haste slowly." Armstrong implemented a "summer outing program," which outsourced students to diverse locations where they would work in fields ranging from construction to domestic service. Armstrong believed this would also teach students "innumerable lessons best learned in a well-ordered home."[5] Because almost all the students at Hampton lived in dormitories, instructors were expected to exert their influence on them outside of the classroom, as well—education at Hampton went on 24/7, creating an environment that would prove too intensive for some of the many students who dropped out well before graduation.[6]

Perhaps the most significant development at Hampton—or, at least, the development that would prove most significant for Elaine—was the decision to begin accepting Native American pupils in 1878, five years before she arrived. General Armstrong was persuaded by Captain Richard Henry Pratt, another Civil War veteran-cum-educator who shared a philosophy of linking a skills-based education to a moral one. This idea prefigured a shift in Indian education occurring in the early years of the twentieth century, moving from the idea that education could "civilize" Native students to one that would give them vocational skills and help to close "gaps" separating races.[7] Pratt, who had commanded a prison in St. Augustine, Florida, of seventy-five Indian warriors from four tribes, believed if these Indians could be taught English and Euro-American methods of farming and other skills, they could more successfully assimilate. Pratt later founded the Carlisle Indian Industrial School with the same idea, most infamously encapsulated in his 1892 saying, "Kill the Indian and save the man."[8] But the ethnocentric philosophy behind this statement wasn't unique to Pratt; indeed, it was a deep undercurrent throughout white America of the nineteenth century. Education for Indians—as well as for Blacks, or other people of color—was thought to be most impactful if it could serve to eliminate as much difference between them and white Euro-Americans as possible. Given the prevailing ideas of Social Darwinism of the day, there was debate about how much it would *ever* be possible to eliminate racial difference completely. Educators like Armstrong and Pratt thought it was worth trying; they did see value in Blacks, Indians, and other people of color, but thought their lives would have more value were they to adhere to Euro-American standards. Therefore, educational instruction at Hampton would be in English only, and the focus would be on Euro-American values, modes of learning, and training "the hand, the head and the heart of selected youths to be examples to, and teachers of their people" to make them "missionaries of civilization."[9] Armstrong came to believe Hampton graduates would be some of the best spokespeople for the school and emissaries for the cause of education for Blacks and for Native Americans; he depended on Hampton graduate Booker T. Washington, among others, to help spread his gospel.

After convincing Armstrong to accept some of his Native American former prisoners so they could receive a fuller education, Pratt recruited additional Indian children to Hampton. Since Hampton was a coeducational school and since Armstrong firmly believed "it is useless to talk of civilizing a nation without civilizing its women,"[10] he was particularly eager to recruit more female Indian students. Between 1878 and 1923, almost 1,400 Indian students, representing sixty-five tribes, would attend the school. The Sioux were by far the most represented of all tribes.

The belief that Black students could help to "civilize" Indians became part of the initial rationale for the "Indian experiment" at Hampton. Indeed, some of the Native students petitioned to have Black roommates so they could learn English faster. Pratt, whose writings often compared Indians to immigrants, believed integrated situations would disperse "foreignness" and lead to assimilation more quickly.[11] However, ties between Black and Indian students soon came to be viewed as something that would *prevent* their collective assimilation to white values; Pratt also began to fear that the American public (by which he meant the white American public) would not accept Indians if they were so closely associated with African Americans, which is part of what led him to begin searching for an educational alternative to Hampton. "No one," writes historian Jeffrey Ostler, "was more sanguine about the uses of social engineering than Richard Henry Pratt."[12] With Pratt looking elsewhere and funders uneasy about the propriety of Black-Indian relations, Armstrong resorted to keeping the education of Blacks and Indians separate, and trying to segregate them socially as much as he could. (This didn't always work: there were numerous documented interracial relationships at Hampton. While Hampton staff did not encourage relationships between students of different races, they didn't exactly discourage them, either.[13]) Nonetheless, as Elaine would later describe it, "Hampton's Indian department . . . was a school within a school. Classrooms and dormitories were entirely separate for the two dark races."[14]

Armstrong came to believe his Indian students were every bit as deserving of the Hampton education as his Black students. His daughter wrote years later, "He threw the force of his personality and influence into the work of convicting the conscience of the nation of criminal negligence toward the red man."[15] Part of his conviction extended to his cultivation of teachers like Elaine Goodale.

As a young woman with no previous formal teaching experience, Elaine wasn't sure what to expect when she arrived at Hampton. Later she would reflect, "Possibly, after all, my lack of any formal preparation for teaching was not wholly a disadvantage. I had early learned to think for myself and was handicapped by no stereotyped ideas or prescribed methods in the effort to devise a fresh and natural approach."[16] Assigned to teach "adult primary," an English class for a dozen Indian men, some of whom were older than herself, Elaine proved early on to be an intuitive teacher, with excellent educational instincts. For example, in an article she wrote for the *Southern Workman*, Hampton's monthly newspaper that served both as a source of information for those at the school and an external public relations tool, Elaine delineated her method for teaching English: "We aim to give them from the first the *use* of the English language—to make it a flexible instrument in their hands. . . . The first step . . . is the teaching of a great number of words, by simple object lessons and the *acting out* of verbs."[17] Ruth Spack notes that the way in which English was taught at Hampton established it in a "superior position to Native languages," and that while literacy wasn't Hampton's central mission, it was close to its central mission because of the belief that the English language would "situate and transmit a superior culture" to Native students.[18] With the centrality of the English language to Hampton's overall assimilatory purpose, Elaine believed language work should happen in every class regardless of subject. In the late nineteenth century, it was radical to think you could teach English in a math class, but it was an educational philosophy the twenty-year-old teacher embraced. She believed in the value of interdisciplinary studies long before this form of education was named and years before it became fashionable. Her reports in the school newspaper about teaching went beyond factual recounting; Elaine's vivid accounts tried to bring her classroom to life for readers by giving specific, sometimes humorous descriptions of her lessons.

In her second year, Elaine was also tasked with teaching natural history and botany. Here she found her approach differed significantly with her pupils' worldview. Elaine attempted to "correct" notions of animal and plant life she viewed as "superstitious" with a more "scientific" approach meant to "encourage habits of exact observation."[19] Elaine failed to recognize that her Native students viewed plants and animals as extensions of themselves, rather than as separate biological systems. She found her students' insistence on their own views "absurdities," clearly unaware at this point in her life that her Indian students could teach her something, too.

Elaine quickly realized the charismatic General Armstrong and his outsized personality affected all aspects of life at Hampton. "The institution as a whole was dominated by the generous conception of human brotherhood implanted by its founder and head," she later recalled. Some of the teachers worked there with no compensation, simply delighted to be involved with this unique social experiment. Armstrong's zeal inspired an almost "religious atmosphere of the school, which was undenominational, bordered on the puritanical, yet without asceticism."[20] The Indian reform movement was more broadly connected to what Ruth Ann Alexander deems the "unspent moral force of evangelical Christian reform." Alexander writes that leaders who "identified Christianity with American citizenship perceived the Indian as a subjugated creature suffering from injustice."[21] The only way to "solve the Indian problem" would be through the dual "civilizing" agents of religion and education. Elaine, too, soon believed education was the "master key" responsible for unlocking all doors to a better life for her students.

Elaine began to recognize that her work with Indian students at Hampton and her writing about it enabled her to question some of the conventional thinking of the day about women's roles, within the socially acceptable and gendered profession of teaching. Quite a few white women were attracted to the cause of Indian rights and Indian education, at Hampton and beyond. While in earlier generations women aligned themselves with the cause of abolition, by the 1880s the Indian reform movement offered women similar opportunities for expression and activism within the "women's sphere."[22] For

FIGURE 2.1. General Samuel Chapman Armstrong. Courtesy Library of Congress.

some women, like writer Helen Hunt Jackson, this movement offered an opportunity for a new kind of activism through literature; for others, like Mary Bonney and Amelia Stone Quinton, a keen interest in Indian reform formed the basis for political action through the Women's National Indian Association.[23] Historian Valerie Sherer Mathes comments, "[The drive] to save others and a desire to live up to society's high expectations" through religious conversion was a key motivation to join the movement.[24] For Elaine, this cause offered possibilities beyond those she'd grown up with at Sky Farm.

Elaine later wrote that Hampton was her "introduction to the world" and that after her parents, General Armstrong was the "strongest influence" in her life; she "caught fire . . . making bold almost at once to spread the new gospel of opportunity for the red man."[25] The education at Hampton became a model for Indian education elsewhere, the forerunner of a system of government schools designed to assimilate Indians into Euro-American culture. U.S. president Rutherford B. Hayes encapsulated the mission of the school, stating Hampton was "destined to become an important factor in the advancement of civilization among Indians."[26] Elaine and the other young teachers at Hampton felt swept up by the sense that they were involved in a "bold experiment," one important not only in the education of their Black and Indian charges but also, more broadly, critical to the mission of an America on the move.

Her employment at Hampton was also formative for Elaine because this was the first time she lived away from any family. She arrived "socially as awkward, shy and unsophisticated as can well be imagined,"[27] but began for the first time to make friends her own age. Some of her fellow teachers remained friends throughout her life, most notably Florence Bascom, who became one of the first and most important American female geographers. Their connection was so deep Elaine named one of her daughters for her.

Elaine also developed close friendships with the Tileston sisters, Laura and Ruth. The Tilestons moved from Massachusetts to Virginia in 1877 and were among some of the first teachers at Hampton. Laura Tileston, who would refer to her friend as "Goody" in her letters home, became Elaine's traveling companion and fellow teacher at both Hampton and later in the Dakota Territory.

Although Elaine's memoir suggested "two or three nascent love affairs" at Hampton and during the summer when she returned to Connecticut to live with her mother and siblings, apparently none were worthwhile enough for Elaine to record them in any detail—or, at least, not worthy enough to be included in the papers she saved. "Absorbed in quite other ideas and plans, I was conscious of no unfulfilled emotional needs and thought hardly at all about marriage,"[28] she reflected. Biographer Theodore Sargent suggests Elaine may have had a serious crush on General Armstrong.[29] While there is no doubt Elaine had been in awe of the general since the moment she met him and wrote rapturously about his work and his influence on her life, there is no evidence of any romantic involvement.

Clearly General Armstrong recognized Elaine's spark, her literary talents, and her outreach capabilities. This must have been affirming, if not intoxicating, for the young woman who had previously led such an isolated and sheltered life. Armstrong's daughter Edith recalled her father had a knack for finding talented young teachers and developing them by "encouraging any reasonable taste or hobby in them, or urging them to develop new lines of work at Hampton."[30] And he did this with Elaine Goodale: by the spring of her first year at Hampton she was writing for the *Southern Workman*; by the winter of her second year, she became the editor in charge. Armstrong commissioned Elaine to write poems used at ceremonial occasions at the school. He encouraged her to write articles about her Hampton experiences and send them out for wider dissemination in national publications like *The Christian Union* and *The Independent*; clearly this was helpful for him in generating publicity and funding for Hampton, but it also started to provide Elaine with a national voice on Indian education, and a way to transition some of her writing from poetry to prose. "It was a short step from verse suffused with serious purpose to prose animated by the zeal of a recent convert," she wrote. "I did not hesitate a moment to enter the lists in public with reverend senators and other solemn graybeards, who in those days regularly inveighed against the shocking waste of public funds in a futile attempt to civilize 'a horde of filthy savages.'"[31] In one such public retort in *The Independent*, for example, Elaine refuted a published report about Indians' "lack of ability to grasp the rudimentary principles of education" with work happening in Hampton classrooms that showed the opposite.[32]

Clearly impressed with Elaine's voice for advocacy, Armstrong sought to widen her platform. "The General saw to it that I had every chance to broaden by knowledge of Indians and deepen by devotion to the cause so eagerly embraced," she recalled. He took her under his wing, bringing her to an early commencement at Pratt's Carlisle Indian School, introducing Elaine to other leaders in the field of Indian education, and arranging for her to attend the Lake Mohonk Indian Conference, an influential gathering of mostly wealthy, mostly male, mostly white people interested in discussing American Indian policies. And when in her third year at Hampton Elaine "confided to him an ardent wish to visit the Great Sioux Reservation in Dakota Territory, from which most of our pupils then came, he arranged for me a six weeks' tour under distinguished guidance and showed me how to finance it by means of travel letters . . . promising to take care of any deficit from a special fund at his disposal."[33]

Instinctively, Elaine knew getting a better understanding of the lives of her students would make her a better teacher for them. Despite the "English only" dictum at Hampton, she began to teach herself some of her students' indigenous languages by looking at books written by missionaries. It is not clear whether Elaine was driven by an intuitive pedagogical desire, an incipient journalist's curiosity, or a sense of adventure inherited from her father—or maybe some combination—but her passion for traveling to Dakota Territory convinced General Armstrong. No doubt the publicity he would receive from having Elaine write about her travels and the potential for this to bring Hampton more students, donors, and revenue also figured into his advocacy.

And so, in fall 1885, accompanied by fellow teacher Florence Bascom, Herbert Welsh—an Indian rights reformer and founder of the Indian Rights Association—and one of his brothers-in-law, Robert Frazer, Elaine set out. She probably traveled by train from Virginia to Philadelphia, where she would have met up with Welsh and Frazer, and from there gone on by train to Madison, Wisconsin, where Florence Bascom, daughter of the university president, joined the group. In the 1880s most white homesteaders traveling from the eastern United States to Dakota Territory would have gone by rail if they could, since it was faster than traveling by freight wagon or stage coach, and gone as far as they could—which would have meant taking the Chicago and North Western Railway to Watertown in present-day South Dakota, and then to the railroad's terminus at the new town of Highmore. They journeyed the next sixty miles to Crow Creek by "dusty overland travel," as Elaine described it, in a wagon. The remainder of the group's travel to all six Sioux agencies included a journey on the steamboat *General Terry* on the Missouri River from Pierre to Fort Bennett (where the boat was temporarily grounded on a sandbank, as frequently occurred during the fall with low water), and by "Indian lumber wagon, lined with a motley collection of buffalo robes and patchwork quilts"[34] to Standing Rock and then Pine Ridge, before going on to Rushville, Nebraska, where they rejoined the railroad network for the journey back East.

Elaine was immediately drawn to the wide-open prairies of Indian Country, so different from the Berkshire Hills in which she'd grown up. The vast landscapes and the varied geography of the West embodied a world of new possibilities for her. The ways in which the landscape changed so dramatically from the gentle flat farmlands east of the Missouri to the open prairies and buttes west of it, with prairie dogs curiously popping up from their dens and pronghorn antelope racing along grassy knolls—and suddenly changed again west of Murdo, to pine-covered mountains with clearly defined rocky ridges—fascinated the young woman. "I wish I could describe our first evening's camp on the Grand River," she wrote reverently in one of her newspaper accounts. "It is sunset; the air is still and cold; the pale-yellow cottonwoods on the riverbank are reflected in the glassy waters; there is a yellow light in the western sky."[35]

She arrived in Dakota Territory at a "critical moment in the history of the West," as she later wrote. Although white Americans had steadily moved west since the founding of the country, migration increased significantly following the Louisiana Purchase in 1803 and the discovery of gold in California in 1849. The Great Plains were largely unsettled by Euro-Americans until the 1870s. And then, as historian Frederick Hoxie writes, aided by railroads and fueled by a sense of what was later called manifest destiny, "west of the Mississippi population was exploding, and rose from 7 to more than 11 million in the 1870s, and much of that took place in areas with large numbers of Indians."[36] During this time period the states of Montana, Wyoming, and Idaho were admitted to the Union. The Dakota Territory, northernmost part of the Louisiana Purchase, remained a sprawling incorporated U.S. territory of almost 150,000 square miles until 1889, when it became divided into the states of North and South Dakota. All these new states triggered increased Euro-American migration and dramatically shifted congressional policymaking and alliances.

The growth of the Northern Pacific Railroad and the 1874 discovery of gold in the Dakota Black Hills rapidly intensified the interest of white settlers in moving to this area. Twice as many Native people as whites lived there in 1870; a decade later, the non-Indian population had increased tenfold. As the white population increased, the U.S. government began to take land from Native peoples in new ways and at unprecedented rates. As the American frontier expanded, Indian lands contracted. The central issue, writes Hoxie, "was not *whether* the reservation system would be changed, but *when* and *how*."[37]

The Sioux, a confederation of several nomadic tribes, divided into several groups under the cover term of "Lakota" and several under the umbrella term of "Dakota," had their territory shrunken dramatically by numerous successive treaties.[38] The Great Sioux Reservation initially covered more than 48,000 square miles. By 1889 the remaining nine million acres had been further subdivided into six separate reservations, and the sacred Black Hills area unilaterally removed from tribal control. In addition, writes historian Pekka Hämaläinen, the white people's westward expansion "taught Lakotas that mass migration of whites harmed the environment, animals and humans by exhausting forage, polluting streams and smuggling in deadly germs."[39]

Though she probably wasn't yet aware of the full picture, Elaine Goodale clearly saw—and recorded—some of the ways in which the Sioux already had their lives and livelihood overturned. "Great suffering seems to be entailed upon the Indians by issuing annuity goods in the severe weather," she wrote in one of her pieces published in the *Hartford Courant* and other newspapers in 1884. She described the difficulties the Sioux, who had not used the Euro-American methods of agriculture or the type of crops until they were forced to do so: "These Indian farmers despair of securing the results of their labor and enterprise." Additionally, she reported, the dearth of medical care was a great problem, with "unrelieved suffering—what preventable, needless disease and death!"[40] she concluded, unaware that undoubtedly much disease originated not with the Sioux, but with their exposure to unfamiliar Euro-American germs.

Part of the trip's impetus for Elaine and her traveling companions was to learn more about education at the various Sioux agencies. In the 1880s, while some Indian children attended boarding schools like Hampton, the great majority did not. This would change; by 1900 about 78 percent of all Indian children who attended school had been removed from their homes and families to attend a boarding school somewhere in the United States.[41] Indeed, once boarding schools for Native children became the dominant educational philosophy, more than seventy-five thousand children were sent to distant schools. As Ned Blackhawk suggests, this policy of forcible removal of children as young as age four, paired with policies such as withholding government rations until parents agreed to place their children in boarding schools, set up a commitment to "eradicat[e] Native Americans."[42]

Along with the prevailing Euro-American philosophy of "civilizing" Native Americans and consistent with the ideas of Social Darwinism gripping nineteenth-century white America, there was a push to educate Native children by trying to erase as many differences between them and Anglo-Saxons as possible. Nathaniel Taylor, appointed commissioner of Indian Affairs in 1867, believed all Indian children should be taught in English, "assuming that a uniform language could fuse the multitude of Native nations into a controllable entity."[43]

Initially the federal government put little money into Indian education, and missionary societies ran most schooling efforts on reservations; inevitably, this meant that government-aided schools also became sites for efforts to Christianize Indians. One of the most prominent missionary educators was Episcopal Bishop William Hobart Hare.

Sometimes called "the Apostle to the Sioux," Hare was appointed to lead the missionary district of the Niobara, encompassing the Dakota Territory, in 1871. Unlike some other leading educators and missionaries, Bishop Hare thought there was inherent value in Sioux culture; the more successful approach to Christianizing and educating the Sioux, he believed, would be to include elements of their own traditions alongside the efforts to Americanize and "civilize" Indians. His reputation was already well known when Elaine and her traveling companions first met him at a convocation of his diocese in Highmore shortly after their arrival in Dakota Territory. This gathering included some Hampton students back home, distinguished by "their quick, frank, manly bearing, their more refined manners and various little evidences of contact with civilization. It was a great pleasure to Miss Goodale and Miss Bascom to revive remembrances of Hampton by meeting with so many of their old pupils and from the welcome which they received,"[44] wrote Herbert Welsh, his attitude about "educated Indians" on full display.

Elaine was impressed by the bishop, "whose finely cut features, not more cordial than stern, nor more stern than cordial, focus the eye."[45] She liked his philosophy about Indian education, respected his knowledge of the Sioux, and came to agree that education for the Sioux would be more impactful if it occurred in locations near their own homes rather than in boarding schools thousands of miles away. The group visited one of Hare's "model" schools at Standing Rock Agency, and another being developed at Pine Ridge.

As Elaine met more people along her journey and learned more about conditions on the Great Sioux Reservation, she continued to write articles: "Mailed at frequent intervals throughout the trip, they described in detail the semibarbaric spectacle of Indian camp and council, new to most readers, not forgetting to stress the effects of mission training with its promise for the future."[46]

Some of Elaine's articles included descriptions of how the conditions of her travels gave her important insights into the lives of the Sioux. For example, she detailed how their Indian guides "dexterously arranged the lodge-poles in conical form . . . then a shapeless roll of white canvas is dragged forward, its peak fastened to the end of another long pole and raised to the apex of the cone—and, as if by magic, the beautiful and convenient Dakota lodge rises complete in the wilderness," and finding, to her surprise, how warm and comfortable the interiors were. Later in the same article she delineated how she adapted the saddle used by Sioux riders to a hybrid more like the type of saddle with which she was familiar, "much to the pony's amazement and the delight of the simple Indian women, who treat me with genuine consideration, quite as though I were not, (and I must be,) an object of very considerable curiosity."[47]

Elaine's "travel letters," as she referred to them, began appearing in newspapers at a time when American newspapers were eager for this type of content. The post–Civil War papers expanded rapidly because of new presses that printed copies more quickly and less expensively, the expansion of the railroads and telegraph that allowed newspapers to be disseminated more widely, and increased literacy rates. With an increased readership including a growing audience of middle- and working-class readers, newspapers expanded their coverage to include local news, human interest stories, and scandals. Content from newspapers was often shared and widely reprinted. All these factors meant many newspapers across the country carried Elaine's well-written accounts of topics most white readers would have known little about and considered almost exotically interesting. General Armstrong's hunch about Elaine's potential to bring more attention to Hampton was borne out. What he probably didn't anticipate was that her journalistic success would soon lead to other opportunities for her—opportunities that would take her away from Hampton.

* * *

Elaine Goodale and Florence Bascom arrived back at Hampton late in fall 1885. Elaine's passion for the cause of Indian education seemed to reach a new fervor after her trip. By January 1886 the staff box under the *Southern Workman*'s masthead bore the bold heading "Indian Department. Elaine Goodale, In Charge." She recruited Herbert Welsh, along with other heavy hitters in the Women's National Indian Association such as Mrs. Amelia Stone Quinton, and Alice Fletcher, a leading ethnologist of Indian cultures, also involved with Indian rights, to be regular contributors to the newspaper. Tamara Berg points out that Elaine used her editorial platform to "craft a forum that offered the American public new perspectives on race."[48] Elaine expanded the topics of articles under her editorial supervision to include not only discussions of what happened in the Hampton classrooms, but also news of the Women's National Indian Association, issues germane to Indian policy being discussed in Washington, and reviews of relevant books. These included a review Elaine wrote of Helen Hunt Jackson's seminal novel, *Ramona*. This book would be credited with drawing wide attention to "the Indian problem" in the United States. But in Elaine's assessment, as one who had traveled to Indian Country and one dedicating her life to Indian issues—and, it must be said, one who at that point had little experience with romance—"As a love story, *Ramona* is a success, except that it is a little overweighted with misery. As a presentation of the Indian problem, it is inadequate."[49]

But Elaine was already starting to think beyond her work at Hampton. As she would later describe it, the trip to Dakota Territory had been transformational. Oddly explaining it in the third person, as if to emphasize the journey's momentous impact on the new educational evangelist she'd become, she wrote:

> One young woman came home in spirit deeply committed to her task as she saw it. She had made up her mind to begin at the beginning, in the heart of a newly transplanted, leaderless, bewildered little community. Others could carry on in more solidly established institutions where there was ample support. Few, perhaps, would care to blaze a new trail in the obscure corner of a wild land, among recent "enemies" speaking an unintelligible dialect. Behind such considerations lurked, no doubt, a taste for adventure and a distinct bent toward pioneering, possibly handed down through a long line of early American forebears.[50]

Elaine was starting to dream of a new endeavor: starting a day school on the Great Sioux Reservation, modeled in part on Hampton and in part on the schools under Bishop Hare's curation. In her mind, such a model would be the best of all possible educational worlds, giving Sioux children vocational skills alongside academic and life skills, but teaching them within the context of their home and community, where she firmly believed education would be more impactful. During her travels to the Great Sioux Reservation, she noticed a school that had been built at White River Camp but never occupied; the treaty of 1868 had promised funding for several day schools on the reservation, which were built but never opened. Elaine started to think perhaps she could take over this school and turn it into a model for other day schools on the reservation. She thought through her ideas before getting up the nerve to pitch them to General Armstrong. When she did describe her vision for a day school combining Armstrong's philosophy of vocational education linked to moral development with her own ideas, Armstrong knew his fledgling teacher was ready to spread her wings.

In Elaine Goodale, General Armstrong found an acolyte. He had conveyed his devout passion for educating non-whites and passed along his almost religious zeal for the cause. She used terms like "the new gospel of opportunity" when talking about this work and referred to Armstrong's "missionary spirit" for which she was the "willing neophyte." In addition to Elaine's teaching duties at Hampton and her editorial stewardship of the *Southern Workman,* Armstrong began to procure speaking opportunities for Elaine. "I would stand up in my plain little traveling dress, without notes and almost without preparation," she recalled, "but too full of my subject to be frightened or self-conscious, and pour out my experiences with a rush, ending with what I fondly hoped was a well-reasoned plea for justice to the first American."[51] Armstrong enabled Elaine to have her biggest platform yet when he arranged for her to speak at the annual Lake Mohonk Indian Conference in fall 1886.

Launched in 1883 by twin brothers Albert and Alfred Smiley, whose Quaker faith led them to grow up with a concern for social justice issues, the Lake Mohonk Indian Conference quickly became a "must attend" event with a veritable who's who of white Indian reformers, philanthropists, and religious and political leaders. Held at the Smiley brothers' Mohonk Mountain House resort in upstate New York, the conference hosted guests who delivered talks over a series of days meant to "uplift and civilize" Indians through land, educational, and other policy reforms. Elaine's talk focused on the need to support Indian day schools on the reservations. She argued that, properly supervised, such schools could monitor student attendance carefully and insist on it by withholding government rations from families who did not send their children, while imparting both academics and industrial training, as well as the lessons Indian children needed to become "civilized" more effectively. She suggested that teachers in day schools would exert a positive influence on the communities they served. Interestingly, she didn't argue that children would be happier or more emotionally stable in their home communities than in boarding schools, although as a product of a home-schooled education herself, Elaine was well aware of how significant it can be for children to learn in a family-supported environment.

The reactions to her Lake Mohonk debut were glowing. An article in the *Hartford Courant* noted, "Miss Goodale is scarcely out of her teens, beautiful, finely educated, refined, intellectual, [and] full of life."[52] Well-known naturalist John Burroughs, who listened to her talk, wrote in his journal, "Met Elaine Goodale, a very sweet and attractive face; serious, self-conscious, genuine. Expect great things from that girl."[53]

That Elaine Goodale should have been such a passionate and gifted public speaker is a bit surprising. Several accounts describe her as painfully shy; she rarely looked at the people with whom she was speaking. An article in the popular *Leslie's Weekly* (originally *Frank Leslie's Illustrated Newspaper*) published a few years after this talk suggested, "To the stranger it simply seems that she is as distant and untalkative as the statue of Liberty in the bay."[54] But apparently her public persona differed significantly from her private presentation.

General Armstrong arranged for Elaine to travel to Washington, DC, to meet with Commissioner of Indian Affairs John Atkins. Armstrong's letter got her a meeting, but Elaine reported she didn't feel "I got far with the whiskered politician. . . . I suspect that he was more amused than impressed by his naïve and youthful caller." She wrote that Atkins insisted she call her day school "an industrial semi-boarding school," since the prevailing practice for Indian education was taking children away from their home environments to yield assimilatory results. The rationale for calling a day school a semi-boarding school, Atkins suggested, could be Elaine's intent to provide students with a midday meal and the fact she proposed to have cots available for emergency use. "A little later," she wrote years later, "the coveted opening as the first

FIGURE 2.2. Elaine Goodale, circa 1886. Eastman-Goodale-Dayton Papers, Smith College Special Collections, Northampton, MA.

Government day-school teacher . . . on the west bank of the muddy Missouri"[55] was approved.

Elaine's friend and fellow Hampton teacher Laura Tileston agreed to become a partner in this bold endeavor. Elaine was grateful for Laura's friendship, assistance, and belief in her dream, as well as for Laura's character. Several years older than Elaine and more "experienced socially," Laura possessed an "unfailing flow of spirits under trying conditions [and would] prove a valuable asset."[56] But the Indian Office refused to appoint two teachers, and certainly not two unmarried women teachers; Laura cleverly subverted the system by procuring from the magnanimous Bishop Hare a commission as a "lady missionary." As Elaine later wrote, the two women faced significant familial and social opposition to their proposed venture: "Young ladies in that era rarely ventured far from the beaten track, and a missionary school in Virginia was quite unconventional enough! Dire consequences were freely predicted in case we persisted."[57] But persist they did, Elaine garnering a salary of $600 for the year but still needing to ask Herbert Welsh for assistance obtaining a discounted railroad ticket for her journey West.

An article in the *Southern Workman* from August 1886 announced their departure from Hampton: "We regret the loss of Miss Elaine Goodale . . . but are happy to say that she will continue her connection as a regular correspondent from her new field of work for Indians. She leaves Hampton, as some of our readers know, with Miss Laura Tileston, whose successful work as a teacher will also be greatly missed here, to take charge of a new Indian school to be established on one of the agencies in Dakota."[58]

Laura went to Dakota Territory first, "to prospect," as she wrote in an account published in the *Southern Workman*. By September Laura was already swept up by the place, the adventure, and the mission, writing home to her sister, "Oh Ruth—I love this land already! It is too beautiful. . . . I feel that I [will] have something proud and beautiful in my life . . . when I can only look back on it."[59] Laura spent her time familiarizing herself with the area and the people, meeting with some Hampton graduates like Chief Medicine Bull, who helped with logistics, working with Bishop Hare and other missionaries to make repairs on "the little day school house, six miles from the agency"[60] and the nearby house she and Elaine would share, and writing letters to her friends and patrons of the Episcopal mission to raise funds.

Elaine remained in the East during this time. She was also busy, between speaking at Lake Mohonk in early October and writing advocacy pieces after, which she identified as excellent ways to gain publicity and raise funds for the new school. She also lobbied Armstrong to view her new school as an extension of his mission and help by funneling some Hampton funds to pay for supplies. She departed from New York for Dakota Territory on November 1.

However, the actual opening of the school at White River Camp didn't occur for a couple of months. Elaine and Laura continued to oversee plans for the expansion and repairs on their school building and on their house, and continued their fundraising activities. They began a sewing circle for Sioux women and reported that before the school officially opened its doors, they already had thirty students registered. The women acquired books, slates, tables and chairs, writing supplies, and soap and towels. When the carpentry to expand the schoolhouse was completed, the cleaning efforts began. In an article in *The Independent* Elaine described the scene: repeatedly sending their local Sioux janitor to haul barrels of water back on his horse, scrubbing walls, floors, ceilings, and windows, Tom Sawyerishly persuading local women and children to help, Laura "playing lively tunes on the [donated] organ to keep up our spirits!" Elaine insisted in the same article, "We determined . . . to keep our own standards, and to reiterate our demands with that smiling persistence for which the 'White River ladies' were already becoming notorious, or so we had playfully been told."[61] Some of these standards included efforts to teach their Sioux neighbors Euro-American privacy practices—Elaine delineated their efforts to impart the need to knock on doors before entering a building. But all in all, Elaine and Laura were thrilled, their quasi-religious fervor building; Laura reported she "felt almost like a priest about to take charge of his first parish."[62]

Elaine described the Lower Brulé Agency in which she and Laura would live and work graphically: "A rude prairie hamlet with only primitive conveniences, its row of cheap frame dwellings relieved from stark ugliness by a border of straggling cottonwoods and an impressive view of the river." Workmen under her supervision added two bedrooms to a "shack" eight miles from the agency and made it "more or less blizzard-proof" and "barely habitable," located several miles away from their nearest white neighbor. But the coldness of the setting contrasted with the warmth with which she and Laura were received by the community. Elaine recalled the "two distinct worlds existing side by side, now in dramatic opposition, now intimately mixed"[63]—the world of Indians converted to Christianity and seemingly embracing Euro-American values and customs, and those who had not. As her writing from that period and onward made clear, this was the duality with which Elaine viewed Native people. Her belief in the necessity of assimilation as the best and most necessary way for Indian survival never waned.

* * *

When the White River School opened on January 11, 1887, Elaine and Laura had enrolled thirty-three children between the ages of six and sixteen; after seven weeks of school, they had almost fifty students. Elaine gleefully described the new white flag they nailed to a pole to welcome children, clearly oblivious to the irony of its other associations in recent Sioux-American military history. "One can scarcely imagine anything more lovely than the scene before us on such a cold winter morning," she wrote in an article in *The Independent*. "The sunshine dazzlingly pure on the snow, the high lights and intense blue shadows of the bluffs, the dark fringe of trees against the dead white river, the thick wreaths of smoke curling lazily upward into the blue from one and another of the rude log cabins about us. Nor could anything see imagined more utterly still, more dream-like, or rather trance-like, in its dead repose."[64] Elaine and Laura waited anxiously: when would the students show up? Elaine knew "Indians are very late risers in the wintertime," and they did not use clocks as she and Laura did, something that gained currency among Euro-American populations in the mid-nineteenth century. They thought it probably useless to insist on a 9:00 start time and hoped an hour later would be reasonable. But as the students straggled in, they realized one of their first tasks would be to try to instill a new sense of time among people whose diurnal clocks were more tied to the seasons than to mechanical timepieces. (After appealing to some of their Eastern benefactors, Elaine and Laura procured and installed a large bell they rang each morning to mark the beginning of the school day.)

Much of Elaine and Laura's effort in the early days of the White River School focused on trying to establish some of the Euro-American principles of dress and hygiene they thought crucial to provide the proper learning environment for their Sioux students and setting ground rules for attendance and discipline. They strongly suggested the boys get their hair cut, but did not insist on this the way teachers at Hampton did.[65] Instead, they began a campaign of not-so-subtle social pressure by praising those students who willingly allowed themselves to be sheared; wrote Elaine, "With the aid of a little gentle ridicule, I do not doubt that a very few weeks will witness the change." Similarly, they praised those students who came to school washed and neatly dressed and "sent them home as object lessons. . . . The results are encouraging. It is my opinion that the Indian is naturally neat about his person, and learns with surprising facility the habits of civilized life in this regard." The students were provided with some clothing donated to the school, and missing buttons came from the box of "forty thousand imported sample buttons. The belles of White River Camp will wear Paris buttons in their calico dresses; and if no two of them are exactly alike, they resemble each other closely enough to give a very stylish effect."[66]

Elaine quickly realized that for many of her pupils the issue of coming to school was not one of desire—most of them as well as their parents seemed readily convinced of the value of education—but rather, their sense of time and consistency was profoundly different from hers. "How can they be expected to realize that it makes any difference whether they come at ten o'clock or at twelve every day, or three days out of five. . . . Even an educated Indian, who is in many respects quite up to the standard of civilization, and who, by his good sense and good feeling and good manners, has fairly led you to forget that he is an Indian, will often betray his inheritance in a manner peculiarly exasperating to the average American, by ineradicable habit of never being on time."[67] Their solution? Have the "benevolent [Sioux] policeman" pay a visit to tardy or absent students at their homes, trying to establish a system of accountability. Enlisting the aid of Hampton graduates living at Lower Brulé Agency to provide peer pressure also helped.

Elaine kept true to her vision of a hybrid curriculum including both vocational and academic elements. "Owing to the primitive and unsupervised state of the Indian school service at that period," she wrote, "we were at least given a free hand—if little more! We introduced sewing, cooking, gardening, music, calisthenics and modern methods."[68] When springtime finally came to the prairies, Elaine requisitioned seeds, chickens, and cows, and drew on her Sky Farm upbringing to try to teach her pupils the farming practices of her youth. She recalled their disbelief when she instructed them that a calf be taken from its mother and shown how to drink from a trough so that the cow could provide milk for human consumption, which she, as other white Euro-Americans, believed crucial for young children's health. "This meant wrestling with an excited calf and a slopping bucket, as I had seen my father do, loftily ignoring a splashed frock and the delighted howls of a ring of masculine spectators."[69]

Classroom instruction was mostly in English. But because none of the students knew a word of the language, and because few of them could read anything in their native Dakota tongue, Elaine and Laura improvised. They first gave their students Euro-American names, using their father's name as a surname and the name of "one of our eastern friends for personal use. These involuntary sponsors were later invited to take an active interest in their Sioux namesakes"[70] (and, of course, Elaine and Laura could then cleverly appeal to these sponsors for additional funding). As Ruth Spack points out, the putatively well-meaning Euro-American teachers of Native students instilling English as the primary language of instruction was clearly part of a colonialist worldview in which "English was not an additional language but rather . . . the only language worthy of acquisition. They were not to become bicultural but rather to substitute the Christian majority culture for their own."[71] The method Laura used at Hampton included giving students definitions of words to memorize, and then sentences, and to try to do this by initially giving them words and sentences related to their past experiences and objects in their immediate worlds—horse, river, butte, and so on.

Elaine, for her part, recognized that were she to become increasingly bilingual, she would better be able to teach her students. She continued her studies of the Dakota language, even though "prim-lipped mentors had gravely advised me not to . . . assuring me that I would often prefer not to understand what was being said. However, I found its acquisition a pleasure, as well as a real gain in promoting understanding and intimacy."[72] Elaine found her facility in Dakota would come in handy not only with her students and with their parents, but also in journalistic work she would later undertake; her ability to subvert translators, whose work was often poor, incomplete, or politicized, proved an invaluable skill.

Elaine and Laura saw the conveyance of Euro-American values as part of their job. They introduced a midday meal consisting of foods their students had neither eaten nor cooked (including raised bread, which Elaine described as "a well-liked novelty"). They taught their students new games and songs. Their close alliance with missionaries (and Laura's technical role as "lady missionary") meant Christianity was an integral part of the educational experience at White River. They handed out medications to ill people, tried to encourage the Sioux to install wooden floors in their lodges because they thought them more sanitary, and sponsored community suppers and magic lantern shows, "wholesome diversions . . . largely supplanting the native dancers."[73] Though Elaine seems to have recognized value in some of her students' ways, she never seems to have doubted that the Euro-American education and lifeways she and Laura disseminated were of greater value. This could be seen clearly through her thoughts on dress. Though Elaine herself cheerfully adopted wearing clothing like her charges, and she wrote, "it seemed really unkind to teach them that they must . . . fashion for themselves dresses with superfluous ruffles and unnecessary button-holes," she and Laura taught this, nonetheless. "And a few months sees starched white skirts, and delicious raised bread . . . which hold forth . . . promise of such finished products of civilization."[74]

Elaine and Laura's hard work and efforts to ingratiate themselves in the Lower Brulé community seemed to pay off. "Among the prophets of disaster, some held that no two women could keep house together and work in double harness without tears and temper," she wrote. "The omens proved mistaken. We divided the duties of school and mission, with each presiding over her own department and the other serving as assistant." The local Sioux called Laura "Miss Owl" for her wise advice and merry temperament, while Elaine was dubbed "Lame Horses." When she questioned a chief, he replied the name derived from a story about a time when his people traveled to a strange country and could go no further, their horses lame. Elaine was never sure whether this appellation was meant as a compliment by aligning her with his people, or as a warning not to push his people too far.[75]

Elaine continued to document their teaching and "civilizing" work through articles she sent back East. In 1887 she acquired a camera and began to take photos to add to her documentary efforts. In the three years she taught at White River School, Elaine published at least twenty-five major articles in Eastern newspapers and magazines on aspects of Indian education, policy, and travelogues from her journeys around the Dakotas. Her late-in-life reflections referred to some of this writing as "propaganda rather than literature"—Elaine was all too cognizant of how she'd turned her writing from poetry to polemic, and how writing that had once been merely a creative outlet had become writing in the service of her causes. These articles clearly served to help raise funds for the school, but they also gave Elaine an increased journalistic presence and a voice as one of the players in Indian policy. Later in life she would wonder why "no effort was made to launch me upon the journalistic or purely literary career for which I had shown most fitness and would seem to offer so much more of congenial association and tangible reward than the obscure and ill-paid pioneer work which I, in fact, undertook."[76] (Like so many, she blamed her mother.) But in the late 1880s, with most of her life ahead of her, Elaine thought only of possibility, thrilled with small victories that can come in teaching and the larger ones she seemed to gain in making her voice heard through print. She felt affirmed by the acclamation she received from the powerful men she so respected after they'd visited the school—Bishop Hare, and General Armstrong, who reportedly wrote to her after his visit, "I congratulate you on having found about the shortest road to heaven of all I know!"[77]

* * *

As Elaine and Laura opened their White River School in 1887, some fifteen hundred miles and a world away in Washington, DC, fellow western Massachusetts scion Senator Henry Laurens Dawes was putting the finishing touches on a major piece of legislation he was sponsoring. Dawes, a Yale-educated journalist turned politician, had been an ardent supporter of antislavery measures during the Civil War. In the late 1860s he became a major stockholder in railroads, and in the early 1870s, a proponent of the efforts to conduct geological surveys in the West. In 1872 he helped to support legislation creating Yellowstone National Park. Dawes shared the beliefs of many Euro-Americans at the time that non-white people would best be served by becoming as much like white people as possible, and that western lands would be best stewarded by white people with a vested financial interest in them. When Dawes became chair of the powerful Committee on Indian Affairs, therefore, it wasn't surprising his efforts to preserve Indians from complete annihilation focused on efforts to assimilate them more integrally into American society.

With his dual interests in preserving land and opening it up for Anglo development, as well as his dualistic beliefs that non-white groups like Indians should in some way be supported to survive but that their survival depended on their ability to let go of what most defined their identity, Dawes felt the system of reservations that had forced tribal groups to move and to congregate wasn't working as well as intended. Something more needed to be done to strip away the corruption, poverty, and lack of "progress" that plagued many Indian groups—at least in the minds of so many Euro-American politicians. Indians needed to become more assimilated, not so they could become integrated into American society, but so they could mimic it. Dawes came up with the idea of trying to break up tribes as social units by trying to instill the value of individual land ownership, encourage farming, secure parts of the reservations in perpetuity by designating them as Indian lands, and, importantly, to open greater tracts of land for white settlers—about eleven million acres' worth. The U.S. president or his designate would have authority about how to divvy up the land. The plan for the Dawes Act—which would ultimately transform the landscape of America and permanently alter the ways Indian people lived on their homelands—was conceived, drafted, and unilaterally passed without any input from tribes or tribal leaders.[78]

There was profound debate leading up to the passage of the Dawes Severalty Act. Proponents of the railroads and white settlers with vested interests in land development expressed support, with caveats. Indian reformers were generally supportive, but with varying rationales. Herbert Welsh of the Indian Rights Association, for example, believed while the Dawes bill would have the effect of reducing the amount of land comprising the Great Sioux Reservation, this would still provide the Sioux with funds for "civilization programs" and would ultimately lead to relationships between Sioux and Anglos that would give the former the "role models" they desperately needed—were they to survive.[79] Dawes himself suggested that the intent of this bill was to "bring the two races closer together" by enabling the American economy, government, and educational systems to assist Indians in getting closer to the standards of Euro-America.

Elaine encapsulated other white Indian reformers' ideas about the pending Dawes legislation after the 1886 Lake Mohonk Indian Conference. In advocating for Indian citizenship, she wrote, reformers endorsed the Dawes bill "as a practical introduction to citizenship." The idea here was that if Indians would "take up land under the conditions of the bill . . . adopt civilized dress and ways," they should then become full United States citizens. Individual land ownership, made possible through the "practical benevolence" of the U.S. government, would make Indians conform to Euro-American ideas and practices. And, as Elaine concluded, quoting from Henry Dawes's address at Lake Mohonk, "We are all agreed upon one thing—the Indian must be made a self-supporting citizen of the United States."[80] Under the Dawes Act, allottees became citizens. But not all Indians were allottees—many Indians would not become official citizens for thirty-seven more years, and it would be an endeavor with which Elaine's future husband would become integrally involved.

When the Dawes Act finally passed, there were many significant consequences. As Frederick Hoxie points out, the assimilationist intent behind the act meant, in theory, Indians "would farm, participate in government and adopt 'higher' standards of behavior. The statute assumed that land ownership, citizenship and education would alter traditional cultures, bringing them to 'civilization.'"[81] But in practice the act was "little more than a statement of intent" with few instructions. It did, however, greatly affect Indian lands. In the ten years after the passage of the Dawes Act, white Americans filed claims for more than twenty-four million acres of Dakota lands alone; between the Dawes Act and the subsequent Curtis Act of 1898, which also imposed privatization of lands on Native people, three-quarters of the Indigenous land base in North America was lost.[82]

Other consequences of the Dawes Act became apparent later. Because of the linkage between land allotment and whether Indians were considered "full-bloods" or "mixed-bloods," there was a new insistence on labeling Indians in ways they simply didn't label themselves, disrupting family and community norms. Allotment policy drew heavily on the nineteenth-century "science" of blood quantum, figuring out how much "pure" Indian blood any individual had, which was not commensurate with the way Native peoples traditionally thought of or classified themselves. The land allotment system didn't consider traditional forms of Indian governance, tribal identity, or systems of respect. Because of the insistence on giving Indians land to farm and utilizing Euro-American agricultural norms, Native women, who had traditionally done many farming tasks, were stripped from these duties as white mentors insisted these tasks should be done by men, disrupting traditional gender norms among many groups. And, as Hoxie points out, the inherent Anglo conformity undergirded a view gathering steam in white Victorian America—the adaptation of Charles Darwin's ideas about evolution to the human society, suggesting some races were inherently superior, along with ideas from the nascent field of anthropology reinforcing the suggestion that some cultures were more civilized than others—meant the Dawes Act would gain wide acceptance because it was seen by both Indian reformers and white land grabbers as a way to make Indians follow the "superior white man's road."[83] Perhaps it is not surprising the Dawes Act passed in the same year the American Museum of Natural History decided to mount exhibits of Indians alongside displays of ancient reptiles and fish—all, increasingly, considered fossils of another era.[84]

The Dawes Act also had ramifications for Indian education, although this was not its original intent. Land taken from Indians that would subsequently be sold to Euro-Americans would—or could—theoretically help pay for the costs of Indian education. Dawes himself did not endorse either a boarding-school model or a day-school model. In fact, advocates of both models found support for their ideas in the underlying notion that land allotment would lead to greater Indian self-sufficiency and, ultimately, a move toward "civilization." Elaine jumped into the fray, publishing an article entitled "The Senator and the Schoolhouse," in which the fearless twenty-four-year-old directly challenged forty-nine-year-old Senator Preston Plumb, then chair of the committee on public lands. Plumb, who believed Indian day schools were "absolutely impracticable," sought to insert language into the Dawes Act that would have given Congress or the president more leeway in how to use funding for Indian education. Arguing on behalf of her day-school model, Elaine challenged the senator: "If you want an utterly 'impracticable' scheme," she suggested, "take the theory of educating the race by putting *all the children* in Eastern industrial schools. The unnatural cruelty of separating the children from their parents to such an extent . . . the expense, the waste, the extravagance of the whole plan . . . condemns it at sight."[85] Her dramatic article garnered page 1 coverage and earned much publicity for the educational model she advocated. Elaine, keenly aware the U.S. government's 1868 treaty promised "a school-house and a teacher" to every thirty children among the Sioux—a promise far from delivered—saw that discussion around the Dawes Act might actually help her in her quest to develop day schools throughout the Great Sioux Reservation.

* * *

Though Elaine spent the summer months of 1887 with her family in Connecticut, borrowing funds against her salary to pay for the trip, she elected to spend her subsequent holidays traveling around the Great Sioux

Reservation. After two years of teaching at the White River School, in late 1888 Laura Tileston decided to return home to her family. While Elaine awaited the arrival of a replacement teacher to take Laura's place, she decided to take advantage of the unchaperoned time. She bought a pony and had a tent made for her, and then traveled across the prairies with different families. Though white people in the towns she visited were horrified, Elaine felt safe traveling with groups of Sioux. "Solicitous white friends urged me never to travel with Indians unarmed," she wrote. "They were poor psychologists and poorer realists."[86] She described her travels in detail, delineating in newspaper articles and, later, in her memoir, evenings spent in tipis with men, women, children, and dogs; the Sioux customs she observed; the sights she saw. Elaine captured some of her trip in a piece published in *The Christian Union,* in which she wrote of the "land of sunshine, sand, and sunflowers." The men hunted deer; the women tanned the hides, put up "teepes," carried water, harnessed ponies, and gathered mint, cherries, and plums. Elaine was accepted as part of the group; indeed, she wrote about how, with her suntanned skin, braided hair, simple dress, and moccasins, she was often mistaken for a Sioux. When the group encountered white settlers, "It has afforded me a good deal of amusement to be accosted with 'Do you speak English?" . . . or 'Why you've been to school, haven't you?' or doubtfully, 'Were both of your parents white folk?'" She concluded this entertaining article by saying, "I can fancy that when I get back again to civilization, after nine or ten weeks of tent life, I shall often dream of these Arcadian days."[87]

Elaine's last stop on her summer travels that year was Pine Ridge Agency. There she made the acquaintance of Reverend Charles Smith Cook, son of an interracial couple, and his wife, Jesse, who'd been educated in the East. The Cooks would become good friends to Elaine, and though she wouldn't have known it when she met them that summer, would play a pivotal role in the future directions of her life.

* * *

"Auntie Ella," Elaine's mother's older sister, hadn't been Elaine's first choice of a replacement for Laura Tileston. Elaine initially asked her younger sister

Dora to take Laura's place. But Dora matriculated at Smith College (mother Dora Read moving herself and the two younger children to Northampton, Massachusetts, to be nearby) and was unwilling to leave. No doubt Dora's refusal—and her college matriculation, something out of reach for Elaine—only added to the dissonance Elaine felt with the sister with whom she'd once been inseparable.

When Elaine returned to Lower Brulé Agency, she found members of the Pratt Commission gathering, seeking to meet with tribal members to procure as many signatures as they could for a follow-up bill to the Dawes Act. The so-called Sioux Bill would divide the Great Sioux Reservation into six separate units, surrendering some nine million additional acres to the U.S. government, which it wished to sell to homesteaders. In return, the Sioux would receive livestock, wagons, farming equipment, and fifty cents an acre for some of the best land along the White and Cheyenne Rivers. It wasn't a good deal, and the Sioux knew this.

Richard Henry Pratt's extreme assimilationist philosophy and supposed familiarity with Native people led to his appointment as head of this commission. Accompanied by Judge John Wright and the missionary Reverend William Cleveland, Pratt traveled across Dakota Territory pitching this new act and attempting to get Sioux buy-in. His previous stop—at Standing Rock Agency—had been badly received and garnered only a handful of signatures.

Ahead of the meeting to be held at Lower Brulé, Elaine fired off an article to *The Independent*. In it, she quoted several Sioux sources who told her that while the "Great Father" got $1.25 an acre for his land, it was an insult to ask the Indian to accept 40 percent less per acre. Another source told her the lands to which the Rosebud Sioux would be shunted were unfit for cultivation. Yet another informed her that once again, the U.S. government was seeking "merely a vain repetition of unfulfilled promises made in former treaties."[88]

In another article, Elaine recognized that part of the haggling over this legislation had to do with differences of opinion between the white people pontificating about it back East and those who saw the situation in the West. "It is unfortunate that our somewhat dogmatic Eastern friends are able to air their views in the newspapers and elsewhere, while the missionaries and agents toil hard" but had little voice in the cultural conversation,[89] she wrote. Elaine increasingly saw herself as the journalist on the ground who could rectify this, someone who could give voice to views not often expressed in print, and perhaps, someone who could help to influence what happened next.

Elaine described the scene at Lower Brulé in which "nearly every man, woman and child in the tribe was on hand when the council opened under a large awning in front of our agency." She felt compelled to attend. "I was not enthusiastic about the bill," she wrote. "I saw clearly, of course, that radical changes were both necessary and desirable, but I was not convinced that to part immediately with almost half their land would be to their ultimate advantage."[90]

Following this meeting came an announcement of another that would take place about a month later at Lower Brulé, with representatives from other Sioux reservations and many important chiefs, including Sitting Bull, invited. The Sioux met among themselves before meeting with the delegation from the U.S. government. Elaine "gained admission to this meeting in the character of a reporter. Sitting among them on the floor in a dense cloud of willow-scented tobacco smoke, I took notes assiduously, translating the speeches as I wrote."

The next morning, she received a visit from Captain Pratt, whom she'd met previously while teaching at Hampton. He eyed her suspiciously and questioned whether she understood the Dakota language. When she said she did, he asked, "What right had I to attend a secret council to which no member of the commission had access? I replied that I was there as a representative of the press. The Sioux leaders, in giving me permission, had indicated their confidence that I would report them fairly to the American public." When Pratt reminded her that she was on the government payroll and should therefore be supporting government policies, she drew herself up haughtily, replying, "I had taken no part in their discussions, but had listened to their views with interest. . . . I am here solely in what I believe to be the best interest of the Sioux and the fact of holding a government post would never stand in the way of expressing my honest opinions. If necessary, I could always resign."[91] At least, this is the way she recalled and recorded this conversation years later.

At the time, she did publish an extensive article about the proceedings in *The Independent*. Describing the ways in which the government representatives pitched the deal, she wrote, "John Wright . . . occupied the whole afternoon session with a long and ill-arranged speech, decidedly patronizing in tone and 'written down' to suit the supposed level of the Indian mind." By contrast, she reported the "pithy discourses from prominent Cheyenne River and Standing Rock men—men who have proved themselves in this matter to be the thinkers and speakers of their nation. They brought forward . . . their reasons for opposing the bill—a series of well-considered . . . objections." She quoted long passages from the Sioux speakers she'd translated. And she quoted Captain Pratt telling the group that their demands were unreasonable, their land not worth the equivalent price they were asking, and that Sioux tribal representatives should come to Washington to make their case. "Let us hope," she concluded, "that the Sioux people will gain such concessions from our Government as will fairly repay them for the thought they have given to this matter. . . . We may also hope that this act may be accepted in the end, and that in it may be found, in the words of one of the own number, 'the promise of life to future generations.'"[92]

This article perfectly embodied Elaine's evolving approach to Native American policy and her Victorian optimism. On the one hand, she clearly saw value in the Sioux way of life, she spoke fluent Dakota (once writing, "I became rather proud of speaking it correctly enough to be occasionally mistaken for a native"),[93] and she understood and supported their quest to retain their lands—or at least, to get a more equitable deal in exchange for them. But, on the other, she ultimately believed in the value of assimilation. The land deals should yield funds for schools, health services, and improvements in home and hygiene that would make the Sioux more Americanized. While critical of some American policies, Elaine firmly believed in the cause of reform. She didn't see her ideas as conflicting or inconsistent; she was a product of the environment in which she had been raised and the time in which she lived. In her zeal for Indian education and Indian policy reform, Elaine found direction in her causes, but in so doing, became lost, torn between the world she knew best and the world she was coming to know.

At the urging and arranging by some of their white advocates like Bishop Hare, several Sioux representatives did travel to Washington to plead their case in fall 1888. An amazing photograph, now in the Library of Congress, depicts the story in sharp relief: in the foreground on the east steps of the U.S. Capitol stand about a dozen older white men in black coats. Behind them, going up the stairs, are perhaps seventy Indians representing the six different agencies. No one looks comfortable. The Indians had made a counteroffer on the price for their land. In the end they did get $1.25 per acre, but the Sioux bill of 1889 contained many complicated provisions in ten single-spaced pages, thirty sections, written in complex language. While they did get some concessions in water rights and agreements about money for schools, the Sioux lost land, and the Great Sioux Reservation was formally divided into six smaller reservations. It's not surprising no one looked happy in that photograph.

* * *

When Pratt arrived in Lower Brulé, he came with a small entourage including two eligible young men who acted as his secretaries. Elaine, more concerned with her work than with her social life, spent the 1888–1889 academic year continuing to teach at the White River School—but she was starting to get restless. She believed the "good results" she'd achieved already placed this school in good standing with the white establishment educational community and with the local Sioux, and provided a model for what could be done with day schools. "I had faith in the day-school, the true community center, and aspired to create little Hamptons, each a focus or rallying point of all good influences throughout the wild Indian country,"[94] she wrote.

Ready for new challenges but uncertain of how to make them happen, Elaine resigned her teaching position and once again sought the council of influential men. Bishop Hare offered her a position teaching a "remote mission outpost among the wilder Teton Sioux," and an invitation to become superintendent of a government boarding school, both of which she declined. Elaine still had "the neglected, the despised day school" as her primary goal, and thought perhaps, were she to travel East, she could "put the whole case before people with influence and see what could be done."

But Elaine's path was meandering. She suggested she would take the summer months to "consolidate[e] my influence with the 'wilder' element" across the Great Sioux Reservation. No doubt having just quit her paid position she was also eager to generate some income from additional travel articles. And she chose a trip route and traveling companions that would generate much unique raw material.

Elaine elected to travel with Whirling Hawk, "an unreconstructed old pagan from the other side of the White River,"[95] and his family on a hunting trip. (Whirling Hawk would become better known as a performer in Buffalo Bill's Wild West Show and through an iconic portrait by photographer Gertrude Käsebier). Many people tried to dissuade her. The trip would be long. It would be dangerous for a single white woman to be traveling with Indians, unchaperoned. It would be uncomfortable and unsanitary. But Elaine was adamant. She persuaded some members of the party to carry her tent and baggage, paid for provisions, and finally convinced Whirling Hawk to take her along.

In one of her travel articles published in the *Christian Union*, Elaine wrote, "I do not really belong here, but here I am—having invited myself to join the hunting party and getting a hearty welcome. I am feeling perfectly at home in this free, open-air life, and . . . should easily pass for one of them." She described the hunting, the ways in which the women's tasks differed from the men's, the types of foods they ate, and the surroundings in which they camped. And perhaps most importantly, she also subtly but strongly pointed out ways in which her Sioux traveling companions dealt with the incursions into their land and their ways by white settlers. The Anglo Americans, she wrote, "are usually quite anxious to overreach the Indians in a horse trade, and make specious offers of old, broken-down hacks, worthless guns, etc., in order to rob them of their only valuable possessions—their ponies." But her traveling companions "are wisely deaf to all such proposals."[96]

In fall 1889 Elaine returned to her native Massachusetts, to her mother's new home in Northampton, which she used as a base from which to plan for and dramatize her next act. Elaine wrote a series of articles and gave a series of talks about Indian education, continuing to speak up in favor of her preferred day-school model. Influential members of the Indian reform movement including Herbert Welsh and Amelia Quinton set up some of her talks. Elaine conceded to get a "platform frock" of brown brocaded silk, in recognition that her talks were indeed giving her an increasingly public platform.

One of the people with whom she shared a stage was Thomas J. Morgan, the newly appointed Indian commissioner. Elaine and the commissioner were on much the same speaking circuit, and they sometimes traveled together from one engagement to the next. This gave Elaine plenty of opportunities to convey her ideas to him—and, as it turned out, plenty of opportunities to impress him. Though she'd procured letters of support from Bishop Hare (who wrote that Elaine's deep interest in Indians and "high skill as an educator" would make her a "valuable auxiliary to your department"), General Armstrong (who suggested Elaine "has studied and been into Indian life as have few in this country"), and W. W. Anderson, the U.S. Indian agent in Lower Brulé (who described the ways in which she built the school at White River into a "high state of perfection" that could "only be attained under the supervision of a person with Miss Goodale's enthusiasm and particular fitness for the work"),[97] she didn't need them. Morgan was more than convinced. But it wasn't until after Morgan was formally confirmed by the Senate that he appointed Elaine to a newly created position—supervisor of education in the two Dakotas. Morgan entrusted Elaine to try to build her vision: a system of day schools modeled on Hampton, that would give Indian children a balance of academic and vocational skills to help to assimilate them—and their families and communities.

Given $376 by the Department of the Interior's Indian Office for a team of horses, a set of harnesses, a "mess chest with dishes and cooking stuff," canvas for a tent, blankets, buffalo robes, "and other articles as may be required to properly equip yourself making journeys over the reservation in performance with your official duties,"[98] Elaine once again set off for Dakota Territory. Galvanized by her new assignment, the twenty-seven-year-old wrote, "Such freedom and power of initiative as I now possessed was thoroughly congenial."[99]

Elaine hired a pair of former Hampton students at Lower Brulé as her cook and driver, and by May 1899, set out on a multi-month journey, covering several hundred miles, to visit more than fifty schools around the Dakotas, and worked to improve them and shape them to her vision of the "model industrial day school."

* * *

Her new position filled Elaine with a kind of determination she'd never had. Fueled by her own initiative more than by funds, powered by her beliefs more than by her means to support them, she traveled around the Great Sioux Reservation. With the authority vested in her by Commissioner Morgan—as well as with his encouragement that she continue to write articles about Indian education to share with a wide readership of potential political supporters and funders for it—Elaine made unannounced visits to schools to observe teachers. She made new hires. She organized a series of conferences for teachers to share best pedagogical practices and instituted some standards among schools that had literally been the "wild west" of individual methods, curricula, and teaching practices. She sent Commissioner Morgan frequent and honest reports, often illustrated with photos. And she endeared herself to elders in the Sioux communities by frequently consulting with them in Dakota.

Elaine clearly articulated her "model day school" prototype in a *Christian Union* article. She described the bedrock principles upon which she thought day schools should be based ("civilization work" including instruction in Christianity, morals, dress and hygiene and manners; manual labor and development of English-language skills); the physical characteristics of the schoolhouse (including a wash room, a "well-fenced garden," plenty of windows, "a reliable clock," and even "plants in the windows and flowers on the table to add to the beauty and suggestiveness of the room"; a description of the midday meal students should be served ("farinaceous and vegetable food with milk"); there should always be two teachers sharing responsibility and a Native policeman to enforce attendance. She stated that self-discovery was an important component for true learning: "The wise Indian teacher never forgets that if her scholars merely recite the prescribed lessons and do not find out anything for themselves . . . her work is a failure." And commensurate with her personal belief that schools, well run, could be models for reservation

FIGURE 2.3. Elaine's camp along the White River, circa 1890. Eastman-Goodale-Dayton Papers, Smith College Special Collections, Northampton, MA.

communities, Elaine wrote of the important but delicate balance of informing parents about curricular reforms and getting them to accept these educational changes by instituting community events to happen at schools to bring people in and value collective recreation as a "civilizing agent."[100]

Sometimes Elaine needed to exercise her authority in unprecedented ways. For example, she described a time when she came to a school in which the teacher attempted to "seat about a hundred children, unwashed, uncombed, noisy, and undisciplined, in a schoolroom planned to accommodate fifty. . . . The man in charge . . . was apparently almost illiterate."[101] Elaine dismissed half the children, rearranged the desks, taught a sample set of lessons to model for the teacher, and followed up with the local Indian agent with her recommendations for changing the structure of the school—and the instructor.

She worked to coach or replace teachers without training who would routinely provide her with excuses for the lackluster performance of their students by citing prejudices about their Indian charges. She "took care to arrive unannounced. . . . A teacher's first intimation of my existence . . . was often my appearance at the schoolhouse door."[102] She advocated for additional funding to pay for the building repairs she thought needed and the additional supplies she felt imperative to move her academic and vocational objectives forward. In doing so, she sometimes felt it necessary to take on members of the U.S. Senate or the Catholic Church, which controlled a large proportion of the funds designated for Indian education at the time. "There are certain gentleman in the United States Senate who have consistently opposed, for many years, the policy of educating the Indians. Their statements that money appropriated for this purpose is money thrown away, and 'the educated Indian becomes a worse savage than before' were uttered at first with considerable effect,"[103] she wrote, questioning the significant appropriations made to Catholic missions for Indian education to the exclusion of supporting government schools run through the Indian Office. Perhaps it was the physical distance between the Dakotas and Washington, or that she was the designee of Commissioner Morgan, or that she was relatively young and idealistic—or some combination—that enabled her to boldly go where her predecessors had not gone before.

In her travels around Dakota Territory Elaine saw what was happening with education, and what was happening with the Sioux. Conditions were deteriorating. Indian land vastly reduced, and incursions of white settlers and the railroads vastly increased; the buffalo absent, disease and poverty more present—the situation in Indian Country was already significantly different from the one Elaine first encountered when she arrived six years earlier.

Elaine observed and wrote about some of this in her dispatches to newspapers. In a prescient article entitled "The Health Question on the Reservations," she stated that since the arrival of white settlers and the Euro-Americans' insistence Indians take up some of their customs, Indian health had greatly suffered. "There were no traces of scrofula or consumption, the fearful scourges of to-day among the Indians of the olden time," she wrote. "The transition period of civilization—the change from airy teepees to close cabins; from warm clothing of skins to shoddy blankets and sleazy calico; from wholesome food to diseased meat and ill-made bread; the excessive use of coffee and other evils incident to this period; among some tribes strong drink and the immoralities of licentious white men—these have ruined the pristine vigor of the aboriginal man!" She also noted, correctly, that the white man's culture had meant not only physical denigration and disease for Indians, but also "mental and moral" problems that "in many instances [show] the struggle of the aspiring soul in the weak body, a truly pathetic sight."[104]

As the young school administrator continued to travel around the reservations, she began hearing of a "new craze" among the Sioux. Curious, Elaine gathered information from her Sioux hosts, as well as from the white settlers she encountered along her journeys. One of the discernible effects of the growing problems and increasing despair throughout Indian Country was the emergence of the Ghost Dance. Though as Elaine wrote, she and other teachers and missionaries who lived among Indians and spoke their languages were not afraid of this "messianic" movement, many other white settlers became increasingly fearful, convinced the Ghost Dance meant Indians were rejecting their "civilizing" ways and signaling problems. They began to call in the troops, further exacerbating tensions.

In December 1890, Elaine arrived at the Pine Ridge Agency in the southwestern corner of the Dakota Territory. "We were practically under martial law," she recalled. "The infantry, in their neat Sibley tents, encamped in our midst, surrounded themselves with trenches and impromptu breastworks. A buffalo-coated sentinel, rifle on shoulder, met us at every turn."[105] For her own safety, Elaine was urged not to camp alongside her wagon, but to stay with her friends Reverend Charles and Jesse Cook at the rectory in Pine Ridge. Although she didn't think it necessary, Elaine conceded, and moved in with the Cooks for what she thought would be the relatively short period of time she'd be observing the school at Pine Ridge. What Elaine had no way of knowing was how profoundly this decision would change the course of her life.

3

From Indian Country to Dartmouth and Back (1858–1890)

The other thing Elaine had no way of knowing when she arrived at Pine Ridge Agency in December 1890 was that there was another person's story she would come to know intimately, another person whose story would join with her own, whose narrative and image she would help to shape and promote. It was another life story she would one day curate to the point of shifting it—even eliminating it—from the permanent record of her life. And though Elaine could not possibly have known or processed it, that person's legacy would come to be known in profoundly different ways than she understood it. That person was Ohíye' S'a, or Charles Alexander Eastman.

* * *

The Sioux creation myth suggests there was another world existing before this one. But because the people of that world did not behave in ways the Great Spirit thought they should, a huge flood washed away much of the earth. The Great Spirit then set out to make a new world. He sent four animals known for their ability to stay underwater as emissaries in search of a lump of mud from beneath the floodwaters to use in making this new world. The loon, the otter, and the beaver failed in the quest, but the turtle brought some mud for the Great Spirit to put into his magical pipe bag. He shaped the mud and used two eagle feathers to overcome the floodwaters, regrowing the earth. Then he took animals and birds from his pipe bag and, finally, made men and women from the remaining mud. The Great Spirit told these people they must live in harmony with their world, with all creatures, or they would again be destroyed. This myth shaped how Sioux would see the world, until they couldn't any longer.

"Sioux" is a historical umbrella term; the people today refer to themselves as *Oceti Sakowin,* which means Seven Council Fires. Each of these seven council fires was composed of bands bonded by linguistic use, kinship, and geography, covering related and allied people: the Sisseton, Mdewakontawon, Wahpekute, Wahpeton, Yankton, Yanktonais, and Teton. Of these groups, the Teton, who ended up living in the westernmost part of their territory, spoke the Lakota dialect and are sometimes referred to as Lakota Sioux, or Lakota. The Lakota were comprised of seven subgroups. The more easterly groups (Sisseton, Wahpeton, Wahpekute, Mdewakontawon) spoke the Dakota dialect and are sometimes referred to as the Santee or Dakota (this included groups which Ohíye' S'a's family came from). In addition, some modern-day linguists suggest the Yankton and Yanktonais spoke a dialect closer to Dakota. In other words, these different groups of Sioux had related cultural practices but somewhat different languages. The groups were also linked by their combative interactions with other tribes, and later, with different groups of Euro-Americans.

Pushed out of the central Mississippi Valley to the Great Lakes and Great Plains in the mid-seventeenth century by warfare with the Ojibwe, the Sioux exodus meant profound changes in their way of life. It put them in greater competition with other tribes for resources. The introduction of horses brought wealth, trade, and new modes of hunting; the introduction of white people brought guns, smallpox, and railroads. Increased contact with Euro-Americans meant more missionaries, more soldiers, and more pressures to assimilate; the decreased lands and buffalo populations meant new environmental and economic pressures. They fought with different Euro-American pioneers for decades when the latter tried to make incursions into Sioux territories. As historian Pekka Hämäläinen writes, "The great paradox of Lakota history is that by helping prevent the realization of other Wests—French, British, Spanish—Lakotas inadvertently paved the way for an American West, and eventually, their own downfall."[1]

The first Treaty of Fort Laramie in 1851, an agreement between the U.S. government and eight Native American groups, ostensibly guaranteed safe passage for Euro-Americans along the Oregon Trail and the ability to build roads and forts in exchange for territory and financial annuities. The Lakota were given exclusive rights to the sacred Black Hills, even though other tribes also claimed this land. The treaty recognized a vast swath of land as under Lakota control, from the Missouri River to the Rockies. It was, as Hämaläinen points out, "by far the largest Native domain ratified."[2] But the treaty didn't last long. After the Panic of 1873, the opening of the Black Hills for Euro-American mining became a national priority, sending miners surging to the area, forcing Lakota to fight to try to keep them out, and ultimately setting up the infamous battle against General George Armstrong Custer at the Little Bighorn in 1876.

In 1858, as white settlers raced to strike their fortunes in the Pikes Peak Gold Rush, on February 19 in a buffalo-hide tipi near present-day Redwood Falls, Minnesota, a baby boy greeted the world. His parents, Wak-anhdi Ota (Many Lightnings), a Santee Dakota, and Wakantakawin or Winona (Mary Nancy Eastman), had four older children before their youngest arrived. Many Lightnings descended from a long line of chiefs. Winona was the only child to come from the union of Wakhan Inazin Win (Stands Sacred), a Dakota daughter of the chief Cloud Man (one of the earliest Sioux to convert to Christianity), and Captain Seth Eastman, a West Point–trained U.S. Army officer and artist stationed in Minnesota. He would later desert his daughter and her mother for a white woman, also named Mary, whom he also married.[3]

Winona's troubled relationships with the men in her life purportedly continued into the time of her own marriage. According to Eastman biographer Raymond Wilson, Winona planned to wed one man whose family could not confer the established set of possessions to hers in the traditional exchange of marriage gifts, so she planned to elope. Enter Many Lightnings, who also sought to marry the beautiful Winona. He learned of her planned elopement and, disguised with a blanket over his head, arrived on the scene before her intended did. They rode away together one dark night, both covering their heads to avoid detection. Writes Wilson, "When she discovered that she had eloped with the wrong man, Mary Nancy decided that Wakan Tanka (... the Great Spirit) ... had punished her for disobedience to her parents. She vowed that she would accept such providence and remain Many Lightnings' wife."[4]

Following the birth of her fifth child, Winona suffered from complications, exacerbated by a throat infection that ultimately killed her. She wanted to call the baby "Mysterious Medicine," because she'd been told by the medicine man attending his birth that one day the baby would also become a medicine man, like her brother-in-law bearing the same name. Instead, because of his mother's fate, the baby was called Hakadah (The Pitiful Last). Many years later, after seeing a couple of sketches of the young mother he'd never known, Charles (as he later called himself) wrote to Mr. H. M. Hitchcock, "Every nursing mother came to my rescue ... until my paternal grandmother was able to feed me." Charles suggested the time of his mother's death was unclear—his grandmother's account differed from his sister's. But it was clear Charles had no memory of his mother. His 1927 letter describes his poignant reaction to seeing these sketches of his mother drawn by Frank Blackwell Mayer. Charles portrayed his mother in mythic, allegorical terms, as "the Demi-Goddess of the Sioux."[5]

Hakadah would be raised primarily by his paternal grandmother, Uncheedah, who stepped in and took charge of the boy. Charles would recall his grandmother as "possessed of as much goodness as intelligence," "remarkably active for her age," someone of "purity and elevated sentiment," and "a wonder to the young maidens of the tribe."[6] He recounted in detail stories he'd been told of how his grandmother raised him to rise with the birds and go to sleep when they returned to their nests, trained him never to cry and always to recognize and appreciate the plants, birds, and other animals around him. Of his first few years of life Charles would write, "My babyhood was full of interest and the beginnings of life's realities. The spirit of daring was already whispered into my ears."[7]

But life's realities for a young Dakota boy in *Mnisota Makoce* (Minnesota) during the early 1860s would soon turn harsh.

FIGURE 3.1. Mary Nancy Eastman (Winona). Courtesy Newberry Library, Chicago.

By the late 1850s the Minnesota Territory had filled with more than 150,000 white settlers; it would become an official U.S. state in 1858. The Sioux grew increasingly dependent on often dishonest agency traders who were "pocketing most of the funds for themselves."[8] To make matters worse, Euro-Americans tried to force the Sioux to relinquish hunting and take up farming, but crops failed and annuities were delayed, plunging the Sioux into poverty and starvation. This, in turn, further depressed Sioux autonomy and made them progressively more economically dependent on the U.S. government.

As white America pushed its boundaries with new westward expansion routes, the Sioux became increasingly embroiled in tensions as their land was compromised or taken over. David Miller writes that the Santee Sioux "became victims both of the desire of the territory for more [white] settlers to meet statehood requirements and the political conflicts leading to the Civil War. The seeds were planted for a future tragedy."[9]

When the Civil War began in 1861, Confederate sympathizers in Minnesota were already organizing and exacerbating the tense situation between the Sioux and the settlers. Seeking to play the Indians against the Union—Minnesota had become the first state to offer to send men to the Union army—Confederates informed tribal chiefs of Northern military defeats in some of the early battles, while Union recruiters attempted to conscript Sioux men. Further escalating tensions, Indian Agent Andrew Myrick refused to let the starving Sioux buy food on credit. Tensions broke open when a Dakota hunting party killed several white settlers. This set off a spree of violence including the burning of white farms, raiding of stores, and killing of hundreds of settlers in the so-called Sioux Uprising (also known as the Dakota War or Little Crow's War)[10] in 1862. In response, President Abraham Lincoln created a new Military Department of the Northwest, installing Major General John Pope as commander in charge. Pope saw this new position as a demotion. His over-determined and misdirected response took the form of his declared intent to "utterly exterminate the Sioux," as his soldiers began raiding villages.[11]

When the troops advanced, Uncheedah grabbed four-year-old Hakadah and fled. Along with her son Mysterious Medicine and a few other relatives, Uncheedah headed north. The group stole a lumber wagon and a team of oxen from a white farmer; as an adult Charles would recall his boyish glee at riding in such a vehicle for the first time, not realizing then the desperation fueling this journey. They crossed the treacherous Missouri River in buffalo-skin boats, towed by men swimming against the strong currents. Their frantic travels took them through lands of hostile tribes, evading Euro-Americans who hunted them, and powerful snowstorms, seeking food where they could find it. "I was now an exile as well as motherless," Charles would write in his memoir. In fact, he believed he was fatherless, too, since it was widely believed both Many Lightnings and Hakadah's two older brothers had been captured; he was told months later his father was among the thirty-eight "hostiles" hanged in the largest mass execution in American history. "There were times of plenty and times of scarcity, and we had several narrow escapes from death. In savage life, the early spring is the most trying time."[12]

Over the next decade, Hakadah would wander with the band of Santee Sioux to which he belonged, the Wah'petons, or "Dwellers among the Leaves," spending part of the year in the upper Missouri region along the Yellowstone River and part of the year going north to Manitoba. Charles later described the uncle with whom he roamed as "my adviser and teacher for many years . . . known as one of the best hunters and bravest warriors among the Sioux."[13] Mysterious Medicine taught him to hunt, ride, and understand the natural world. He also instilled in his nephew a belief that someday it would be his responsibility to avenge his father's death with the white men who had killed him.

Charles later recorded many of his memories of this time in two autobiographical books and a series of additional books recounting Sioux traditional stories and customs. Drew Lopenzina writes of the collective impulse behind these books, "Not only is he a literal orphan, but he is a cultural orphan as well, compiling his family scrapbook with whatever reference points or memorabilia he can gather."[14] It is difficult to assess the accuracy of Charles's remembrances, but what's clear is the voice of these stories. "One result of the Dakota practice of storytelling," writes historian David Martínez, "is that Eastman deepens his portrayal of the Dakotas' relationship with their Minnesota homeland—as well as the Great Sioux Nation—by demonstrating the extent to which this relationship is integral to the people's collective memory and knowledge." The way Charles relates his memories, says Martínez, gives them a "Dakota-centered agenda."[15] In addition, as Eastman descendant Yvonne Wynde points out in a 2023 publication of some of Charles's previously unpublished retellings of traditional Sioux creation stories, traditional Indigenous storytelling forms link families across generations in powerful ways.[16]

Of the many stories emanating from this period of his life, three stand out as tales giving insight into Hakadah's childhood and adolescence.

The first story, a chapter in Charles's autobiographical *Indian Boyhood*, is entitled, "Hakadah's First Offering." Written entirely in the third person, it delineates how his revered grandmother tells young Hakadah that after eight summers the time has come for him to transition from being a child to becoming an adult hunter. Tradition had it this passage involved making a sacrifice to the Great Mystery of something that the child holds most dear. For young

Hakadah, that "something" is his beloved dog, Ohitika. Charles details the rituals leading up to the sacrifice; of his own feelings, he writes only, "He swallowed two or three big mouthfuls of heart-ache and the little warrior was master of the situation."[17] While some contemporary critics suggest Charles wrote of this painful situation in third person to make it seem more distant, a type of deference to his largely white reading audience (and omitted that the dog was likely eaten after being sacrificed as part of the ceremony), others posit writing about this seminal event in his life as if it had been an event that happened to someone else serves to universalize it, making it part of a larger Sioux tradition. The self-sacrifice involved in this tale, encapsulating a personal experience as part of a larger collective, speaks to the role that such virtues play in Sioux culture.[18] Interestingly, questions about what constituted self-sacrifice would loom large throughout Charles's life.

The second major event Charles recounts from his days as Hakadah is the time he earned his second name, Ohíye' S'a. As Eastman descendant Kate Beane points out, it is customary for Dakhóta to change names at points of significance in their lives.[19] Charles recounts a lacrosse game between men of two villages; it's promised that should his village beat their rival, he will be rewarded by receiving a new name. When his village wins, the young boy is brought into a circle and given the name Ohíye' S'a (The Winner). He is told, "Be brave, be patient and thou shalt always win!"[20] The boy goes on to live up to his name, becoming a stellar athlete and consummate competitor. Although he would change his name one more time, he never completed abandoned Ohíye' S'a, though the way he wrote it and the order in which he would list his names would shift.

The third major story Charles recounts from this part of his life is the day his life turned upside down.

One day after turning fifteen, Ohíye' S'a returned from hunting to find a couple of unfamiliar men—Sioux, but dressed in white man's clothing. Confused, Ohíye' S'a turned to his uncle, Mysterious Medicine. "My boy, this is your father, my brother, whom we mourned as dead." Ohíye' S'a could barely fathom this. His father, who had been imprisoned in Davenport, Iowa, following the Dakota conflict, was taught English in prison, converted to Christianity, and subsequently pardoned by President Abraham Lincoln. Jacob Eastman, as he then called himself, took his two older sons and moved to Flandreau, Dakota Territory.

"Your brothers have adopted the white man's way; I came for you to learn this new way, too," Jacob told him. Reluctantly, Ohíye' S'a agreed to go with his father—his grandmother would come as well—to put on the garments brought for him, and to listen as his father read from his Bible and told his son that Jesus was the son of God. It was because of Jesus, said Jacob, that he journeyed to find Ohíye' S'a. "This conversation made a deep impression upon my mind," wrote Charles.

He described the trek from Canada to Jacob's home, the encounters with hostile tribes along the way, and his tremendous surprise and fright at seeing a train for the first time (his memory was of "a monster with one fiery eye"). He thought about running away and returning to the only life he'd known, but as he later wrote, "I could not doubt my own father, so mysteriously come back to us, as it were, from the spirit land."[21] And when they arrived at Flandreau, "my wild life came to an end, and my school days began."[22]

* * *

Sixteen different verbs in the Dakhóta language all describe the experience of returning home.[23] We do not know which of them, if any, young Ohíye' S'a used upon arriving at his father's homestead in Flandreau, Dakota Territory. Flandreau, in the far east of present-day South Dakota, was settled by Euro-Americans in 1857. They soon abandoned it out of fear of the Yankton Sioux. In 1869 the town was resettled by a small group of Christianized Sioux. The flat lands on which the township was built are tucked into the curve of the Big Sioux River. Along with his two older sons, John and David, Jacob came to Flandreau, filing for land under the Homestead Act of 1862 and the Sioux Treaty of 1868.

When Ohíye' S'a arrived at his father's 160-acre farm in 1873, he didn't know a word of English. Jacob strongly believed the only way for Indians to survive was to adapt. During his incarceration, Jacob took his first name from the Bible and his surname from his dead wife's Euro-American family.

His conversion to Christianity made him devout; he sang hymns and read the Bible to his youngest son every day, something the boy would one day come to believe a seminal influence. But at first, he recalled, "In accordance with my training, I asked few questions, although many arose in my mind. I simply tried silently to fit the new ideas like so many blocks into the pattern of my philosophy."[24]

Many of the new ideas didn't fit easily. Jacob insisted Ohíye' S'a become baptized and take a Euro-American name. Charles Alexander supposedly selected his new names "at random from a book of names presented to him by a preacher in the community,"[25] wrote one of his grandsons, Ernst Mensel. Jacob also stipulated that Charles learn how to farm; though the teenager was adept at hunting, he had never touched a plow and didn't know how to drive yoked oxen through a field. And finally, Jacob required his son to attend school. Uncheedah was concerned her grandson would "get lost on this new trail," but Jacob told his son, "The way of knowledge is like our old way in hunting. You begin with a mere trail—a footprint. If you follow that faithfully, it may lead you to a clearer trail—a track—a road. Later on there will be many tracks, crossing and diverging one from the other. Then you must be careful, for success lies in the choice of the right road."[26]

For Charles, the footprints didn't seem too distinct at first. His second memoir, *From the Deep Woods to Civilization*, describes his confusion in attending the mission school two miles from his home. He wrote poignantly of being in a classroom where he did not understand a word said. His fellow students played games whose rules he didn't know. Days were divided into distinct units of time alien to the boy who'd risen with the birds and patterned his life by the seasons rather than by a calendar. His peers teased him because of his long hair. He was ready to abandon this new venture, but Jacob persisted, cutting his son's hair so at least that social pressure would abate. When Charles returned to school the next day with shorter hair and a new attitude, he began to learn the new language and the new ways. He proved such an adept student that it was soon decided his education must continue beyond the little mission school. Jacob's unshakeable conviction in the importance of education impressed itself deeply on the teenager.

Charles would attend the innovative school in Santee Agency, Nebraska, founded by Congregational minister Dr. Alfred Riggs in 1870. The school trained Indians who came from throughout the Great Plains to receive education in a Euro-American curriculum that included both humanities and natural sciences. Many of the graduates became ministers, missionaries, teachers, nurses, and engineers. Charles described the school as "at that time the Mecca of the Sioux country."[27]

In 1874 Charles set out for school with another boy, walking the 170 miles between Flandreau and Santee. When his traveling companion decided to turn around and go home, Charles briefly considered fleeing and returning to Canada. But he recalled his promises to his father, and so he continued by himself for several days until he arrived at the school. His brother Hinhan Duta (Red Owl), baptized as John Eastman, was studying for the ministry under Dr. Riggs and was an assistant teacher at the school.[28] He, along with the avuncular principal, a man with a kindly face and a full beard, greeted Charles in Dakota. Riggs would become an influential figure in Charles's life. Literature scholar Drew Lopenzina writes that Charles would take on several white father figures throughout his life: "His desire to please his own father was sublimated by a need to not displease the white families who took him in and helped him on his new path."[29]

Although his memoir documented his early frustrations at school ("I hardly think I was ever tired in my life until those first days of boarding-school"), Charles once again proved himself an eager and facile student who quickly mastered all he was taught. By the end of the second year his English was so good he could easily translate anything from English into Dakota, and his command of math so dominant he soon studied with boys three years ahead of him. Riggs became convinced the young man could serve as a model of Americanization, the epitome of what could be achieved through the government's educational philosophies and assimilation practices. Convinced Charles could go on to teach other Indians the ways of "civilization" and thereby contribute to his people, Dr. Riggs took it upon himself to write a series of letters to President Aaron Chapin of Beloit College in Wisconsin, on Charles's behalf. "This will introduce you to Charles A. Eastman. . . . He is one of our most promising scholars and is an earnest Christian," he wrote. "Could you interest someone particularly in Charley Eastman who would be his advisor and tutor?" Adding that while it would be helpful if President Chapin could find funding to help defray the costs of his education, "Charley Eastman goes to paddle his own canoe. He must make his way chiefly by his work."[30]

Beloit's program consisted of three years of study in English, Latin, Greek, math, history, bookkeeping, geology and minerology, and mental and moral philosophy. It was designed to prepare students for college " under the immediate and constant charge of a principal, and the discipline is conformed to the usage of the best academics."[31]

Just before Charles arrived at Beloit, he received word his father had died after a short illness. "This was a severe shock to me," he wrote, "but I felt even more strongly that I must carry out his wishes. It was clear that he who had sought me out among the wild tribes at the risk of his life, and set my feet in the new trail, should be obeyed to the end."[32] Charles resolved to go forward and begin the next phase of his education.

Taking a train for the first time in his life, seeing a city whose streets seemed teeming with people moving impossibly quickly, and going to an "eating house" where he was served by a "pretty waitress, whose bright eyes and fluent speech alarmed me" were among the salient memories Charles recorded about his journey to Beloit. Historian David Martínez points out that the way in which Charles wrote about these memories in *From the Deep Woods to Civilization* began a theme he would develop in much of his other writing: the phenomenon of strangeness. Charles described himself as a "young blue heron . . . entirely uncertain of his perch"; Martínez adds that Charles was caught between the world he knew and the one he came to know, and the thought that "the day of the Indian has passed forever." Charles would spend his life trying to reconcile these thoughts.[33]

Once on campus, though Charles was greeted warmly by President Chapin, he was soon exposed to the first blatant and virulent racism he had encountered. He recalled hearing a young man shout to someone else across the college common, "Hurry up Turkey . . . we have Sitting Bull's nephew right here, and it's more than likely he'll have your scalp-lock before morning!" Charles wrote of his shock, pointing out that the incident occurred "less than three months after [the Sioux annihilated] Custer's gallant command." Charles added, "When I went into the town, I was followed on the streets by gangs of little white savages, giving imitation war whoops."[34] It's hard to know how to read Charles's word choice here. Was "Custer's gallant command" meant as ironic, or as a phrase deferential to his white publisher or reading audience? Kiara Vigil believes Charles Eastman's entire narrative should be read as a "gesture to an American nostalgia for this past," but also as a missive meant to persuade readers of "the lasting relevance of Indian people"[35] going forward.

Charles's three years at Beloit were filled with his studies and athletics (he spent not less than three hours a day exercising or participating in sports). He cut wood for professors to earn money and worked on local farms during the summers. While there were many ways in which he excelled at and embraced this new life—and felt, through his increasing facility with English, that he increasingly thought like a white man—he always perceived a two-ness that separated him. "I was now a stranger in a strange country, and deep in a strange life from which I could not retreat."[36]

This sense of being between cultures that Charles described would later be famously personified by Black historian and sociologist W. E. B. Du Bois in *The Souls of Black Folk*. But it would also become part of the theory of cultural pluralism, fueled by white philosophers and anthropologists like Horace Kallen and Franz Boas. For Charles Eastman, though, this idea was central to his lived reality.

* * *

Charles felt ready to move on from Beloit, especially after additional Sioux students arrived, as he believed he could "progress faster where I was not surrounded by my tribesman." Dr. Riggs arranged for Charles to attend Knox College in Galesburg, Illinois, his own alma mater. The "Knox Academy" preparatory curriculum was like the one at Beloit, consisting of both "classical studies" in English, Latin, and Greek, and natural science courses, math, bookkeeping, and history.[37] Charles's time at Knox was marked by continued academic success, and by his first exposure to "pale-face maidens" whom he found to be "very winning and companionable." Charles apparently taught an exercise class for these young ladies as a way of earning money and having regular contact with women. Raymond Wilson adds, "He grew more self-confident around the admiring women and throughout his life would remain comfortable in the presence of women."[38] There would be times later in his life when members of his family would question what Charles's high level of comfort with women might mean.

Charles attended Knox from 1879 to 1881. After that time, like so many beneficiaries of a liberal arts education, he wondered what to do with his life. But for the young Sioux man who felt he'd been singled out to receive this education as a beacon for his people, the confusion about his purpose seemed to illuminate him more than any answers. "I wished to share with my people whatever I might attain, and I looked about me for a distinct field of usefulness apart from the ministry which was the first to be adopted by the educated Sioux," he wrote. "Gradually my choice narrowed down to law and medicine . . . but the latter seemed to me to offer a better opportunity of service to my race."[39]

The notion of what constituted a proper medical education was changing in late nineteenth-century America, along with requirements for what one needed to do to get into medical school. Earlier in the century one could become a doctor by shadowing one; years of college study were then not required. By midcentury, students could directly begin medical training in medical schools, without having first attended college. Shifting from a largely rote memorization philosophy delivered in classrooms at stand-alone medical schools, after the Civil War medical educators began thinking it more important to train doctors by giving them a "progressive education" based on problem-solving skills garnered from clinical training in hospital settings. As this idea took hold, so did the idea that medical schools should be separate but dedicated parts of universities. And beginning in the late 1870s, possession of a college degree started to become a prerequisite for admission to medical school.

When Charles decided he wished to pursue medicine as a way of serving his people, he realized he would first need to gain a degree from a program that would grant him a bachelor of sciences degree. He was just uncertain of how best to attain this goal.

Charles returned to Flandreau in 1881. He worked as a clerk in the store his brother-in-law owned and taught a term at the mission school he'd once attended, where his brother John now served as principal. That fall, he met up with his old friend and mentor, Dr. Riggs. For the first time, Charles heard about Dartmouth College, and, encouraged by Riggs, he decided this should be his next educational step. Dartmouth, founded in 1769, was chartered as an institution to educate Native Americans in Christian theology and liberal arts, with funds raised partly by Native American minister Samson Occom. But given that Dartmouth's founder, Eleazer Wheelock, shifted Occom's funds away from the idea of an "Indian Charity School" and toward an elite college to train white Congregationalist ministers, and given Dartmouth's location in Hanover, New Hampshire, far removed from much of the Native population, Dartmouth's focus became educating Euro-Americans. Indeed, when Charles Eastman matriculated in fall 1883, he was the only Native American in his class.

Charles departed Flandreau in January 1882 for the East. Taking the train to Chicago, where he spent the night, Charles was once again surprised by the hurry people seemed to be in on the streets, as well as by the "faces of the people [that] were not happy at all." Friends warned him to be on the lookout for pickpockets, an idea that was an anathema to Indians, who "seldom found it necessary to guard our possessions." Soon he was on the train heading to Albany, New York, and from there on to western Massachusetts, directly crossing the rail line Elaine Goodale would have taken on her journey to Hampton. Charles got off the train at its terminus in Boston, where he was greeted by Frank and Annie Wood, friends of Dr. Riggs who were heavily involved in the Indian Rights Association and the Boston Indian Citizenship Committee. The Woods would become surrogate parents for Charles, people with whom he would stay when in Boston, people who helped him financially and who introduced him to influential reformers and other people who would become his financial patrons. Wilson writes that Frank Wood "counseled [Charles] on everything from proper dress to proper deportment. He was greatly impressed by what Eastman had already achieved and was mightily concerned that nothing should impede the young man's progress or shorten his reach."[40]

There was probably something about the young Sioux so determined to help his people that spoke to Frank Wood. Wood, born in Ireland, was brought to Boston at the same age young Hakadah had been when he was brought to Canada. As a boy Wood apprenticed in the print trade. He worked his way up in the business, eventually opening his own print shop and being so successful he became a millionaire, an unusual attainment in the 1880s. His wealth gave him the ability to turn his considerable energies to many progressive causes of the late nineteenth century, including work on behalf of Native Americans.

Boston, long a focal point for progressive causes in America, was a hub for Euro-Americans passionate about Indian issues. The Boston Indian Citizenship Committee formed in 1879 after an event sponsored by newspaperman and abolitionist Thomas Tibbles highlighted some of the travails facing Native American groups. Members of the Ponca tribe who had been removed from their traditional lands by the U.S. government accompanied Tibbles. Tibbles knew how to harness the power of the press to draw attention to the causes he was passionate about; he also understood how to galvanize liberal, monied Euro-Americans. Drawing in people ranging from the mayor of Boston to abolitionist Wendell Phillips to poet Henry Wadsworth Longfellow, Tibbles and his Ponca colleagues inspired prominent Bostonians to organize. They soon branched out from supporting the Ponca cause to issues affecting other Indian groups. Frank Wood lent his support—and opened his checkbook—on behalf of this organization, too.

Wood was also passionate about women's education. As a trustee of Wellesley College, he arranged for his articulate and handsome young house guest to give a lecture at the college. This talk, the first for which Charles received compensation, would launch his career in public speaking. The Wellesley talk also served to introduce him to other influential white Indian reformers, one of whom suggested if Charles were to forgo going to college at Dartmouth and attend Harvard, instead, he could procure a generous scholarship for him. But in consultation with Frank Wood, whose judgment Charles implicitly trusted, he decided to stick with the original plan.

Charles found the Dartmouth campus imposing. The Green, probably covered by snow when he first arrived, was the vista in front of buildings with their Georgian-style architecture and distinctive mansard roofs. The Old White Church, built in 1795, commanded its classic New England presence among the few other buildings, all so different from any Charles had ever seen. In some recollections, Charles wrote that shortly after he'd gotten settled in the dormitory in which he would be staying, he found himself drawn to a great pine tree out beyond the Green. "I stood there silent. I don't how long after a while I felt I was rather cold but up to that time, my spirit seemed to run back hundreds of years—long long before the white man's advent in America. I was not judging, but I tried to reconcile the whole thing in my spirit while it in Indian fashion rose from all those beautiful attributes to the unseen God."[41]

After consulting with Dartmouth President Samuel Bartlett, Charles was directed to spend yet more time in yet another preparatory program before he was deemed ready to begin his studies at Dartmouth. He attended Kimball Union Academy in nearby Meriden, New Hampshire, for a year and a half before returning to Dartmouth in fall 1883, starting as a freshman at the age of twenty-five. During his first term at Kimball, Charles was accused of plagiarizing a portion of a paper he'd written. When confronted, Charles reported he had never been asked to write something like that and did not realize copying passages from another book was wrong. His repentance and commitment to Christianity convinced his instructors he could remain at Kimball and be on track to attend Dartmouth upon completion of his studies.[42]

During the intervening summer on the East Coast, Charles caught his first sight of the ocean (and his first taste of saltwater when he inadvertently swallowed some), hiked mountains in Maine and New Hampshire, and spent time with the Woods in Boston, a place he came to consider the "metropolis" of New England and "home of culture and art, of morality and Christianity."[43] During the next few years, Charles would have occasion to meet and speak with a number of Bostonians centrally involved in literature and reform movements of different kinds, including Longfellow, Francis Parkman, and Mary Baker Eddy. In this time of relative leisure before he began his studies at Dartmouth, Charles was introduced to some of the popular literature of the day in white America, including a much-admired book of poetry published four years earlier—*Apple Blossoms*—written by two sisters who had been proclaimed childhood poetic prodigies.

Although considerably older than most of his peers and certainly from a very different place and background, when Charles finally entered Dartmouth as a freshman, he seems to have relatively quickly found ways to take full advantage of the college's educational opportunities. He later wrote that it was at Dartmouth that he first became interested in both literature and history; significantly, he recalled, "Here it was that civilization began to loom up before me colossal in its greatness."[44]

Charles's choice of words here was probably not meant to be ironic. The idea that Indigenous people were "savages" and the opposite of "civilized society" went all the way back to ancient Greece. In the United States, Thomas Jefferson, fascinated by Indians and the reports coming from Meriwether Lewis and William Clark, who he had dispatched to the West, wrote at length about these "savages" whose culture seemed so different. When ethnologist Henry Lewis Morgan's work was published in the mid-nineteenth century, ideas about how "savage" Indians were obstacles to "progress" and what they would need to do to become "civilized" became even more entrenched. Roy Harvey Pearce writes, "A lot of American thinking about the Indian was based on an explicit comparison between savage and civilized life—in the mid 19th century this took the form of comparing whites with Indians, who, as savages, had all past and no future."[45] No future, of course, unless they would assimilate. The distinction between "savages" and "civilization" became a useful justification for land and educational policies. And as a Dakota studying in the white man's world, Charles, too, learned to use this language strategically.

Yet it's also clear Charles was acutely aware of his own first language and his own cultural roots. He did not abandon it entirely for the "civilized" language of literature and history he studied. In a 2023 book of previously unpublished retellings of Sioux creation myths, Kate Beane notes Charles first began recording some of these stories during his time at Dartmouth. "He first wrote them down in Dakota in 1885," she writes. "Five years later, he committed to confirming the twelve lessons with Weyuha, one of only three men then capable of repeating the full legend." Elsewhere in this book, another Eastman descendant, Gail Johnsen, who inherited a typed manuscript of these retold legends from her grandmother, Eleanor Eastman, stated that Charles apparently continued to work on this project for many years, though it is not clear with whom he might have worked on the typed version of this manuscript his descendants ultimately edited and published; we know from some of Charles's immediate family that he did not know how to type.[46]

At Dartmouth, Charles undertook a diverse liberal arts curriculum. He studied classical languages, French and German, philosophy, history, and political science, as well as chemistry, physics, zoology, botany, and geometry. Since learning English when he was fifteen, Charles picked up at least a working knowledge of five other languages. While pursuing this broad education, it is not clear that his academic record was as stellar as it had been at the other educational institutions he attended. According to a Dartmouth publication, Charles "excelled at oratory and debate."[47] In a remembrance, one of his classmates quipped, "To those who experienced Charlie's classroom work, it is quite interesting to read that he graduated with honors. Truth to tell, we think the case might more veraciously be put by varying a Shakespeare passage to read, 'God made him an Indian; therefore let him pass for a scholar.'"[48] Something meant to be a fond recollection written after Charles died in 1939 is read differently today, but it is clear even his friends at Dartmouth never stopped viewing Charles as fundamentally different from themselves.

Charles recalled himself as a "sort of prodigal son of old Dartmouth," someone whose extremely different perspective was sometimes embraced by his professors and his peers. "I was often encouraged to ask questions and express my own ideas. My uncle's observations in natural history, for which he had a positive genius, the Indian standpoint in sociology and political economy, these were the subject of some protracted discussions in the class room." He added, his dry wit apparent, "This became so well understood, that some of my classmates who had failed to prepare their recitations would induce me to take up the time by advancing a native theory or first hand observation."[49]

Charles also took advantage of his time at Dartmouth by participating in several extracurricular activities. He was inducted into the Phi Delta Theta fraternity. He seems to have enjoyed much of the social life offered to him at this elite college. "He was a great favorite with the whole college, from the president down," wrote a journalist in a feature story, "and received more social invitations during his first year than any other in his class. He appeared to great advantage in evening dress, and is said to have been extremely popular with the other sex."[50]

But Charles seems to have spent most of his time out of class involved with sports. He was appointed captain of the freshman football team, and during his years at Dartmouth played competitive baseball, tennis, and football. He also boxed and ran track, where he set many Dartmouth records. A classmate recalled, "The surviving members of 'Eight-seven can see him today in their mind's eye coursing with steady, graceful strides the course of the two-mile run, leaving his competitors despairingly in the rear."[51]

Historian Colin Calloway writes that Charles's experiences at Dartmouth in some ways mirrored the complicated Indian-white relations in the United States of the time: "Surviving Dartmouth in the 1880s, like surviving in the United States, exacted a heavy toll on an Indian."[52] Although Charles's public recollections of his Dartmouth years trend positive, some of the other materials recording his time there demonstrate those years must have left him keenly aware of the worlds he straddled. For example, one summer Charles tried to earn some money for the upcoming year working as a traveling salesman. He "donned a scarlet fez, and with a basket on his arm went on a pilgrimage through the country towns of Vermont and New Hampshire, peddling his wares. His appearance excited much curiosity, as he was taken for a real live Turk."[53] Charles certainly recognized that whenever and wherever he was seen in this world, though not always identified as an Indian, he was always thought of as separate, different, othered.

Although they clearly liked and respected him, Charles's Dartmouth classmates also never saw him as an equal. In an unsigned book review of *From the*

Deep Woods to Civilization, published in the *New York Sun* in 1916, a Dartmouth classmate wrote,

> Owing probably to innate modesty, Dr. Eastman also fails to mention that never to be forgotten cane rush between his freshman class and the sophomores, when he and his fellows stripped to the waist and covered with oil, fought such a battle as Hanover New Hampshire never saw before and never has since, and of that dramatic moment when a piercing war whoop rang out above the din and confusion while a dusky, powerful figure with blazing black eyes and streaming black hair plunged through the mob of fighting students gripping the precious cane and bolted down College Street with four husky sophomores clinging to his back and shoulders.[54]

Another classmate wrote in the *Dartmouth Alumni Magazine*, "I cannot refrain from recalling those freshman days. . . . Then the ancient call of 'Eight-seven up' carried a species of terror to the sophs because of our cherished Indian. In the cane, high hat, and football rushes, Ohiyesa seemed as good as a score of our New England youth—lusty and muscular though they were."[55] Similarly, when the freshman football phenom inadvertently tackled a hapless young faculty member who had ventured too close to the field, the campus newspaper reported the incident, picked up by other papers running the story with headlines like "New Sioux Student at Dartmouth Tries to Scalp One of the Professors."[56] Revered for his athletic prowess but clearly seen as the Indian Other—which surely accounted for his physical agility—Charles no doubt knew throughout his time at Dartmouth that the affection his classmates had for him was always tempered.

An infamous episode epitomizing Charles Eastman's duality at Dartmouth is the story about when famed British poet and cultural critic Matthew Arnold came to Hanover. Charles's recitation of this meeting simply stated, "At Dartmouth I had met the English man of letters Matthew Arnold, and he was kind enough to talk with me for some time." Charles's classmate Stanley Johnson wrote that upon learning there was "an honest-to-goodness Indian" at Dartmouth, Arnold requested to meet the curiosity. "So Ohiyesa appeared arrayed in evening clothes, and with that unruffled poise that has always been with him constantly as his hands and feet. It was reported the great English essayist was himself embarrassed, since he had expected to view war-paint, feathers and wampum."[57]

And Dartmouth as an institution continued to alternately present Charles as a product of a successful Dartmouth education—a physician, writer, public speaker, and important spokesman for Indian affairs who had achieved the highest ranks among the assimilated—or to portray him as an Indian, separate from and othered in significant ways by the rest of his Dartmouth cohort. Historian Kiara Vigil suggests, "As 'Dartmouth's Indian,' Eastman could not escape the association others made between his Indianness and his body."[58]

The two portraits and many photos of Charles held at Dartmouth depict him in traditional Sioux dress. The photos of him at his fortieth college

FIGURE 3.2. Charles Eastman at his fortieth Dartmouth reunion. Courtesy Dartmouth Libraries.

FIGURE 3.3. Julius D. Katzieff, *Dr. Charles Eastman, "Ohiyesa,"* about 1927–1929, oil on canvas, Hood Museum, Dartmouth.

reunion show both how the college wished to portray him and perhaps how Charles then thought of himself. In one photo, he is riding a horse in a parking lot surrounded by black automobiles, as if a vintage paean to another era. In another, Charles is posing in buckskin and headdress alongside a white classmate dressed in a formal black top hat and starkly contrasting white trousers, sporting a cane in one hand and a cigar in the other. Whether this reunion photo was meant to be interpreted as the Gentleman versus the Indian, or perhaps, more generously, as a way in which their college class contained men of different backgrounds, is not clear. Nor is it clear whether Charles's Sioux regalia and accoutrements were meant by him to claim his own identity, or to accede to his classmates' stereotypes.

Charles would be invited to Dartmouth on a couple of occasions to dress up and play the part of Samson Occom, something Charles seemed willing to do although he certainly did not need to. Indeed, Occom was Mohegan, not Sioux. Historian Philip Deloria writes pointedly of how Charles Eastman was able to "play Indian" when it served a function in his life. "When Eastman donned an Indian headdress, he was connecting himself to his Dakota roots. But he was also—perhaps more compellingly—imitating non-Indian imitations of Indians."[59] In playing an Indian from a different tribe in this very public forum, it is possible Charles was doing exactly what Deloria suggests.

Despite these ambiguities, Charles Eastman's Dartmouth experiences were seminal for him. During his years in Hanover, Charles developed some of the ideas that would govern his thinking and the relationships that would guide his professional development. He saw in stark relief the ways in which he was accepted by his classmates, but how they focused on his athleticism or viewed him as not quite like themselves. He learned when it was beneficial for him to look like an Indian as well as when he needed to appear more "civilized." Dartmouth, it turned out, would also serve as the launching pad for Charles's many subsequent crossings into and out of Indian Country.

4

From Boston University to Pine Ridge Agency (1887–1890)

When Charles Eastman began medical school in fall 1887, he embarked on a curriculum including anatomy, physiology, and dissections.[1] The Boston University School of Medicine, which opened its doors in 1848, embraced a homeopathic approach. The training had a holistic focus, viewing the art of healing as a set of interconnections among body, mind, and the context in which patients lived. This philosophy no doubt matched well with Charles's worldview informed by traditional Dakhóta beliefs in the interconnectedness among people and their environments.

Unfortunately, little detail about Charles's three years of medical school exists. He lived with Frank and Annie Wood in their enormous, towered Italianate house on Alban Street in Dorchester. Widely considered one of the finest examples of Victorian architecture at the time, the home's interiors were lined with luxuriant draperies, fine paintings, and expensive books; the winding, tree-lined drive to the house led to exterior grounds including a gazebo and a carriage house. No doubt it was the most ornate and richly Euro-American decorated place Charles had ever seen, much less lived in.

Before Charles began his medical studies, Annie Wood wrote on his behalf to J. D. Atkin, commissioner of Indian Affairs, seeking information about possible scholarships that might cover the cost of his books, lab fees, and other living expenses, which she estimated would run about $600. When no funding was forthcoming, the Woods covered Charles's expenses themselves.[2] Charles wrote elliptically, "I was very happy when . . . it was made possible for me to study medicine at Boston University. The friends who generously assisted me to realize my great ambition were of the type I had dreamed of, and my home influences in their family all that I could have wished for."[3]

In his second year Charles studied medical chemistry, surgical anatomy, obstetrics and gynecology, and dentistry (in the nineteenth century, dental procedures were often performed by general physicians rather than dentists); in his third year, surgery, "insanity and nervous diseases," among other topics. The medical school experience at this time shifted from classroom-based approaches to clinically based ones. Boston University insisted its students participate in both daily and weekly clinics on several topics, ranging from surgery to cardiology, dermatology to pediatrics. "In these, as in other departments, special efforts will be made to familiarize the students with the best methods of examining patients, and to instruct them in all the details of diagnosis, prognosis and treatment,"[4] claimed the school catalogues.

During his second two years of medical school, Charles worked with low-income and impoverished people in Boston's South End. Without question, this training provided him experience that would prove useful in some of his postings after medical school, working with Native populations who also suffered from ailments coinciding with and exacerbated by poverty, poor nutrition, and substandard housing.

The comfortable, even luxuriant life with Frank and Annie Wood, who Charles referred to as "a father and mother to me at this period of my life," contrasted greatly with the world he saw in the clinics. The Woods also provided him with many enriching extracurricular opportunities. Charles wrote that they were "very considerate of my heath and gave me opportunity to enter into many outdoor sports, such as tennis and canoeing, besides regular gymnasium work."[5] Through the Woods he met "society people of an entirely different sort to those I had hitherto taken as American types." Charles didn't record much about his social life, but did note, "at . . . seaside hotels" he met many white women. "I was, I admit, particularly struck with the audacity and forwardness of the women. Among our people the man always leads. I was astonished to learn that some women whom I had observed to accept the most marked attentions from the men were married ladies. . . . I was surprised when I entered the ballroom to see the pretty women clad so scantily." Charles

FIGURE 4.1. Charles Eastman in the late 1880s. Courtesy Dartmouth Libraries.

also wrote in his second autobiographical book about his surprise when a journalist encountering him on the beach at Nantasket published a gossip column in which he referred to Charles as "the hero of the Boston society girls . . . a Sioux brave."[6] Clearly the reputation he'd started to earn among the "pale faced maidens" in exercise classes at Knox continued during his time at Boston University.

But whatever social dalliances Charles may have had outside of medical school were tempered by his continued and increasingly diligent embrace of Christianity. He attended church with the Woods during the school year, and each summer spent time in seminars given by Dwight Moody in western Massachusetts. Moody, an evangelical minister and publisher, gained fame during the Civil War for his work with Union troops. After the war Moody became involved with the Young Men's Christian Association (YMCA), preached, and traveled internationally to spread his brand of Christianity, outside of traditional denominationalism. Moody denounced the evils of cities, industrialization, and congestion and suggested true spirituality would come from finding ways to mitigate these problems. This philosophy was compelling to Charles, whose observations on the American cities he'd seen centered on their dissonances, and whose personal and professional focus highlighted physical activity as a key to health.

It is also apparent Charles and Dwight Moody shared a concern for Native Americans, and a dry sense of humor. In an anecdote he recorded in *From the Deep Woods to Civilization*, Charles described a walk with Reverend Moody: ". . . We came to a stone at the roadside. 'Eastman,' said he, 'this stone is a reminder of the cruelty of your countrymen two centuries ago. Here they murdered an innocent Christian.' 'Mr. Moody,' I replied, 'it might have been better if they had killed them all. Then you would not have had to work so hard to save the souls of their descendants.'"[7]

Perhaps through the influence of Reverend Moody, as well as through his own interest in athletics, Charles started to become active in the YMCA. This was the beginning of an institutional relationship he would cultivate throughout his life.

During Charles's final year of medical school, he wrote a thesis on aneurysms. Like much of the documentation of Charles' life, this thesis no longer exists.[8] This document would be of interest not only for its medical value, but also for its symbolic one. Aneurysms, weakening of arteries that cause them to bulge and sometimes to rupture, often are asymptomatic until the point at which they become a problem—sometimes a life-threatening problem—for a patient. As a third-year medical student Charles probably did not see his choice of subject as a metaphor for his own life; this would not become apparent until much later.

Similarly, although his classmates selected Charles as their commencement orator, nothing other than the title of the talk—"Comparative History of the Art of Healing"—listed in the graduation program remains in the written record of his life. Did he speak of the differences between the practices of medicine he had been studying and the practices of healing he'd learned from his uncle, Mysterious Medicine? Did he attempt to enlighten the almost exclusively white audience that healing practices differ across cultures? Was he able to offer a perspective suggesting that non–Euro-American medical practices are efficacious? Did he reference his experiences with immigrant and low-income patients and discuss ways healing must consider people's life experiences?

Charles's graduation from medical school in 1890 at age thirty-two did merit special mention in the *Boston Daily Globe*. An article entitled, "He's a Winner: Sioux Indian Who Got a Boston University Degree" described his early life and various educational attainments, and concluded with his intent to "carry the benefits of civilization among his people for whom he cherishes a brotherly affection."[9]

Throughout Charles's sixteen years of premedical education in Euro-American schools, he was often the subject of curiosity—if not pointed othering—by his teachers and his peers. And though he had always maintained a belief that the education he received would be useful someday in enabling him to contribute to his people, he doesn't seem to have taken a formal role in either educating white people about Sioux culture or political advocacy on behalf of his people during this time. However, the years he spent with Frank and Annie Wood began to change this.

From his own participation in progressive causes, Frank Wood knew the best way to disseminate information and build a following and a financial base in the late nineteenth century was to give public talks. The popular nineteenth-century lyceum movement set the stage for talks with educational, philosophical, or political intent, and increasingly, for talks with commercial intent. Frank Wood began to arrange opportunities for Charles to lecture to friendly, low-risk—and largely female—audiences. He also introduced Charles to Harriet Hemenway, a wealthy Boston socialite who would help to establish the Massachusetts Audubon Society and was involved with other reform movements; she, too, arranged for Charles to give a series of talks about Indian history. He turned out to be a very good and natural public speaker (he later suggested, "It may be that I shared the native gift of oratory"); his handsome face and graceful demeanor, as well as his clearly identifiable features marking him as "different"—even "exotic" to the Euro-American audiences of the time—made him instantly popular. Even so, in *From the Deep Woods to Civilization* he wrote, "None of my earlier friends who knew me well would have believed that I was destined to appear in the role of a public speaker!"[10] Frank Wood began grooming him for this role he later embraced.

Wood also decided that after Charles graduated from medical school, it was time for him to speak on a larger stage. In a letter to Indian Commissioner Thomas J. Morgan, Wood wrote of his plan "to take him [Charles] to the Lake Mohonk Conference with me, that he may meet the friends of the Indian and get additional education on the Indian question."[11] At the time, Wood served as treasurer of the organization that put on the yearly conferences and raised funds to support its political and educational initiatives.

The Lake Mohonk Indian Conference was truly the place to be for white people interested in Indian reform. No one seemed to think of their work as paternalistic; participants believed their work would save Indians from annihilation by finding policies helping them to assimilate. Historian Margaret Jacobs reflects that within a few years after white reformers started Lake Mohonk, "They had abandoned the most direct forms of restitution. . . . Instead, they developed a near consensus about what would truly bring reconciliation between settlers and Indian people . . . the allotment of Indian lands to individuals as private property and boarding school education for Indian children."[12]

Earlier in 1890 organizers put together the first Lake Mohonk Conference on "The Negro Question," but most conferences focused on Indian issues. Despite this focus on people of color, for the first several years no non-white people were active participants. Prior to 1890, not a single Native American person had been invited to speak at this conference purportedly about Indian education, policy, and welfare.[13]

But on the evening of October 8, 1890, at the eighth annual Lake Mohonk Conference (the second conference in that year), Charles Eastman became the first Native American to address the conference. Though Charles left no record of how he felt about speaking at this event or what he said, and in his autobiographical book only mentioned the names of some of the prominent people he met, the *Proceedings of the 8th Lake Mohonk Indian Conference* provide a transcription of his remarks. "I resolved upon pursuing a more liberal education a little over ten years ago," he began. "Before deciding on that, I had a sort of personal revival. My constant prayer was that I might understand the American people—their language, their mode of life and their ways—that I might be more useful among my own people." He stated he did not see how he could attain these goals until he went to the schools he did. He explained his decision to study medicine, saying, "I believed that I might do good by helping my people to take care of their health." And he concluded, "I have faith that sooner or later the white people will recognize the wrongs that we have suffered, and right them. From Sky-top this morning, I looked down upon the floating clouds all around us. But way up on the sides of the hills I could see specks of light here and there between the great clouds. The clouds were breaking up, and I had faith that they would move away. So I have faith that the clouds that shadow our people will move away."

After Charles spoke, conference convener Albert Smiley stated that Charles "had been pursuing his studies in Boston as a protégé of Mr. Frank Wood," and that Dr. Eastman had received a commission to serve as the reservation physician at Pine Ridge Agency. From perhaps the most important public platform at the time on Native issues, Charles was held up as an example of what education could do for the American Indian. "So," concluded Smiley, picking up on Charles's metaphor and layering it onto his own, "the light really has broken upon him today."[14]

These few paragraphs of their remarks both encapsulate and problematize the larger issues of Indian education in that era. Clearly Charles recognized, as had his father, that for Indians of his generation the way to survive was to learn the language and the ways of Euro-Americans. Charles needed to "understand American people" so he could be more "useful" to his own. Charles also recognized the role white colonialism played, expressing his fervent hope white people would right the wrongs Indians had suffered at their hands, while also acknowledging the role white patronage played and delivering his gratitude to those who had made his education possible. It was a complicated message. But it did not seem to fully register with everyone. Mr. Smiley, for his part, saw Charles only through the lens of his own privilege. Charles's success and career path had only been made possible by a rich white man. It could not have happened any other way.

* * *

There was another way in which Frank Wood worked behind the scenes to help launch Charles's career.

In May 1890, a month before Charles graduated from medical school, Wood began to send letters seeking employment for Charles. He wrote to Indian Commissioner Thomas J. Morgan, telling him of Charles's accomplishments in medical school, his standing among his class of sixty, and the oration he gave at graduation, and asking that he be given a position in the Indian Service as an agency physician.

When no job was immediately forthcoming, Wood hired Charles as a bookkeeper in his Steam Printing Firm for the summer. Wood wrote to Morgan again, as well as to other influential friends. "Dr. Eastman possesses all the qualities to make him a very useful man among his own people," he wrote. "He has a good mind with remarkable powers of persistence and application for an Indian. He is in love with his profession and I think will make a very skillful physician."[15] In another letter Wood repeated this message, adding, "He has been in my family for more than three years and neither my wife or myself have been able to see fault in him."[16]

By August, Charles finally received a letter offering a position with the Indian Health Service of the Office of Indian Affairs at Fort Berthold, in present-day North Dakota, with the Gros Ventre tribe. This was concerning to Charles, who knew neither the language nor the customs of this group; in fact, the Gros Ventre people had often been in direct conflict with the Sioux. Wood stepped in, writing again to Commissioner Morgan. Instead of this placement, Wood suggested, might Charles be placed at Sisseton Agency, where his older brother John served as minister, or perhaps at Santee Agency, where Dr. Alfred Riggs, Charles's former mentor, advocated for a placement? Wood also mentioned that Senator Richard Pettigrew, who represented Dakota Territory, might be contacted to help arrange an appointment for Charles among his own people. Wood ended with a plea to place Charles where his work could "do the most good." As David Miller writes, "Frank Wood's salesmanship waxed a blend of progressive ideology and New England moralism."[17]

Charles himself wrote to Commissioner Morgan. He was explicit in his desire to be assigned to an agency where he knew the language and the culture. With his brand-new MD as a calling card, Charles explained the doctor-patient relationship worked optimally when both physician and convalescent could communicate effectively, and in which the physician had a cultural context to explain treatments in a reassuring way.

Charles went even further in making a case for himself, describing his desire to make a difference among his people through education. He intended to do more than simply dispense pills and tonics, he wrote. In accordance with his homeopathic training, he wanted to improve Indian health by improving the conditions in which the people lived. He planned to provide classes in disease prevention and hygiene. He concluded his letter with a plea. Though he knew that people at Sisseton Agency, where his brother worked, were "desirous of having me as their physician," he wished to be placed "among the less civilized Sioux," such as those at Rosebud, Pine Ridge, or Standing Rock Agencies. It was there, he said, that his influence could be greatest not only in medicine, but "in all the civilizing and educational work."[18]

All the lobbying worked. Charles was reassigned to the Standing Rock Agency. He was grateful; he'd also met the Indian agent in charge there, James McLaughlin, whose wife was of mixed-blood descent and somehow related to Charles's family. He "would not be a stranger." But in late September, Charles found out he had been reassigned to Pine Ridge Agency. It seemed some people in the Indian Service protested Charles's appointment and Morgan changed his mind. This was the first time Charles's presence and approach managed to aggravate people in the Bureau of Indian Affairs; it would not be the last.

* * *

What did Charles Eastman think as he journeyed back to Dakota Territory after his Lake Mohonk debut in October 1890? He had not been among his own people since he left Flandreau for Dartmouth eight years earlier. As the train chugged westward and the landscapes of eastern cities and deciduous forests yielded to the plains and prairies of the Midwest, the more open vistas must have triggered memories. Was he excited or apprehensive? Did he worry how he might reconnect with the Sioux? Was he pondering how to apply his Euro-American education and westernized homeopathic approach to medicine? Did the words he had heard uttered at Lake Mohonk feel paternalistic, shoehorning him into well-meaning but uninformed white men's ideas about who he was and what he could achieve, or did he sit on the train inspired, ready to prove their faith in the training he'd received?

At this moment Charles was at a cultural borderland. As Frederick Hoxie writes, "The chauvinism and hubris embedded in . . . triumphant American nationalism offered only one alternative to young men like Ohiyesa: leave your Dakota lifeways behind and take on the habits of American 'civilization.'"[19] But intent on returning to his people with his new medical degree, Charles knew he had to find ways of melding his past and present with what he viewed as a necessary future. Despite knowing the Euro-American philosophy of assimilation, despite his periodic embrace of Victorian-era optimism and his immersion into Euro-American cultural practices, Charles knew he could not completely leave behind his Dakhótaness. He would become someone who used his life's work to define a future where traditional values could survive—someplace, somehow—in the cultural borderland of a changing America.

We cannot know for sure how Charles thought about his own role, or how he planned to use the experiences and knowledge gained throughout the many years of his Euro-American education. Certainly, he was all too aware of how he had come to be viewed by his white mentors, who saw in him the epitome of the Indian who could be molded by Euro-American education and values and embrace of Christianity, someone who as a thoroughly assimilated Indian could model this for others. Indeed, he would be hailed by Commissioner of Indian Affairs Thomas J. Morgan as "one of the finest specimens of Indians . . . [and an] example of what can be done . . . by education."[20] This is what white politicians, educators, and ministers wanted to see, the embodiment of an Indian who'd given up "savagery" and the backwardness of his old life for "civilization," a "specimen" rather than a man. Yet as contemporary historian David Martínez writes, Charles Eastman would turn out to be much more than "living proof of the reforms' faith in progress."[21]

What we do know, for certain, is that as Charles Eastman crossed back into Indian Country, it was a perilous moment in the history of his people. The dust storm encasing Pine Ridge Agency as Charles arrived in early November was perhaps emblematic; obscuring his vision from what he would later describe as a "bleak and desolate looking place,"[22] preventing him from initially seeing the stark realities leading to the life-changing events that would soon unfold.

5

The Wounded Knee Massacre (1890)

When Charles Eastman arrived at Pine Ridge Agency in November 1890, the situation was fraught. By the time Elaine Goodale arrived a month later, conditions had further deteriorated. By the time the two of them commenced their relationship mid-December, the escalation of tensions had almost reached its apex.

Relations between the Sioux and Euro-American settlers were never easy. After the Siouan exodus from the central Mississippi Valley to the plains, and after they received guns and began utilizing horses, the Sioux's world was made "smaller and its boundaries more accessible,"[1] historian Pekka Hämäläinen points out—so that they came into increasing contact and conflict with white Americans pushing ever westward. A series of military conflicts, paired with a long and growing list of broken treaties, ratcheted up tensions. Land deals diminished the Sioux's overall territory, and legislation attempting to get Indians to use Euro-American definitions of land ownership further enflamed the embers of conflict. By the mid-1860s most Euro-Americans already viewed the Sioux as enemies; the U.S. military responded by continuing to build forts at the outer edges of Sioux land, which led to a cycle of more tensions, more conflicts, and more tensions.

Throughout the 1870s a bad situation got even worse. The U.S. government placed Indian agents on reservations and charged them with overseeing subsidies, education, and general compliance to U.S. policies. The system, however, was deeply flawed. Many Indian reformers back East, like the well-meaning but sometimes misguided people running the Lake Mohonk Indian Conference, believed the system broken. A few publicly stated the quiet part out loud: the caliber of some of the agents was questionable, at best. Their salaries were low, and there was no standardized training and little oversight, which all too often led to high turnover rates and provided enormous potential for grift.

And when gold was discovered in the Black Hills in 1874, white settlers poured in. There was greater demand for railroads to be built, and consequently, more environmental pressures on the land. Unwilling to support the prior treaty made with the Lakota giving them sovereignty over lands now sought by railroad entrepreneurs, President Ulysses S. Grant used the Doctrine of Discovery to justify taking Native lands.[2] By 1876 the U.S. Army had deployed more than 15,000 soldiers in the Great Plains. Conflict of some sort seemed inevitable. Grant decided Indian attacks could be used "as a pretext for US military action," writes historian Gretchen Cassel Eick. And such attacks were entirely predictable, since Indians shunted onto reservations, their food procurement entirely dependent on U.S. rations, were left with little leverage. The federal government effectively weaponized food.[3]

Sioux leaders Sitting Bull and Crazy Horse resisted efforts to confine their people to decreasing territory and believed the U.S. government continued to ignore previous treaty agreements. Tensions increased, and Native groups mobilized, including an alliance of Sioux and Cheyenne. These problems culminated in the Battle of Little Bighorn in 1876, where General George Armstrong Custer's Seventh Cavalry was roundly defeated by a coalition of Lakota, Northern Cheyenne, and Arapaho.

The Sioux may have won that battle, but they were losing the overall war. Throughout the 1880s their land holdings continued to diminish as increasing numbers of Euro-American settlers filed homesteading claims; "Dakota fever" reached almost epidemic proportions among white pioneers. The signing of the Dawes Severalty Act in 1887 affected many Native groups but "signaled a renewed assault on Sioux lands,"[4] writes Jeffrey Ostler. The Sioux became ever more dependent on U.S. subsidies, and increasingly subjected to efforts to assimilate through policies ranging from reservation police forces paid—or coerced—into implementing U.S. policies, to continued efforts toward Christianization, to educational policies meant to reduce tribal influences on children. In 1889 Congress admitted North and South Dakota as states, further dividing the territories, and dispatched the ironically named General George Crook to get the Sioux to agree their territory would now be limited to seven smaller reservations. Crook, like some of his predecessors, promised to try to improve food rations and to improve the wages of Indian police forces in exchange, but it was clear Congress would go ahead with this policy with or without Sioux sign-on. Coupled with a two-year drought, poor supplies, and broken promises, food insecurity became a major issue. Food, once so bountiful across the Lakota world, once viewed as a system of which humans were a part, once gathered or hunted collaboratively, became scarce, became a commodity, became a coercive tool to force starving Sioux into submission.

Politics in Washington further complicated the deteriorating situation in the Dakotas. Keen to get votes for his Republican Party and bring new western states into the union to increase his party's influence, President Benjamin Harrison furthered a culture of politically appointed and poorly trained Indian agents, exacerbating an already tense situation.[5]

Into the deepening despair and increased cultural anxiety among Siouan peoples came word of a revivalist ceremony sweeping across Plains Native groups. Inspired by the teachings of a Northern Paiute spiritual leader named Wovoka (a.k.a. Jack Wilson), the Ghost Dance was considered a way of reclaiming traditional practices to unite Native people with spirits of their dead relatives, end American expansionism, and reclaim Native American sovereignty by returning Native peoples to a time of pre–Euro-American existence. Wilson later told anthropologist James Mooney he'd seen a vision of what could be with people who died long ago "engaged in their oldtime sports and occupations," and "by performing this dance at interval," contemporary Native people "would secure this happiness to themselves."[6]

The Ghost Dance ceremony could include as many as 400–1,000 dancers who would ritually prepare themselves by fasting or eating only certain foods, purifying themselves in sweat lodges, wearing special clothing, and decorating themselves with body paint and eagle feathers. Given all that was going on in their dealings with white Americans, it is not surprising that the Ghost Dance would have piqued Sioux interest. "Like many similar movements throughout the world," suggests Ostler, "the Ghost Dance is best understood as an anticolonial movement."[7] But that is not the way it was understood at the time.

The Sioux probably were attracted to the idea of connecting with their dearly departed; the idea that it might bring back the buffalo and the old ways of life would also have been compelling. But contemporary analysts suggest the Sioux would also have wondered about whether the Ghost Dance customs, emanating from other tribes, were consistent with their own cultural beliefs and religious practices; that women could be included, for instance, might have made them wonder about the efficacy of the dance for themselves, because women had largely separate domains in Siouan culture. But regardless of any concerns they may have had, Sioux groups began participating in this ceremony in large numbers. It's estimated about one-third of the Lakota became Ghost Dancers.[8]

White Americans did not understand the Ghost Dance as an anticolonial movement; they understood it as an anti-American movement. They viewed it as an insurrection, and as a threat. In early December 1890, newly reelected South Dakota governor Arthur C. Mellette issued a statement carried by many newspapers: "In view of the wide-spread alarm for fear of an Indian outbreak I assure all settlers . . . they are in no possible danger. . . . The ghost dance is subsiding and turbulent Indians are being set apart by themselves and are under complete control of the United States troops, large forces of which are stationed at strategic points, completely commanding the situation,"[9] read a prominently placed article in the *Wessington Springs* (SD) *Herald*. He wasn't exaggerating: by mid-November, the government had authorized deployment of a massive number of troops, converging from their home bases in many states to the new state of South Dakota. Not since the Civil War had there been so large a military operation.[10]

On one of his first days at Pine Ridge Agency, Charles recalled a conversation with Captain George Sword, the Oglala Sioux head of the Indian police force. "I fear we are going to have trouble," he told Charles, explaining a "Mountain religion" proclaiming a Messiah was starting to take hold among his own people. "Our reservation has been free from this new teaching until the last few weeks. . . . It has been rapidly gaining converts." Captain Sword concluded, "The agent says that the Great Father at Washington wishes it stopped. I fear the people will not stop. I fear trouble."[11]

Elaine Goodale had seen instances of the Ghost Dance during the summer and fall of 1890 as she rode around the Dakotas. She visited with Sitting Bull, the important Hunkpapa Lakota leader at his home at Grand River, where she "passed several nights alone in my tent within sight and sound of the ghost dancing."[12] Elaine knew the Ghost Dance was causing a huge amount of anxiety among white settlers, and throughout her travels around the territories she noted the increasing military presence. She recalled, "There was no secrecy about the dance which had caused such frantic alarm. It was held in the open, with neither fire nor light. . . . Anyone might look on."[13] Not only did she look on, but she also felt compelled to write about what she saw for Eastern white readers whom she knew would have interest in the unfamiliar ritual and concern about what it might portend.

Elaine cast the Ghost Dance primarily as an expression of longing for dead family members. "Nowhere is the obligation of kinship stronger, the family tie more sacred, friendship more loyal, hospitality more uncalculating and universal," she wrote. She described the Ghost Dancers as a combination of those Indians who had already embraced Christianity and those who had not. She delineated the fasting that preceded the "ample feast" that followed, the ways in which "everything is decorated—even the bails of the kettles and the handles of the new tin dippers are wound with ribbons of brilliantly colored corn-husk, and finished with gay little tassels," and the outfits the participants wore.[14] Nowhere in this article, published in *The Independent*, would readers have found any evidence of a threatening presence or practice. Elaine estimated about 10 percent of the Sioux were Ghost Dancers.

Tracking the uptick in Ghost Dancing throughout her travels around what had been the Great Sioux Reservation, Elaine eventually arrived at Pine Ridge, westernmost of the Dakota agencies. It was there, she wrote, "my personal fortunes, strangely enough, reached a turning-point with this dramatic crisis in the history of the Sioux."[15]

* * *

Charles's first few days in Pine Ridge were challenging. Upon his arrival he was shown his quarters—a bedroom, sitting room, office, and dispensary in the same barracks as the police quarters and Indian agent's office. "There was no carpet, no furniture save a plain desk and a couple of hard wooden chairs, and everything was coated with a quarter of inch or so of fine Dakota dust," he wrote. "An old-fashioned box stove was the only cheerful thing on the premises." There also was a hole in the wall, where his "predecessors had been wont to deal out pills and potions to a crowd of patients standing in line."[16] One of Charles's first actions was to close the hole and put a sign on the door inviting potential patients to discuss medications with the doctor, instead of simply receive them.

Indeed, the "Indian white doctor," as he came to be known, did things differently than his predecessors. Not only did he insist on seeing patients before doling out medication, but he also spent time with them. "It surprised them that I insisted upon examining each patient and questioning him in plain Sioux—no interpreter needed! I made a record of interesting cases and took note of the place where they were encamped, planning to visit as many as possible in their teepees."[17] Charles was especially reluctant to use any curative alcohol, quickly seeing the toll it took on many Pine Ridge residents who sought liquor as a panacea for their many physical and emotional ills. He rapidly became busy, seeing "hundreds of patients who left me but few leisure moments." He soon needed an assistant to help him in the dispensary and hired mixed-blood George Graham to help with the mixing of salves, ointments, and syrups.

After a short time in Pine Ridge, Charles received an invitation to a tea party at the rectory of Reverend Charles Smith Cook. The "gracefully worded" invitation asked him to celebrate "my birthday and your coming to Pine Ridge." Charles gladly accepted. He had been working long hours and admitted to "pangs of homesickness." The source of his homesickness wasn't obvious—was it the world of Euro-American education and culture in the East that had been his home most recently, or the world of pre-white Sioux existence he'd known as a child?

Elaine Goodale, who had been staying with the Cooks, also looked forward to the tea party, as well as to meeting the young Sioux physician everyone was talking about. The combination of his unique educational path and the people he and Elaine knew in common had heightened her sense of anticipation.

It is not difficult to imagine the electric shock of attraction when Dr. Eastman was introduced to Miss Goodale, the handsome young doctor with close-cropped dark hair and an athletic build, and the petite young woman with intensive gray eyes, her light brown hair in a bun with curly entrails. That Charles was already familiar with her writing would have immediately endeared him to her. That they already knew of one another's work with the Sioux only added to the allure. They were two people doing unconventional work in conventional professions; their reputations as young people pushing the envelope of their respective careers preceded them. Their connection was clear from the start.

As they began to get to know one another, Elaine and Charles also found in one other a passion to help Indian peoples mirroring their own fervor. Elaine was impressed when Charles worked to reorganize his inadequate office space, advocated with the U.S. government to procure additional medical supplies to supplement the meager and insufficient stockpile he'd been given, and "bought a saddle horse with his own money in order that he could respond to distant calls."[18] Charles admired Elaine's dedication to her work, too—her mastery of the Lakota language so she could communicate more effectively and her genuine desire to travel about the Great Sioux Reservation on horseback to learn more about its people and come up with better ways to educate its children. He believed her to be "absolutely sincere in her work for Indians."[19]

A week after their first meeting at the Cooks' home, they rode together to a Catholic mission near Pine Ridge. Their conversations deepened the initial connections they felt. Along the way, Elaine learned Charles had been up all night tending to a sick baby. "I was deeply touched by this quite ordinary incident," she wrote.[20] This moment of clarity sharply contrasted with the confusing time unfolding around them. The only thing becoming ever clearer was that the situation was anything but ordinary.

* * *

Among Indian agencies in the late nineteenth century, Pine Ridge arguably had the worst reputation. Writes historian Robert Utley, Pine Ridge "exhibited a more conspicuous personification of the evils of the spoils system"[21] than any other agency. And given the well-known grifting, thievery, and bribery so rampant among those assigned to work with Indians on reservations, this was saying a lot. Utley reports Pine Ridge was widely known as "Pettigrew's Place," a facetious nod to Senator Richard Pettigrew's patronage placements. One of these placements—perhaps the one that would prove most disastrous in the eye of history—was the installation of Daniel F. Royer as Indian agent at Pine Ridge.

By fall 1890, Royer's checkered résumé should have given anyone checking plenty of pause. Royer had no credentials for being an Indian agent. He'd trained as a teacher but taught only briefly, gone to medical school but practiced medicine a scant few years before mysteriously abandoning his practice, and opened a drugstore without training as a pharmacist.[22] Like so many men seeking a reversal of fortune, he came to Dakota Territory in 1884, where he worked as a pension examiner, may have briefly been a newspaper editor or publisher, and somehow managed to get elected and served two terms in the Dakota Territorial Legislature. An article in the *Wessington Springs Herald* described him as "a man below medium height, round and snugly built, and decidedly hansome [*sic*]. Dark brown hair, a love of mustache of the same color, fair complexion and blue eyes that talk whether the lips move or not."[23]

Once Royer came to Pine Ridge it wasn't only his eyes or lips that spoke; so did his hands, as he busily wrote letters and telegrams ever more urgently requesting the protection of troops. "Indians are dancing in the snow and are wild and crazy," he stated emphatically on November 18 to the commissioner of Indian Affairs. "I have fully informed you that employees and government

FIGURE 5.1. U.S. troops surrounding Indians at Wounded Knee, 1890. Courtesy Library of Congress.

property at this agency have no protection and are at the mercy of these dancers. Why delay by further investigation? We need protection, and we need it now."[24] Troops began to flood into Pine Ridge; ultimately numbering five thousand, with four thousand or more in adjacent areas, fully a third of the U.S. Army at the time.[25]

Royer repeatedly ordered the Ghost Dancers to cease and desist, to no avail. He was no more effective with this than he had been a month earlier when he tried to stop Buffalo Bill Cody from recruiting Lakota for his Wild West Show. In both instances, Royer displayed a pitiful lack of understanding about the Sioux culture around him, as well as about the conditions of hunger, economic insecurity, and cultural deprivation leading to the activities he found so threatening. Royer, writes Utley, "was weak, excitable, and easily panicked, so much so that the Sioux named him 'Young-Man-Afraid-of Indians.' He quickly made himself a target of contempt and ridicule, and he proved utterly wanting in any ability to stem the drift to anarchy."[26] Heather Cox Richardson adds, "It would have been hard to find a worse Indian agent than Royer," under whose watch conditions at Pine Ridge "deteriorated with breathtaking speed."[27]

Elaine found Agent Royer's actions almost inexplicable. "None of the missionaries, speaking the language and knowing the temper of the people as they did, had the least fear of an uprising," she pointed out. She wrote that General Nelson A. Miles, the more conciliatory veteran soldier who had replaced General Crook as commander of the Military Division of the Missouri and had oversight over what *should* have been happening in Pine Ridge, advised Agent Royer to let the Ghost Dance craze run its course; he felt it would end without incident.[28] Charles, for his part, later wrote, "The 'Messiah craze' in itself was scarcely a source of danger. . . . Other tribes than the Sioux who adopted the new religion were let alone, and the craze died a natural death in the course of a few months."[29]

But Royer could not let it alone. He was culturally ignorant of Sioux practices. He didn't know the language, and he misread their actions. And he was incredibly fearful. His nephew, Lewis McIlvaine, who Royer had brought to Pine Ridge, inexplicably, to teach baseball to the Sioux, reported his uncle always kept a loaded rifle close by. With Royer constantly trying to bring in armed guards and arming himself, tensions around Pine Ridge ramped up significantly between October and December.

At the same time, conditions continued to deteriorate. Charles later wrote, "Rations had been cut from time to time; the people were insufficiently fed, and their protests and appeals were disregarded. Never was more ruthless fraud and graft practiced upon a defenseless people. . . . Never were there more worthless 'scraps of paper' anywhere in the world than many of the Indian treaties and Government documents! Sickness was prevalent and the death rate was alarming, especially among the children."[30]

Although the situation was bad in Pine Ridge, it wasn't the only place where the combination of terrible conditions for the Sioux paired with missteps by the American military created a veritable tinder box, ready to implode.

At Standing Rock Agency, almost three hundred miles to the north of Pine Ridge, straddling the South and North Dakota borders, Agent James McLaughlin sought to seize Sitting Bull and keep him in custody until the Ghost Dance wound down. McLaughlin viewed him as a potential agitator, believing his presence would further encourage and perpetuate the Ghost Dance. When Elaine visited with Sitting Bull only weeks before, she found the situation tense but not out of control. Agent McLaughlin was someone she described at the time as "one of the steadiest and most experienced men in the service."[31] But something went horribly wrong in the raid McLaughlin ordered on Sitting Bull's cabin on December 15. Sitting Bull was awakened in his home early in the morning but refused to leave with the police who tried to remove him. A crowd gathered; shots rang out. When the melee was over, three Indian police officers and a dozen Sioux were dead, including Sitting Bull. Elaine would later reflect, "The dictator of Standing Rock . . . insisted throughout that he could handle the situation without help and that his well-trained police might be trusted to carry out his orders." In retrospect, she added, this tragedy led "as a fairly direct consequence—to the many times multiplied tragedy of Wounded Knee."[32]

* * *

Despite the growing tensions all around them, Elaine and Charles unexpectedly, miraculously, admitted their love for each other. "I had planned to enter upon my life work unhampered by any other ties," he later wrote. "At last, however, I had met a woman whose sincerity was convincing and whose ideals seemed very like my own. . . . I do not know what unseen hand had guided me to her side."[33] Elaine, for her part, expunged any record of how she felt about falling in love with Charles from the record of her life. She left no comment about fate or destiny, no witness to the romance of it all. Instead, she sought to cast their relationship as part of her career trajectory: "In reality . . . [it] followed almost inevitably upon my passionate preoccupation with the welfare of those whom I already looked upon as my adopted people."[34]

Christmas was almost upon them. Elaine and others working at Pine Ridge felt perhaps their holiday preparations could help to ease some of the apprehensions everyone felt and provide some measure of joy for the suffering children. Elaine and Charles spent evenings working side by side sorting through the boxes of donated clothing and toys and purchasing candy and oranges to distribute. They gathered with others at Pine Ridge Agency practicing carols. Their preparations would culminate in decorating the tree.

On Christmas Day 1890, Elaine and Charles announced their engagement. "We became engaged under the Christmas tree he had helped me trim for the children of 'our people,'" she later wrote, "who, shivering in their cotton tipis, still awaited we knew not what disaster."[35] Wrote Charles, "I had laid my plans carefully and purposed to serve my race for a few years in my profession . . . and I had decided that it would be wise not to think of marriage for the present." However, he added, "I had not given due weight to the possibility of love."[36]

"When, only a few weeks after our first meeting, I promised to marry Dr. Eastman, it was with a thrilling sense of two-fold consecration," recalled Elaine. "I gave myself wholly in that hour. . . . At the same time, I embraced with a new and deeper zeal the conception of life-long service to my husband's people."[37]

Elaine knew her own people would be more perplexed. Interracial relationships were rare in those days, even more uncommon among the Goodales' circle of acquaintances in rural western Massachusetts. Charles wrote to Elaine's sister Rose that perhaps their engagement had "sicken[ed] you all," but he wanted the family to understand, "We are comparatively corresponded in many ways. We have many common ideas, desires, and purpose of life. It seems rather hasty, but the fact that we know each other's purpose and objects of life . . . gained a spontaneous respect, and love came on both sides."[38]

But whatever concerns Elaine and Charles had about how news of their engagement would be met were soon overshadowed, and the joy they felt in their newly admitted love, overtaken.

* * *

Following the disastrous murder of Sitting Bull, many Hunkpapa fled south, where they met Sitting Bull's half-brother, Big Foot, and his Minconjou Lakota followers. The uprising General Miles feared Sitting Bull might stoke almost happened when the botched raid killed the Hunkpapa leader. Big Foot embraced the Ghost Dance and was thus on the U.S. military's unofficial list of "troublemakers who should be arrested." He had been invited to Pine Ridge by Chief Red Cloud to try to broker peace before the situation escalated further. But in the last days of December, as these two bands of Sioux approached Pine Ridge, the U.S. military prepared for further action. The Seventh Cavalry—Custer's old unit—under the command of Colonel James Forsyth, came into position along Wounded Knee Creek, joining the additional troops who had arrived at Agent Royer's vehement urging. There were almost five hundred well-armed soldiers. Charles noted he planned to go investigate the situation there but "my fiancée pointed out that my duty lay rather at home with our Indians, and I stayed."[39] Elaine's suggestion probably saved Charles's life.

On the morning of December 29, Elaine, Charles, and others at Pine Ridge were busily marking gifts to be distributed and filling candy bags "when the distant thunder of big guns, some eighteen miles away, sent cold shivers down our backs. Within an incredibly short time came first reports of the slaughter at Wounded Knee. We were told, indeed, that the cavalry had been cut off from reaching us and that we were at the mercy of a maddened horde of Indians!"[40] Elaine wrote.

"We were all straining our ears toward Wounded Knee," Charles remembered, "and about the middle of the forenoon we distinctly heard the reports of the Hotchkiss guns." There was confusion at the agency, with reports coming from messengers of the military and the Sioux. Some "hot-headed young braves fired on the sentinels" at the agency, Charles wrote, and when the Indian police attempted to answer their fire, General John Rutter Brooke (who had ordered the Seventh Cavalry to come to Wounded Knee) told Charles to instruct the Sioux police not to fire until ordered to. "I did so, as the bullets whistled by us, and the General's coolness perhaps saved all our lives."[41]

The situation remained tense in the days afterward. Charles's office filled with the wounded and the sick. He asked a friend to take Elaine and Jesse Cook to the railroad, believing they would be safter outside of Pine Ridge, but they refused. "Miss Goodale would not leave while there was a chance of being of service," he wrote. Elaine remembered, "Mrs. Cook and I, inwardly strung up, moved among the fugitives with hot coffee and sandwiches and comforting words."[42] But that was only the beginning of the horror.

The next day, the Seventh Cavalry appeared with their dead and wounded. Wounded Sioux straggled in. "I can never forget Mr. Cook's incredulous horror when he came upon the poor creatures in their bloody rags, huddled on the bare boards of several army wagons, chilled to the bone and too stunned in their culminating misfortunes to utter a sound, until the torture of fresh movement wrung from them screams of agony," Elaine wrote. The church was turned into a makeshift hospital, Elaine and Jesse called into service as nurses. Charles worked around the clock trying to save the victims. "Our patients cried and moaned incessantly, and every night some dead were carried out. In spite of all we could do, most of the injuries proved fatal. The few survivors were heartbroken and apathetic. . . . The tree was dragged out, but joyous green garlands still wreathed windows and doors, while the glowing cross in the stained-glass window behind the alter looked down in irony—or in compassion—upon pagan children struck down in panic flight."[43]

On the next day a blizzard forcefully overtook Pine Ridge. Snow piled up and drifted, blanketing the area, replacing the dreadful booming of the Hotchkiss guns with an eerie wintered silence. Charles and several Indian police rode out in search of a wounded officer who they did not find. When it stopped snowing two days later, they again rode from the agency in search of any wounded Indians who might have remained behind on the battlefield. Charles was placed in charge of an expedition of about one hundred men in wagons. With difficulty, they traversed the landscape until they began to uncover horrific sights. "Fully three miles from the scene of the massacre we found the body of woman completely covered with a blanket of snow, and from this point on, we found them scattered along as they had been relentlessly hunted down and slaughtered while fleeing for their lives," he wrote. They found burned tents, frozen bodies, women, and children. Some among Charles's rescue and recovery workers found their own relatives' corpses. "It took all my nerve to keep my composure in the face of this spectacle,"[44] he recalled. Though Charles's training at Boston University had not included dealing with mass trauma on the scale he faced it, Doug Hughes, a contemporary dean at the university's medical school, writes, "Eastman's physician skills must have been excellent, to have saved so many lives under such dire circumstances is remarkable." Hughes points to records showing that of fifty-one patients under Charles's care following the massacre, forty-four survived.[45]

Charles instructed those working with him to inspect every single body they found. As it turned out, not all the bodies were dead—even though they had been lying in the snow for a couple of days there were some survivors, miraculously including an infant. Charles described the baby as wrapped in a blanket and "entirely unhurt." He brought the child back with him. The infant—a girl—was nursed and cared for by a series of Sioux women, one of whom—Annie Yellow Bird—wished to raise it as her own. The infant unwittingly became a symbol of both the Lakota maternal resistance that saved her life (including the birth mother who'd covered the child in red, white, and blue grease paint to protect her from frostbite, either not knowing the sad irony of her color choices or mistakenly thinking that they would protect her), and also the Euro-American paternalism that changed the course of it.

Buffalo Bill Cody and his public relations man, John Burke, who happened to be at John Yellow Bird's trading post outside of Pine Ridge, heard about the baby discovered in the snowdrifts. A post-Christmas miracle, perhaps, but also an opportunity. Never one to pass up an occasion to get his boss's name in the news, Burke seized on the idea of procuring the child and presenting her to one of Buffalo Bill's wealthy patrons.[46] A dramatic situation ensued when Burke managed to get the child baptized with a Euro-American name, standing in himself as godfather. Determined to hold onto the baby, Annie Yellow Bird ran off and hid the child. Brigadier General Leonard Colby intervened, tracking her down, and bargained with Burke so he could keep the child himself, and present her to his wife. The white men saw this baby as a kind of "trophy of war,"[47] writes Renée Sansom Flood. Years later this story would serve as the basis of Elaine's novel *Yellow Star*. But in the immediate wake of the Wounded Knee Massacre, the baby simultaneously served as an emblem of Lakota resilience in the face of tragedy and the ways in which white Americans would seek to impose their will and their culture and change the narrative.

Today it is estimated that 250–300 Sioux men, women, and children were murdered at Wounded Knee. The army buried at least 146 Sioux in a mass grave. "The total number of fatalities was undoubtedly higher, for survivors and their friends removed some of the dead and dying before the burial party arrived,"[48] writes Richard Jensen. There were also significant differences in the language used to describe essentially the same events in some of the newspapers in the western part of the United States versus newspapers from eastern states. For example, under the screaming front-page headline "The Situation Is Serious/Short Bull Determined to Capture Pine Ridge if It Costs Him His Warriors/Grave Times Being Expected," an article from early January 1891 published in the *Madison Daily Leader* from South Dakota read in part, "The party sent to Wounded Knee to bury the dead Indians returned late night. They found and buried 84 bucks and 63 squaws and children. It was also found that five had been buried by Indians. . . . Buffalo Bill is on his way here and there is every prospect that his expert shooting will be pressed into war service the moment he arrives."[49] The *Pittsburgh Dispatch* in Pennsylvania reported a few days later, "Those who buried the dead report 84 bodies of men and boys, 44 of women and 18 of young children. Some were carried off by the Indians. A number of prisoners, chiefly women, have since died of their wounds and more will soon follow."[50]

Almost immediately after the massacre ended, the marketing, commodifying, and branding began. Some of the objects left in the wake of the tragedy were collected and sold as curios; more than a century later some of these artifacts held by collectors and museums in disparate locations began returning them to descendants, while other objects were found to be inauthentic.[51]

No fewer than eighteen newspapers stationed either reporters or stringers at Pine Ridge Agency just prior to the massacre. The number of journalists in that remote outpost reflected the expectation of a dramatic story, cast with forces of "savages" and the U.S. Army pitted against one another, a story that would undoubtedly sell newspapers. The presence of the telegraph and railroads in Rushville, Nebraska, only twenty-one miles away, meant news could be dispatched quickly—and it was. By the evening of December 29, the day of the massacre, families of the Seventh Cavalry had gathered at the Fort Riley telegraph station awaiting news of casualties; by Tuesday, December 30, the first reports about the incident at Wounded Knee appeared in daily newspapers across the United States; by the following day, news had reached papers overseas. The presence of Buffalo Bill Cody and John Burke in Pine Ridge undoubtedly stoked the publicity. In fact, a group of Sioux performers in Buffalo Bill's Wild West Show were returning from Europe and traveling by stage to Pine Ridge along with a journalist from the *Omaha Bee* when news of the massacre broke.

It wasn't just print journalists and public relations guys who'd gathered in Pine Ridge; it was also photographers. The group included an entrepreneurial paparazzo named George Trager. Trager, who had experienced a downturn in livelihood during the drought that year, which had depressed the overall economy in the Dakotas, happened to be in Pine Ridge at the end of December. He and *Omaha World Herald-Tribune* photographer Clarence Morledge were present for some of the battle and its aftermath. They widely marketed their grotesque, wrenching photos of twisted Indian corpses in the snow, deliberately mislabeling some in the interest of spiking sales, and selling them along with "souvenirs" like moccasins from fallen Sioux, taken from the battlefield. "Some of the pictures developed new associations, ones never intended by their makers," writes Jensen. "The historical accident of a blizzard two days following the massacre cast an icy specter that the camera recorded; people frozen in death, on a land frozen by cold, in pictures frozen in time."[52] These iconic photos helped to shape a narrative about Wounded Knee suggesting Ghost Dancing "savages" who rejected the white man's "civilization" engaged American soldiers in battle but lost pitifully; more broadly, these photos suggested metaphorically that Indian culture, itself, was an artifact of the past, getting buried by the snowdrifts of time.

Because of the high drama and near instantaneous marketing of the tragedy, Wounded Knee took on almost mythic qualities even at the time. David Treuer suggests, "In the American imagination and, as a result, in the written record, the massacre at Wounded Knee almost overnight assumed a significance far beyond the sheer number of lives lost. It became a touchstone of Indian suffering, a benchmark of American brutality, and a symbol of the end of Indian life."[53] But the mainstream American press at the time certainly interpreted the events differently. For instance, an article in the *Washburn Leader* from North Dakota led with descriptions of the American casualties, did not mention the number of Sioux killed, and stated, "To say it was a most daring feat, 120 Indians attacking 500 cavalry, expresses the situation but faintly. It could have only been insanity which prompted such a deed. It is doubted that before night neither a buck or squaw out of all of Big Foot's band will be left to tell the tale of this day's treachery. Members of the Seventh Cavalry have once more shown themselves to be heroes in deeds of daring."[54]

An editorial appearing in the *Aberdeen* (SD) *Saturday Pioneer* typified what was being published in the days and weeks following the massacre. "The *Pioneer* has before declared that our only safety depends upon the total extermination of the Indians. Having wronged them for centuries we had better, in order to protect our civilization, follow it up by one more wrong and wipe these untamed and untamable creatures from the face of the earth."[55] The author of this incendiary editorial wasn't the Wicked Witch of the West—it was her creator, L. Frank Baum, then publisher of this weekly newspaper.

As a journalist, Elaine knew the press's power to influence public opinion. With the encouragement of her mentors, that is what she had been trying to do for several years. Despite the horrendous sights she'd seen, and regardless of how physically and emotionally exhausted she must have been, Elaine was determined to push herself to write some of the story that wasn't getting sensational front-page coverage in the wake of the massacre. "It fell to my lot, at that heart-shaking Christmas season, not only to nurse the wounded prisoners in the church turned hospital, but to bear public witness to their tragic and undeserved lot,"[56] she recalled. She immediately put pen to paper, churning out at least a half-dozen articles published in numerous newspapers, some of them picked up by the wire services and reprinted, at least in part, across the country. In addition, Commissioner Morgan solicited Elaine's account of the events at Wounded Knee, which he subsequently publicly released.

In this widely reprinted article, Elaine sought to correct some of the misinformation being spread by the "official" military version of the battles, some of the fake news of 1890. For example, she disputed claims Sioux women had been armed and active participants in the battle: "There is no doubt that a great majority of the women and children, as well as a number of unarmed men, had no thought of anything but flight," she wrote. She pointed out that most of the bodies of women and children were discovered two miles or more from the scene of the battle. "They were pursued up the ravines and shot indiscriminately by soldiers." She stated that most of the Sioux were unarmed and cooperated with the troops when asked to turn over their weapons. She also attempted to correct the widely disseminated story that hostilities had been set off by a well-planned and broadly executed coalition of Sioux: "The irresponsible action of one hot-headed youth should not be the signal for a general and indiscriminate slaughter of the unarmed and the helpless."[57]

Some newspapers carried more of Elaine's letter to Commissioner Morgan than others. Not surprisingly, Eastern newspapers, including the *New York Times*, were more likely to carry most of the story, sometimes featuring her comments as part of their headlines. For example, the *Boston Post* ran the headline "'Had an Old Grudge to Repay': Miss Elaine Goodale's Version of the Wounded Knee Battle," calling attention to her conclusion that "I think there is no doubt that [the killing of Sioux] was in many cases deliberate and intentional. The Seventh Cavalry, Custer's old command, had an old grudge to repay."[58] These sentences were not included in many versions of her comments published in newspapers in the West.

In *The Independent*, Elaine retold the story of the events leading up to the massacre from her perspective. As Tamara Berg suggests, Elaine's language here—the "rhetoric of domesticity and reform"—likely made her points not only more palatable to her readers, but also more convincing.[59] Elaine's article couched grotesque details of the massacre in terms of the plight of Sioux children. Leading with, "In the mind of the average reader, that battle-ground of the hostile Sioux is undoubtedly a place of unrelieved terror and desolation," she urged her readers to "look at the other side of the shield." She described the destitution of the Sioux, the "neglected little children that swarmed about the hundreds of tepees silently pleading for a gleam of Christmas brightness," the stark contrast between the "Christmas bells that pealed out at five o'clock on that holy morning" and the Indian and white worshippers praying for peace and the "authoritative tidings of the carnage at Wounded Knee" that came only a few days later. "We can hear the screams of the suffering children, the moans of the women and the laments for their dead." She wrote of the fright of the survivors brought into the church-cum-hospital, the irony of seeing cheerful Christmas decorations in the face of unbelievable tragedy. She concluded, "War is provocative of brutalities, of indecencies, of avarice, ambition, hate and all deadly passions; but here too flourish heavenly pity and heroic courage." But those she commended were the "dark faces of loyal, tho plundered and suffering Indians," including the "Indian doctor of healing"[60] who tended to the victims.

An article Elaine published in *The Independent* later that year about Wounded Knee also stirred controversy. In arguing against the efforts being made to conscript Sioux into the U.S. Army, she noted that the "events of last winter" disproved any notion the Sioux were anxious to fight, except as a last resort. "Do I not know something of the moral degradation which inevitably results from the presence of troops at or near an Indian Agency, and which was observable even in the short time during which they were quartered upon us last winter?"[61] she wrote. In one response to her strongly worded indictment, Major George W. Baird replied, "Miss Elaine Goodale's article . . . warrants, if it does not require, a few words of comment." His comment included a denial that the "force" sometimes used by the military against Indians should be equated with the "violence" she claimed, that soldiers should not be referred to as "accomplished murderers," and that "it is an axiom among those well informed that the Indians have no better, wiser friends than army men."[62]

But other articles seemed to give more credence to Elaine's charges. "The version of the Wounded Knee affair given by Elaine Goodale . . . makes a serious charge of inhumanity against the troops," wrote one reporter in an Eastern newspaper. He repeated Elaine's claims about unarmed Indians and indiscriminate killing by the American troops, concluding, "The criticism of brutality of the troops in this encounter seems to have a basis of truth."[63]

Elaine wasn't the only person trying to counter the widely circulated misleading and sometimes blatantly inaccurate press reports about what had occurred at Wounded Knee; Charles did this, too. Though his official report of his work trying to save the victims of the massacre to the government was clinical, he also wrote a lengthy letter to his "white father" Frank Wood, which Wood subsequently circulated for wider publication. Charles wrote he'd been to the field of battle shortly after the event, where he found eleven people still living, including children. He confirmed that survivors told him the Sioux had given up their arms to the soldiers, and that it was only one Indian ("known as good for nothing") who fired the first shot. But then the result was, literally, overkill. "They fired upon the Indians instantaneously. Shells were thrown among the women and children so that they mutilated them most horribly."[64]

Charles returned years later to the events of December 1890 in his autobiographical book *From the Deep Woods to Civilization*. "I have tried to make it clear that there was no 'Indian outbreak' in 1890–91," he wrote, "and that such trouble as we had may justly be charged to the dishonest politicians, who through unfit appointees first robbed the Indians, then bullied them, and finally in a panic called for troops to suppress them." He recalled that although he tried to dismiss stories of corruption and grift whispered in his "reluctant ears," eventually he could not. "At that time, I had not dreamed what American politics really is."[65] He concluded, in destroying much of the Sioux economy, the actions of white Christians had little to do with the intent of the religion he'd adopted as a young man. Martha Viehmann points out how Charles's writings about Wounded Knee show both his sympathy for the Sioux and the reality of his work as a U.S. government employee, suggesting once again his two-ness as a Native American man who saw up close the violations against his people alongside the reality of who his employer at the time was.[66]

What Elaine and Charles saw and experienced at Pine Ridge Agency stayed with them their entire lives. Elaine would continue to publish articles reflecting on what she'd seen in the wake of the Wounded Knee Massacre periodically for decades; her last published article about the Ghost Dance and Wounded Knee appeared in 1945. In the early 1930s in a letter to Rose, Elaine reflected on how, despite her front-row seat to this piece of history, she had never cashed in on it. "Wounded Knee is sad and shameful enough, in all conscience," she wrote, "but . . . I see a new book which exaggerates this same affair viciously, for effect, and gets a long, respectful review on the first page of today's Times Book Review," which she contrasted with her own account that she had not been able to publish.[67]

It is difficult to know if what Elaine and Charles witnessed had psychological effects on them at the time, or in the years afterward. But there are clues about the residues of post-traumatic stress each of them must have experienced.

A little more than a week after the massacre, *The World* published a letter Elaine wrote under the headline, "Elaine Goodale's Plea: Her Appeal through *The World* for the Desperate Sioux." In this letter she wrote of her years of living among Indians and how "the present crisis in Indian history is certainly unexpected to most of us who have been intimately acquainted with the Sioux." She described some of what she had observed: "The mind refuses to conceive of the horrors of this prolonged journey."[68] Many years later she wrote, "Stunning as was the impact upon our nerves of the spectacle of extreme agony and violent death, there was still deeper tragedy in the psychological reactions of Dakotas."[69]

Charles, for his part, did not leave much of a written record about whatever emotional impact or post-traumatic stress the Wounded Knee Massacre left on him. But surely it did. David Martínez suggests Charles's "close acquaintance with travesty" reflects his placement as a doctor at Pine Ridge right after getting his medical degree. How incredibly frustrating it must have been for the young doctor to be thrown into a situation of mass casualty, where the tools of the trade he'd learned were of little use, where the desire to have medical training so he could be of service to his people was so futile. The irony could not have been lost on him.

Martínez points out that in his autobiographical book, Charles refers to what happened as a "massacre" rather than a "battle," that he withholds judgment but doesn't offer forgiveness, and that he clarifies that what happened at Wounded Knee was a complete contradiction to the Christian ideals he'd learned from his Euro-American mentors. Charles suggests, in contrast, that his own job was to try to ease the pain of those around him.[70] Gerald Vizenor is certain Charles Eastman must have been "haunted and mortified by the atrocities of the cavalry soldiers. Wounded Knee caused even more post-traumatic burdens than other horrors of war because the stories of survivors were seldom honored."[71] In his 1916 autobiographical book Charles understatedly reflected that the massacre at Wounded Knee came to be a "great disappointment" to both Elaine and him.[72] But its impact would prove far deeper.

Whatever the enduring nightmares Wounded Knee would create for Elaine and for Charles, whatever the shadowy remnants of trauma that would from time to time rear their ugly visage in their lives, the massacre did impress two concrete visions upon them. First, it solidified their determination to devote their lives to the causes of Indian identity and reform. And second, it hardened their resolve to do this work together. By the time she wrote her memoir (which would not be published until a quarter-century after her death), Elaine no longer viewed her decisions as romantic, no longer thought of herself as in any way being swept up by the impetuousness or optimism of youth; she viewed these decisions as being about something beyond herself and Charles. At least, this is how she chose to cast it for history at a time when her own history with Charles was fraught. "The gift of myself to a Sioux just at this crisis in their affairs will seem to some readers unnatural," she wrote. Because it wasn't just about Elaine and Charles: it was about their work.[73]

In the years to come, the tragedy at Wounded Knee would come to be seen as a prominent symbol—an emblem of Native American suffering, an icon marking the end of the period of the white frontier, a representation of Indigenous resilience in the face of unspeakable tragedy. Wounded Knee, writes David Treuer, "stands for an end, and a beginning."[74] The same might have been said of Elaine and Charles's relationship: Wounded Knee certainly marked a turning point for them as individuals and as a couple. It unquestionably was both a conclusion—to their time as single people, to the initial phases of their careers, to the relative optimism of youth—and a beginning—to their life as a couple, to the changes in their professional circumstances that followed, and to a more tempered view of what life would bring.

PART II

Coming Apart

6

From St. Paul to Washington (1891–1899)

After the Wounded Knee Massacre, the complicated prevailing politics and their strong crosscurrents continued to affect Elaine and Charles. Charles maintained his work as an agency physician at Pine Ridge but found the job increasingly fraught. Pressures grew not to speak out about the many problems he saw. Elaine continued to work and write about what they had experienced but resigned her administrative position in March 1891. It is not clear whether she resigned in protest of government policies she viewed as unhelpful at best, destructive at worst, or whether she was resigned to embark on what she later termed the "well-worn road, trodden by women's feet throughout the ages" and "abruptly relinquish[ed] all thought of an independent career for the making of a home."[1] Besides, there were difficult family issues to negotiate.

To say that Elaine's family was unsettled by the news of her engagement is an understatement. Her sister Rose wrote to her fiancé, Redington Dayton, that their mother "takes it very hard." In a subsequent letter she described Uncle George, Henry's brother, as "completely horrified"[2] and that Aunt Ella, Dora Read's sister who taught alongside Elaine at the White River School and witnessed Elaine's close relationships with Native Americans, was "shocked beyond words." Sister Dora later wrote, "Elaine's marriage shocked, shocks, and will shock me as long as I live."[3] Rose, though more accepting of the engagement, later confessed she was reticent to speak of it. There is no surviving record of what Henry thought. But it was clear his brother, at least, gave voice to some of the truly racist rhetoric of the day, suggesting any children that came from the marriage would be "halfbreed brats."[4]

Elaine did not preserve the correspondence she likely received from her parents and siblings about her engagement. But from the scant written record that does exist, we know she and Charles were aware of the resistance their union was meeting back East. Charles wrote to Rose in January 1891 and assured her that though the couple had not known each other long, their love was certain. Once they recognized the things they had in common, he said, "this of course assured us opportunities of closer acquaintance and when this was gained, we suited each other well and a spontaneous respect and love came on both sides." Charles told Rose the bonus of gaining two sisters-in-law "exceeds all of my expectation in the deal." He also sought to impress on Rose that press reports of their engagement "were full of errors" about him and "you can judge for yourself in case of Elaine's—they have made some erroneous statements about her. . . . We are very much amazed in many instances the account of our engagement."[5] This may have been the first time Charles and Elaine were astounded by the inaccuracies about them in the press; in fact, misinformation about them, their children, and their work would follow the Eastmans their entire lives.

Charles and Elaine would probably have been even more amazed if they knew how many accounts of their engagement there actually were. Articles appeared in hundreds of newspapers across the country: East to West, from the *Vermont Watchman and State Journal* to the *Honolulu Advertiser*; North to South, from the *New North West* in Deer Lodge, Montana, to the *Piedmont Alabama Inquirer*. There were numerous articles in Canadian papers and newspapers overseas, as well.

Beyond the number of articles written about Elaine and Charles's engagement, the content of some of them was extraordinary. A notice in the *Buffalo* (NY) *Evening News*, presumably chiding Elaine in a light-hearted manner for her work on behalf of the Sioux, read, "The interesting announcement is made that Elaine Goodale, who commenced writing verse a few years ago before shedding her pinafores, has at last taken a matter-of-fact view of life and is to be married to Dr. Charles Alexander Eastman at the Pine Ridge Agency—scene of the present Indian war. It is hoped the cruel war will not come near the poet. . . . The Sioux should spare her for the weariness she has made among the white people."[6] An article in *The World* entitled "The New Idyl of Elaine" suggested Elaine's childhood in rural western Massachusetts, removed from much of "civilization," had in some way prepared her for marriage to an Indian and served as "a presentiment of what life had in store for her."[7] Other newspapers chose to focus on Charles, mentioning his educational background (and often incorrectly suggesting he'd gone to medical school at Harvard or college at Cornell), frequently discussing his physical attributes, and sometimes making him seem as if he belonged in a museum more than in a marriage: "He is as nearly a perfect type of manhood as can be found in his generation. As a specimen of physical health and strength he enjoys as much admiration as for his moral traits, and he has the reputation of being an accomplished athlete."[8] (The sheer number of times Charles is referred to as "a specimen" speaks to the systemic othering and dehumanizing he experienced.) A brief notice in *The Indian Helper*, Carlisle Indian School's newspaper, quipped: "The papers have it that Miss Goodale is about to marry Dr. Eastman, an educated Sioux Indian at Pine Ridge Agency. Mr. Standing sighs and says, 'Another brilliant career ends in Sioux-i-cide.'"[9]

In a lengthy article titled "Elaine Goodale's Indian Lover," a writer in the *Boston Herald* began, "A pretty romance is that of Dr. Charles A. Eastman, the young Indian medical student who has been so well known in Boston and vicinity over the past few years, and Miss Elaine Goodale, one of the two sister poetesses of the Berkshire Hills, whose engagement was announced on Christmas Day." The article delineated both their backgrounds—incorrectly suggesting that "they were prepared for each other in temperament, education, sympathies and age—he is twenty-eight and she is twenty-seven" (he was thirty-three)—and concluded were they to marry and leave Pine Ridge, "she chooses to take her husband from among the very people to whom she has given her young years, no one can say that she is not in earnest."[10]

Teresa Dean, a reporter for the *Chicago Herald*—the only female reporter at Pine Ridge at the time of the Wounded Knee Massacre—often wrote columns of beauty advice and gossip. Her pieces from Pine Ridge represented a major change of genre, and her views of what occurred were somewhat ill-informed and reflected her derogatory opinions about Indians. She was also off the mark when she wrote of Elaine and Charles's engagement. "Miss Elaine Goodale is about 36 years old. The Sioux she is to marry is said to be 28." Charles "is a full blooded Sioux, but was adopted and educated by a wealthy family in the East. He is very considerate, and as attentive as a white man." In response to this piece, the *Buffalo* (NY) *Courier* responded, "The *Chicago Herald* has a correspondent in Pine Ridge named Theresa Dean who seems to have taken a contract not only to abuse the Indian but also to present their friends in the most unflattering light possible."[11] Elaine and Charles must have been astonished but not altogether surprised at the misinformation, gender discrimination, ageism, and racism expressed in this and other articles widely disseminated by a press eager for profitable tabloid copy.

And it was not wholly surprising their union generated such interest. In late nineteenth-century America, interracial marriage was still relatively rare; it wasn't fully legal in all U.S. states until 1967. There aren't reliable figures about the percentage of marriages that happened between Euro-Americans and Native Americans, but it was certainly true marriage between Native American women and white men was far more common than between Native American men and white women. As Margaret Jacobs points out, gender played an important role in the extent to which an interracial marriage might have been deemed more or less acceptable; marriages between white men and non-white women were discouraged but considered to be more suitable than marriages between white women and men of color.[12] But even marriages between white men and Native women were often laden with problems; Anne Hyde states that this "frontier mingling" often had a violent edge to it, with Native women forced into marriage, raped, and sometimes held captive.[13]

And yet as the nineteenth century wore on and assimilationist attitudes became more widespread, white women intermarrying became somewhat more acceptable because it was seen as a way to "convert" men of color to Euro-American practices: "Notions of class and gender shaped public acceptance in ways that precluded federal policies. Perhaps it is more accurate . . . that assimilation policies provided additional opportunities for Indian men to portray class and gender ideals, and that those portrayals made their marriages acceptable or at least tolerable in mainstream society,"[14] writes C. Joseph Genetin-Pilawa. Charles's medical training would therefore have made him a more "acceptable" match for Elaine, at least in some minds. And yet intermarriage was still so unusual it often merited press attention.[15] This was certainly true when the bride had been a well-known child poet, the groom received an elite Euro-American education, and the pair had been centrally involved with the dramatic story at Wounded Knee so recently in the news. It was a story made for tabloid coverage.

Elaine traveled back East sometime after resigning her position. Unfortunately, like so much else about her life with Charles, she conspicuously removed from the written record details about what happened when she returned. Did she spend time with her mother, and did Dora assist in wedding preparations, although she initially refused to attend? How did Elaine manage to persuade her sisters to be bridesmaids when they so clearly expressed grave reservations about their future brother-in-law; or were their misgivings concealed from Elaine at the time? How did the cash-strapped Goodales manage an elaborate wedding, and why did this happen given their doubts about the groom?

We do know that later in life Elaine suggested that if it had been up to her, she would have been happy to marry at Pine Ridge in a ceremony officiated by their friend Reverend Cook. But according to her, Charles had insisted on a wedding back East. And then Henry Sterling Goodale stepped in. He offered his apartment at the Windermere Hotel in New York as the reception site and arranged to have it decorated with mountain laurel blossoms brought from Sky Farm. He likely procured the services of Reverend E. Winchester Donald at the grand Church of the Ascension on Fifth Avenue and West Tenth Street. And he was no doubt responsible for some of the notable guests, including *St. Nicholas* editor and author Mary Mapes Dodge, *Springfield Republican* editor Charles Whiting, abolitionist minister and writer Moncure Conway, and celebrated minister, social reformer, and *Christian Union* editor Lyman Abbott.

While there are no known photographs from the June 18, 1891, wedding (Sargent suggests some were destroyed in a fire, but because "no one, including Elaine, herself, felt that the photos should be kept [is] a sad commentary.")[16]

many rich accounts of this most unlikely wedding can be accessed. One article in the *Madison* (SD) *Daily Leader* stated that two hundred people were in attendance; another article suggested, "The great edifice would have been packed by an eager and expectant audience had it not been for the provision of issuing cards of admission."[17] An article in the *Boston Daily Globe* running under the headline, "An Indian Princess: His People Are Her People—Their Gods Are the Same; The Child Poet of the Berkshires Is Now Ohiyesa's Bride" described the "simple but beautiful" decorations in the church—"graceful palms, roses and lilies in pots . . . arranged along the chancel rail, while the altar was banked with the same flowers." The ceremony began at noon with the organist playing Mendelssohn's wedding march.[18]

The wedding party consisted of Charles's ushers and best man, three Dartmouth classmates, and Rose's fiancé, along with the bridesmaids. Elaine's sisters Rose and Dora wore pink and yellow and carried roses. Charles was escorted down the aisle by a Boston University Medical School classmate. According to an article in the *Watertown* (NY) *Times* under the headline "A Poetess Weds a Big Injun": "The groom was dressed in a frock coat and dark trousers; he is very dark, has high cheek bones and straight hair, and looked an Indian very much." Another article mentioned Charles was "a splendid specimen of manhood" with looks that "characterize his race, but notwithstanding this fact, is a handsome man."[19] The bride was described as a beautiful woman "of medium height, with gray eyes and chestnut hair, a graceful figure with a sweet poetic face." In "Wedded a High-Born Sioux; Poetess Elaine Goodale the Bride of Dr. Ohiyesa, Unique Wedding at the Fifth Avenue Church This Afternoon" we learn that "leaning on the arm of her father, the bride was dressed in a long white satin dress, with long veiling. She held a bunch of lilies of the valley in her right hand."[20]

The ceremony itself was alternately described as "beautiful," "simple," and "all of fifteen minutes." The couple traveled uptown to Henry's "Sky Parlor" for the small reception and late breakfast. Elaine's mother apparently relented and attended; one newspaper account reported that "Dr. and Mrs. Eastman were assisted in receiving by Mrs. Goodale, the bride's mother, who was attired in a toilet of gray silk and velvet." The rooms at Henry's apartment were "tastefully dressed" with the flowers from Sky Farm.[21] After the reception Elaine changed into a "travelling dress of gray cloth and silk . . . and a straw bonnet trimmed with white roses," and she and Charles departed for Sky Farm, where they spent their wedding night and the next days, before traveling to Boston.

They were in Boston by June 23, where they attended the Wellesley College commencement and heard the Reverend Herman Lincoln Wayland speak about "The New Education." His address would have resonated with both Elaine and Charles, elucidating the need to blend a classical education with more practical elements, and the importance of studying history not merely to understand the past, but to prevent elements that should not be repeated.[22]

On the afternoon of June 25, Frank and Annie Wood hosted an elaborate reception for the newlyweds. A lengthy, gossipy article about this event appeared in the *Boston Daily Globe*, discussing what Elaine was wearing ("a lovely gown of creamy white surah which fitted her slender figure exquisitely; it was trimmed with bands of white ostrich feathers") and identifying Charles as of "a goodlie aspect" with a "bronzed face," "pompadour of the blackest hair" and a "lithe, well-developed grace of form." The journalist described the "whole of the first and second floors of the Woods' spacious mansion . . . thrown open for the reception . . . the lovely grounds so attractive with their wealth of vines and flowers and trees that one almost wished it had been made a 'fête champêtre' so that one could have stayed out among them in the perfect June weather." Indoors were a profusion of roses and more mountain laurel brought by Elaine and Charles from Sky Farm, along with a feast of "cool ices and creams, dainty cakes and sandwiches, refreshing drinks, berries and other delicious refreshments" served by a squad of waiters. The writer listed many of the three hundred or so guests who attended, including members of the press, literati, academia, and officers from the Boston Indian Rights Association. The article concluded, "With this perfect unanimity of sentiment and purpose, with their hands full of the work they choose and love, with youth and health and free opportunity to do this work side by side, one can feel sure that one's warmest wishes for the happiness of this young couple will be fulfilled—that they will themselves work out the fulfillment thereof."[23] These words would prove ironic in several ways.

* * *

From Boston, Elaine and Charles traveled west again by train, first to Montreal and then crossing back into Indian Country, stopping at Flandreau to meet members of Charles's family. Charles recalled his brother John "had gathered all the family and the whole band of Flandreau Sioux to welcome us."[24] At the same time, his brothers arranged for the unveiling of a memorial to their father.

When Elaine and Charles returned to Pine Ridge in summer 1891, it must have been with some trepidation. Not only were memories of the Wounded Knee Massacre relatively fresh, so were the reminders about omnipresent corruption at the agency. For Elaine, who had worked professionally in education since the age of twenty, it was exciting to shift her focus to part-time writing and more full-time assistance building Charles's career and their home. But this surely also felt a jarring turn. And it would not always be a decision she thought wise.

They moved into Charles's forlorn suite of rooms in the barracks until the new home being built for them was finished. Elaine busied herself planning and furnishing the new home, which she later referred to as "the center of so many loving hopes."[25] Charles recalled the early days of their marriage spent entertaining both "chiefs and leading men" and "humbler Indians and poor old women." He wrote, "We kept [an] open house, and the people loved to come and talk with us in their native tongue."[26] (Historian David Miller mentions that later, when the Eastmans left Pine Ridge, they were filled with thoughts about visitors "like Teddy Roosevelt who had sat before a roaring fire in the Eastman home."[27] It is indisputable Roosevelt visited Pine Ridge at that time and certain that Charles met him at a later point, but there isn't documentary evidence that the man who would become president visited with the Eastmans.)

Elaine didn't leave behind many contemporaneous recollections of this time. Later in life she wrote, "I won't say that the adjustment was easy or that

I was never lonely, restless, and haunted by a secret sense of frustration. Every woman who has surrendered a congenial task and financial independence will understand."[28] The other reason Elaine probably felt conflicted but not wholly sorry was that in August 1891, she became pregnant.

* * *

In the beginning of their time as a newly married couple in Pine Ridge, Charles worked to build his practice on the reservation. He frequently made house calls, sometimes with Elaine in the carriage, sometimes by himself on horseback, even in blizzards or at night, at times traveling many miles to reach patients in remote locations. In so doing he earned the broader community's trust. He noted that occasionally "the white residents and even the border ranchmen" called him for medical assistance. In her roles as publicist, cheerleader, and journalist, Elaine documented Charles's work. In an article titled, "A Day with an Agency Physician," she wrote of the many patients (he was responsible for 5,000–6,000 agency residents) without commensurate support, the "inferior quality" of drugs provided, the endless bureaucracy of government paperwork, and the dingy office. And she described the difficult task of navigating between traditional Sioux folkways and modern Euro-American medicine, such as the case of a dying man recently returned from a stint as a performer in Buffalo Bill's show. He'd spent all his family resources on "native medicine men" and their cures. When nothing worked, he turned to "mysterious white man's medicine as their last hope." The agency doctor attempted to save the man while allowing him to retain his faith in the cures of his elders—no small task.[29]

Though Charles seemed to be starting to build his reputation, in the first few months of married life it became clear his annual salary of $1,200 would barely cover their expenses. Charles wrote, "There was nothing I called my own save my dogs and horses and my medicine bags, yet I was perfectly happy."[30] Like a small but growing number of other Native men, Charles's Euro-American education seemed to promise a remunerative career. But unlike other Euro-American–educated Native men like Sherman Coolidge or his own brother, John, Charles's job came with no demonstrable institutional support. At the time Elaine seemed to justify it ("The Agency doctor receives a fixed salary—it is needless to say a small one— . . . he never feels at liberty to refuse a call, although fatigue, distance and bad weather might, under other circumstances, induce him to do so."[31]) But her word choices reveal the beginning of her recognition that his fixed salary was problematic. Even at this early juncture in their lives together, Elaine and Charles's attitudes about money started to diverge. Later in life, Elaine wrote to Rose that from the start, money was a key source of dissent in her marriage: "During the early part of our married life I felt it was his right as 'head of the family' to decide what we should do, where to live, and so on, and only after a great deal of painful experience learned that I MUST oppose these ideas of his and MUST try to guide the family fortunes."[32]

On top of the challenging conditions at Pine Ridge and financial pressures that seemed to grow along with Elaine's waistline, there was another issue brewing that became a major source of conflict for the couple. This issue prefigured what would become a series of unfortunate events embroiling Charles in scandals of different sorts—scandals that would figure prominently throughout much of his adult life.

Captain George LeRoy Brown, a Civil War veteran and West Point graduate, came to Pine Ridge Agency in December 1891. After Daniel Royer's disastrous stint as Indian agent (he was relieved of his duties in early January 1891), he was supplanted by a series of temporary replacements. It was a job no one wanted, Brown possibly among them. Brown became the Indian agent who couldn't seem to shed various controversies. One of them involved Charles Eastman.

After the losses of property and livestock that the "friendly" Sioux suffered at the hands of Euro-Americans throughout the build-up to Wounded Knee, Congress awarded them a compensatory appropriation of $100,000.[33] Commissioner of Indian Affairs Thomas Morgan put special agent James Cooper in charge of the disbursements. Witnesses were supposed to be present when money distributions to the Sioux occurred, and Cooper asked Charles to stand in as a witness. At first Charles was reluctant. He probably should have listened to his gut sense.

As soon as he began serving in this capacity, Charles noticed irregularities. Claims were extremely delayed in being paid out. Charles observed clerks handing Sioux bills and silver but not counting it, and saw Sioux approached by traders who stood outside of the office informing those who'd received cash that some of it was owed to them. Numerous Sioux later reported to Charles they had not received the full amount of money to which they were entitled. David Miller writes that other people at Pine Ridge, including Reverend Cook, believed many Sioux were shortchanged 10–15 percent of what they were owed.[34] Because Cooper left Pine Ridge immediately after the disbursements were made, there was intimation he had absconded with some of the missing money. In addition, Agent Cooper was associated with a "ring" of white men who appeared to be stealing supplies from a government warehouse.

Charles did not report his suspicions to Captain Brown, who by this time had assumed his post as acting Indian agent at Pine Ridge. Instead, Charles wrote directly to Philip C. Garrett in Washington, DC. Garrett, a wealthy Philadelphia financier turned philanthropist and Indian reformer, had served as president of the Indian Rights Association and was appointed by President Benjamin Harrison to the U.S. Board of Indian Commissioners. Garrett would have been well known—and well respected—among people Charles and Elaine knew. Charles's letter to Garrett subverted the chain of command, and in so doing, likely alarmed Agent Cooper. Upon learning of Charles's letter, Cooper wrote directly to Commissioner Morgan, accusing Charles, "who [had] been educated and should be taught to set an example for the more ignorant to live, and not be pilots to the . . . system of back-biting, manufacturing groundless charges against those who are trying to do what is just and right and inciting others to believe false rumors."[35] It is plausible to think part of Agent Cooper's indignation wasn't only because Charles disrupted the normal reporting structure; but because he was an Indian with more formal education than his white supervisor and had ties to some of the most powerful people in the Indian Service, Charles upended what Cooper would have assumed to be the natural and correct social order.

Agent Cooper returned to Pine Ridge and began procuring affidavits to exonerate his actions. Charles refused to sign one of these documents, which only further inflamed the already combative Cooper. Cooper then appointed Indian Agent Brown to investigate. Brown's work set off a series of internal and external investigations and established a highly contentious relationship between himself and Charles.

Raymond Wilson details the entire sordid story of accusations and counteraccusations, investigations, and counterinvestigations, some petty (like Agent Brown accusing Charles of riding his horses too hard), some more significant (like Charles accusing Agent Brown of harassing him and treating him "very wickedly").[36] Brown tried to use the authority of his office to undermine Charles in any way he could; he even refused Charles's request for additional medical supplies, leading Charles to complain that Agent Brown was preventing him from doing his job. In September 1892 Brown began suggesting to Commissioner Morgan that Charles be transferred to another agency. Two months later Charles received an offer to transfer to Fort Lewis in Colorado or to some other agency, which he refused; later he was offered a position at Flandreau, a placement he originally thought acceptable, but which he subsequently declined. When Brown subsequently learned that Charles refused to leave, he wrote Morgan, again, to ask if Charles could be transferred someplace—anyplace—without delay.

In the escalating battle between Charles Eastman and Agent Brown, both solicited help from influential individuals. Commissioner Morgan and Senator Dawes, as well as Frank Wood, were firmly in the doctor's corner, while Herbert Welsh of the Indian Rights Association and Theodore Roosevelt, then a Civil Service commissioner, sided with the agent. (When Welsh, one of Elaine's traveling companions on her original trip to Dakota Territory, sided against Charles, she resigned from the Indian Rights Association, writing to Boston papers that she would not "continue to aid with my name and money an association of which Mr. Welsh is the secretary."[37]) The proxy wars went all the way up to President Harrison, with Frank Wood arguing on behalf of Charles.

The cascade of letters and telegrams continued. In a subsequent letter to Commissioner Morgan, Wood questioned why the commissioner was permitting Agent Brown to "continue his outrageous persecutions of a man who is his superior in every respect" and spoke ardently of Charles as one would defend one's own son. Morgan, writing to Secretary of the Interior John Noble, wondered if Charles's "inexperience, youth and heavy workload" had contributed to a situation in which he might have acted intemperately, though he believed Agent Brown was "playing the role of a petty tyrant."[38]

Not surprisingly, the press caught a whiff of the continuing controversies at Pine Ridge, and many newspapers ran articles containing sensationalized, often misleading, and sometimes blatantly inaccurate information. For example, an article in the *St. Paul Daily Globe* ran a short piece under the headline "Elaine Is Discharged" reading, "Dr. Eastman and wife (neé Elaine Goodale) and the principal of the Indian schools at Pine Ridge Agency, have been discharged from the employ of the government for sending out sensational reports to the effect that the Indians were preparing for an outbreak. This will put an end to the Indian scare reports from this agency."[39]

Elaine, too, jumped into the fray. As she'd done in the aftermath of Wounded Knee, she hoped to correct some of the misinformation in the press and clear both her own and Charles's names. She wrote a series of letters, published in newspapers around the country, in which she defended Charles and continued to try to shed light on the corrupt practices of Indian agents at Pine Ridge Agency. She denied the insinuations that the conditions would lead to a coming "Indian outbreak." "It is uncharitable to suggest that such a theory may have deepened the shadows in the doctor's picture,"[40] she wrote. Several articles bore subheadings like "the white wife of Dr. Eastman has vigorously sustained her husband in the controversy, and as vigorously denounced Captain Brown"[41] in the newspapers that ran them.

One of the inquiries into the allegations and counterallegations made by Charles and Agent Brown held in Pine Ridge was adjudicated by Inspector James H. Cisney, brought in to "impartially investigate" the situation. His investigation turned out to be anything but impartial. Cisney, appointed by President Harrison as an Indian agent before picking up this assignment as an inspector, apparently asked Elaine, "By what right do you send out these dispatches and letters to the eastern papers?" Insulted by the question, which she felt Cisney had no right to ask, Elaine indignantly responded, "By the right of a justice loving American woman, sir."[42]

But Elaine was often excoriated for her defenses of Charles and accusations against Agent Brown. An article in the *Sioux City Journal* claimed she "still wields her pungent pen and doubtless has earned the enmity of the Pine Ridge administration." Indeed, Inspector Cisney, who ultimately recommended to Commissioner Morgan that Charles be removed from his post at Pine Ridge, suggested Elaine was partly to blame, calling her a "tartar." "She bosses her husband entirely," he said. "On the witness stand I asked Dr. Eastman if he was obliged to do exactly as his wife said, and he frankly admitted that he was. Eastman's trouble was caused by his wife, who simply tried to run the reservation."[43] Cisney's rhetoric insinuated that any man who allowed his wife a voice in his actions was no man at all.

Charles attempted to hit back. He wrote directly to Commissioner Morgan, telling him he believed Inspector Cisney began his investigation biased. He added, "It appears to me very necessary to come east at once in order to effectively push the matter."[44] He requested a leave to come to Washington and plead his case. Although Charles responsibly arranged for another doctor to fill in for him, Agent Brown wrote to Morgan complaining that the temporary replacement Charles found was unacceptable and tried to prevent him from going to the nation's capital.

But Dr. Eastman did go to Washington. Through the connections he had with Frank Wood and through Elaine's personal relationship with Commissioner Morgan, he secured meetings with Morgan and with Secretary Noble, several influential senators, and even President Benjamin Harrison. However, as David Miller writes, "No champion emerged to defend his cause nor was any dramatic defense aroused on his behalf."[45]

It became an untenable situation with no good solution. In the end, Secretary Noble sided with Agent Brown but gave a nod to Charles, praising his service and his training. Ultimately the words of corrupt white Indian agents took precedence over the Eastmans'. News about this dispute made it into many papers of the day. The *New York Times* reported, "Captain Brown charged Dr. Eastman with insubordination. Dr. Eastman charged that Capt. Brown was tyrannical, overbearing and generally unfitted to fill the position he holds . . . the Secretary's conclusion is that the good of the service requires that Dr. Eastman shall be suspended from acting as physician at Pine Ridge, and that, unless Dr. Eastman can be assigned or appointed to another place that he is willing to accept within the next fifteen days, he must resign or he will be removed."[46]

Charles refused to accept any of the transfers offered to him. According to Raymond Wilson, Charles viewed such acceptance as akin to an admission of guilt. Instead, he believed the most honorable course of action would be to resign.

Apart from the horrendous political pressures on them, the growing financial problems, and the attacks on their character and actions that both Elaine and Charles sustained, the Eastmans had another concern to contend with: protecting their new baby, Dora Winona Eastman. Baby Dora's parents joyously greeted her on May 31, 1892. But they quickly saw how differently the world greeted their child. Headlines like "Improving the Race: A Daughter Is Born to Mrs. Elaine Eastman," "Elaine Goodale's Grandchildren Who Rue Their Looks Will Wish She Had Married a White Man," and "An Interesting Baby" ran in newspapers throughout the country. Most of the articles were even worse. "The baby born to Elaine Goodale, the New England poetess, and her Indian husband is of course a mixture of red and white," read an article in the *Herald-Advance* from Milbank, South Dakota. "Mrs. Elaine Goodale Eastman, the New England poetess, who married a full-blooded Indian in the west, is now glorying in the possession of a little papoose" stated an article in the *Cortland* (NY) *Standard*. An article in the *Berkshire Eagle* suggested, "Mrs. Elaine Goodale Eastman, erst of Sky Farm and now the wife of an Indian physician, is receiving the congratulations of her friends on the birth of a red and white baby. The child can boast an American ancestry that beats us all, running back to centuries before Christopher Columbus was thought of."[47]

It's almost impossible to imagine how Elaine and Charles, protective as new parents are, would have felt about the portrayal of their child in the press. Or to know what it might have meant to Elaine to be attacked so virulently for using the tools of her well-honed writing skills to defend her husband, particularly when she had been so critical of her own mother for not promoting her father's work more. Or to understand how Charles must have felt,

FIGURE 6.1. Charles with his firstborn child, Dora Winona. Courtesy James W. Dayton; Raymond Wilson.

hamstrung in his abilities to treat his patients effectively, unjustly accused by Indian agents, punished for blowing the whistle on blatantly unscrupulous practices being perpetrated by government employees. Or to know their feelings when both, as young, idealistic people doing work they believed in, must have had some of whatever faith they still had after Wounded Knee shattered by the reality and extent of the corruption they encountered. They didn't leave a lot of explicit answers.

In one of his autobiographical books Charles wrote, "It was a great disappointment to us both to give up our plans of work and our first home, to which we had devoted much loving thought and most of our little means; but it seemed to us then the only thing to do."[48] If there were contemporaneous reflections Elaine wrote, she destroyed them, but a clue comes from a letter she wrote to Rose in 1933. In it, she claimed that Charles had made "on several important occasions . . . unfortunate and really disastrous [decisions], without consulting me at all." Later in the same letter she suggested that the decision to leave the Indian Service after the "war with the Pine Ridge agent" to "open practice in a strange city with a family and no money nor friends" was "almost a pure gamble" and stated she "had nothing at all to do with [it] except to try to make the best" of it.[49]

Charles resigned his position on January 26, 1893. Somehow then, in the middle of winter, Elaine and Charles packed up their meager possessions, whatever little money they'd saved, and along with their eight-month-old daughter, moved to St. Paul, Minnesota, returning, as Charles suggested, to the "home of his ancestors" thirty years after he'd left it.

* * *

The Eastmans arrived in St. Paul on February 8, 1893. If they thought they had left the controversies of Pine Ridge behind them, they were mistaken. The next day the *St. Paul Daily Globe* ran an article with the headline of "Fears Indian War: Dr. Eastman of Pine Ridge Looks for a General Uprising." The article purported to be the story from Charles's point of view and quoted him saying, "A serious conflict would wipe out many of the Oglala Sioux, and women and children would be murdered. . . . Those people were never conquered. The cold-blooded butcher at Wounded Knee didn't conquer them. Their animosity has neither been stamped out nor conciliated." The lengthy article recounted the problems between Charles and Agent Brown, but concluded with Charles suggesting, "I was born in Renville County, Minnesota, and have been away from my native state about 30 years. I am glad to be here."[50]

Shortly after they arrived, Charles took a three-day exam to become a licensed doctor in that state. He passed, though up to half of those who took it did not.[51] Charles attempted to set up an independent practice, but patients proved scarce: white patients were loath to see a Native American doctor—even one with Charles' credentials—and Indian patients were leery of a Native doctor dispensing "white man's medicines." There was also a lot of competition: as Teresa Swanson, Sydney Beane, and William Beane point out, by 1899 there more than 150 physicians in the city of St. Paul.[52] Charles joined the Twin Cities Medical Association, which yielded offers to join other people's practices as an "Indian doctor," but this was not how he wished to be pegged. He was determined to make his way as a solo practitioner.

It is not surprising Charles wished to disassociate himself from "Indian medicine." The Minnesota newspapers of the day were filled with ads for so-called Indian remedies for common ailments, offering fake cures to bilk unsuspecting consumers. One such ad read, "Don't be deceived by ignorant, unscrupulous fakirs [*sic*] and confidence men, assuming to offer 'Indian Remedies' and who pretend their nostrums are made by the Indians. Kickapoo Indian Sagwa is THE ONLY GENUINE INDIAN REMEDY MADE AND SOLD IN AMERICA!"[53] These ads capitalized on a Euro-American stereotype; Indians might have mysterious natural cures but they were distinct from conventional medicine.

But Charles was not very successful attracting new patients after hanging out his shingle as a mainstream doctor outside their rented rooms at 227 E. Tenth Street. He later wrote that waiting for patients to come was "the hardest work I had ever done." He was "persistently solicited for illegal practice, and this by persons who were not only intelligent but apparently of good social standing. . . . They were astonished when I refused to consider anything of the sort."[54]

Strapped for funds and sidelined at home with the care of her baby, Elaine once again turned to writing to bring in much-needed cash. Only it wasn't her own writing that finally began to bring in some funds—it was Charles's. When he began telling stories of his childhood to young Dora, Elaine "Urged him to write down his recollections of the wild life." She added that she "carefully edited and placed [them] with *St. Nicholas*."[55] Charles recalled this a little differently. In *From the Deep Woods to Civilization* he wrote, "While I had plenty of leisure, I began to put upon paper some of my earliest recollections, with the thought that our children might someday like to read of that wilderness life. When my wife discovered what I had written, she insisted on sending it to *St. Nicholas*."[56] The difference in their recollections is slight but significant. In later years the question of just how responsible Elaine was for Charles's writing, and just how much editorial influence she exerted in her husband's publications, would become a major source of contention.

After his first magazine piece was published in December 1893, Elaine and Charles realized this could be a way to raise income and, importantly, disseminate Dakhóta culture to a broader and mainstream white audience. "Recollections of the Wild Life: Hakada, 'the Pitiful Last'" told the story of Charles's earliest days. "Some persons value their earlier recollections and experiences much more than others do," he wrote. "Many children are very inquisitive, and forget the object of their apparent interest as soon as they receive the information they seek; but there are a few who have the gift of memory, and store up truths pure and simple. One would naturally think that this could be true only among the children of the more advanced races. But we can say for the children of uncivilized nations that they hear very little from their parents that can be called instructions, what they receive coming direct from Nature—the greatest schoolmistress of all."[57] The story recounted how the baby Hakadah was raised by his wise grandmother but taught how to survive by the birds and other animals around him. The success of this article, and its successor articles published the following year, set Charles along a path that would lead to the publication of his first memoir, *Indian Boyhood*, and eight other books putting traditional Sioux stories and lore into forms popular with a mostly white, mostly middle-class reading audience.

Although Charles's stories were pitched and thought of as children's tales, some contemporary analysis suggests a careful reading provides a "serious in-depth examination . . . [of] Dakota ways written as a first-hand account." Swanson, Beane, and Beane point out that most of the so-called factual accounts of Indian life in the late nineteenth century came from Euro-American writers, but Charles's stories provided "among the first published accounts that lent agency to Native people."[58] In another interpretation, Christopher Pexa suggests that though many of Charles Eastman's writings were labeled children's tales, they were strong critiques of "US settler colonialism on the basis of tribal epistemologies that were probably missed by his largely white audience."[59]

In addition to his writing, Charles began to find other opportunities outside of his medical practice. In summer 1893 he was invited to give a talk at the World's Columbian Exposition in Chicago. His speech about Sioux mythology, given under the aegis of the International Folk-Lore Congress, focused on how Sioux religion was inextricably tied to a worldview founded on beliefs in the primacy of the natural world. "Each animal, each thing, has just so much purity and holiness," he said. "The mighty river and the little brook, in proportion to their strength and wonderfulness, show the power of the god."[60] As David Murray points out, anything having to do with the religions of non-white people was segregated from presentations about western religions, as in the separate exhibit in the International Folk-Lore Congress at the 1893 Columbian Exposition.[61] Oddly enough, *Popular Science Monthly* published a revised version of Charles's talk the following year.

By May 1893 Elaine was pregnant again. The Eastmans' second child, Irene Taluta, was born on February 24, 1894. Elaine would write to Rose she'd had "a pretty hard time" with Irene's birth and felt "thankful to be safely through the ordeal." Irene, she wrote, is "a dear little creature, plump and healthy, one thinks she will be fairer than Dora but her eyes are quite dark."[62]

Charles's medical practice in St. Paul continued to suffer during this time, even though he was elected secretary-treasurer of the Twin Cities Medical Association. He began casting about for other opportunities, writing letters to U.S. senators and the new commissioner of Indian Affairs, Daniel M. Browning, to see if there might be any possibility of returning to the Indian Service as a physician. Wilson suggests Charles emphasized his "overwhelming desire to help his people," but it is also clear things in Minnesota weren't exactly going as he and Elaine had hoped. No new opportunities were forthcoming, and their financial situation continued to be precarious when an unexpected door opened for Charles. He received a visit from Charles Ober, secretary of the International Committee of the YMCA. Ober, an alumnus of Reverend Moody's summer revivalist seminars—the same seminars Charles attended during his medical school summers—sought to expand the YMCA's influence among Indians. He believed Charles, with his educational credentials, nascent publishing experience, and public speaking ability, paired with his Sioux background, was just the man for the job.

The YMCA was founded in 1844 in England as a way of providing "healthy activities" for young men in cities. By 1851 the movement had spread to several other countries, including the United States. Closely connected to the evangelical Christian movement, the YMCA provided a range of opportunities for young men in sports, vocational pursuits, and other activities designed to promote morality and "good citizenship." Massachusetts-born Ober came to this work after having been almost lost at sea and rescued off the Newfoundland coast. After this traumatic experience he decided to devote his life to Christian work. He tried to persuade Charles Eastman to do the same.

Charles initially hesitated. "My first thought was that it was out of the question to sacrifice my profession," he wrote. "Then, too, I doubted my fitness for religious work."[63] But induced by the promise he could name an Indian successor as well as, no doubt, the promise of an annual $2,000 salary, Charles accepted the position. On June 1, 1894, he started as Indian secretary of the International Committee of the YMCA, tasked with traveling to reservations throughout the western United States and Canada, getting an understanding of work being done, and organizing new YMCA associations among Indian groups.

To his surprise, Charles found the YMCA work engaging. He "felt that the spiritual guidance to young Indians would be of 'far-reaching importance.'"[64] As he traveled to different reservations, he realized how differently Christianity had been received among Indian groups. Some believed the white men who brought Christianity to Indians did not themselves practice its precepts; others devoutly accepted the faith; some attempted to integrate it with their own Indigenous beliefs. This was exemplified by one old man who told Charles after a week of Bible study he'd concluded, "Jesus was an Indian." The YMCA work caused Charles to reconsider his own religious beliefs, he later wrote.

It also caused him to be away from his young family for long stretches of time, causing Elaine endless aggravation and much grief. After the first summer of 1894, when Charles was on the road and Elaine at home with a toddler and a new baby, she wrote to Rose of how difficult the summer had been, between the heat in St. Paul, her separation from her own family, and how "dreadfully" much she missed "the Doctor" during this time.[65] In the annual reports of the YMCA listing "Charles A. Eastman's Work Among American Indians," it becomes clear that between 1894 and 1896 when he worked for the association, Charles was on the road almost constantly; in 1894, traveling back to the Dakotas and Nebraska; in 1895, returning to these places and also going to Manitoba (where he visited the grave of his grandmother and reconnected with his uncle), Pennsylvania, Texas, and New York; and in 1896, returning to many places with already existing YMCA groups and journeying to Kansas, Indiana, Illinois, and Ohio to establish new ones.[66]

Charles was on the road so often that rumors began circulating that he and Elaine had split up. At a conference in Pierre, South Dakota, Charles Ober felt compelled to pair his remarks about the new YMCA Indian project with the comment, "Rumors regarding the separation of Dr. Eastman and his white wife (Elaine Goodale) are untrue. Dr. and Mrs. Eastman are living in St. Paul happily. . . . Their whole time is spent in trying to better the Indian race."[67] This may have been the first public suggestion of problems in their marriage; it wouldn't be the last.

Charles also began giving frequent public lectures in association with his YMCA work. In addition to speaking to existing, fledgling, or new Indian YMCA groups, Charles made formal public addresses to Euro-American audiences to gain publicity and raise funds for the new "Indian initiative." His talks were widely covered, often running under headlines such as this in the *Omaha Daily Bee*: "Evangelizing the Indians' Dr. Eastman Describes the Work Now Being Carried on Among Them." This article described "Dr. Eastman, the educated Sioux Indian" as a "calm, even speaker, with the grave manner usual with Indians, but in his case this is softened considerably by his smiles." Describing Charles's remarks as focusing on young Indians who needed the guidance emanating from YMCA activities, "Dr. Eastman closed with an urgent plea that his hearers forget the 'pigment of the skin' and help the Indians by prayer."[68]

Elaine also assisted Charles with publicity; she published an article in *The Independent* in which she wrote about Charles's work for the YMCA, describing the focus on bringing young men together using sports, religion, and civic work to "teach the young men, in time, to protect themselves against dishonesty and double-dealing on the part of Government agents and others." Her assimilationist interpretation included stating, "The YMCA does not encourage the Indians to remain Indian; it tends to break up their isolated position and to unite them in manly and Christian fellowship with neighboring white communities." She concluded, "Dr. Charles A. Eastman, International Secretary for the Indians, St. Paul, Minn., will be very glad to correspond with any whose interest is aroused in this new movement toward making *men* of the Indians."[69]

That spring an article ran in the *Cook County Herald* in Grand Marais, Minnesota, 260 miles north of St. Paul. Headlined "Wedded to a Sioux and Finds that Marriage Is a Success; Elaine Goodale, Who Married a Full Blooded Indian, a Happy Wife and Mother—Her Husband Now Occupies an Enviable Position," this lengthy article focused on the question of whether Elaine made a mistake in her marriage. "Was her marriage a sacrifice, socially considered? Was it an end to her usefulness as a brilliant contributor to literature? Would her pen continue to surprise and charm the world of literature with sonnets and sketches, or would it be laid aside with her assumption of wifely and matronly responsibilities and care? In brief, was the girl poet's marriage a failure?" Interested readers wanted to know. And they probably wanted to know in several locations across the country because this wasn't the only place the article ran. What readers would have read painted a rosier picture than what Elaine herself would have shared at this particular juncture, as the Eastmans struggled financially with Charles's medical practice on hiatus and Elaine not writing as much as she had been: she "accepted the situations as they unfolded to her, philosophically, even enthusiastically, and to-day she finds herself a welcome guest at the homes of the wealthy and cultivated citizens of St. Paul; the proud mother of [a] bright little girl a couple of years old, the wife of a physician with a growing practice in the same city, and a contributor in her leisure moments to the current publications of the country."[70] To Elaine, these descriptions of her life would have been ironic, even laughable.

In summer 1895, the Eastmans rented a cottage along the eastern shore of Bald Eagle Lake, sixteen miles north of St. Paul. The cooler temperatures, abundant fishing, and other recreational opportunities and convergence of two railway lines made this a popular and fashionable summer retreat in the 1890s; newspapers in St. Paul and Minneapolis were filled with articles mentioning those who decamped to Bald Eagle Lake and lists of the season's social events. While the Eastmans existed outside of the whirl of white Bald Eagle Lake society, that summer and the subsequent summers they spent there would be among the least stressful times of their marriage. By 1903 the place had become important enough to them that they purchased a small cabin; however, their residency would prove short-lived.

In Fall 1895 the Eastmans traveled East with Dora, leaving Irene in the care of friends in St. Paul. Although Elaine left no record, they apparently went first to New York, where they visited with Henry as well as "many callers from among her literary friends." One newspaper summed up their trip with a series of headlines and subheads: "Back from the West; Elaine Goodale Eastman Revisits New York with Her Indian Husband; Happy Life of the Gifted Poetess Among the Nation's Wards; She Will Go Back to Them; Urged by Her Friends to Settle Down Here, but She Refuses to Do So." The body of the article continued in the same vein: "Her marriage with the son of a Sioux chief not only excited surprise among the many friends and admirers of the gifted poetess, but some of them, on account of the unconventional character of the union, predicted the reverse of an auspicious future for the pretty bride. Happily, their apprehensions have not been realized, as the presence of the blooming matron sufficiently indicated." The article described Charles with some of the usual misinformation ("a student at Yale College where he was graduated with class honors") as well as the work he was now doing for the

YMCA. Another article delineated Charles and Elaine's addresses to the Harlem branch of the YMCA, concluding, "Elaine Goodale Eastman addressed the conference with perfect composure and simplicity that told of strength and culture" while Charles "has left a good medical practice to help his race by means of organization."[71]

From there they went to Lake Mohonk for the thirteenth annual Indian conference. There they met up with many mentors and colleagues, including Frank Wood, Reverend Riggs, and former commissioner Thomas Morgan. On the evening of October 10, Charles spoke about his work with the YMCA. He discussed the need to provide young Indian men with physical education to keep their bodies well, and Bible study "to arouse their sympathy for one another." Elaine, who spoke on October 11, focused her remarks on the roles of Indian women. She described the "three quite distinct stages" of Indian women's lives, in which they passed through girlhood "as a butterfly" with no responsibilities, became "a loving drudge," and ended up as a "feminine autocrat." She explained Indian grandmothers as "the tyrant[s] of the community—sharp, shrill-voiced, and determined always to have the last word." And yet she concluded her talk by saying that people at the Lake Mohonk Indian Conference should realize that "it is through the women that we can reach the heart of the people."[72]

Sargent suggests Elaine's remarks at the Lake Mohonk Conference were "very angry" and that the focus of that anger was Charles's grandmother. Citing an unpublished paper by Marion Copeland, Sargent theorizes Elaine felt resentful about Charles's recent visit to his grandmother's grave, which caused him to be nostalgic in a way Elaine found threatening.[73] It is true that Charles's return to Manitoba became a significant event in his life. In one of his autobiographical books, he remarked on the journey, both practical and spiritual for him, on seeing his grandmother's grave, which he described as "one of the great moments of my life," and the importance of reconnecting with the uncle who'd raised him. It's possible that revisiting the site of his boyhood reignited in Charles a deeper connection to his Dakhóta heritage. David Martínez importantly suggests that despite the years away from his homelands, and apart from his Euro-American education, Charles always retained "the Dakota sense of self that can come only from remembering where one is from, whom one's relatives are and the stories they told, and in the language in which they were recalled. Such a sense of self becomes an act of survivance when maintained against a society that does not see a place for such being."[74] There aren't any extant indications of Charles's recognition at that time that he might start to turn from the Euro-American trends of his education back to a more Dakhóta-inspired philosophy, or of Elaine's recognition that he did so. But it seems reasonable to think, given Elaine's clear and staunch assimilationist ideals, that a dawning realization that her husband might be electing a different path would be unsettling.

Following the Lake Mohonk Indian Conference, the Eastmans traveled to Boston, where they stayed with the Woods, saw many old friends, and gave a joint talk at the Shawmut Congregational Church that Charles had attended while a medical student. The article about this talk in the *Boston Globe* quoted Charles discussing the impetus behind his YMCA work: "The very efforts at civilization have brought about conditions which are most perplexing to everybody who has the welfare of my people at heart." He added, "the very worst things which hold us back are those instituted by the government in its intended kindness. They give us provisions and clothing and charge us with being lazy. . . . No permanent progress can be hoped for until measures are taken to improve the health of the people on the reservations." He suggested the YMCA work would help to stave off some of this, but more work was needed. Elaine, for her part, spoke about her experiences as a teacher, focusing on the YMCA as "the only method to teach the young men to feel that they were an integral part of the American people."[75]

When the Eastmans crossed back into Indian Country and returned to St. Paul, they moved for the third time in three years, taking an apartment at 102 N. St. Albans Street. This move, near an area of the city dominated by large Victorian houses (rather than by row houses), represented something of a change in lifestyle for them. Though the Eastmans did not live on Crocus Hill, considered then as today to be among the most elegant addresses in St. Paul, it was an easy walk and, for Elaine, an aspirational one. At the beginning of 1896 Charles was on the road again for the YMCA. Elaine joined the newly formed Crocus Hill Mother's Club, where she attended talks and, starting in

1897, presented on topics like "Child Study—Imagination." By 1898 she was writing a regular column for a magazine called *The Interior* on topics relating to child-rearing, such as "The Possibilities of a Back Yard," "Sunday Amusements for Children," and "Undesirable Traits in Childhood." It is not surprising she shifted her focus from Indian education to parenting; as the mother of three young children with the birth of daughter Virginia in February 1896 and as a woman who was often a single parent without really being single, Elaine had a restless mind and a constant need to be busy beyond the constant needs and busyness of motherhood. Later in life she stated how Charles's perpetual travels left her "inevitably house-bound." "I won't say that the adjustment was easy or that I was never lonely, restless and haunted by a secret sense of frustration," she wrote.[76] Reflecting on her life, Elaine knew resentments were already building in the early years of her marriage. "Up to a year or two after my marriage, I was reasonably happy and content—full of enthusiasm and large plans," she wrote to Rose in 1940. "The years after were sort of an endurance test. . . . No one can deny that I had a pretty tough time!"[77] But like so many women, particularly those of her era, her overriding priority was to support her husband and his needs and sublimate her own. "For many a year every early dream and ambition was wholly subordinated to the business of helping my talented husband express himself and interpret his people," she reflected. "Obviously, it was far from modern."[78]

* * *

Parents of young children organically find themselves drawn back to their own childhoods. Perhaps it is reflecting on our past and wanting to replicate it—or differentiate from it—with our children; or perhaps, when hearing our young children's thoughts and observations on the world, we're triggered to recall things from childhood.

By 1896 Elaine and Charles were the parents of a four-year-old, a two-year-old, and an infant. For Elaine, tasked with primary care of the children, this meant only occasional forays back to her own writing, which tended to focus on poems like "Papa's Kisses," illustrating a little girl's disappointment when her father went out the door and she was left with her mother ("He kissed the little maid good-bye, When to his daily task he went; Then to her mother turned—but no! The baby would not have it so.")[79] Paired with some of her early writing in *Journal of a Farmer's Daughter* about how, during busy seasons on the farm, she would see Henry at only certain times of the day, it's easy to imagine how Elaine might well have seen the little girl "with pouting lip" and "jealous eye" who watched her papa go out the door in her poem from the 1890s and recalled scenes from her own childhood.

But Charles was probably brought back to his childhood in a somewhat different way.

The Santee Sioux lived on land in what became the state of Minnesota for many years before white settlers appeared. But the increasing Euro-American population settling there in the mid-1800s led to a series of treaties with the Sioux that were subsequently broken, and then land claims by the Santee that were effectively liquidated. They received little of the money they had been promised. And by the late 1850s, they had been driven out, in the period during which young Hakadah fled to Canada with members of his family. Those who remained were situated "on miserable reservations at Crow Creek" and expected to use unfamiliar techniques to farm.[80] Moved again to the Santee Reservation by the mid-1880s, members of these Sioux groups began organizing to try to present their annuity claims to Congress. It took until the 1890s for the Santee Sioux to begin to get some traction on this issue.[81]

At this time Charles was starting to tire of the constant travel and need to raise funds for his YMCA job and thinking more seriously about how he might return to medicine in a way that could support his growing family. "At this juncture," he wrote, "I was confronted by what seemed a hopeful opportunity." A few Sioux leaders, including his brother, John, "argued that I was the man of their tribe best fitted to look after their interest in Washington. They had begun to realize that certain of these interests were of great importance, involving millions of dollars. Although not a lawyer, they gave me power of attorney to act for them on behalf of these claims, and to appear as their representative before the Indian Bureau, the President, and Congress."[82] Charles and a Sioux colleague signed a ten-year contract with the Santee authorizing the pair to represent them; for their services, they would get up to 10 percent of all monies brought in. To do this lobbying effectively, Charles knew he would have to have more regular face time in the nation's capital.

Charles once again moved his young family, crossing out of Indian Country to Washington, DC. In a short article announcing this move—riddled, as usual, with misinformation—the *Black Hills Union* in Rapid City, South Dakota, reported, "Dr. Charles Alexander Eastman, a Flandreau Sioux Indian graduate of Cornell University, husband of Elaine Goodale, will live in Washington hereafter as the representative of the Standing Rock (Pine Ridge) Sioux before the Interior Department. He has been looking after the Flandreau Sioux for some time, but this occupied him only occasionally. Heretofore when the Indians wanted anything done in Washington they sent a delegation here to urge the President."[83]

This period in both Elaine and Charles's lives is somewhat of a mystery. It is not clear exactly when the family moved to DC; their fourth child, Ohiyesa Charles Alexander Eastman II, known as Ohi, was born in September 1898 in Redding, Connecticut, but there is no record of whether the three girls or Charles were present. In Washington the family lived in a boarding house on Third Street NW, not far from the U.S. Capitol. During their Washington year Elaine began trying to place essays in magazines to earn extra cash, writing about child-related topics such as "Child-culture in the Home," which appeared in the *Women's Home Companion* in April 1899. She also occasionally sold pieces about child-rearing to newspapers, in which she doled out advice such as "let a child play alone a portion of each day" and "don't think that your child is going to love you the same way you love them." Charles continued to give some public talks for the YMCA, such as one he gave about "The Moral Effect of the Indian Young Men's Physical Training on His Uncivilized Life," in which he described the deleterious effects of rum and tobacco introduced by the white man, but concluded, "When you take the young men and put them to the schools, such as the Carlisle Indian School, and give them proper physical training, they once more take on the physical qualities of their powerful ancestors" rather than the unfortunate qualities of "civilized life."[84] But the majority of his efforts shifted to his political work.

In 1898–1899, Charles worked as a lobbyist on behalf of the Sioux. He met with congressmen and senators, spoke before the committees on Indian Affairs in both houses, and met with President William McKinley. Though he later wrote he'd gone to Washington hopeful his work would be met fairly and "our wrongs corrected," he ended up believing, "I had overmuch faith in the civilized ideal, and I was again disappointed."[85]

Part of Charles's disappointment came from the passage of the 1898 Curtis Act. Named for then congressman Charles Curtis, a mixed-blood member of the Kaw Nation who would become vice president under Herbert Hoover, the legislation was originally intended to amend the 1887 Dawes Act. Curtis's intent, according to his autobiography, was to do more to help Native groups transition to a system of private land ownership, something Curtis, despite his Indian heritage, believed critical for Indian survival given the dominant Euro-American influence. But in practice, the Curtis Act served to break up communal lands held by the Five Civilized Tribes of Indian Territory (because of previous treaties, the Choctaw, Chickasaw, Muscogee, Cherokee, and Seminole had not been included in the Dawes Act), called for the abolition of tribal governance, and resulted in a federal definition of who could be counted as "Indian" and qualified to be eligible for tribal citizenship. In disenfranchising tribal courts and placing further restrictions on land allocation, the Curtis Act paved the way for the admission of the state of Oklahoma. Today the Curtis Act is recognized as a significant moment in the ongoing marginalization of Native peoples; after its passage there were lawsuits regarding its constitutionality and the Interior Department admitted to multiple ways in which it was having difficulty actualizing some of the act's provisions. Contemporary assessments also suggest despite Charles Curtis's spin in his autobiography, his own political motives for this legislation trumped any belief in shepherding Native people toward a system of land ownership. Charles Eastman left no record of his public thoughts about it at the time, though in later writings he alluded to this act and the later Burke Bill of 1906 as legislation resulting in "much discouragement."

Indeed, apart from the factionalism, self-interest, and certain prejudice Charles faced during his time in Washington, there were also efforts being made to thwart his work. Some of these efforts were led by white men working in the halls of government who weren't quick to arrange the meetings Charles requested and stymied his lobbying endeavors. But some of the efforts to stalemate him were spearheaded by other Santee, like James Garvie, a clergyman and former teacher (and a cousin of John and Charles Eastman's), who accused Charles and his colleague Charles Hill of misrepresenting themselves as attorneys, procuring illegal signatures and purposely confusing some Santee so they could garner higher fees. Once again Charles became embroiled in controversy. An investigation into these claims ultimately exonerated both Charleses, but the damage was done. Their lobbying efforts continued to founder, bringing no annuities for the Santee—and no 10 percent to the lobbyists.

Charles also managed to make time in February 1899 for a gala Dartmouth alumni event. The guest list included President McKinley, toasted by the Big Greeners present. An account of this event in the *Washington Evening Star* noted, "The most entertaining address [was] that of Dr. Charles A. Eastman of the class of '87. . . . Dr. Eastman spoke in the most interesting manner and held closely the attention of all his audience." The article recounted Charles's tale of how his education at Dartmouth had launched him into "a civilized career."[86]

Despite his star status at the Dartmouth gala, after a year it was clear to the Eastmans that once again, Charles wasn't earning enough money to support their large family. Receiving no remuneration for his work on the Santee claims case, and desperate for income, Charles leased the land in South Dakota he had received as an allotment—as well as the land claims he had made in the names of his children—to an ironically named German farmer called Hans Lien. Lien became convinced Charles had no right to lease him this land in the first place and, in fact, owed him return of the rental funds.[87] The Eastmans also owed $500 to their DC landlady. In debt, with few clear sources of income and four children under the age of seven, it was clearly time for a change. It wouldn't be the end of Charles's work on behalf of the Santee claims, but when Elaine was offered a position at the Carlisle Indian School, she grasped it. It was time for the family to move, once again.

7

From Carlisle to Amherst (1899–1903)

Elaine began her adulatory 1935 biography of General Richard Henry Pratt with the story of how, as a child, he emerged from a near-death bout with smallpox. He lived, she wrote, "to round out nearly four score and four years as the maker of a new highway—a builder not of locks, but of men."[1] More contemporary and contemptuous assessments of Pratt refer to him as an architect of social engineering, the designer of an assimilationist agenda, even a draftsman of cultural genocide. "Pratt and other Friends of the Indian thought of themselves as protectors of natives," writes Alan Trachtenberg, but "lacked only a sense of irony and were unable to see anything odd about their campaign to 'Americanize' the original inhabitants of the place they called America."[2]

Pratt, the Civil War veteran who fought alongside freed slaves in the Tenth U.S. Cavalry, also later led several military engagements against Native Americans. His involvement with both Blacks and Native Americans led him to develop extremely strong and sometimes contradictory views on what he believed best for them. On the one hand, he opposed racial segregation, but on the other, he wasn't sure allowing Blacks and Indians to co-mingle in educational settings would benefit either group. He believed there was value in Native American culture, and yet he was certain the only path for Indians' survival meant conforming to Euro-American customs. He'd fought for institution of the Dawes Act and traveled to Dakota Territory to procure signatures to divide up land into reservations, only to later believe—equally vociferously—the reservation system made Indians wards of the state and prevented their complete educational and cultural assimilation. Despite these contradictions, and maybe because of his success in promoting his views,

Pratt was an enormously influential figure in Indian education and policy in the late nineteenth and early twentieth centuries.

It was Richard Henry Pratt who had convinced General Armstrong to begin admitting Indians to the Hampton Institute in 1878. And it was Pratt who decided a year later that ties between Blacks and Indians at Hampton would threaten future funding opportunities, if not the ultimate goal of Euro-American conformity, and convinced the Bureau of Indian Affairs to allow him to turn an unused army barracks in Carlisle, Pennsylvania, into an off-reservation boarding school. Pratt, by this time promoted to lieutenant colonel (he would achieve the rank of general upon his retirement), pitched the school as a cross between a military academy (uniformed students marched and were subjected to severe discipline including corporal punishment and solitary confinement) and an assimilationist school (instruction was in English, and students had to cut their hair and become Christians). Pratt even found a way to monetize assimilation: he hired photographer John Nicolas Choate to take a series of "before and after" portraits of students, which Pratt then used as a form of visual propaganda he sold. In one of the most widely disseminated photos, the "before" image depicted a student named Tom Torlino as a "savage" with dark skin, long flowing hair, in Native dress; the "after" photo showed a young man with short, cropped hair, a Victorian-era suit and cravat, and "his skin tone has undergone a seemingly miraculous shift from its former dark brown to a much lighter tone," according to art historian Peter Hayes Mauro. Decades before photoshopping or AI-generated images became so commonplace that discerning consumers know not to believe all they see, nineteenth-century viewers of images had far less reason to doubt them. The Torlino image became iconic, serving to visually demonstrate the efficacy of the Pratt education to turn "savages" into "civilized" humans, and furthering the commodification of Indian images.[3] Disseminating these images widely worked: congressional funding and private donations rose sharply.

Like Hampton, Carlisle offered a blend of classroom instruction and vocational education. Its rigorous athletics program included development of a stellar football program under the coaching of Glenn "Pop" Warner and spawned several award-winning Indian athletes who achieved national and international fame, including Jim Thorpe, the first Native American Olympic gold medalist.

Given Pratt's goals for the school, it is no surprise he turned to the Eastmans. The combination of Elaine's writing skills and Charles's ability to articulate the advantages of a Euro-American education to Native Americans, along with both of their connections to people in the Indian advocacy community, made them an ideal set of employees. After the Washington, DC, debacle they were actively looking for inexpensive housing with built-in childcare and salaried positions, making Pratt's offer one they couldn't refuse. In 1899 the Eastmans moved to Carlisle, where Charles would serve as an "outing agent," finding students summer placements with white families, acting as a liaison for the school, and traveling to different reservations to help recruit new students. Elaine was put in charge of the *Red Man*, the school's monthly magazine, which, like the newspaper at Hampton, served as both an in-house news source and an external public relations and fundraising vehicle.

Apparently the Eastmans were invited for a trial run during the summer. The July 1 issue of *The Indian Helper*, the weekly school newspaper, ran a short news item stating, "Dr. Charles Eastman and wife Elaine Goodale Eastman with their four children . . . arrived on Saturday evening for a few weeks stay with us during the heated term. Dr. Eastman is a Sioux Indian, a College graduate, and a man of wide information and experience in Indian affairs. . . . The Doctor is a most interesting and intelligent speaker from the stand point of his race, and is thoroughly progressive, believing the only true salvation for the Indian is for him to become a voting citizen as speedily as possible. Mrs. Eastman is widely known as a poetess and writer on Indian matters."[4]

The trial proved a success; Pratt hired the Eastmans for a year. He wrote to the commissioner of Indian Affairs in 1899 suggesting the outing philosophy created "quite a school in itself." To supervise the program, he had hired Charles Eastman, who "with both a college and a medical education" would be the ideal role model. Charles's yearly salary of $800 was less than he had made at Pine Ridge but more than he'd brought in during the entire year in Washington.[5] In addition to editorial stewardship of the *Red Man*, Elaine

FIGURE 7.1. Carlisle Indian School's "outing program." Courtesy Library of Congress.

would supervise the students who worked with her as part of the school's industrial training program. The school administration had a heavy editorial hand in evaluating content, which usually included items about school events, sports recaps, and alumni news.

Within a short time, the Eastman family became part of life at Carlisle. In July 1899 the school newspaper reported, "Dr. and Mrs. Eastman are croquet and tennis players and employ some of their spare moments in wielding racket and mallet with a purpose." In early November came notice of a Halloween party, at which "one of the most grotesque ghost stories we ever listened to was given by Dr. Eastman in his inimitable way. What the Doctor does not know about primitive Indian customs is not worth knowing." The same article noted Elaine reciting some "fortune poems" from her "fertile store." Even the children made it into the paper: "Little Virginia Eastman calls the man on the bandstand's chief clerk 'Buggy,'" and "O-hi-ye-sa, the baby boy, is as happy as happy when on the ground, down among the girls. . . . Dora is a girl of seven, and makes herself quite at home among her little Indian sisters, and curly haired Irene is always manifest with her pointed questions and baby-like logic."[6]

Pratt commissioned Elaine to write a school anthem. "Comrades All" had a rousing chorus that clearly hit the marks Pratt intended: "Comrades all, A loyal hearted band, True to each other, And to our native land!"[7] The song was performed for the first time at the twentieth anniversary of the school; by the following year its performance had become a regular commencement feature.

Pratt must also have been pleased with Elaine's ability to get his school in the news. In November 1899 she published "Song of the Carlisle Indians" in *The Independent*, a poem reading more like a cheerleader's chant than lyrical verse. The first stanza ends: "The prize of honor doth beguile, Each warrior's heart—Carlisle! Carlisle!"[8] In January 1900 she published an extensive article on Pratt's outing system, explaining, "The Carlisle outing is by no means a summer holiday; it has become a fundamental part of the Carlisle training, a definite method—perhaps *the* method—of Americanizing Indians."[9] This was exactly the publicity Pratt sought; he must have been thrilled.

Even during the period he worked as an outing agent, Charles was engaged with other jobs. He continued working on the Santee claims case and gave occasional talks for the YMCA. Charles also continued to write. The most notable piece from the year at Carlisle was an article about the 1876 Battle of the Little Bighorn, published in *The Chautauquan* in July 1900. The subhead of the article, a parenthetical "Told from the Indian standpoint by one of their race," encapsulated the way the press discussed this article. Though Charles's main points suggested there was no "massacre," that there were far fewer Indians fighting Custer and the Seventh Cavalry than had been widely reported, that the Indians were not as heavily armed as reported, and that Custer made strategic decisions leading to his defeat—he had been "out-generaled"[10]—press reporting didn't recapitulate them. Some newspapers ran stories on the article framing it as "Dr. Eastman tries to claim Indian numbers exaggerated at Little Big Horn." Because Charles's well-reasoned arguments contradicted the burgeoning American myth about Custer's last stand, this article got a lot of play across the country. Interestingly, some of Charles's arguments about Custer's tactical mistakes were later borne out by research, accepted today as major factors contributing to his defeat. But in 1900 few gave such arguments much credence.

More contemporary critiques of Charles's piece on Little Bighorn center other reasons why this piece, often overlooked among his books and articles, is an important one. First, as David Martínez points out, the incident at Little Bighorn was probably of great interest to Charles because of what he experienced at the Wounded Knee massacre. He also had relatives who fought at Little Bighorn and probably conceptualized the battle in ways that were both personal and part of a longer, broader narrative, connecting his own story to his people's. And second, the way in which Charles constructed this article epitomizes Indigenous storytelling: the use of questions, and conditional language linking information known about the battle with Native histories. Though the largely white reading audience might not have realized it at the time, says Angela Calcaterra, Charles's writing about a battle that occurred years earlier linked Native experiences in a way that made a quiet but bold political statement.[11]

Between supervising the outing program and trying to recruit new students, Charles spent much of his time on the road. He didn't leave much record of this work. In his 1915 book, *The Indian Today,* he reflected that although Pratt's outing system had been attempted at other schools, it was "not always with equal success." He suggested criticisms of the school were made "usually from political or purely selfish motives" and concluded, "It is the impression of the most advanced members of the race that he [Pratt] has rendered to [Indians] and to the country a particular service, and that the wonderful progress demonstrated by the Indian in recent years is due in large measure to his work, and to its results as seen at Hampton and Carlisle."[12]

Charles's laudatory commemoration of General Pratt and the education he promoted perhaps ran contradictory to Elaine's belief that the best education for Indian students would be in day schools on reservations. And none of the Eastman children were ever sent to Carlisle. It's possible one of the reasons Charles felt so indebted to Pratt was the role he believed Pratt played in saving his life.

In December 1899, Charles traveled throughout South Dakota recruiting students. When he returned, students in tow, he fell ill. "I am sorry to report that Dr. Eastman is dangerously ill," Pratt wrote to Commissioner of Indian Affairs William A. Jones. He sent Charles to the hospital after a local doctor treated him unsuccessfully. "Today and tomorrow are the turning points and he is now in very great danger," Pratt continued. But the real point of Pratt's letter came at its conclusion: "It is plain even if he recovers that he will not be of any use to me for weeks as an outing agent," he wrote, and proceeded to ask Jones for funds to hire someone else.[13]

Indeed, Charles was so ill that Elaine summoned his brother, John, to his bedside. But by the end of January, according to the weekly health bulletins appearing in *The Indian Helper*, "Dr. Eastman is up and around almost as usual, although he is still somewhat weak after his very serious illness and will need to take good care of himself for some time to come."[14] Whether he or Elaine knew of Pratt's mercurial, self-interested response to Charles's illness is not clear, but they probably didn't—both of them would heap praise on Pratt for years to come. Charles did recover sufficiently to get back out on the road for Carlisle by later that spring, so Pratt had no immediate need of a replacement.

Elaine, too, managed to do some lecturing away from the school after Charles recovered. In early March 1900, she traveled to New York and then to New England to address women's clubs "on topics pertaining to the Indian and to the duties of a mother."[15] In addition, she wrote articles for the *Woman's Home Companion* and sold some of her poems to newspapers.

But the joys of motherhood, publication, and whatever satisfaction Elaine derived from her brief trips were not enough to compensate for problems that continued to fester in her relationship with Charles. His salary was insufficient to meet their family's needs—it's not clear how much Elaine received for her editorial work, but probably less than Charles's $800 salary; in any case, both appeared on the Carlisle rosters as "irregular employees," so their positions weren't meant to be anything other than temporary. Charles continued to be away from home more than he was there. Their immediate situation was far from ideal, with no clearly good prospects for their future. In a 1938 letter to Rose, Elaine admitted toward the end of the year at Carlisle that she considered separating from Charles: "I should have gone to work on my own responsibility and in my own way even if it meant a separation, as it probably would have done," she wrote, adding she considered this but since she had four young children, didn't think it a viable option.[16]

Elaine must have conveyed to Charles her grave concerns about their financial status because he began seeking another job with a higher salary in spring 1900. However, no job was forthcoming until the beginning of September, when he was offered a position as an agency physician at Crow Creek in South Dakota at an annual salary of $1,200. Charles gratefully accepted the position and prepared to move the family back to Indian Country. As Raymond Wilson points out, political patronage seems to have played a disconcerting role in Charles's appointment: "Partisan influence often dictated who received appointments, and the Indian service remained a bastion of patronage" often resulting in incompetent people being hired or placing those who were competent in positions in which they were bound to clash with others.[17] Once again, this is what happened with Charles Eastman.

* * *

Laura Ingalls Wilder wrote about the South Dakota droughts, dust storms, and grasshopper plague she experienced in the 1880s. While not as severe, the Eastmans, too, had trouble traveling to South Dakota two decades hence because of poor weather and dust storms—undoubtedly reminiscent for Charles of what he had experienced arriving at Pine Ridge. This was not the only parallel they would be able to draw to their previous stint in South Dakota.

The period the Eastmans spent at Crow Creek Agency between mid-September 1900 and March 1903 is not well documented in their own writings but can be pieced together from letters and newspaper accounts. Apparently, Elaine wrote weekly letters home, but almost none of them survived. There is one written to her sister Dora in which little details open large insights into what Elaine must have felt and experienced. Beginning the letter by apologizing for missing her weekly missive twice, Elaine explained she was simply too busy and too exhausted to write. "I work until I simply *have to rest*," she wrote. Elaine feared she would have no help at all once the new baby was born—"what will become of the children.... They need such constant watching!" Her short descriptions of the homeschooling she provided for the older children suggested she enjoyed teaching them and felt they were learning well, but this duty added to her strain, happening in cramped quarters and without sufficient supplies. She also felt life on the Crow Creek reservation "is not a good place for me in any way, yet I had no choice in the matter. The strain at Carlisle was even worse—and there we had no home life at all—here there is at least a flavor of domesticity and privacy."[18]

In their first year at Crow Creek, Charles spent much of his time initiating a smallpox vaccination program on the reservation. Despite being the first vaccine invented, the smallpox vaccine was not widely used on Indian reservations, and many Native Americans were extremely reluctant to receive it.[19] Charles's work included disinfecting all agency buildings and, importantly, educating Sioux about the benefits of vaccination. He spent a great deal of time riding to distant locations across the reservation, attempting to convince the Mdewakanton Dakota of the need for and safety of vaccination. The medical reports he filed with the government indicated he also spent a great deal of time making house calls. And just like his first stint as an agency physician, Charles experienced significant frustrations dealing with meager supplies and massive bureaucracies. He would later write, "The drugs supplied by contractors to the Indian service were at that period often obsolete in kind, and either stale or of the poorest quality."[20] Despite trying conditions, Charles was more successful than not, reporting no Indian deaths from his vaccination program, and that in 1903, for the first time in years, the number of births outstripped the number of deaths on the reservation.

Charles and Elaine were also busy with another endeavor—putting together his first book.

The work on *Indian Boyhood* began when the Eastmans moved to St. Paul and *St. Nicholas* published his first set of stories. That proved an important launching pad because, as Gretchen Cassel Eick writes, "More Americans read *St. Nicholas* than read the leading national magazines for adults combined. . . . Writing in *St. Nicholas* placed his stories alongside those of the recognized great writers of the time—Mark Twain, Henry Wadsworth Longfellow, Rudyard Kipling, Robert Louis Stevenson, Alfred Tennyson and William Dean Howells."[21] The encouraging reception Charles's stories received, paired with the knowledge that a book contract could bring much-needed funds, led Charles and Elaine to pursue the project further, though as Charles would write, part of his purpose remained educating Euro-American readers about the Sioux.[22]

Starting with the unforgettably evocative phrase, "What boy would not be an Indian for a while when he thinks of the freest life in the world?" *Indian Boyhood* consists of a group of stories divided into a dozen sections, some describing Hakadah's early memories and life, some retelling traditional tales. The book was widely appraised—Elaine pasted more than seventy separate reviews in a scrapbook—and sold well from the start: a royalty statement from his publisher McClure, Phillips shows Charles received almost $500 in the first year of its publication (more than $18,000 in 2024 dollars).[23] Not surprisingly, many of those extolling *Indian Boyhood* couched their praise in ways that made as much of the author's otherness as of the book's content and furthered the Native-to-civilization narrative. "A book of very great interest and such as nobody else could have written," said the reviewer in the *New York Sun*. "Dr. Eastman is a full-blood Sioux Indian who . . . can tell his own red-skin experiences and feelings in the language of the paleface." The *Washington Evening Star* reviewer wrote, "Students of ethnology, those who are any way interested in the several phases of Indian life, will no doubt be much entertained and not a little instructed by a perusal of *Indian Boyhood*." And the *Brooklyn Daily Eagle* led with, "Dr. Charles Alexander Eastman, who is a full-blooded Sioux Indian, born in a wigwam in the Northwest, has just published a volume entitled *Indian Boyhood*, in which he gives an account of his infancy and boyhood up to the time that he was brought into contact with civilization. It is the only book that has ever been published of Indian life as seen from the inside and is especially valuable on that account."[24] (This was incorrect: the first published Native American autobiography, *A Son of the Forest*, by William Apess [Pequot], came out in 1829.)

Present-day views of *Indian Boyhood* run the gamut from those who believe Charles Eastman "offers little apparent challenge to the dominant colonialist discourse of his time," to views that "in *Indian Boyhood* we see how Ohiyesa was taught to understand himself, his community and the world around him in a way that melded the natural world with humans, [and] look for patterns of connectivity" in ways distinctively Indigenous. Some analysts suggest that even in this first book, the complexity of Charles Eastman's writing—and the subversiveness of it—is apparent.[25]

The success of *Indian Boyhood* and the amount of publicity it generated helped to launch Charles's writing career, buoyed his speaking career, and added to the family coffers. But it had some unintended consequences for the Eastmans, as well. These came principally through a series of articles appearing in the press across the country, reintroducing Charles and Elaine to the reading public, often containing untruthful elements, perpetuating stereotypes, and defaming their children.

An article in the *St. Paul Globe* from December 1902 under the headline "Romance Worthy of Cooper" stated, "J. Fenimore Cooper himself could have wanted nothing more romantic for an incident in one of his novels than the meeting of Charles A. Eastman, the full-blood Sioux author of 'Indian Boyhood,' and his wife—then Miss Elaine Goodale. The thing, as it happened in real life, was quite as adventurous as anything Cooper ever produced." The article delineated Elaine's career as a childhood poet turned teacher, who "roughed it for some years in the Dakotas," found herself at Pine Ridge, and then "the young Indian educator and poetess worked beside the swarthy native, ministering to his patients and helping at operations." The natural result, claimed the unnamed journalist penning this article, was Elaine and Charles's marriage and five children, the youngest of whom "had not inherited any of the attractiveness of the mother. It was a veritable old squaw miniature. It was a queer sight, this beautiful woman holding the homely pappoose, [*sic*] with its glittering eyes, every move and every expression marking it as an Indian. It seemed a changeling from the tepees, but the mother crooned to it as mothers always have done and the mother love was not dimmed."[26]

Another version of this article appearing in the *Portsmouth* (NH) *Herald* began with the local angle of Charles's background as a Sioux who came to Dartmouth, became a doctor, "dressed like a white man, and used his talents and influence to arouse ambition for better things in the breasts of the Brule youths." This article told a truly bizarre and false story of Elaine and Charles's meeting. One day, when called to visit a "sick squaw in a far-off Indian village, at the door of the tepee Charles was met by a beautiful young girl. Dressed . . . in Indian fashion, in blanket and mocasins [*sic*], her eyes were dark and her tresses, raven, but the creamy white and the oval of her face proclaimed her not of that race. She spoke a few words to him in Sioux and slipped away." Who was this Cinderella in moccasins? "He was told that she was Elaine Goodale." According to this article, the girl poet "dropped out of sight. She had turned to the life of the Indian and was living a strange life in the tepees of the Sioux, dressed like them and eating of the same food."[27] This strange story was apparently good copy because it appeared in scores of papers.

Neither Elaine nor Charles left any written indications of how these types of stories made them feel. Perhaps they were already inured to the press's wild exaggerations and false news. Perhaps such widely circulated stories enhanced the animus Elaine's family felt and created further tensions. Such stories also served to underscore differences that were becoming increasingly apparent between Elaine and Charles, with prejudiced descriptions of their children another unwanted, unneeded reminder of the obstacles their biracial children and their interracial marriage would face. The world the young couple believed they were creating for themselves and their optimism about it, imperceptibly, began to disintegrate.

The other unintended consequence of *Indian Boyhood*'s publication was the questions it began to raise about how much editorial influence Elaine had. These questions continue to percolate in the twenty-first century as scholars and fans alike read books and articles with Charles Eastman's byline. But in 1902, with five children under the age of ten who she was nursing, caring for, and teaching, trying to supplement the family income and further her own career by juggling everything and finding some time to write, dealing with family finances and soon with other large political tribulations, Elaine didn't have the bandwidth to wonder much about whether her editorial stewardship of Charles's writing would create problems. These would come later, and they would haunt her, always.

* * *

Elaine and Charles found that life back on an Indian reservation meant grappling once again with U.S. governmental policies meant to speed up the assimilation and Americanization of Indians. Some of these policies were misguided at best; others, truly draconian. They found the grift and corruption they'd seen at Pine Ridge extended to other reservations in ways they could not previously have imagined. And they started to realize they didn't always agree with each other about what might be best for Indian people in the long run.

"I feel bound to send you some items, the most interesting, perhaps, being the recent withholding of rations from many of the young, able-bodied men,"[28] Elaine wrote in a letter published in the *Red Man and Helper* back at Carlisle. She thought the ration system rational, not unlike the argument that would be made years later by conservative politicians about the welfare system. She believed handouts had potentially damaging effects for those who could work; withholding rations from everyone save the elderly and most infirm Indians was therefore a good idea, incentivizing work. The entire system of rations—which usually consisted of flour, salt, bacon, and beef—developed in the wake of a reservation system that had completely upended Native American patterns of food procurement. Rather the feeding those who most needed nourishment, it often resulted in disease and starvation. As writer William Least Heat-Moon points out, the ration system became a symbol "of conquest and devastation" that "meant native, nomadic tribes could live neither like white men—unless those whites were indigents—nor like the red men they had so recently been."[29] But Elaine, always a firm believer in the gospel of assimilation, did not see it that way. She blithely suggested withholding of rations was "certainly a step in the right direction."

Charles's view regarding the withholding of rations differed from his wife's. He would write in 1915 that the ration system had deleterious effects:

"The self-respect of the people was almost fatally injured by these methods," and the ration system was "demoralizing."[30] In addition to the rations program, during Charles's time at Crow Creek he continued to see enormous problems in the ways in which U.S. governmental policies set up systems on reservations that didn't work, often exacerbated by people put in charge who engaged in all sorts of corrupt behavior.

When the Eastmans arrived at Crow Creek Agency, James Stephens, the Indian agent in charge, was already embroiled in significant controversies involving allegations of illegal trade and neglect of his official duties. His replacement, Harry D. Chamberlain, did not move quickly to clean up the messes left by his predecessor and did nothing to heal the distrust existing among Sioux at Crow Creek. Tensions continued to rise.

Noting Charles's fluency in Dakota, Chamberlain became suspicious of Charles's conversations with tribal elders. Chamberlain's apprehensions crystallized around White Ghost, a local leader known as the most influential chief, who had written to Commissioner of Indian Affairs Jones about the conditions at Crow Creek and laid blame directly on Chamberlain. White Ghost wished to travel to Washington to spell out his charges directly and wished a "good interpreter" to travel with him to make sure he was properly understood. Catching wind of this, Chamberlain inferred that the "good interpreter" must be the good doctor, and wrote to Commissioner Jones himself, requesting first that Charles be instructed to focus on his medical duties, and then, that he be transferred immediately.

Frictions between the two deepened when Charles questioned whether annuity money meant for the Sioux had been diverted. Chamberlain wrote again to Commissioner Jones accusing Charles of insubordination, neglecting his duties, caring improperly for his patients, making rounds across the reservation without notifying Chamberlain of his whereabouts, and generally stirring up trouble. Chamberlain coerced the two senators from South Dakota to write to the commissioner requesting Charles's removal. Instead, Jones commissioned an investigation.

Indian Inspector J. E. Edwards was tasked with seeing if the allegations Chamberlain made against Charles had merit. These allegations included "taking undue liberties with a female patient and attempting the same with others."[31] Charles denied all the charges. He wrote the commissioner stating he had never attempted to instigate problems by stirring Sioux resentments; he was not required to report his comings and goings to the Indian agent but always left word with Elaine about where he would be in case of an emergency; and he had never neglected his patients and certainly never acted "immorally or unprofessionally." He presented a statement from the woman in question, corroborated by her husband, both statements witnessed by clergymen.

Meanwhile, further complicating the situation, back East, the Indian Rights Association was busily complaining to Secretary of the Interior Ethan A. Hitchcock about rife corruption within the Indian Service, and suggesting several individuals who should be investigated. One of these individuals: Harry Chamberlain at Crow Creek. An article about this case reprinted in many newspapers across the country stated, "The charges against Indian Agent Chamberlain include dishonesty and various other offences. . . . It is pretty well known that . . . grave irregularities have been committed under the jurisdiction of Agent Chamberlain," whose appointment had been opposed by some senators who believed him "a tin-horn gambler and utterly unfit for a place of trust." Noting that Chamberlain sought to cast Charles Eastman as the scapegoat, the article suggested, "Charges more insinuating than definite were made," and the "attempt to charge Chamberlain's irregularities to Eastman is there regarded with grave suspicion as being a further demonstration of the same enmity."[32] Because this article was published in numerous papers, it certainly reached the eyes of Agent Chamberlain. Aware of Charles's past ties with Philip Garrett of the Indian Rights Association (the same person to whom Charles had written about problems at Pine Ridge) and distressed by how Charles was referenced in these articles compared to himself, Chamberlain redoubled his efforts to get Charles dismissed.

And just when it seemed a complicated situation for Charles and Elaine couldn't get more complicated, it did.

Before Inspector Edwards issued a finding in this investigation, Agent Chamberlain struck again. He accused Charles of yet another sexual impropriety, this time with Augusta Hultman, superintendent of the Grace Boarding School on the reservation. Three teachers at the school accused Charles and their supervisor of having an immoral relationship. This drama played out like a bad soap opera.

Charles attempted to defend himself against the attacks on his character. He wrote directly to Commissioner Jones, denying the charges. He explained that the women who had "blown the whistle" on the alleged relationship were Augusta Hultman's enemies, teachers who resented her authority. Charles once again solicited letters of support to bolster his case.

Though both Charles and Augusta denied any relationship and Inspector Edwards agreed they hadn't had one, he concluded Miss Hultman had "not conducted herself as becomes a lady," allowing Charles to examine her without the presence of a third party. He recommended her removal, though not Charles's. Edwards suggested since Charles was treating patients, he should be reprimanded, though any further "dishonorable actions" would merit his removal. But Miss Hultman complained about the unfair and sexist double standard. Commissioner Jones agreed she had been treated differently than Charles and allowed her to return to her duties. The Eastmans might have been able to heave a collective sigh of relief, but trouble again reared its ugly head.

In mid-December 1902, Charles returned to the Grace Boarding School to examine a sick student. As he was leaving, he witnessed an altercation between Miss Hultman and another teacher, who hit her several times before being restrained. This incident, reported to Agent Chamberlain and to Indian Inspector Frank Churchill, who'd been dispatched separately to investigate ongoing problems at Grace, resulted in the school's closing. But Churchill went further: he recommended that Charles, whom he viewed as "a dangerous man to have on a reservation where the Dakota or Sioux language is spoken," should be transferred.[33] Several newspapers ran articles, like one in the North Dakota *Courier Democrat*: "Charles Eastman, the well-known Indian doctor, will be transferred from the Crow Creek reservation, where, it is said, he has been a disturbing element."[34]

How Charles and Elaine dealt with these issues is unfortunately something that can only be surmised from their actions, because there are no extant writings from that time. We know Charles did not appeal Churchill's findings; he requested a thirty-day leave in the beginning of January 1903, during which time he traveled to the East. Notices in newspapers help to track his actions. "Dr. Charles A. Eastman is at present in the city," reported the *New York Tribune* in mid-January. "He is understood to be at work on another book of Indian life as seen from the inside, which is nearing completion."[35] He met with his publisher, McClure, Phillips, and he gave several talks. Shortly after Charles returned to Crow Creek, Agent Chamberlain reinstituted his poison-pen assaults, complaining to Commissioner Jones again that Charles was fomenting problems. Charles tried to remain at Crow Creek to treat an outbreak of grippe, which Chamberlain insisted to the commissioner was not the epidemic Charles labeled it. Chamberlain was not satisfied in his campaign to undermine Charles's authority and discredit him until Charles resigned in early March 1903.

Commissioner Jones offered Charles a different position helping to revise the Sioux allotment roles, assigning Euro-American surnames for administrative ease. Charles accepted this job—in truth he had no other options. Having run into political debacles in both of his jobs as an agency physician and not having been able to sustain a living as a physician in private practice, it seemed clear some career rebooting was necessary. Elaine later wrote, "I should have much preferred that Dr. Eastman continue to practice medicine and think I felt worse about his leaving it finally than he did."[36] We don't know what Charles felt. He maintained an interest in health and wellness throughout his life, later writing about and developing fitness programs for the Boy Scouts of America and camping programs, devoting a chapter of his 1915 treatise on the state of contemporary Indians to "The Indian's Health Problem," and sometimes lecturing on how "civilization" had brought about many poor health consequences for all people. Historian Sarah Pripas-Kapit suggests it is possible Charles's medical training ultimately left him disillusioned, believing "'civilization' had caused widespread health catastrophes," and left him questioning more broadly "the tactics—and indeed the desirability—of assimilation policies."[37]

Indeed, this entire period of Charles's life must have been supremely frustrating and disillusioning, though he made no mention of it in his autobiographical *From the Deep Woods to Civilization*. He skips from 1897 to 1910, not mentioning his time at the Carlisle Indian School and expunging the time spent working at Crow Creek.

David Miller hypothesizes that by 1903, at forty-five years old, Charles "had not yet found his 'place' in life. Frustration stalked his career, constantly raising the question of whether 'civilization' transformed the Indian for . . . most of his wishes and goals lay dashed and unaccomplished."[38] He'd been professionally thwarted in numerous ways. Powerless to sustain a job in which he could use his medical training to help his people, stymied by governmental bureaucracies, punished for blowing the whistle on corrupt practices and practitioners, and unjustly accused of wrongdoing in most every job he had held, Charles had been unable or unwilling to stay in any position more than a few years. He'd been poorly compensated for his work. He'd been the subject of numerous erroneous and often racist newspaper articles. And perhaps most ironically of all, his fluency in the Dakota language and customs, which he had always believed would be assets in working with his people, were made into knowledge his Euro-American superiors weaponized against him.

We don't know what Elaine thought because she excised any record from the written documents she left behind. Theodore Sargent writes, "One can only speculate that the nature of the charges leveled against Charles must have mortified Elaine. . . . She must have resented the publicity and anything that Charles might have done to fuel the suspicions that swirled around him. Her public silence in this case, so unlike her behavior at Pine Ridge, might be read as a lack of support for her husband."[39] But years later she wrote to Rose that the responsibility of making responsible decisions for her family largely fell to her. "We went back to the [Indian] service as a matter of absolute necessity, neither of us really wishing it," she wrote. "After about ten years of this, I began to plan, and the decision to come East, push writing and lecturing, educate the children . . . were on *my* initiative. . . . He appeared amazingly indifferent to higher education of the children, however. Of course, this is all is ancient history."[40] Hindsight may be 20/20, but in this case, Elaine came to blame Charles for all the failures of their life at Crow Creek.

* * *

The situation at Crow Creek Agency became so fraught that the Eastmans believed they could no longer live there. Charles's new job, revising the Sioux allotment rolls, would probably have been more easily accomplished using Crow Creek as a base, but it was no longer tenable. They left and spent some time with Charles's brother and his family in Flandreau. And then, although well ahead of the summer season, they decided to decamp for their small cabin on Bald Eagle Lake in Minnesota. That had been one place where they'd known more carefree days; perhaps they could be recaptured. As of mid-April, they were living in the cabin full time.

We know a little about the seven months the Eastmans lived at Bald Eagle Lake from the recollections of a neighbor, published in a newspaper years later, and an interview conducted by David Miller in the early 1970s with a niece of Charles's who lived with the family that summer. The one-time neighbor, William Miller, wrote a letter to the *New Bedford Standard Times* recalling Dr. Eastman "was a Sioux of remarkable intelligence for one of his race. . . . This man entertained us often by relating his early boyhood experiences. . . . My, my, how we listened to stories of the Doctor's Indian boyhood!"[41]

From Grace Eastman Moore we learn that each day, Charles would rise early and work on the tedious project of copying names from the Indian allotment rolls. His afternoons would be spent walking in the woods, jotting down ideas for a new book on a pad he carried with him, and taking the children swimming and fishing in the lake. Elaine would encourage the children to collect plant specimens and then teach them about botany during the day; in the evenings she typed Charles's notes and worked with him as he composed chapters of a manuscript that would become *Red Hunters and the Animal People*.

Despite the idyllic setting and more relaxed pace of life, Elaine and Charles still contended with numerous difficult problems. Some were stressors they had faced since the beginning of their marriage while others were newer issues. But all their problems were like molten lava, bubbling, boiling, just under the surface, present and noticeable when sulfurous fumes leak up to the surface but not quite ready to erupt.

Money was always tight, always a source of contention. "Personally I feel that I should have been happier if I had never been compelled to think about earning money after my marriage," Elaine wrote to Rose, but this was never to be the case.[42] There were the constant needs of five young children, and Elaine felt most of the burden of their care. "Your remark about having thought the Doctor particularly helpful with our children was one that has recurred to me," Elaine corrected Rose, because "he took NO responsibility for them, either when they were small—and he used to boast that he left them entirely to me, therefore anything that went wrong MUST be altogether my fault. But of course, you had no way of knowing his attitude as he was very careful to make a good impression in company, and I never failed in loyalty until [later when] I thought it about time some of the truth be told."[43]

Newspapers continued to publish the ridiculous story about the Eastmans' mythical meeting and their "pappoose" who "unfortunately" bore none of her mother's characteristics, as well as stories about Charles's less-than-noble departure from Crow Creek. None of this could have been easy.

A short poem Elaine published in the *Buffalo Enquirer* after they'd moved to Bald Eagle Lake perhaps gives some insight into her feelings at the time:

> Why should we mourn
> When life is gone,
> This life so mixed with sorrow?
> What though our May
> Goes out today
> Our June comes in tomorrow.[44]

And, truth be told, Charles was probably having a difficult time, too. Apart from whatever disillusionment felt from his most recent stint as an agency physician and whatever disappointment he felt at leaving behind his practice of medicine, he had agreed to a contract with the Indian Service on yet another project with a wholly assimilationist intent.

The idea that Native Americans needed to change their names to conform with Euro-American styles and practices of naming was an extension of the "Americanization/civilization" policies the U.S. government had long been enacting. Without "proper" names "accurately" reflecting family lineage, the rationale went, it would not be possible for Indians to pass private property along to their kin, and the ownership of private property was seen as key to breaking down Indian ways. The 1887 Dawes Allotment Act put in place the mechanism for dividing land to make Indians into farmers; the next step was thought to be breaking up reservations, seen in the last years of the nineteenth century as a flawed experiment whose true outcomes allowed Indians to congregate together too much, made them too dependent on subsidies, and did not achieve the ultimate goal of assimilation. But for land allotment to work, you needed to instill a system of private ownership, and for private ownership to happen efficiently, you needed to have a westernized system of names.

As Francis Paul Prucha points out, this logic was inherently flawed because it neither recognized nor acknowledged many important aspects of Indian cultures. For instance, many Indian groups gave people different names throughout the course of their lives (as Hakadah became Ohíye' S'a). Some Indian groups followed naming practices honoring matrilineal rather than patrilineal clans and lineage. Many tribes named people in symbolic ways: names of animals respected for particular characteristics, names of ancestors, names made in reference to a special achievement.

The overarching governmental assumption posited that Euro-American systems of naming were not only more logical, but superior; a Christian name like "John" (or "Charles," for that matter) was inherently better than even an anglicized version of an Indian name, like "the Winner." In addition, many Euro-Americans "found Indian names confusing and, because they rarely spoke any Indian languages, difficult to pronounce."[45]

Some of the earlier attempts to give Indians Christian names reflecting a father's lineage resulted in much confusion. In 1890 the commissioner of Indian Affairs stated all Indians living on reservations should be given an English Christian name but retain their own surnames. The surnames would be translated into English, too, and shortened if deemed too long. However, this allowed way too much leeway for Indian agents, who would sometimes shorten names in ridiculous ways, give offensive names, or select contextually inappropriate ones like "William Shakespeare" or "George Washington." Indian students in boarding schools such as Hampton and Carlisle were also given Euro-American names, which might bear no relation to names given to the rest of their family back home.

There was no uniformity in the U.S. government's attempts to rename Indians, no overall strategy, and poor records. There was also no person in charge. This changed when Hamlin Garland came along.

By the turn of the century, Garland was already a well-known writer, prolific in both fiction and nonfiction. He had published short stories and novels, a biography of Ulysses S. Grant, and a book about the Klondike Gold Rush. A true multipotentialite, his interests ranged from farming to psychic phenomena. Fascinated by Indians, Garland's writing offered a vision of Native Americans combining a romanticized view of Indians as a "backwards" race yet worthy of Euro-Americans' help and empathy. His 1902 novel, *Captain of the Grey Horse Troop*, serialized in the *Saturday Evening Post* and made into a silent film in 1917, added to Garland's already considerable audience and advanced his essentialist views of Indian life. The combination of Garland's interests and his connections to a range of influential people led to his appointment by President Theodore Roosevelt as director of the Indian naming project.[46]

Garland quickly got to work, consulting with white men whose expertise included ethnology, biology, and literature. By the beginning of December 1902, he had developed a plan and a set of guidelines. Indian names had to be easily pronounced; the translation of Indian names into English words must exclude words or phrases thought to be offensive to white sensibilities (no similar concern evinced about offensiveness to Indians); the original names should be retained if possible. Garland thought it best to begin with the Sioux at Crow Creek Agency. This seemingly random choice appears to have been guided by Garland's association with Charles Eastman, though exactly where the two encountered one another is unclear. They had been corresponding about Garland's appreciation of *Indian Boyhood*, and Charles's appreciation of some of Garland's stories about Indians in magazines.[47] They may have met in person when Charles went to New York in January 1903; he'd written a letter to Garland asking if he planned to be there. In February 1903, Garland requested to Secretary of the Interior Ethan Hitchcock that Charles be named the renaming clerk at Crow Creek; Hitchcock wrote to Garland that Charles could be hired at a salary of $100 per month and "during the time he is thus engaged, he will devote his entire time to the same, and not do literary work."[48]

It's easy to see how, from the start, this was a job with conditions bound to land Charles in trouble again. A low salary (which did not include the cost of his travels to reservations to do the actual work), the caveat that he "not do literary work" in which he was already engaged and needed to generate additional income, and the eventual need to spend time traveling to many different reservations, set him up for problems with both his employer and his wife.

It's also easy to see how the substance of the work would place Charles in uncomfortable, sometimes untenable positions. Even before his appointment became official, Charles wrote to Garland about concerns. He pointed out that among the Sioux, "The family name is pretty generally adopted. . . . that is to say, the children bear the father's name, but it is usually a translation of the Indian name. I certainly prefer the native appellation if available."[49] As he got into the work, Charles realized many names that were "highly regarded among us" weren't easily translated into English names. "I had many difficulties with questionable marriages and orphaned children whose ancestry was not clear. Then there were cases of Indian women who had married United States soldiers and the children had been taken away from the tribe in infancy, but later returned. . . . I was directed not to recognize a plurality of wives, such as still existed among a few of the older men."[50]

The ways in which the popular press discussed this work no doubt added to Charles's discomfort with the tasks at hand. Indian names were described as "fanciful, sometimes unpronounceable, and offtimes vulgar . . . their English translation unfit for publication," claimed a reporter in the *Washington Evening Star*. "There is nothing now as a rule to show the family relationship."[51]

And there was, not surprisingly, deep suspicion among many of the Sioux with whom the reporter spoke. They believed that "the revision of names was another cunning scheme of the white man to defraud them of what little land still left in their possession."[52] They weren't wholly incorrect, as Charles would learn. But in his initial work on the naming project, he found himself again placed in a position of straddling cultures, negotiating between worlds.

* * *

When Commissioner of Indian Affairs William Jones and Secretary of the Interior Hitchcock agreed to switch Charles Eastman from being agency physician at Crow Creek to becoming the "renaming clerk," it was certainly convenient. The very skills that had rendered Charles suspect in the mind of Agent Chamberlain were thought to be assets for his new job. They needed a graceful way of easing him out of a job in which so much controversy had arisen. They did not anticipate he would wish to leave Crow Creek along with the Indian rolls to write up his report.

And they were probably blindsided when he announced his intent to move. Charles wrote that his decision was triggered by "inadventures" including the loss of housing on the Crow Creek reservation when he lost his agency physician job and the unwinterized cabin in which the Eastmans were living at Bald Eagle Lake.[53]

As summer turned to fall and the weather began to change, the Eastmans knew they could not spend the months ahead in Minnesota. Unable to afford appropriate lodgings in St. Paul, Elaine at this point decided it imperative to move back East. "It was never my way to wait upon circumstances or take the line of least resistance," she wrote to Rose. And this time she didn't wait. She reached out to her beloved father for assistance, and Henry Sterling Goodale was only too happy to provide it. In November 1903, Elaine and Charles packed up their belongings and their children, and left Indian Country once more, traveling 1,300 miles to Amherst, Massachusetts, where Henry had rented a spacious home for them.

8

From Amherst to London (1903–1911)

Amherst, Massachusetts, was a small college town with a big literary reputation. Helen Hunt Jackson, author of two of the most influential books that launched the nineteenth-century Indian reform movement (the nonfictional *A Century of Dishonor* and the novel *Ramona*), was born and spent her girlhood in Amherst. She was a childhood friend of another Amherst literary giant, the poet Emily Dickinson, whose first volume of poetry was published posthumously in 1890, the same year as the Wounded Knee Massacre. Noah Webster of dictionary fame called Amherst home for part of his life, as did poet Robert Francis and journalist Ray Stannard Baker. True to Amherst's literary reputation, the years during which Elaine and Charles Eastman lived there would be their most productive in written output: between them, they would publish thirteen books and dozens of articles and poems. But the Amherst years also had many twists and turns in terms of Charles's occupations and in the Eastmans' relationship.

As it turned out, Amherst was also a town with interest in Native American issues. The Amherst Indian Association formed in 1890, dedicated to "do what we could toward the solution of the Indian problem."[1] Composed of women, many of them wives and daughters of Amherst College professors, the association brought in speakers like Amelia Quinton, president of the Women's National Indian Association, Captain Richard Henry Pratt from the Carlisle Indian School, and Angel de Cora, a Winnebago student at nearby Smith College (who would work with the Eastmans at their summer camps) to discuss aspects of Indian education, policy, and culture and raise money for Native American causes. Merrill Gates, president of Amherst College from 1890 to

1899, served on the Board of Indian Commissioners for almost three decades, and often spoke of his dual beliefs in allotment and education as the best paths forward for Indigenous people. Amherst's reputation as a town known for education, literature, and civic participation of different kinds made it even more appealing to Elaine and Charles.

The house Henry rented for them on Snell Street was not far from the main part of the college campus and an easy walk into the town. Owned by Mary Stearns, widow of a former Amherst College president, the large, rambling Victorian was shaded by mature trees; several porches wrapped around the home, speaking to an ease of living the Eastmans had previously not known. David Peck Todd, an astronomy professor known for his international eclipse-chasing expeditions, and his wife, Mabel, Emily Dickinson's first editor, lived next door. On the other side of the Todds' house rose the newly constructed Wilder Observatory, housing the world's largest refractor telescope. It was an unusual neighborhood, and one representing a very different environment for the Eastman family.

For the first time, the Eastmans were living in a place not connected to an agency or a school, with a kitchen, furnace, and bedrooms for each of the children. Henry also paid for a live-in servant to help Elaine—a luxury almost unimaginable in her former life. The differences between life in a small cabin on a Minnesota lake and a large house in Amherst altered patterns of family life in significant ways.

The move to Amherst also represented other enormous changes for the Eastmans. They were back in New England, ensconced in a college town steeped in traditional values derived from a Puritan past, and not exactly known for the diversity of its citizenry. The 1900 U.S. Census showed that of Amherst's year-round population of 5,200, only a tiny fraction were people of color. Six people were listed as "Indian," but not delineated as either South Asian Indians or American Indians. Elaine endorsed the public schools' quality, and so the children attended school for the first time, exposing them to classmates from backgrounds different than their own.

And they were back among Elaine's family: her father, brother, and sister-in-law lived three miles away they in a house were rebuilding on a piece of property Henry purchased years earlier; her mother and two sisters were living in Redding, Connecticut, 110 miles to the south. After almost two decades of infrequent visits and somewhat more frequent letters, Elaine and Charles were suddenly thrust into situations in which they had to confront the long-simmering tensions with her family.

It didn't take them long to reestablish themselves in their professional endeavors. Within a month of their arrival in Amherst both Elaine and Charles were giving public talks. In early December 1903, Charles spoke in Amherst on "A School of Savagery." According to the write-up of this talk in the *Springfield Daily Republican*, Charles discussed his early life, his Euro-American education, and "many stories of Indian life which interpret Indian character in a new light to most of his audience." Apparently, despite the Eastmans' need for income, he gave this talk gratis, with proceeds of the tickets going to "settlement work in New York City."[2] His neighbor Mabel Loomis Todd wrote in her diary that she had attended this talk about "his Indian boyhood" but "his wife, Elaine Goodale, did not go."[3] This talk was a trial run for many others he would subsequently give.

Charles signed on with the J. B. Pond Lyceum Bureau. Pond, whose clients included P. T. Barnum, Arthur Conan Doyle, and Mark Twain, built a career representing famous authors and celebrities. Charles's engagement with the agency took a little while to arrange; he had begun exchanging letters with Major Pond at the end of his time in Crow Creek. Charles wrote to Pond that he could give talks on a number of topics, including "When I Was an Indian Boy," "The Last Stand of the Sioux," "Indian Wit, Music, Poetry and Eloquence" and "Indian Athletics and Physical Training," and that his name on the publicity circular should be "spelled in full, Charles Alexander Eastman (Ohiyesa)."[4] In the promotional materials Pond developed, an elegant photo of Charles in a suit jacket and tie graces the cover; he looks directly at the camera but does not smile. "Here is a man with a story to tell—a story which has never yet been fully told," the text begins. "It is the story of a race which has hitherto remained for the most part silent, under persistent mistreatment and misunderstanding. Dr. Charles A. Eastman, a Sioux Indian, stands as the first competent interpreter between the aboriginal American and the American people." After an abbreviated, exaggerated summation of Charles's life are two pages of testimonials, including one from Hamlin Garland reading, in part, "I regard him as far and away the ablest living expositor of Sioux life and character." Another page contains excerpted reviews of *Indian Boyhood*, and yet another lists the various topics of Charles's talks for hire.[5] At the time Charles gave his first talk in Amherst he announced he would be giving many more public lectures, including upcoming talks in Philadelphia and at the Geographical Society of Baltimore. Clearly, he was not adhering to Secretary Hitchcock's admonition he focus only on the allotment rolls.

Elaine, too, seems to have almost immediately taken advantage of having some childcare. A notice in the local newspaper announced she would be speaking about "How can we help the Indian help himself" in December 1903.[6] Soon she placed more articles in various newspapers and magazines, including one piece of note—a short story called "Life of Little Yellow Star," picked up by many papers in the early months of 1904.[7] This sad tale describes a Dakota girl named Yellow Star who is sent to a school on her reservation. Her white teacher takes a great interest in her, inquiring at her home when Yellow Star fails to come to class, showering the girl with special attention, sending a doctor when she falls ill. Apart from the obvious parallels to the white teacher who becomes overly involved with her Indian students, this story prefigured themes Elaine would return to in her novel, also called *Yellow Star*, published in 1911.

Throughout the early years of their time in Amherst, both Elaine and Charles juggled numerous professional projects as they tried to support their large family. In addition, they still owed hundreds of dollars to their Washington, DC, landlady, who was busily complaining to the various officials in the Indian Bureau about Charles's delinquency on his debts. This created additional tension between him and his government employers. It also, no doubt, created additional tension between Charles and his wife.

Charles's "official" main job was working on the Sioux allotment roles and the naming project. Between 1903 and 1909 Charles worked to revise names of approximately 25,000 Sioux, earning him the moniker "the Name Giver."[8] This work often involved weeks of travel back to Indian Country, which also meant weeks of separation from Elaine and the children. The work was also stressful because Hamlin Garland frequently had to act as an intermediary between Charles and the commissioner of Indian Affairs, who expressed ongoing concerns about the other very public work Charles continued to do when he ostensibly only had this one official job.

No doubt adding to the difficulties of this endeavor were the unremitting newspaper articles published about it, including an extensive piece that appeared in the local *Daily Hampshire Gazette* in 1907. Stating, "Dr. Eastman looks very well tamed, not merely for an Indian, but for a man, with his impeccable store clothes, his library jammed with books, an outdoor entourage of college buildings, approximation to the college professor type in mental habit, and the slightly reserved courtesy of the best New England type," the article suggested his work on this project was necessary because "the past that fitted the old Indians' names is dead. New names are required to suit actual conditions." The writer added that traditional Indian names were a "fantastic and chaotic nomenclature, a handicap to the red man in competition in white society."[9] Another article appearing in the *Boston Globe* under the headline "Renaming the Indian: Interesting Work by Dr. Charles Alexander Eastman; the Unpronounceable Red Man's Name to Go" stated, "Dr. Eastman, himself a Sioux Indian, has been appointed by Uncle Sam to bring order out of the chaotic state of the red man's nomenclature."[10]

But beyond this, the work left Charles with profound ambivalence. In his 1911 book, *The Soul of the Indian,* widely regarded as one of his most significant treatises, he wrote, "Names of any dignity or importance must be conferred by the old men, and especially so if they have any spiritual significance."[11] Knowing this, it is difficult to see how he reconciled his knowledge of the ways in which Indians gave themselves names with his own task of assigning them Euro-American ones. Some historians believe Charles likely thought of this work as a way of acclimating the Sioux to the inevitabilities of changing life in America.[12] But it couldn't have been easy; it was a bad choice among bad choices for Native Americans.

Charles's lecture schedule kept him on the road much of the time. After Major Pond died in 1903 Charles fulfilled the events at which the agency had booked him and continued to accept many additional speaking invitations. Elaine assisted him with management and bookkeeping for his lecturing career, and for a time, clipped notices of his talks in a scrapbook she kept. She subscribed to the Luce Clipping Service, one of several started in the late nineteenth century, to obtain articles about Charles's talks. Luce provided its clients with what founder Robert Luce referred to as "a single nugget in a cradle-full of gravel."[13] In addition to keeping records of his talks, for over a decade Elaine handled all the correspondence and publicity for them, which often amounted to twenty-five or more different events in different locations in a single calendar year. The lecturing increased his public profile and brought in much-needed income, but it also kept him away and while furthering his public profile, did nothing for hers. Undoubtedly, she came to see these talks with ambivalence.

She also continued to assist him as he put together his second book, *Red Hunters and the Animal People*, published in 1904. Timed to come out ahead of holiday sales, this book garnered strong reviews. "The work as a whole is valuable aside from its romance," wrote a reviewer in the *Brooklyn Daily Eagle*, "as an evidence of the Indian's viewpoint, shown by one who speaks from the intimate knowledge of one reared in the culture which these tales represent." The reviewer in the *New York Tribune* agreed: "In the book which Dr. Eastman has written of the relations of the Indian and the animal people we have the benefit of a trained and educated intelligence brought to the interpretation of the legendary and acquired lore of the red man. The volume has, accordingly, a double interest—that of the stories as stories and as representations of the Indian point of view."[14]

Some contemporary Indigenous perspectives on this book suggest although white reviewers of the day might have missed it, this wasn't just a book about talking animals. Nor should its author have been thought of as some kind of ethnological object himself. Christopher Pexa writes that Charles Eastman's motives in writing this book may well have been more complex than simply recounting traditional tales and suggesting how humans learned behaviors from animals. Charles's "talking animals recover and rearticulate Dakota peoplehood and kinship based ethical relations" and symbolically use animals as “exemplary peoples” who maintain “kinship norms of inter-generational respect and obedience.”[15] Viewed as a continuum, Indian people and the animals in their world make a very different statement.

How much and what kind of input did Elaine have on this book? Years later she engaged in serious dialogue with Rose about how much assistance she provided Charles. When Rose suggested to Elaine it was wrong for Charles to have published them with himself listed as the sole author, Elaine responded, “He was and is the author—although he wrote very carelessly and would not even try to correct or revise, therefore I did ALL the drudgery—but took conscientious pains to preserve his style and tone and not to introduce my own.” Clouding this picture is a letter Elaine wrote to one of Charles’s Dartmouth classmates a few years later: “As most people realize from internal evidence, I collaborated on all nine of his books.”[16] But in 1904 questions of collaboration were far less pressing for Elaine than questions relating to the immediate and direct needs of her growing children. And at the end of that year, it was clear the family would be growing further: at the age of forty-one, Elaine was once again pregnant.

* * *

World-famous photographer Ansel Adams once wrote that photos aren’t just images taken with cameras: they are acts that include our background, the people we know, the various cultural experiences we’ve had, the time in which we live. Photographs are not simply images of those who appear in them; they are not simple, at all. The photographs of the Eastmans from the early part of the twentieth century open fascinating parts of their stories, both for what they say about Elaine and Charles as individuals and for what they tell us about the larger context in which these photos were staged, shot, and disseminated.

In 1904 Elaine commissioned formal portraits of the children to be taken for Christmas. The girls are all wearing lacy, ruffled dresses; Ohi wears a high-collared white shirt and jacket, hair streaming past his shoulders. Dora, Irene, and Virginia have large bows in their hair; Eleanor is wearing a white eyelet

FIGURE 8.1. Five of the six Eastman children, circa 1901. Courtesy James W. Dayton; Raymond Wilson.

baby bonnet. Biographer Theodore Sargent writes, "These are delightful images, but there is a curious ambiguity about them that seems to underscore Elaine's efforts to comply with her new Amherst standards. . . . It is hard to imagine that Charles had anything to do with these getups."[17] It's not clear whether Elaine's standards were any different in Amherst than they had been anywhere else or if Charles, who often dressed in Victorian jackets and shirts with cravats, would have seen anything wrong with these portraits. Yet Sargent is on to something about the contextual ambiguities in which the photographs were shot.

The children's Euro-American Victorian clothing and hairstyles in these photos speak to a degree of staged Anglo-conformity. Though neither Elaine nor Charles left behind any written thoughts about these portraits or what inspired them, it's not out of the realm of possibility that Elaine wanted for her children what children often want for themselves—to fit in with their peers. In the photos under discussion Dora Winona was twelve, Irene ten, Virginia eight, and Ohi six—all in public school for the first time. A few years later in adolescence the peer pressure to be like everyone else would only have intensified. By the time the 1910 census rolled around, not one of the Eastman children was listed as "Indian"—they were all listed as "white." This almost certainly emanated from Elaine filling out the questionnaire sent ahead of an enumerator's visit to their home. In fairness, as Anne Hyde points out, multiracial families were "a problem" for census takers.[18] Some of Elaine's complicated thinking about her biracial children is found in a letter to Rose written in the late 1920s in which Elaine discussed a recently published book called *American Minority Peoples* and added, "The notion that 'Indian traits,' for example, might be detected in my children, has always seemed to me nonsense."[19]

The issue of the biracial Eastman children appearing "too Indian" was no doubt also complicated by the images of their father that increasingly appeared on book jackets and in newspapers across the country. Since his Dartmouth days, Charles knew there were times when looking "like an Indian" could be beneficial. As historian Phillip Deloria writes, perhaps beginning with the Boston Tea Party when white insurgents chose to dress up as

Indians because only Indians would be thought of as tempests of tea-tossing trouble, there have been many times throughout American visual iconography when "playing Indian" served both Native and non-Native people wishing to use costume to make a point. "Indians, it is clear, are not simply useful symbols of the love-hate ambivalence of civilization and savagery. . . . To understand the various ways Americans have contested and constructed national identities we must constantly return to the original mysteries of Indianness."[20]

As Charles began to depend more on his writing and lecturing for income, he realized appearing in Native dress could increase sales. Kiara Vigil suggests Charles knew the ways in which he dressed functioned as an advertisement for his work. She argues that his choice of attire was strategic: "Eastman's ability to dress up as an Indian, or not, enabled him to address diverse audiences and their expectations."[21] Indeed, the photographic portraits of Charles in first editions of his various books varied greatly. His 1911 *The Soul of the Indian* shows a highly stylized and spiritual Charles shirtless, wearing a feathered headdress, looking up at the sky. His 1915 *From the Deep Woods to Civilization* depicts a different formal portrait of Charles, graying at the temples, wearing a starched white collar, tie, and suit jacket, looking off to the side in a classic "author shot."

Similarly, Charles would sometimes appear at public talks attired in suit and tie, sometimes in feathered headdress and fringed buckskin. And the way he chose to present himself often dominated the coverage he received. For instance, an article in the *Lewiston* (ME) *Sun* ran under the headline, "Ohiyesa Came in Real Sioux Costume and told Story of Genuine Heart Interest." "His headdress was a genuine war bonnet," the reporter stated, "made of spotted eagle feathers. . . . His costume was of tan colored skins, with wonderful bead trimmings, light blue forming the background for the bead work. Woven into this, were all sorts of symbols. The tomahawk which he carried was once owned and used by Crazy Horse."[22] Whether this was true was almost beside the point; there was more ink given to Charles's attire than to what he said. Many articles appearing in the popular press over the course of Charles's public speaking career would call out when he wore "full Sioux regalia." Historian Lucy Maddox comments that Charles's frequent and strategic use of wearing dramatic Sioux attire in his public talks shows he "knew and understood well the white public [he was] addressing, [and he] specifically set out to correct stereotypes and misconceptions . . . acknowledg[ing] that changing public opinion was a necessary prerequisite to changing Indian lives for the better."[23]

Conversely, when Charles appeared for his public lectures wearing Euro-American clothing, newspaper reports were more likely to focus on things such as a "remarkably clear and instructive lecture by Dr. Charles A. Eastman," as one headline from the *Barre* (VT) *Daily Times* read.[24] As Tony Dykema-VanderArk points out, Charles "reversed the game of 'playing Indian' to 'playing white,' and in so doing subverted common images of conflict." He suggests that through the curation of Charles's image and through his writing, Charles deliberately tried to find the common ground between Indians and white people, often using the common experiences of childhood to do so.[25]

Charles Eastman was not the only Native American speaking on public stages in America to dress differently according to the audience or topic being addressed. Paiute author and educator Sarah Winnemucca sometimes gave talks wearing traditional dress and, at other times, Euro-American Victorian gowns. There were also instances in which Euro-Americans would insist the Native Americans with whom they worked wear traditional clothing: in Buffalo Bill's Wild West Show, Native performers were sometimes asked to don tribal costumes like full war headdresses that were only supposed to be worn in particular ceremonial occasions; photographer Edward Curtis sometimes dressed his subjects in traditional clothing they no longer wore and had them shave off facial hair, wear wigs, or add fake nose rings to make them look "more authentic."[26]

But Charles's costume shifting wasn't as simple as dressing one way for some audiences and one way for others. Perhaps slyly and deliberatively, Charles used his Indian identity to make a point: sometimes his Indian appearance would signal a real connection to his people, and sometimes, an image of what Euro-Americans would *think* an Indian should look like. Philip Deloria and others believe Charles's "hybrid life" produced a man aware of both the implications of his Dakhóta roots in shaping the person he was and the implications of the ways in which Euro-Americans saw him as an Indian Other. Moreover, this cross-cultural awareness wasn't limited to the ways Charles could monetize it; it was something he used to make it difficult for observers to figure out what was authentic and what was not.

This confusion about who and what the real Charles Eastman was may also have extended to his wife.

* * *

For Elaine and Charles, the years 1905–1910 were as packed with life events as the lives of families can be. Their last child, Florence, was born in September 1905. Henry Sterling Goodale died in 1906, and Dora Read Goodale in 1910, the same year her namesake granddaughter, Dora Winona Eastman, graduated from high school. The Eastmans moved to a different rental home in Amherst in 1906. And within that same five-year period, between them, Charles and Elaine published four books. Money continued to be tight, Charles's various occupations continued to keep him on the road a lot, and Elaine continued to juggle the demands of her large family while managing part of Charles's career and trying to jump-start her own. And the tensions between Elaine and Charles grew, the resentment often repressed but simmering.

We get some idea of what was going on during this time from the letters Rose's son James, a freshman at the Massachusetts Agricultural College (later UMass/Amherst), wrote home to his mother starting in 1909, when he moved in with his aunt and uncle in exchange for help with chores. From these letters it's easy to discern the small flashpoints that would later ignite.

The house at 25 College Street, painted yellow with orange trim, had a distinctive gambrel roof and two chimneys (today it houses Amherst College's Keefe Health Center). Though not as large as the house on Snell Street, it provided ample space for the Eastman family, and its upkeep provided Elaine with many tasks to assign. Even with all the children and James there to help, Charles was usually not present, and this became an ongoing issue for Elaine. "Even after I was doing three-fourths of his work, he reluctantly and ungraciously, if at all, vouchsafed the least help with mine. That one partner should sit around smoking and playing solitaire, most of the day, while the other worked somewhat beyond her strength and without relief at tasks which he could quite well spell her at, surely can't seem to you right," wrote Elaine to Rose in 1933. In another letter from 1937, Elaine suggested Charles's "career is a pretty good example of [what] we often see—the success of the egotist in getting most of what he demands out of life and in imposing on those who are more yielding or more considerate."[27]

But Elaine's complaints about what little Charles did when he was in Amherst were at least matched—if not eclipsed—by her thoughts about the problems caused because he *wasn't* there a lot. "Having six children and not enough means to employ housekeepers or nurses, I carried two or three separate jobs and was a good deal overburdened. My husband, on the other hand, led a very easy life, with abundant leisure and recreational opportunities, often traveling for pleasure for months at a time, while we at home had great difficulty in paying for absolute necessities," she wrote to Rose in 1939. "Usually, he was away from home, but if not, he appeared very indifferent."[28] To be sure, Elaine's later-in-life recollections were probably tainted by what would happen in the final years of her marriage to Charles, and to be fair, it's clear some of what she didn't get "the Doctor" to do she delegated to her nephew, so it isn't as if she had no help at all. James, too, commented in letters to his mother about many chores "Aunt E" would assign to him, and how, when "the Doctor" returned from his trips it seemed to have a calming influence on his boisterous cousins, writing, "things will be more peaceful for a while now!"[29]

The other moderating force in the first years of the Eastmans' Amherst life was Elaine's father. Henry had been their financial savior, renting the first two houses in which they lived in Amherst and paying for some help for Elaine. From Elaine's earliest writings we know of Henry's poetic soul, the ways in which he carefully encouraged his daughters, the strong bond his eldest child felt with him. Henry seems to have been an unyieldingly supportive force in his children's lives, whether arranging for Elaine's wedding to Charles when Dora and others in the family had such opposition to it, or working to build the stone home in Amherst that he would live in with his son, Robert, and daughter-in-law Helen Brennan—a union Dora had also vehemently opposed and actively tried to prevent, perhaps in part from prejudice about Helen's Catholicism. Henry must have adored and indulged his grandchildren, too: a *New York Times* article about his management of the Windemere apartment buildings in New York describes his own dwelling as "a cozy nook at all seasons" filled with "books and pictures of Mr. Goodale's three charming daughters and of the little grandchildren."[30] In 1926 Elaine speculated to Rose, "Wouldn't Papa have enjoyed being a great-grandfather?"[31]

Henry's decline and death in 1906 from heart disease proved heartbreaking for his family. His obituary in the *Springfield Republican* noted Henry's "true literary gift and . . . rich vein of Yankee humor" as well as his "sincere, gentle, delicate and honorable nature."[32] Elaine left behind no contemporaneous thoughts about the impact of her father's death, but over the years she conveyed in letters to Rose something of the emotional vacuum his death left for her. In 1931 she recalled she'd recently written "a tardy tribute to our father, whom I, at least, utterly failed to appreciate at that time."[33] Fittingly, Henry's memorial service was held at Lodestone, the home built by his own hands, where he spent his last years. He was buried in an unmarked grave in Amherst's Wildwood Cemetery. Late in life Elaine wrote to Rose that Henry's wish had been to be returned to nature, and that she, like her father, "dislike the idea of any stone, and indeed of associating a grave in any way avoidable with a loved one departed."[34] Even without a gravestone marker Elaine mourned her father for years; the final poem in her final collection is titled "For Those Dear Dead" and clearly references her father:

> Now those dear dead, whom we misprized
> Their meek and late revenges take;
> So tenderly our bosoms ache
> For sad, remembered smile of theirs,
> And in our thoughts, and in our prayers,
> So sweetly are they canonized![35]

Henry's death not only left an emotional hole for Elaine but also left a gap in whatever financial aid he had been able to provide for her family. Elaine later recalled to Rose, "We were living there in actual poverty and the Doctor earning almost nothing!"[36] The Eastmans' expenses increased along with the size of their family; Irene Taluta, who showed great promise as a singer, needed lessons, and with children in high school, the issue of college tuition loomed. With the Sioux renaming project only bringing in $100 a month and the Santee claims work yet to bring in any money at all, Elaine knew their writing would provide additional funds. She also knew she needed to do more than ensure Charles would produce manuscripts that could be sold; she needed to find a way to produce additional pieces herself.

* * *

Whether through inspiration of the muses or motivation of the dollar, the Eastmans went into high gear on their respective writing projects. In 1906 Charles sold articles to *The Craftsman, Harper's Bazaar, Ladies' Home Journal,* and *Outlook,* among others. In 1907 McClure published his third book, *Old Indian Days,* dedicated to his four daughters. In 1909 came *Wigwam Evenings,* a group of "Sioux Folktales Retold," collaboratively written by Charles and Elaine and published by Little, Brown; this was followed by *Smokey Day's Wigwam Evenings,* published the following year. And in 1911, Charles published *The Soul of the Indian.*

Elaine was also busy writing under her own by-line. Between 1906 and 1911 she sold poems and articles to *Harper's Bazaar, Outlook,* and *The Independent.* In addition to the two books of folktales written with Charles came her *Little Brother O' Dreams* in 1910, followed by *Yellow Star* in 1911. According to Sargent, the protagonist in *Little Brother O' Dreams* "is clearly modeled after Elaine's father, Henry, to whose memory she dedicates it." Little Brother has a mother who is a bit sharp and overprotective and lives in an old farmhouse on the side of a mountain, near a large and fantastic waterfall, just like Sky Farm. Little Brother meets a little girl who becomes his childhood companion exploring the natural world around them, and eventually becomes his wife. Sargent notes this tale honors Henry by enshrining his best qualities in the hero and the home he built his family in the setting.[37]

In *Yellow Star,* Elaine returned to the Wounded Knee Massacre and told a fictionalized story about the baby whom Charles rescued from the snow, later adopted by a white family. The subtitle of this book, "A Story of East and West," prefigures the cultural struggles faced by the heroine, called Stella by her adoptive parents, as she tries to reconcile her Ojibwe roots with the Euro-American world in which she'd been raised. A reviewer in the *San Francisco Call* observed when Yellow Star grows up with her adoptive family, "Every racial trait vanishes. In this environment (which may or not be true to experiences) . . . when the girl has grown up she returns to her people. . . . The story is fiction, but founded on fact, for Mrs. Eastman has had much experience among her adopted people."[38] Even though Elaine clearly recognized some of the push-and-pull in interracial adoptions and Yellow Star is tugged in different directions, she ultimately selects choices guided by her adoptive culture rather than her birth culture; as ever, Elaine's conclusion that assimilation is the best response to tumult in the Indian world prevailed. In Elaine's rendering, Stella's life was the better for adoption; the real child on whom Stella was based didn't fare as well.[39] No doubt Elaine would not have applauded the U.S. Supreme Court's 2023 decision upholding the notion Native American adoptees should optimally be placed with tribal or family members.

Elaine later somewhat disparagingly referred to these books as her "pot-boilers." "Our income was never at all adequate to the family needs, in spite of my husband's varied activities and growing reputation," she wrote in 1930. "In odd hours I wrote several fanciful plays and pageants and published . . . books for young folks."[40] Contemporary literary analyst Sarah Ruffing Robbins further explains having these books "pigeon-hole[d] . . . as children's literature with a pedagogical bent" put them into a genre of another time period that was starting to fall out of fashion, perhaps another reason Elaine felt defensive about them.[41] Additionally, for someone who early in life had been told she had almost unlimited literary potential, the fact that she had forsaken the possibility of becoming a great poet, a well-credentialed journalist, or a well-known writer for becoming someone who churned out prose for profit must have been an enormous source of disappointment. Elaine, like so many women before and after her, knew that in becoming a mother she had shifted her primary responsibility from anything she could do for herself to everything she needed to do for her children. Whether this also included an increasingly heavy editorial hand in Charles's writing is a question also worth raising.

* * *

Between 1905 and 1910 Charles's movements can be best tracked by the many newspaper articles that appeared about him. He gave talks on several topics in Maryland and Pennsylvania in 1905; in 1906–1908 he spoke across the Midwest; in 1909 his lecture locations ranged from Wilkes-Barre, Pennsylvania, to Champaign, Illinois, to Guthrie, Oklahoma. Many newspaper articles also followed his ongoing work on the Sioux naming project, which continued to take him to the Dakotas and Nebraska for weeks at a time. While noting the "remarkable achievement" of renaming nearly 30,000 Sioux, many of these articles continued to print incorrect information about Charles, such as an article in the 1910 *Caney Chronicle* from Kansas that noted, "The doctor was a member of the faculty of Amherst College for many years. He has degrees from Dartmouth and Harvard universities. . . . He is an interesting talker and his store of information relative to the Noble Red Man is apparently limitless."[42]

Charles's reputation as an authority on Indian cultures, as an author, and as a speaker grew rapidly in the early part of the twentieth century. In one measure of how his fame increased, in 1905 he was invited to a celebration of Mark Twain's seventieth birthday at the famous Delmonico's Restaurant in New York City. Charles attended this event along with many leading literary figures of the day, including Frances Hodgson Burnett and William Dean Howells, as well as many other famous people like naturalist John Burroughs (who years earlier had heard young Elaine Goodale speak at the Lake Mohonk Indian Conference and commented she was one to watch), industrialist Andrew Carnegie, and mannerist Emily Post. *Harper's Weekly*, host of the gala, published a special supplement with photos of the luminaries at each table. Charles, gazing away from the camera, was seated at the same table as Carnegie, and beside Margaret Sutton Briscoe Hopkins, a Southern writer married to an Amherst College professor. But the tiara she's wearing, along with the flowing white gown, makes her look more like a princess than an academic spouse. While Charles attended this fête, his own wife was back in Amherst with their six children. Even if they viewed this event as possibly advancing Charles's career, it probably didn't seem like a very good trade-off to Elaine.

The opportunities for Charles to add to the family coffers almost always seemed to involve travel. As the allotment/naming project wrapped up, Charles received another opportunity that also necessitated months away from Amherst.

Like many museums and universities, the University of Pennsylvania Museum began collecting artifacts from different cultures in the late nineteenth century. Although its website today begins with the land acknowledgment, "The Penn Museum respectfully acknowledges that it is situated on Lenapehoking, the ancestral and spiritual homeland of the Unami Lenape," such recognition of the what the museum owes to Native peoples was not always the case. Consistent with a nineteenth-century philosophy that Native Americans were a race bound to disappear between intermarriage and practices of forced assimilation, museums like Penn's began to gather apparel, artwork, sacred objects, and skeletons to document cultures their Euro-American curators believed belonged in exhibits of the soon-to-be-past. George Gustav Heye, a banker with a keen interest in Native American cultures, decided to invest in collecting artifacts from various tribes. He loaned some of his vast collection (estimated in his obituary in the *New York Times* to have consisted of approximately three million items) to the University of Pennsylvania. In 1910 he agreed to finance an expedition to collect additional artifacts from the Ojibwe. Somehow—and it's not clear through what channels this happened—Charles Eastman was put in charge of the effort to gather artifacts for Penn, although the Sioux were traditional enemies of the Ojibwe. That summer he set off for northern Minnesota and Ontario and spent three months traveling, collecting "ethnological curios," and visiting with Ojibwe who "kindly welcomed" him, despite his Sioux heritage.

Perhaps the most lyrical chapter of Charles's *From the Deep Woods to Civilization* is the one describing his summer of the artifacts expedition. For example, of Rainy Lake, which straddles the border between International Falls, Minnesota, and Fort Francis, Ontario, Charles wrote, "The clear black waters have washed, ground and polished these rocky islets into every imaginable fantastic shape and they are all carpeted with velvety mosses in every shade of gray and green, and canopied with fairy-like verdure."[43]

But beyond his poetic, sometimes ecstatic, descriptions of the environment and the traditional practices of the Ojibwe, whom Charles believed were largely untouched by Euro-American culture and "almost unconscious of the bare pathos of their survival," the 1910 trip may have rekindled in Charles a desire to return to some of his own past. Writes David Martínez, "The further Eastman pursued his museum work, the more the Ojibwe reawakened in him the deep connection he once felt for the woods and the life he lived there."[44] This "reawakening" would have many consequences for Charles in the years to come, both personal and professional. David Miller suggests the journey also had a component of renewal: "At fifty-one years of age, Eastman remained in many ways a frustrated and disillusioned man, still not having found his 'place' in life. In his restlessness, he sought some sort of renewal of identity," and found it along the way on this trip.[45]

Contemporary analysis of this piece of Charles's work varies widely. Some suggest Charles's work collecting Indian artifacts was the ultimate sellout, viewing Indian culture as commodity and decisive evidence of his own assimilation. Neil Schmitz writes this work "marks the extent of Eastman's conversion. He has come a long way from the deep woods, from his tribal childhood. . . . [He] finds himself in the wrong place in this story, put in the white man's place in his subject category."[46] But others interpret Charles's work as recognition of the importance of preserving Native cultures and as part of the journey he had to take to get back to his own Sioux roots. Martínez believes, "Rather than being a tale about the expropriation of sacred items, Eastman's real story is about how the Ojibwe are the only true Indians left. . . . In a world where Eastman and many of his intellectual peers regarded the old ways as gone, maintaining a traditional life is nothing short of extraordinary."[47] Elsewhere, Martínez adds that though the explicit purpose of Charles's journey was to procure artifacts from those who owned them for a

Euro-American collector, "Eastman did not hesitate at indigenizing the collecting process. He approached Indian leaders and showed them respect, smoked the pipe with them, stayed in their camps and villages, ate with them," and exchanged gifts with them. In so doing, he notes, "Eastman's spirit is rejuvenated" and he is "less of a scientist and more of a traveler, perhaps even a pilgrim."[48]

The period of Charles's 1910 sojourn was unquestionably a time Elaine experienced differently as she dealt with a myriad of stresses. She was home with all six children and her nephew, James; her own mother's health declining; her oldest child about to depart for college, albeit at nearby Mount Holyoke. She'd published the first book she had written in years, and though *Little Brother O' Dreams* garnered good reviews ("a tender poetical story," wrote one reviewer; "It brings back vividly the two little girl poets that astonished every one, we will not say how many years ago. It is a difficult task in these matter-of-fact days for an author to hold true to one note of sentiment that will stir the reader, but that task Mrs. Eastman has carried out brilliantly," wrote another)[49] unlike Charles, Elaine had no ability to go on the road to promote her book.

The difficulties of 1910 continued for Elaine as reports of her mother's deteriorating health came from her sister Dora. Dora had broken off her engagement to stay in Connecticut and care for their ailing mother, and tried to continue her writing career as she accepted a job teaching at a local school to help pay the bills and wasn't above guilting the sister who didn't live close by to help. "My dear sister," wrote Dora to Elaine in June 1910, "It will be a shock but, I think, scarcely a surprise to you, to hear that Mother is almost certainly suffering from a malignant abdominal tumor, which already renders her almost helpless, and must be increasingly painful to the end. . . . The worst thing about it is that there will probably be a period—perhaps a long period—of intense suffering—from Mother. I do dread it for her!" Dora concluded she knew Elaine would ask what she could do, "but I can't think of much to suggest."[50] For Elaine this letter must have triggered intense and complicated feelings—her mother was dying, her own ambivalent feelings about her, unresolved, and the sister with whom she'd long had a somewhat competitive relationship was the one taking care of their mother—and telling her there wasn't anything Elaine could do to help. If there were other letters in which Dora attempted to instill guilt in her sister, Elaine didn't save them. Dora Read lingered until the end of December; Elaine left no record of what she felt when her mother eventually died.

When her will was unsealed, it turned out mother Dora left her house in Connecticut to daughter Dora along with all of its contents and half of her china, silver, and linen; her interest in the Lodestone house in Amherst to Rose (not to Robert, who had been living there), along with the other half of her silver, china, and linen, and gave Robert first choice of her books, pictures, and other articles. To Elaine, she bequeathed her "Indian curios, also my mosaic brooch with the motto PAX."[51] Whether this was meant as a peace offering isn't clear, but the inequities in the ways the elder Dora divided her estate surely continued to divide her children.

Early in that turbulent year of 1910, Elaine published a poem about Halley's Comet in *The Independent*. It is unlikely she would have seen it at that point (her former neighbor, astronomer David Peck Todd, reported a sighting in Amherst in mid-May), but it does seem likely Elaine's language was also symbolic given everything else going on in her life at the time:

> Even so, my Life, thou cam'st to me
> From deeps no man can measure;
> Dread night and chaos wait for thee—
> And must I lose my treasure?[52]

* * *

In 1911, issues about race figured prominently in world news. In the Torreón massacre in Mexico, a mob killed more than three hundred Chinese residents; in Russia and Ukraine, anti-Jewish pogroms were on the rise; in Canada, "anti-Oriental" riots broke out. In the United States, the tragic fire at the Triangle Shirtwaist Factory in New York City shed light on the deplorable conditions in which immigrants worked; it was the height of the Jim Crow era, and the massacre of perhaps a hundred Black Americans in

Slocum, Texas, the year before had ramped up racial tensions across the country.

Poor conditions on Native American reservations, exacerbated by limited economic and educational options and numerous systemic health issues, underscored the inequities Indigenous peoples in America faced. Acutely aware of this, Charles, along with his brother John and the Reverend Sherman Coolidge, an Arapaho who, like the Eastman brothers, received a Euro-American education, met to discuss the idea of forming some kind of pan-Indian rights organization. The idea didn't go anywhere at the time. In 1908 Charles, Coolidge, and Dr. Carlos Montezuma, an Apache who similarly received both undergraduate and medical training in Euro-American schools, were invited to speak at a conference at the Ohio State University run by sociologist Fayette Avery McKenzie. Discussions about forming a pan-Indian alliance emanating from this conference moved the idea forward. And in April 1911, several prominent Native Americans, including Charles Eastman, met and announced the formation of the American Indian Association. This organization would work to find "large scale" and "systemic ways" to bring Native Americans into "modern life," and to find ways of getting Native Americans better able to help themselves. A few months later they held a conference that attracted many prominent Native Americans and white people interested in Indian issues; the organization changed its name to the Society of American Indians (SAI). Charles was nominated for the position of executive committee chairman but lost out to Thomas Sloan, a mixed-race Omaha educated at the Hampton Institute. Charles's affiliation with SAI would wax and wane as the organization took positions with which he did or did not agree, but he would become an active contributor to its signature journal and eventually its president in 1918.

Charles's increasingly high and increasingly political profile continued later in 1911 when he was asked to be the lone Native American representative at the First Universal Races Congress to be held that summer in London. The congress, brainchild of two prominent humanists of the era, was a large convening meant to bring together representatives of different races to discuss "general relations between peoples of the West and those of the East" as well as relations between people of various racial backgrounds. Representatives from more than fifty countries attended, and the program included talks given by people ranging from anthropologist Franz Boas to Abdu'l Bahá, founder of the Bahá'i faith, to African American sociologist and activist W. E. B. DuBois. Other individuals in attendance at these meetings included author H. G. Wells, social reformer Jane Addams, and founder of anticolonialist passive resistance, Mohandas Gandhi. An album of "portraits of readers of papers" from the congress, held in the Dartmouth College Archives, shows that all but two of those asked to give papers were male, most were European, and most were white. Within this group, the portrait of Charles Eastman is notable.

The opportunity to appear at the conference became important to Charles for several reasons. It was a high-profile appearance at a prestigious event coinciding with a time when his personal financial pressures were escalating, and he undoubtedly viewed this as an opportunity to enhance his own marketability. But beyond that, he viewed this opportunity as "a political project," suggests historian Kyle Mays—a chance to showcase Native cultures, demonstrate their plight in the face of ongoing Euro-American oppression, and continue to advocate for Native American citizenship.[53]

Charles's paper is every bit as far ranging as its title, "The North American Indian." It is an extraordinary document in which he took on the considerable task of explaining topics as diverse as Indian thought about owning possessions, to gender roles, to tribal governance. It's filled with simplistic explanations of complex cultural concepts crafted for the international audience (for example, explaining that an Indian chief's influence was limited to his clan and "was in reality merely the authorized spokesman of his clan, save as he might acquire unusual authority by rare personal qualities, or, in later days, by the recognition and favour of the white man"). The paper offers brief but pungent explanations of why numerous U.S. policies were failures: the method of educating Indians by segregating them in separate schools was "a mistake, except as a temporary expedient," and the entire reservation system was "a radical misapprehension of the red man's native capacity." The intrusion of white Euro-Americans ruined the Indian's environment with "the pollution of streams, the destruction of forests, and the levelling of hills [which] were to him a sacrilege," and brought a "train of whiskey and drunkenness [with] debauchery and diseases caused by immorality; then the hitherto unknown and frightful small-pox, decimating many tribes and wiping out whole bands; and finally the white plague, tuberculosis, following inevitably upon a sedentary and indoor life in unsanitary dwellings (whose use was suggested or compelled by the white man), together with poor and insufficient food."[54] It was a stunning indictment, arguably the strongest political statement Charles had made publicly to this point. And yet his remarks rendered remarkably little press coverage, perhaps because of the enormous scope of the conference as well as its large number of prominent speakers.

Given that this was his first trip to Europe and given the distinguished platform, it's surprising this event merited only two paragraphs of reflection in Charles's *From the Deep Woods to Civilization*. In the first paragraph he wrote about the "great privilege" of attending this event with such noble goals, where he was "entertained by some well-known men." Of perhaps greater interest is the second paragraph, in which Charles described a meeting to draft the congress's platform. Charles noted use of the word "Christian" being used to the exclusion of mention of other religions. He suggested they "substitute a term to which we can all subscribe," and his suggestion was heartily embraced by some of the Jewish, Hindu, Bahá'i, and other representatives there.[55] He reported he then received invitations to speak in different countries by "some oriental representatives" but he had already committed to many speaking engagements back home.

Truth be told, there was another reason Charles needed to get back to the United States. After Henry Goodale's death the previous year, the primary source of the Eastmans' ability to pay the College Street house rent disappeared. Fortunately, there was the option to move into Lodestone rent-free thanks to Rose, who'd inherited the property. A series of letters James wrote home to his mother describe Elaine's frenetic attempts to get the home prepared for occupancy by her large family and the effort it took to downsize from the houses in which they had been living in Amherst to Lodestone, which had no indoor bathrooms and far less space. Once again, Charles was absent from a major family effort.

FIGURE 8.2. Lodestone. Courtesy Jones Library, Amherst MA.

Elaine later wrote a poem she entitled "The Woman's Challenge." The last verse gives voice to the resentment she had and the ways in which she began making this increasingly clear to her family:

> I have burst a hundred barriers, I have blazed a hundred trails;
> The sun's on my blowing banners, the wind's in my swelling sails;
> Hearken to me, my maters, for the patient past is past;
> Now she that was dumb has spoken and lifted her voice at last!
> Ready to counsel as comfort, comrade in work as in play,
> And fit for an honest sharing in the tasks of a nobler day,
> She that was cramped and hindered is come to her waiting prime—
> Room for the larger woman—a woman to fit the time![56]

9

From Camp Oáhe to Northampton and Detroit (1912–1921)

A lodestone is a kind of magnet. Like every magnet, its polarities attract—negative poles join with positive ones and vice versa, but put the same types of poles together and they repel one another. During Elaine and Charles's years at Lodestone, the house's name became all too ironic: the differences magnetically attracting them to one another at the start of their relationship became negative polarities, consistently dividing and pushing them apart.

Lodestone is a two-story cottage made of stone and weathered shingles. For many years this house of less than two thousand square feet was heated only by a large stone fireplace and a wood-burning stove. Nestled in the woods three miles from the center of Amherst, its relative isolation provided a life more akin to the Eastman family's time at Bald Eagle Lake than to their years at either of the other Amherst homes.

Once they made the decision to move to Lodestone, Elaine put everyone to work with myriad home improvement projects, which were documented in detail by letters James wrote home to his mother. Elaine, too, marked these projects in her correspondence with Rose, frequently complaining. As usual, most of her complaints centered on how little Charles was around and how little disposable income they had to make necessary upgrades to the house, many of which involved trying to make the drafty cottage warmer. "Isn't this terribly shivery weather in our cold country houses? We are simply perishing here and I hope it will moderate soon," Elaine wrote in December 1914.[1]

James's brother Theo enrolled at Amherst College in 1914, and both Dayton brothers frequently visited Lodestone. Their letters home demonstrate that while "Aunt E" often put them to work on the frequent occasions "the

Doctor" was away, there were many times they and other young people convened there for picnics, campfires, and games. Lodestone seemed to be a magnet for them, too.

The Lodestone years continued to be productive ones for Charles's writing. Amazingly, he published books in four consecutive years from 1913 to 1916, and another in 1918. Of Charles's books churned out during this period, two focused on Sioux and other tribal stories (*Indian Child Life*, 1913; *Indian Heroes and Great Chieftains*, 1918); one was a guide for scouting (*Indian Scout Talks*, 1914); and the other two were arguably among his most important works of nonfiction: *The Indian Today* (1915) and *From the Deep Woods to Civilization* (1916).

The Indian Today focuses on a wide range of topics, including the agency system, Indian education, and Native arts industries. The book delves into the American Indian's past and explores the status of Indian affairs in the early twentieth century, delineating many of the ways in which Indian people were negatively affected by the "onslaught" of Euro-American culture and policies, echoing themes Charles discussed in earlier writing.

The book also reflected some of the ways in which Charles's thinking about U.S. Indian policy had evolved. He'd previewed this in his talk at the First Universal Races Congress, but the essays in the book lay out his thoughts in greater depth. Calling *The Indian Today* Eastman's "most overtly political book," historian Kiara Vigil argues that because Charles intended a broad reading audience, the book "emerges as one of Eastman's strongest pedagogical pieces and represents him as an Indian intellectual and educator." Vigil suggests that part of Charles's goal was convincing other Native American leaders "to see education as a means to an end because advanced schooling could ameliorate some of the differences and prejudices that separated Indian people from white Americans given hierarchical understandings of class and race."[2]

Apart from his insistence on education for Indians despite its often assimilationist emphasis, another of Charles's major arguments is a push to extend full citizenship rights to all Native Americans. The impetus for Indians to become official citizens of the nation that colonized them, pushed them onto reservations, and imposed efforts to change their cultural and religious practices might seem ironic. But many Native Americans viewed citizenship as an answer to ongoing questions and concerns about Indian status, the promise of participatory democracy and a way to have a voice in their own future rather than depending on federal paternalism. A simultaneous affirmation of American nationalism and emergent Native nationalism found voice in the Society of American Indians. Cristina Stanciu writes that SAI members, including Charles Eastman, "appropriated the rhetoric of American patriotism to convey an unquenchable Indigenism."[3] When he became president of this organization in 1919, Charles argued vociferously for Indian citizenship, declaring, "We are not a 'dying race,' we are alive and asking for our share of the liberty and democracy that we have fought for." Many SAI members more broadly believed only citizenship would deliver justice and equality for Native Americans.[4] It would take until 1924 to achieve this goal, but Charles's early call to arms in *The Indian Today* helped to lay the groundwork for this movement.

At least some reviewers at the time of the book's publication seemed to recognize its scope and importance. "Those who are interested in the American Indian as he was and now is, who wish to review his early treatment at the hands of the white settlers, and his condition under our government agency system . . . should read Dr. Charles Alexander Eastman's authoritative book," wrote a reviewer in the Philadelphia *Evening Public Ledger*. "He shows . . . an intimate acquaintanceship with the political abuses which have wreaked as many hardships on the red man under the U.S. government."[5]

The title page of *The Indian Today* lists the author as "Charles A. Eastman (Ohiyesa), author of *Old Indian Days, Indian Boyhood*, etc." These other two books were published by McClure, a division of Doubleday, which published *The Indian Today*. But the "etc." is also significant, signifying Charles's growing prominence as an author. By 1915 when this book was published, Charles had published books with four publishers, and several had been translated into other languages, with editions published in France, Germany, Austria, Bohemia (modern-day Czech Republic), and Denmark, among other countries.[6]

From the Deep Woods to Civilization, published in 1916, covered some but not all of Charles's life, from the time he and members of his family escaped to Canada through some of his work in the first decade or so of the twentieth century. There are many elisions, including entire years of his life, and details about his romance with Elaine, their marriage, children, and financial woes are scant. And yet the book contains many important insights into the events of his life and how he interpreted them.

The final paragraph of this book might be among the most discussed and carefully analyzed passages of anything he wrote:

> I am an Indian; and while I have learned much from civilization, for which I am grateful, I have never lost my Indian sense of right and justice. I am for development and progress along social and spiritual lines, rather than those of commerce, nationalism, or material efficiency. Nevertheless, so long as I live, I am an American.[7]

In assessing this passage, many scholars suggest Charles perfectly encapsulated his life philosophy, the ways in which he reconciled elements of his Indian life from "the deep woods" with "civilization." And it may not be the contradiction it sounds like upon a cursory reading, because Charles saw himself as someone who could embrace a "new Indian-ness," as Malea Powell points out, melding his Dakhóta self with the man who had gone to Euro-American schools, worked for the U.S. government, and advocated for Indian citizenship.[8] The message is more nuanced, explaining strategic ways he sought to bring together worlds he often straddled. Biographically, this paragraph also previews a more direct claim Charles would make on his indigeneity later in life.

The chapter about Wounded Knee is also important. This chapter is the longest and most detailed of the book; its heft alone says something about the impact the event had in Charles's life. His writing style also differs in this chapter. Literature scholar David Brumble suggests the chapter shows the evolution of Charles's writing with less romanticizing and a greater sense of irony. Lisa Tatonetti thinks it important to read Charles's descriptions of this life-altering event carefully because they "are more complex and contradictory than [they] might appear upon an initial reading."[9]

Even the title of this book can be read either as indication of Charles Eastman's assimilationist journey or, more subtly, an ironic indictment of the journey Euro-Americans *suggested* Indians should make.[10] But at the time of its publication, *From the Deep Woods to Civilization* was read by its Euro-American reviewers as a book written by a thoroughly assimilated Indian. In fact, this became the focal point of their praise. Wrote the reviewer in the *Boston Globe*, "Dr. Eastman's book is one of the great testimonials to the reward for courage and perseverance in America. Even with his own seven-league boots, the step from teepee of the savage to the home of culture was a long one." The *New York Times* reviewer concluded, "The vital thing about Dr. Eastman's autobiography is not its adventures, its transitions from 'savage' boyhood to manhood as an American citizen. It is the psychology of that transition, its unblinking judgment, its artful summing up, its loyalties, its choice."[11]

In addition to ramped-up book writing, the period in which Charles lived at Lodestone was the time he most busily engaged with lecturing. A little news item in the *Springfield Union* in July 1912 modestly announced, "Dr. Charles A. Eastman in his home in the Belchertown Road is preparing for a lecture tour."[12] Around this time Charles became one of the featured speakers on the Chautauqua lecture circuit; the "circuit Chautauquas," founded in 1904, featured talks given in tents traveling across the United States. Charles's reputation as an exceptional lecturer grew as the volume of his talks increased; in 1917, an article in the *Christian Science Monitor* declared, "Dr. Eastman is the most educated and prominent Indian in America. . . . He is an exceedingly eloquent, witty speaker whose lecture is also full of pathos as he truly pictures the real Indian. Dr. Eastman has very remarkable ability as an orator."[13]

Writing about Charles's work as a lecturer, Lucy Maddox highlights a flier promising that "'Dr. Eastman will appear upon the platform . . . in the full-dress costume of a Sioux chief, beautifully made in the old style of beaded, Indian-tanned deerskin, with a war-bonnet of eagle feathers'" and that his talks would be "'setting forth in a fashion as convincing as it is picturesque THE TRUTH about the much misunderstood red man.'" These promotional fliers stated Charles had lectured in "nearly a hundred different towns and cities in New England alone."[14] This doesn't seem to be an exaggeration: a 2021 electronic perusal of newspaper stories about Charles's talks between 1912 and

1920 yields hundreds of hits. He spoke before clubs and college audiences, YMCA assemblies, and women's organizations; he addressed politicians, book readers, Boy Scouts, and Camp Fire Girls. Sometimes his audiences numbered a couple of dozen people, sometimes, several hundreds.

The scrapbook Elaine kept of clippings about Charles's talks reveals not only the astounding number of lectures given across the country, but also the variety of topics. Charles spoke about Indian history, religion, philosophy, and culture; he discussed Sitting Bull, Little Bighorn, "The Last Stand of the Sioux," and "The Changed Indian"; he lectured about the need for Indian citizenship and spoke about Native education, health, and economic conditions. He also gave many talks based on the series of books he published.

In addition, many of his talks were titled "The Real Red Man," including lines such as "The Indian is a true philosopher, and as such he has never been surpassed by any representative of civilization. He has his high ideals and lives up to them." Sounding less like an assimilated Indian wasn't always well received: "Ohiyesa's remarks were distinctly prejudicial to the vainglory of the Christian paleface, though evidently not designedly so," assessed one reporter. But sometimes his tone was lighter, displaying Charles's dry sense of humor: the *Boston Herald* reported Charles quipped in a lecture to Harvard students, "palefaces are incubator hatched. The soil in which they are brought up is too artificially fertilized with tenderloin and baked potato."[15]

During these years Charles would sometimes be accompanied by daughter Irene, who opened and closed the program singing traditional Native American songs. Adopting her Dakhóta middle name, Taluta, as her stage name, Irene dressed in doeskin dresses and a beaded headdress and wore her long hair in braids. Irene's performances beside her famous father helped to boost her own singing career. She earned many good reviews for her concerts and was starting to build a reputation as a crossover singer, as facile with Indigenous music as with opera. "If the melodies of the American Indian are someday recognized as classic music," wrote a reviewer in the *South Bend* (IN) *News-Times*, "the recognition will be due in large measure to a Springfield schoolgirl, Irene Eastman, or Taluta, the daughter of the Sioux Indian Dr. Charles A. Eastman. Her mother, a white woman, is well known as a poetess under her pen name of Elaine

Goodale."[16] After attending one of Charles's talks at a church in Greenwich, Connecticut, Hamlin Garland wrote, "At the close of his fine talk, his daughter Irene sang the songs of her people delightfully. . . . Together they gave a singularly clear and noble concept of the Sioux."[17]

More broadly, performances like Irene's of traditional Native music became part of a larger debate that ensued among leaders of the Fourth Annual Conference of the SAI in 1914. Although performances had become a standard feature of SAI conferences, they were also an internal source of dispute.[18] Some Indian leaders worried that while of great interest to non-Native participants, performances might serve to trivialize some of the issues of greatest concern to Indian reformers and left Native culture open to appropriation and misinterpretation. Conversely, SAI members like Charles Eastman believed demonstrations of Indian culture helped advance their political and social goals through artistic expression and preservation while advancing Indian civil rights.

* * *

The 1897 Santee claims case dragged on without any payout. Elaine wrote a letter to Rose in 1912 stating that despite the delays, she still encouraged Charles to pursue it because if it ever came to pass, each of their children stood to receive funding, apart from anything he would earn.[19] In 1917 Charles attempted to draw up a new contract compensating himself $25,000 for his ongoing efforts, but by this point with so little demonstrable progress, few Santee wished to have Charles represent them.[20]

Occasionally other jobs seeming to offer more money or greater stability appeared tantalizingly in the offing. In 1912 Charles was considered for the position of commissioner of Indian Affairs. He began lobbying for this job, procuring letters from influential supporters, including Ernest Seton, founder of the Boy Scouts of America and an old friend of President William Howard Taft. Seton wrote on Charles's behalf, imploring, "He is better qualified to understand and face the numerous problems [of the Indian Bureau] than any other man in America. . . . The mere fact that he is an Indian would guarantee the loyalty of all his people. It would convince them of our desire to do the fair thing and it would redound to the lasting honor and glory of your administration if you should avail yourself of this opportunity, to do for the Redman what Lincoln did for the Negro."[21] But in the waning days of Taft's administration, it became clear an appointment—especially such a controversial one—would not receive Senate confirmation. In 1913 newly elected President Woodrow Wilson also considered Charles for the post, garnering headlines such as "A Poetic Choice" and "Well-Known Sioux Educator May Be Wilson Appointee." Although Charles would have been only the second Indian to hold the position, his checkered history with government positions meant he was soon out the of the running.

With Charles off lecturing, writing, and trying to get other salaried jobs, Elaine attempted to supplement the family income in whatever ways she could. During the Lodestone years she continued to sell poetry and articles on parenting. Her childhood poem "Ashes of Roses" was set to music on three different occasions. And yet none of the Eastmans' combined ventures earned enough money for the family. However, another possibility for revenue opened with the expansion of the American scouting movement.

In 1901 a wealthy British ex-pat named Ernest Thompson Seton, a writer, naturalist, and illustrator living in Cos Cob, Connecticut, found his property vandalized repeatedly by a group of boys. Seton thought the boys would learn more from positive example than from prosecution and invited them to participate in a unique experiment. Seton set up "Indian camps" on his property and engaged the boys in outdoor work, games, and activities loosely modeled on Native American practices. The boys took on Indian titles—"chief," "second chief," and "keeper of the wampum." Seton found them engrossed and excited—and they never vandalized again. Encouraged, Seton published a series of articles about his experiment. In 1902 he decided to expand the program into something called the Woodcraft Indians. Historian Abigail Van Slyck points out Seton's work introducing Euro-American boys to Native Americans ways started what became a long-term association between camping and "playing Indian . . . in very selective ways."[22]

Seton's ideas linking Indians and children underscored ideas circulating more widely in American culture. As historian Philip Deloria writes, the precedents of associating Indians with children had a long history; both were "thought of as natural, simple, naïve, preliterate and devoid of self-consciousness."[23] Additionally, in the first decades of the twentieth century, many Euro-Americans started to think about Native Americans' connections to nature nostalgically; Indians led a simpler, more pastoralist life that if recaptured could help to counter some of the ills of modern industrial life. By mimicking Indian life and practices, Euro-Americans could find freedom and fulfillment in an unadorned life. Kiara Vigil concludes this linkage of children, nature, and Indians glorified ideals of pristine wilderness and innocent childhood for those who would mourn the passing of both.[24] Scouting offered a way to reclaim them.

Seton channeled all these thoughts as he developed ideas about a camp for white boys utilizing Indian culture. He turned to Charles's books as a source of inspiration and information. By 1910, when Seton merged Woodcraft Indians with the new Boy Scouts of America, he actively channeled Charles's "inspiring accounts." Seton believed that "American Indian spirituality and character would save white Americans from materialism, urbanization and over-civilization."[25] That same year Luther Halsey Gulick and his wife, Charlotte, began a parallel organization for girls, the Camp Fire Girls. Gulick, a physician, physical education educator, and outdoor enthusiast, shared many interests with Charles; they'd also both been involved with the YMCA. Soon ideas about scouting merged with ideas about extending experiences during the summer at sleep-away camps.

Summer camps took off in the early part of the twentieth century; in 1900 there were fewer than a hundred camps in the United States, but by 1918, that number had increased tenfold.[26] Many of the camps tapped into the growing American nostalgia for "simpler times" through the adoption of Native American traditions like council fires, sleeping in wigwams, and Indian storytelling, thought of as temporally outside of modernity.

Charles was immediately intrigued: Seton's philosophy of outdoor, Indian-themed physical and moral education appealed to him, and he also realized the potential to monetize this. He began writing and placing articles in publications like *Boys' Life*, the Boy Scout magazine, and speaking in support of both the Boy Scouts and the Camp Fire Girls. *Indian Scout Talks,* published in 1914, cemented Charles's reputation as a national authority for the scouts, with chapters on "how to build wigwams and shelters," "how to make and follow a blazed trail," "the language of footprints," and more. The photograph of Charles in the first edition of this book shows him facing the camera, wearing a full feathered headdress and an ornate beaded shirt—he couldn't possibly read more "Indian."

He included talks about scouting in his lecture repertoire as he traveled the country. Charles also began consulting with various summer camps up and down the East Coast. Sometimes Charles was brought in as the "resident Indian"; a brochure for the Pine Island Camp in Maine depicts Charles as "the greatest Indian and better fitted than any living man to bring to us the glorious past of that vanishing race."[27] In summer 1914, Charles was hired as the director of Camp Archibald Butt, a large Boy Scout camp on Chesapeake Bay in Maryland. To have a camp director who *was* a Native American and could authentically teach archery or how to start a fire with sticks became a boon for camp recruitment, as well as to garner significant publicity. An article in the Washington, DC, *Evening Star* recounted Charles's opening comments to the Scouts: "I want you to know nature as the Indian knows it. . . . I want to prove to you that if you treat nature right, nature will treat you right."[28]

Based on this experience, Charles and Elaine began investigating sites in nearer-by New Hampshire with the idea of opening their own Indian-themed summer camp. They leased a seventy-acre lakeshore property north of Keene in 1915, and got to work designing a program, figuring out how to fund it, and recruiting the first season of campers. Anne Morgan, daughter of financier J. P., became one of their primary financial backers. In a promotional article that ran under the headline "America's Only Indian Camp for Pale-Face Girls," Elaine suggested not only would "all the usual land and water sports, music and dancing" be featured at the camp, but also "specifically genuine Indian games, dances, woodcraft and nature lore, signaling, ceremonies and council fires," along with a "grand final event."[29] These ideas became key to how the Eastmans marketed their new endeavor.

FIGURE 9.1. Archery lesson, Camp Oáhe brochure. Courtesy Jones Library, Amherst, MA.

The camp's headquarters adapted a 1797 farmhouse at the end of a dirt road. An adjacent field housed tents with wooden platforms in which campers would sleep on cots. A nearby icehouse refrigerated the meat, vegetables, milk, eggs, and butter supplied by local farmers. Surrounded by towering pines, pristine mile-long Granite Lake was just steps away from the lodgings. At the time the Eastmans opened Camp Oáhe, "the Hill of Vision," there were only five or six houses spread out around the lakeshore.

Irene, who had worked as a counselor at a Camp Fire Girls camp in Pittsburgh and taught swimming and folk dancing, along with sisters Dora (a rising senior at Mount Holyoke College) and Virginia (about to enter Wellesley College), would serve as counselors and role models. They also served as sources of inspiration for the advertising campaign.

The first brochure for the "School of the Woods: The Summer Camp with a Difference" emphasized that with five daughters of their own, the Eastmans were "deeply sensible of the responsibility involved in the care of young girls."[30] Other articles printed in newspapers picked up on this theme: for example, a lengthy article in the *New York Sun* under the headline "Training American Girls in Indian Woodcraft" included a subhead exemplifying "Guiding Future Mothers of the Race Back to the Love of Nature Is Plan of Dr. Charles A. Eastman, Who Is a Sioux Chief." The reporter wrote, "In a year of surprising developments all over the world comes an announcement from the interior of New Hampshire, from the old Indian kingdom of Monadnock, bordering on a forest lake, that will have special interest for those who have led the way in the education of women. It is that Ohiyesa, descendant of many generations of Sioux chiefs, has established in the New Hampshire woods a school where he proposed to train American girls after methods which, he says, gave to Indian maidens in time past wonderful vitality, mental and spiritual power and ability to take care of themselves." The article quotes "Big Chief" Charles discussing his thoughts on how white America "is not progressing" but "retrograding" because men and women have lost touch with nature. To remedy this, he says, we must "train our boys . . . and especially educate our girls, who will be the mothers of the coming generation. . . . For that reason I am making the experiment at Monadnock."[31] Apparently Charles's aspirational statement became widely known; a 1920 publication, *A Handbook of American Private Schools*, described Camp Oáhe as "the vision of an idealist made real."[32]

Unquestionably, Charles and Elaine were big supporters of women's education and had been for years. Elaine always regretted her own inability to attend college; Charles's association with Frank and Annie Wood, women's education advocates and on Wellesley College's board of trustees, led him to hope someday he would have daughters there. Women's education was becoming more prominent in the United States in the early twentieth century; in 1900 women earned 60 percent of the high school diplomas awarded but represented only 23 percent of the college graduates, but by 1910, 40 percent of Americans getting a bachelor's degree were female.[33] But the Eastmans also shrewdly realized that recruiting a group of girls for their first year of summer camp was clever branding. Emphasizing the camp was led by a medical doctor who also happened to be an Indian offered parents of prospective campers a

FIGURE 9.2. Elaine with campers. Courtesy Cheshire County Historical Society.

degree of comfort and a guarantee of authenticity. Girls could be safe, but they could also push the boundaries by playing Indian.

An article from the *Boston Sunday Post* suggested at the new School of the Woods, "The best educated Indian in America, author of a dozen widely read books on Indian life and history, a practicing physician, lawyer, businessman and educator, is going to show wealthy white girls the little conveniences of life which native Americans seem to know by instinct. And here are some of the things the back to nature school is going to teach the pretty palefaces, most of them daughters of wealthy New Yorkers." These skills include "how to make a fire when the grocery man forgets to bring matches; how to cook a porterhouse steak without a skillet; how to make a baby stop crying at night so that the landlord will not receive complaints from adjacent flat dwellers," as well as other "Indian skills" encapsulated with strangely citified applications. The captions under the photos in this article emphasize the Eastmans'

Indianness and otherness: "Dr. Charles Alexander Eastman, the Sioux chieftain, in costume of civilization" reads the one under the photo of Charles in a suit. "Miss Eleanor Eastman, shooting with native American weapons, on her father's estate in Amherst, Mass." and "Miss Mabel 'Great Cloud' Eastman, youngest daughter of the famous Ohiyesa. She is adept with the bow and arrow" inexplicably reads the caption under Florence's photo.[34]

The Sioux quotient of the Eastman girls' mixed-raced heritage was clearly played up by the press, but their parents also deployed it strategically. Just as there were times when Charles knowingly and tactically dressed in Sioux regalia, the Eastman sisters appearing in Indian dress were moments of "redfacing as tactic," drawing attention to their Indianness to help market the new family endeavor.[35]

It is important to emphasize that while the dress and the Indian-themed activities tapped into popular cultural trends and augmented the camp's marketability, the Eastmans' intent wasn't only to make money. Charles, especially, evinced a genuine sense that white women would be better served by learning Indian values. It was a sincere effort to impart and preserve Indigenous values. Charles envisioned the American scouting movement as a way of teaching young people tenets of citizenship exemplified by Native peoples. Kiara Vigil suggests the Eastmans' camps should be considered "a critical aspect of Charles Eastman's intellectual oeuvre and activist work" because of the centering of Dakhóta cultural practices and philosophies.[36] Penelope Myrtle Kelsey adds that Charles's summer camp work demonstrates he sought "a place and a way for American Indian cultural practices to live on within the dominant society."[37]

Encouraged by the success of the initial summer, the Eastmans decided to expand "the Monadnock experiment" the following summer. For summer 1916 they recruited a larger cohort of campers with a new brochure. "Camp Oáhe: The Hill of Vision" featured an expanded staff, including Angel DeCora Dietz, a member of the Winnebago tribe, Hampton Institute and Smith College graduate, and well-known artist, who would teach sketching, Indian beadwork, and basketry. The promotional material promised Euro-American families a safe mixture of familiarity with a dash of Indianness. The brochure is bountifully illustrated with photos depicting Charles alternately in Sioux regalia and suits, girls wearing bloomers or Indian costumes engaged in outdoor activities, and the final elaborate pageant of the summer, "an Indian play, the Eagle and the Star." Oáhe is "an enlargement of our family circle" which will "preserve the normal, wholesome atmosphere of family life, as opposed to the institutional and pedagogic." Under the direction of "Doctor Eastman, widely known as the author of many Indian and nature books, and as a speaker and leader in Boy Scout and other 'Back to Nature' movements," the camp will give "special attention" to "delicate children." And parents shouldn't worry: Oáhe's location and elevation meant "mosquitos are seldom seen here, and hay fever is unknown."

The typical daily schedule features the "moose call" rising bell at 7 a.m., morning exercises and a dip in the lake (optional), camp duties, games and sports, nature study, handicrafts, swimming, canoeing, and meals all before lights out. Running July 1 to September 2, the cost was $300. Girls could purchase a "full ceremonial Indian outfit" for just $1 extra. A couple of pages announce the concurrent opening of Camp Ohiyesa for boys, a mile and half away from Oáhe. The brochure concludes with a lengthy list of endorsements, including parents of campers from the first year, professors, and, notably, Hamlin Garland.[38]

The camp work seemed a good meshing of Elaine's interests in child development and Charles's interests in using outdoor and physical education for moral development. In a 1933 article, Elaine wrote of how the camp movement presented "the much-needed antidote to our increasingly complex and mechanized civilization" and with the combination of nature, sports, arts, and time to play, also provided for children's "self-expression . . . as an essential factor in education." In many talks on behalf of the Boy Scouts and Camp Fire Girls, Charles articulated his philosophy of the alignment of traditional Indian teachings and scouting and outdoor education as an important key to the soul. Running Camp Oáhe might have been good for the Eastmans' souls, too—at least for a while.

Camp Oáhe and Camp Ohiyesa ran each summer from 1916 to 1928, when Elaine sold the camps; they were run by the Carter family until 1934. But not every summer was as halcyon as those first couple seem to have been. Theo

Dayton, who worked several summers, reported back home the "rather strained atmosphere." And whatever Dayton noticed early on, it's safe to say the atmosphere became rather more strained during the summer of 1918 and its aftermath.

* * *

Financial shortcomings were a constant source of stress between Elaine and Charles, but this was not the only thing putting pressure on their relationship. As Charles's reputation as a writer grew, so did Elaine's resentment. She felt she was partly responsible for his success and that every hour spent helping his career was an hour taken away from developing her own. He was frequently on the road, ceding all responsibility for their collective existence to her. His increasing national reputation meant more opportunities for him, which, though healthy for family finances, was unhealthy for their marriage.

Just before the start of the second camp season in June 1916, Elaine and Charles were to celebrate twenty-five years of marriage. Of her silver wedding anniversary, Elaine wrote years later to Rose, "We had all six children at home. . . . I entertained quite a party of our neighbors, with flowers, music and ice cream—Irene and her teacher, Madame Mitzlaff, sang for us. It was the only anniversary I ever tried to mark specially—and would have been quite successful except for the fact that Dr. Eastman—rather characteristically—forgot all about it and failed to return in time from Boston! We tried to turn the bridegroom's absence into a joke!"[39] But it was a joke that wasn't very funny. It stung Elaine, even almost three decades later.

During the late 1910s, Ohi was having trouble in school. Like his father, he excelled in sports, commended in the Amherst High School yearbook for his accomplishments in football and baseball; unlike his father, he struggled mightily with academics. With America's entrance into World War I in 1917, Ohi threatened to drop out of school and enlist in the Navy. Opposed to this notion and terrified of losing her only son, Elaine pulled Ohi out of public school and sent him to Kimball Academy in New Hampshire, the school Charles had attended prior to entering Dartmouth. Much to Elaine's horror, immediately after his graduation the following year, Ohi enlisted anyway.

If financial woes, problems with their children, tension in their marriage, and a World War weren't enough, there was another threat facing the Eastmans and enveloping the world even as World War I was being fought to its bitter conclusion—another offensive, invisible but deadly, raging worldwide: the influenza pandemic. This virulent strain of the flu started wreaking havoc the previous year but by 1918 had intensified and spread, leading to a pandemic stage declaration. Although often referred to as "the Spanish flu" (a misnomer falsely attributing its source), the virus spread rapidly across the globe. Fully a third of the planet's population at the time became infected; at least fifty million people would die.[40]

In spring 1918, doctors in the United States started reporting the first cases, spread principally by troops gathering at military bases. The disease disseminated quickly from soldiers to the general population, and it became clear no one was immune, the young and otherwise healthy included. Sometimes it inexplicably seemed as if young people were even *more* likely to become victims of the pandemic.[41] Estimates suggest up to 675,000 Americans died, but mortality rates may have been higher, in part because deaths in highly affected low-income and communities of color went largely unreported—not unlike the COVID-19 pandemic a century later. In addition, just like in the most recent pandemic, mortality rates among Native American populations were about four times higher than among the general population.[42]

Aware of the disease's virulent spread, the Eastmans seemed to believe they would stay healthy if they remained in relatively isolated places. Ohi and Eleanor were enrolled at the Kimball Union Academy in Meriden, New Hampshire, and rather than returning to Amherst, Charles and Elaine stayed in Munsonville, where Florence attended the local grade school. Dora, having graduated from college, was teaching at an Indian school in Nebraska, and Virginia attended Wellesley College. But one of the Eastman children was not far removed from a virus epicenter: Irene Taluta was living with a cousin in New Jersey, commuting to New York City to study voice.

In early October 1918, Irene called her parents to let them know she would visit. She had big news to share: the Metropolitan Opera had offered her a contract. Elaine, Charles, and the two youngest girls were in Washington, DC,

FIGURE 9.3. Irene Taluta Eastman. Courtesy Cheshire County Historical Society.

when Irene arrived from New York along with her friend, Esther Shoop. Elaine and the younger girls contracted the flu, delaying their return to New Hampshire. When Irene arrived in New Hampshire she felt ill; she was soon taken to a hospital in Keene, twelve miles south of Munsonville.

Although many influenza cases had been reported in large U.S. cities, until September 1918 there were no cases in New Hampshire. But once it arrived in the Granite State it spread quickly. Within a week of the first reported case, the Board of Health in Manchester, the state's largest city, ordered all schools and public facilities closed. Ill patients occupied every bed in every hospital. Overwhelmed public responders pleaded with owners of the few private vehicles to help transport the sick. By the pandemic's end, this small state had suffered a large toll: more than 2,700 influenza deaths out of a population in 1918 of 440,000.[43]

Poolrooms and theaters closed in Keene in late September 1918. By early October, schools were shut. "With a patient capacity of around 40 people, Eliot Hospital was overwhelmed," reported the *Keene Sentinel*.[44] An emergency satellite hospital was set up in the Keene Normal School to take the overflow patients, but soon it, too, filled. In two short months, Keene recorded at least 153 deaths from the flu. One of those deaths, on October 23, was twenty-four-year-old Irene Taluta Eastman.

Irene's death was an unbearable and devastating tragedy for her parents. Theodore Sargent hypothesizes Irene's death was crushing for "Charles, the doctor who had been unable to help, and Elaine as the mother who was not at her daughter's bedside when she died and had had no opportunity for "even a look or word of farewell."[45] Years later Elaine poignantly reminisced to her sister Dora, "And all in a second of time, overtaking a young, happy woman like an avenging fate. . . . All we have to cling to is the 'undefeated human heart.'"[46]

Her father buried Irene under a large tree overlooking the lake at Camp Oáhe, a place that had held special meaning for her.

Irene's tragic death generated a significant amount of news. An obituary in the *New York Times* noted that Irene's "soprano voice of unusual quality" had highlighted and promoted "understanding of the various Indian tribes." *Musical America* wrote, "As an interpreter of Indian song, gesture, language and dances, Miss Eastman was singularly gifted by birth, ancestry, voice and training. Her desire was to make the Indian race, its music and its customs better understood and appreciated."[47]

Of the many touching tributes, perhaps none was more poignant than the one in the *American Indian Magazine*:

> Since the last issue of this magazine the Great Spirit has taken away from the world a rare, sweet soul of great promise. Taluta, the young Indian singer, whose voice has so often charmed and thrilled her hearers with her interpretations of Indian music is dead. So young, so talented, so loyal to her Indian blood and her Indian traditions, her race looked to her with hope and confidence that she would do great things for them. . . . All who love the Indian race and have grieved with them over many hopes deferred and promises unfulfilled, must grieve with them once more over this latest loss.[48]

The loss of a child is an almost inconceivable tragedy. It upsets the natural order of life; it is a profound, horrendous burden that inevitably, devastatingly, affects every member of a family. Some couples can pull together in the wake of such a loss. But the loss of their second-born seemed to crack open a fissure that had been widening in the Eastmans' marriage for many years. Rather than turn to one another in their grief, they drifted further apart. Much of what we know about what happened with Elaine and Charles after Irene's death comes from a very unlikely, somewhat ironic source: it comes from the source that would prove to be the ultimate wedge in the fault lines of this marriage.

* * *

Henrietta Martindale was the eldest daughter of Sophie and Stephen Martindale of La Crosse, Wisconsin. Stephen had been a Beloit classmate of Charles's, though it's unclear whether they kept in touch. Henrietta's mental and physical health were always a bit precarious: she entered Smith College in fall 1907 but didn't graduate until 1913, some undefined illness forcing her to take two years off. Henrietta's Smith College portrait depicts a lovely young woman, her dark hair styled in a bun. She looks poised, serene, and somehow naïve. During summer 1918, Henrietta's family sent her to work at Camp Oáhe at the end of the camping session; her father thought his former classmate's emphasis on outdoor education, health, and Indian ways of well-being might improve Henrietta's strength and vigor.

In a series of letters she wrote home to her parents and her sister Katharine, Henrietta, then thirty years old, described her impressions. She arrived in August and wrote of the beautiful approach through the mountains, the festival going on at Oáhe when she arrived, the costumed Eastman girls dancing and singing. Her first letter mentions swimming in the lake, hiking, sleeping in a tent, and becoming integrated into all the camp's activities. "You are grand to let me come here. I know it will make me healthier than anything else would. And then I'll have pep enough to see that you all have a vacation in the woods too."[49]

In subsequent letters, Henrietta described her impressions of the Eastman family: Ohi, on furlough from the Navy, "is such a nice boy"; Irene, "the second oldest, is awfully nice and so talented"—Henrietta couldn't wait to hear her sing; Dora, the eldest, "is so very kind to me." Elaine, however, had "a terribly *nagging* disposition and makes things *very* unpleasant sometimes, but we all try to keep out of her way." She described Charles, in contrast, as "a poet and an artist [who] can tell wonderfully beautiful tales around the fire."[50]

For some reason when the summer camping season ended, Henrietta chose to remain in New Hampshire rather than return to Wisconsin. It's not clear what she was doing.

On November 9, Henrietta sent a telegram to her parents. "Take no chances with Katharine. Have doctors friend or nurse to help. Keep quiet. Warm. Plenty fresh air. No draft. Wear masks. Gargle . . . Influenza hardest on strong girls of her age. Please be very careful." Henrietta had good reason to send this telegram. "Planning write you today. I have had flu two weeks. Been in hospital, now all well but weak. Dr. Eastman here. . . . His Irene and her chum both died of it. Am here at Cheshire House Keene."[51]

In a long, rambling, disjointed letter to her parents and sister in which the chronology is a bit opaque, perhaps deliberately so, Henrietta detailed the

FIGURE 9.4. Henrietta Martindale, circa 1911. La Crosse Area Photograph Collection, University of Wisconsin-La Crosse Murphy Library Special Collections/Area Research Center, La Crosse, WI.

"terrible things" she'd experienced over the past few weeks and Irene Taluta's final visit to Camp Oáhe. Through reading her letter carefully and mapping on which dates events she mentioned occurred, the narrative becomes clearer. This is the story she told:

Irene and her friend Esther planned to stay in New Hampshire for a while before returning to New York. Henrietta was staying in the home of a Mrs. Scott, about a mile and half from the camp, when Esther notified her on Monday, October 14, that Irene had taken ill. At the time, Charles and Elaine were both in Washington, DC, with two of their other daughters, both of whom had "terrible cases of the flu"; when they recovered, Elaine came down with it. According to her letter, with Charles and Elaine away, Henrietta called a doctor in Keene who suggested Irene might have influenza and should be brought to the hospital. "I was the only one who could help them at all," Henrietta wrote. She wired Dr. Eastman to return to New Hampshire immediately. "Poor Doctor Eastman has had a terrible load to bear."

Charles returned to New Hampshire on Wednesday, October 16, to find the hospitals at capacity. Irene had been taken to the overflow facility; Henrietta volunteered to help because they were so short-staffed. During the next week, Henrietta saw terrible things at the satellite hospital: staff stretched to its limits, tensions running high, death abounding. She reported, "I did everything I could to help but it was of no use. Irene died Wednesday morning at five o'clock." This was October 23.

She wrote that Dora Winona arrived from New Jersey the following day, and then Ohi. The family members held a service at the camp that Friday, October 25, "and they buried Irene on a beautiful hill there under a tree, and Doctor Eastman offered a silent prayer into the heavens." Elaine, ailing in Washington, was unable to attend. Henrietta's report was second-hand, though, because she, too, had fallen ill. Henrietta suggested it was her own fault she succumbed because "I had not worn my mask the night before, when I went down to Mrs. Aldrich's to put Irene's white dress on her and to comb out her beautiful beautiful long black hair. Somehow it seemed sacrilege to wear a mask and I couldn't do it." Henrietta, who had a mild flu case, spent a little time in the hospital and then recovered at the Cheshire House hotel.

Sometime in this same awful week, Esther Shoop became afflicted and died. Charles was devastated. Then he, too, developed a high fever, but Henrietta stated, "he nursed himself out of it in Nature's way." In several places in the letter, she insisted she "was the only one able to help him. I know if you had been here you would have had me do just what I did. . . . I did everything for the Doctor that I could. He was absolutely stunned and broken-hearted but very brave." And then, she added, "He is a wonderful man and I love him very much." Elsewhere in the letter she mentioned that when she was ill, only "Dr. Eastman's warming could keep me warm." She also suggested, "Doctor Eastman was just like a father to me, Dad. I know you would love him for what he did for me. He seemed to think almost so much of me as his own daughter, and it was a great load off from him when he saw that I was really well." She urged her parents to write "just a little to Dr. and Mrs. Eastman, it would relieve them, I know, as they felt so sorry to have me sick."

Henrietta's meanings in this letter are ambiguous, confused, and confusing. It's not clear when, during this bewildering and highly emotional time, Henrietta was truly the "only one there" to console Charles—right after Irene died, or in the week or two after? Although she mentions several times being the only one there, by her own accounting, she became ill two days after Irene died and was in the hospital, herself, until November 2, at which time she returned to Cheshire House. She stated Charles stayed with her at the hotel right after Irene died, and then again after Dora and Ohi departed. But during the times he was with her in the hotel, did he act "like a father" to her, or was his behavior like something else? And what were Henrietta's feelings for Charles; did her admiration change to something else? Henrietta's language is also confusing: was being "perfectly lovely" a doctor's bedside manner to a young woman recovering from the flu, or did Henrietta mean "perfectly lovely" as one might report a lover would be? Was Henrietta suggesting to her parents they would forgive her for risking her own life to help nurse Irene and then prepare her body for burial, or for consoling her father's old college friend in a way that might not have been appropriate? And when Henrietta wrote, "Our country has great need of a man like that. He is a poet, artist, writer, orator, and first of all, a man of truth and honor, and a lover of little children. He has given me more than I can ever tell,"[52] what did she actually mean?

Perhaps Henrietta was being quite literal. Because a few months later, she realized she was pregnant.

* * *

"I appreciated your very considerate letter," Elaine wrote to her brother-in-law, Redington Dayton, in April 1919. "My wonderful, gifted girl who was so near to me in spirit, whom I had not dreamed could go before me—she is gone! Life is very strange. I have never yet expressed my grief, never let myself go, because it would hurt the others if I did, and yet it seems sometimes as if it would be a relief to give way." She stated she was glad she had the camp and all the work associated with preparing for the upcoming season "because it compels me to meet people to exert myself which I might not do if I did not have to. The Doctor finds an outlet in his Indian work."[53] Elaine's grief for the loss of her second child followed her for the rest of her life, hugging her closely as her daughter could no longer. She would write to Rose years later that she felt Irene had been nearer to her in outlook and spirit than any of her other children, and even that none of her other children were as important to her as the one she lost to the flu pandemic.

Charles left behind no writing offering insight into his feelings. Though several sources describe Irene as Charles's favorite among his children, the basis for this seems to be an assumed closeness from their several trips together when Irene would "open" for him. From what can be reconstructed, Charles reacted to Irene's death by retreating. Based on an interview he conducted with Munsonville resident Earl Barrett, David Miller recounts tales of Charles "living alone," "tramping in the woods," and hunting ducks on Granite Lake after Irene's death and in the following spring. There is an amusing anecdote in which the newly constituted New Hampshire game department's warden arrested Charles for hunting out of season; Barrett reported when a judge asked Charles how he pled for poaching, Charles pled "Indian." "He explained as an Indian he had a right to wildlife for the use of his self-subsistence.

The judge agreed, and the chagrined warden had to return Charles the eighteen miles back to the lake."[54]

Irene no doubt played a special role in the Eastman family. Close to both her mother and father, Irene may also have best embodied a blend of her parents' passions—Elaine's flair for artistic expression, and Charles's desire to preserve and promulgate Indigenous cultures.[55] There's no record of how the other Eastman children reacted to Irene's death, but unquestionably, it left a huge hole in the family and upset the dynamics of sibling relationships.

During the months following Irene's death, Elaine and Charles tried to carry on with life. He was consumed with his SAI duties and gave talks in different locations about Indian citizenship; she with organizing the upcoming camp season and the release of her book *Indian Legends Retold*. Ohi returned from his stint in the navy, which was presumably of some consolation to his bereaved parents and sisters, but the family remained devastated. It's not hard to imagine how their respective grief, expressed in such different ways, continued to drive a wedge between Elaine and Charles.

And then sometime during summer or early fall 1919 came a message—we do not know when or to whom—that pushed tensions in the Eastman household to a point of implosion.

* * *

In October 1921, Henrietta Martindale wrote to her sister Katharine, "Three years ago today Irene died, and then came to life."[56] The baby, who came to be known as "Bonno Hyessa," was originally called "Irene" by her mother; she still referred to the baby as "Irene" when the little girl turned two. Henrietta seemed convinced that magically Irene Taluta had been reborn. Theodore Sargent and Raymond Wilson pieced together the bizarre story of how Henrietta managed to conceal her pregnancy from her parents, informing only her sister in sealed letters marked "Private," traveled to California, and lived there for the duration of her pregnancy. Henrietta miraculously kept the baby's existence from her parents for the first couple of years of her life so she could retain their financial support.[57] But sometime after the child was born—and it is not at all clear when this was—Henrietta notified the person she referred to as the baby's father. And, possibly, informed the father's wife.

Charles denied he was the father. But in a series of letters to Rose in the 1930s, Elaine revealed she had "ample proof" of Charles's paternity. "You remember, I suppose, that it was I who investigated, and that he flatly refused to do so or to accept my findings, though . . . they were entirely convincing." In another letter she referred to the "letters and evidence regarding the affair that broke up our home." She said she'd shown a couple of them selectively to her children—"just the bare facts, making it as easy on their father as I could"—but she ultimately decided to "preserve just a very few of the 'key' letters and statements" and burned all the rest. Sargent reports that none of these "key letters" have ever surfaced.[58]

But there were still more bends to this decidedly twisted tale.

There are some suggestions in Henrietta's letters to her sister that the Eastmans were sending her funds to help support the baby until they might take her. "I am hoping to have a telegram . . . from Irene's father saying that they wish me to bring Irene back to care for as their adopted daughter, until they can take her themselves . . . however, I am not *sure* of this." And there are some intimations in Elaine's letters to Rose that she might actually have been considering this: "I was ready to make any sacrifice to that end. . . . The door has never been closed."[59] Elaine may have only been referring to a desire to help Henrietta with the child financially, which would have involved sacrifice for the cash-strapped Eastmans. Given Elaine's fiction about Yellow Star, it's clear she believed the adoption of Indian (or part-Indian) babies by white families a good idea, and we know Elaine considered her own children to be mostly white. But it wasn't so simple with this part-Indian baby. Charles refused to acknowledge paternity, and it was Elaine who insisted he needed to accept responsibility.

The second twist to the story is that Charles apparently visited Henrietta in the Midwest. And he went more than once. What transpired at these meetings remains shrouded in mystery. Sargent and Wilson report Henrietta stated she saw him "on a number of occasions between 1919 and 1925, both at her lodge in the Indiana Dunes . . . and at a hotel in Chicago."[60] Adding to the soap opera-esque element of this story is the third twist, a letter from Henrietta's husband, Paul Wilson (who she married in 1926) while he was incarcerated in San Quentin. "Not 2 weeks after we were married I found that she went to the hotel La Salle to see Mr. Eastman," he wrote. "She stayed with him for 1-night, next day she asked me to let him come live with us. I to stay in the little place in the woods. She to live at the lodge with [Charles]. I refused. And told her I'd kill him if I ever caught him near the place. Him a married man too. And the father of Bonno."[61]

Elaine, who made numerous references to "Dr. E's illegitimate daughter," apparently went out of her way, more than once, to find out about the girl as she grew up, even attempting to contact her directly. Elaine also traveled to Chicago in 1925, where she met Henrietta and saw her daughter. Elaine wrote to Katharine Martindale, suggesting she had done what she could to get Charles "to do what he could for the child." This may have included agreeing to divorce him so he could marry Henrietta if he wanted to. Elaine also revealed that Henrietta had written to her and that Elaine felt there were things in these letters that raised "serious doubts of her sanity." She claimed to have no ill will toward Henrietta.[62]

The final twist to this story is the set of unanswered questions about who Bonno's father was. Sargent and Wilson cite several people who had contact with Henrietta and were told unequivocally Charles Eastman was the father. Gretchen Cassel Eick suggests some sources state Bonno's father was a Rainy Lake Sioux named Hyessa Hyessa, but also that this person "may be Eastman using another name" (coming from O-hieysa, perhaps). In a 1923 letter to her sister Katharine, Henrietta wrote, "Bonno is being known now as Anpah Martindale Hyessa and I am being known as her mother, Mrs. Henrietta Martindale-Hyessa." And Theodore Sargent tracked down one of Bonno's daughters, Maya Cramer, who suggested, "The family believed that [Bonno's] father was a Rainy Lake Sioux named Hyessa Hyessa. If, as seems to be the case, Hyssa Hyessa was actually Ohiyesa, then the living family members have not been so informed."[63]

Despite the mysteries surrounding Bonno's birth, one thing became transparent: Elaine Goodale Eastman came to believe her marriage could not continue. It wasn't necessarily the strong possibility Charles had been unfaithful to her as much as that he was unwilling to take responsibility for the child. She enlarged upon this thought in another letter, stating, "I have known breaks to result, one might say, inevitably, from injury or insult by one to the other so deep as not to be overlooked—and in my own case I have been able to forgive such an injury and still be unable to avoid the break on a difference of principle—a matter of personal integrity and honor, which you should know, was the sole ground on which I parted from the Doctor." In another letter she wrote she felt her own children were "inclined to feel that their half-sister is none of their affair, and . . . resent the wrong their father did to THEM, more than what he did to her and to her unfortunate mother."[64]

In August 1921 Charles Eastman left New England, moving eventually to Detroit, where Ohi lived. Elaine prepared to move in with one of her daughters in Northampton. The Eastmans abandoned Lodestone, its magnetic pull no more. "Life is always preparing us for these bitter and ironic surprises," Elaine wrote to Rose sometime after this. "Since I lost Irene without even a look or word or farewell—and then my husband's behavior poisoned not only the present and future but all my memories of married life, I have at least the cold comfort of feeling that nothing worse CAN happen to me."[65]

PART III

Separated but Tied Together

10

From Detroit to Lake Huron (1921–1939)

"Every age, every race, has its leaders and heroes," Charles Eastman wrote in his last published book, *Indian Heroes and Great Chieftains*. "The names and deeds of some of these men will live in American history, yet in the true sense they are unknown, because misunderstood."[1] He was writing of the fifteen Indian leaders he profiled in this 1918 book, but it is hard not to think there was some sense in which Charles was also writing of himself.

In the final eighteen years of his life, Charles Eastman returned to the Midwest. He also returned to many of the Dakhóta traditions he had put aside or abandoned in his life with Elaine. As ever, he held numerous jobs—money remained a struggle—and controversy never seemed far away. He railed against the authority of the Indian Bureau and pushed for its abolition even as he accepted one final job within it; he championed the politics of gaining Indian citizenship but worked largely outside of any organizational structure; his on-again, off-again relationship with the SAI was mostly off after the one year in which he served as its president; he continued to lecture widely until he could no longer. And although he attempted to maintain some career as a writer, after 1918 he would never publish another book. His early life may have followed the path he delineated of going from "the deep woods" to "civilization," but his last years brought him back in the other direction. The final decades of his life were marked by numerous ironies—ironies that most certainly would have been noted by this introspective, thoughtful man with a wickedly dry sense of humor.

In some ways the most intriguing questions about Charles Eastman's final years are the ones that remain unanswered, many of the most interesting parts of his story the ones that can be guessed at but not told with any certainty.

If Charles Eastman is in some ways ultimately unknown, he may have been right—because, ultimately, he may have been misunderstood.

* * *

There is no extant written record of what happened between Elaine and Charles after Henrietta Martindale confirmed the birth of her daughter and Elaine's investigator supposedly confirmed Charles' paternity. We don't know what either of them thought or said or felt; Elaine expunged any record of this time from her papers, and Charles left no paper trail. Throughout most of 1920 and 1921 he spent an enormous amount of time on the road; newspapers report talks he gave throughout New England, New York, and the Midwest. Occasionally he led hikes for local Boy Scout troops. Sometime in 1920 he sat for sculptor Eugenie Shonnard, who created a mahogany piece called "Chief Ohiyesa Communing with the Great Spirit" that now resides in the New Mexico Museum of Art, but the circumstances under which this artistic effort commenced are not known.

On August 1, 1921, Charles deeded Camp Oáhe to Elaine for $1. After that, it becomes more difficult to track his movements. David Miller suggests Charles "immediately left for Detroit"; Raymond Wilson says Charles spent at least "the winter months after 1921" in Detroit; Gretchen Cassel Eick reports he "moved to Stone Lake, Wisconsin, 177 miles north of La Crosse, where Henrietta Martindale . . . lived."[2] He was living with his son, Ohi, by the later 1920s, at least some of the time, but whether Charles actually had a place he called home between 1921 and 1924 is something of a mystery. It is certain Charles attended his daughter Virginia's wedding to Sterling Whitbeck at Camp Oáhe in September 1921. Though neither the mother nor the father of the bride left behind any record, it's easy to imagine how awkward the situation must have been. This also might well have been the last time Elaine and Charles ever saw one another.

* * *

Charles served as president of the Society of American Indians from September 1918 through October 1919. Early in his tenure he'd been involved with one of the more contentious issues within the SAI, regulating peyote use in religious ceremonies. Several prominent SAI members believed peyote was integral to many tribes' religious practices and therefore should not be legislated; Charles, along with General Pratt and Gertrude Bonnin (Zitkála-Sá), believed peyote a dangerous substance likely to do Indians more harm than good. Headlines such as "Dr. Eastman Says Peyote Will Ruin the Red Race" underscored Charles's belief peyote was a narcotic that negatively affected both physical and moral health; he agreed its use should be curtailed under the bill proposed by Congressman Carl Hayden. Historian Hazel Hertzberg's assessment of the fight over this bill revealed some of the divisions in the developing pan-Indian movement: peyote use was variously seen as a throwback to a Native past that would effectively prevent contemporary Indians from a healthier embrace of a more integrated future, or a way of reclaiming Indigeneity.[3] The Hayden Bill passed in the House but lost in the Senate.

Peyote regulation wasn't the only issue dividing SAI members. There was debate over the call to eliminate the Indian Bureau; controversy over the drive to increase SAI membership that yielded new members but somehow left the organization with a funding deficit; and arguments over how best to achieve full citizenship for Native Americans. Charles, who had signaled his belief in the importance of citizenship in his speech at the Universal Races Congress, advocated for a citizenship bill introduced by Representative Charles Carter of Oklahoma. This bill provided citizenship for all Indians with the caveat of restrictions based on whether Indians were "full blood" or not. With the knowledge gleaned from his years of work on the Indian renaming project, as well as the personal investment of someone whose maternal grandfather had been white and whose children were half-white, Charles understood the complexity of this issue. He felt Carter's provisions would mean some Indians would be granted full citizenship while others would be subject to restrictions imposed by the Indian Bureau. Yet he supported it anyway, once again leaning into a position that more Native Americans would benefit from the bill's passage, even if it required additional work.

After Irene's death, Charles set out across the country, frequently speaking about the need for Indian citizenship. A partial recitation of one of his talks, given in Wilkes-Barre, Pennsylvania, quoted Charles saying, "The citizenship of the Indian is the one thing most desired. We feel that the time is past for us as a dependent and competent race to be governed by the Bureau at Washington. We want to enter upon the work of educating the public to the true condition on the Indian reservations showing how they are managed and what disadvantages in the way of their progress are met in these reservations." He pointed out that citizenship would add both manpower to the armed services and voters who could more fully participate in American democracy if they could exercise their voices.[4] In the *American Indian Magazine*, the SAI's general publication outlet, Zitkála Sá commented, "Our president, Dr. Charles A. Eastman, spent about three months this spring on a lecture campaign on behalf of American citizenship for the Indian. Sacrificing remunerative engagements to give himself up to strenuous public speaking, delivering three and sometimes four addresses in a day."[5] In fact, Charles was speaking about this topic a lot, but he didn't stop giving lectures on other topics that tended to be more remunerative.

Charles also gave many talks focusing on the need to abolish the Indian Bureau. Some of these lectures, not surprisingly, produced inflammatory headlines and articles, such as one in the White Earth Indian Reservation (MN) newspaper, *The Tomahawk*: "Charges Indians Fleeced: Dr. Charles A. Eastman Asserts Federal Bureau Must Go." According to the paper, "Charges that the United States Bureau of Indian Affairs is 'squeezing the blood' from the Indians whose affairs it administers, 'stealing whatever they have' and destroying the old high idealistic morality of the race, were made by Dr. Charles A. Eastman, president of the Society of American Indians, who spoke at the Little Theater at the University of Minnesota."[6] A lengthy article in the Carlisle Indian School's *The Red Man* gave a fuller articulation of Charles's argument: "The fact of the matter is that the reservation system is outgrown. Whatever benefit it may have been at the outset in the way of sustenance and protection, and as a nursery of civilization, at their present stage of development it is nothing but a hindrance. It makes children of [Indians] and so perpetuates itself. Full citizenship is necessary now, in order to save the young men."[7]

FIGURE 10.1. Charles at the Dana Hall School, Wellesley, MA. Courtesy Dana Hall Archives.

In October 1919 the SAI held its annual meeting in Minneapolis. Wilson describes Charles's presidential address as "an extremely romantic presentation on Native Americans, their place in history, and their contributions to America," paired with a pageant he had written about Pontiac, an eighteenth-century Odawa chief who'd led a war against the British. Wilson suggests Charles wrote and starred in this pageant at the meeting; Elaine later emphatically stated to Rose she had co-written this play and attached her byline to it.[8] The performance of "The Conspiracy of Pontiac" was open to the public. The cast included Charles, playing Pontiac, joined by other delegates to the convention such as Gertrude Bonnin and Carlos Montezuma. The horses and canoes envisioned in the original script were cut since the pageant was performed indoors. According to Lucy Maddox, Charles hoped this play would get picked up by the city of Minneapolis for use as a "centerpiece of planned annual carnival." Though local commerce officials came to the SAI performance, they envisioned a possible use of the play differently from Charles: "Minneapolis wanted a carnival; Eastman wanted a historical pageant."[9] Like so many of Charles Eastman's ideas, this one was never realized.

It was not a good SAI meeting for Charles for another reason: he couldn't hold onto the SAI presidency, losing out for the second time to Thomas Sloan, an Omaha who advocated a pro-peyote stance. After this defeat, Charles declined to do much with the SAI again.

The long-running Santee claims case, two decades after Charles's initial engagement, remained another ongoing frustration, even though his intermittent involvement now lacked any official capacity. When the U.S. Court of Appeals finally rendered a decision about monies due the Santee in June 1922, it awarded the Santee about $387,000, far less than the Santee thought they were owed. Charles tried to step back into the picture, suggesting were the Santee to reengage with him, he would attempt to lobby Congress for a higher fee. But the Santee declined, already represented by different attorneys. Instead, Charles began to lobby various senators, reiterating his long association with the case and arguing he was due some of the funding the court had awarded in attorney fees. "When the Santee discovered that Eastman was attempting to get legislation passed which would take an additional $15,000 from their settlement, they protested,"[10] writes Raymond Wilson. In the end, Charles obtained no additional money, augmenting both his disillusionment and his financial woes.

Desperate for a salaried position that offered at least a modicum of security, Charles accepted an offer to return to the Indian Service. In summer 1923 he became a U.S. Indian inspector. The irony of having been the *subject* of inspections on at least two different occasions in his prior work for the Indian Service could not have been lost on him; that his salary wasn't even 50 percent higher than it had been when he'd last worked for the government must also have been disheartening. However, during the year and a half he worked as an Indian inspector, Charles undertook several projects, including a few special assignments that probably held some inherent interest for him.

Charles traveled far and wide in this role. He investigated issues on seventeen reservations in the West, traveling back to familiar places such as Lower Brulé and Rosebud Agencies in South Dakota and the Shoshone Reservation in Wyoming, as well as to places he'd not been, such as the Umatilla and Klamath Reservations in Oregon, the Tulalip Agency in Washington, the Mackinac and Chippewa Reservations in Minnesota, and the Osage Reservation in Oklahoma. He issued reports calling for better health programs and increased medical care, worked on allotment issues, and attempted to resolve personnel disputes.

Several of his "special assignments" involved events. He observed the Illinois Indian Day Celebration in Chicago in 1923, finding it inauthentic and a poor representation of Indian life and culture. He participated in a ceremony honoring British prime minister David Lloyd George in Minneapolis; Charles helped to organize the Sioux participation, and his efforts were later praised by President Calvin Coolidge. He was part of the so-called Committee of One Hundred, a distinguished group of Native Americans, white Indian reformers, anthropologists, military officials, and ministers who convened in Washington, DC, in December 1923 to discuss a wide range of issues. They called for many reforms aimed at improving Indian education, removing bans on various Indian religious ceremonies, protecting Indian ownership of mineral rights on their lands, and resolving land claims. While not resulting in any policy changes, these discussions helped to frame some of the Indian policies later crafted during the New Deal.

Given his employment history with the Indian Service, it probably would have been miraculous had Charles gotten through his nineteen months as Indian inspector without controversy. He did not.

In 1923, Frank C. Rogers, who was a special officer in the Indian Service tasked with monitoring alcohol use at the Rosebud Agency in South Dakota, observed a celebration with a traditional ritual involving a clown dance. Misunderstanding the purpose and meaning of the ceremony, Rogers deemed it was an outlawed practice and ordered it to cease. When the Sioux protested, he drew a gun. Charles investigated the complaints against Rogers and found them legitimate; Rogers should not have interfered, he concluded. But when Agent Rogers found out about Charles's investigation, he threatened him. Charles suspended Rogers, who in turn complained to the commissioner of Indian Affairs. Another special inspector investigated this, concluding Rogers should be transferred to another agency. But Charles did not get off without rebuke; he was chastised for somehow having overstepped his authority, an inspector who couldn't inspect.

Senior Indian Services personnel also critiqued Charles's administrative work. As Wilson writes, "Eastman found it extremely difficult to submit his reports on time," and his superiors criticized "his tardiness in filing weekly reports and expense vouchers . . . though many people at the bureau considered his actions dilatory or explained the delays as 'Indian time.'"[11]

* * *

In some ways the last project Charles undertook in his role as Indian inspector was the most interesting and controversial, drawing his attention back in time.

A young Shoshone girl named Sacagawea was either sold into a nonconsensual marriage to French-Canadian trapper Toussaint Charbonneau or, as some versions of the story have it, won by him as part of a bet. In 1804 when Meriwether Lewis and William Clark embarked on their cross-country exploratory expedition commissioned by President Thomas Jefferson, they hired Charbonneau and his teenage wife as guides and interpreters. Sacagawea's assistance became the source of legend; her presence as a young woman with a young child no doubt helped signal to Native groups the expedition's peaceful intent. She died sometime in the 1800s after marrying a second time and possibly having one or more additional children.

There was not much definitively known about Sacagawea, ranging from the exact spelling and pronunciation of her name to her marital status, to when and where she died. During the early part of the twentieth century Sacagawea's legacy became of great interest to suffragists; she was viewed as an independent, (literally) trailblazing woman seen as a symbol for what women were trying to achieve in pursuing formal recognition of their rights and campaigning for the Nineteenth Amendment, giving women the right to vote. With increasing attention being paid to her and calls for some kind of commemorative monument to be erected, the question of where Sacagawea was buried, and whether she died in 1884 at the age of ninety-five, or in 1812 at the age of about twenty-four, came into question.

Grace Hebard, a University of Wyoming professor, believed Sacagawea died in 1884. An active supporter of the Nineteenth Amendment, Hebard worked to get federal legislation passed to erect a Sacagawea memorial. Hebard theorized the Shoshone woman left her first husband because he'd abused her, regretted having led white men into Indian Country, and chose to live independently and anonymously for the remainder of her life. This narrative fits the suffrage cause. Hebard suggested she based her ideas on interviews with both Indian and white informants, though numerous historians disputed her claims. The issue started to garner a lot of press interest; numerous articles appeared across the country. Hoping to settle an issue that was starting to be a bit of a political hot potato for the Indian Bureau, the commissioner of Indian Affairs assigned Charles to investigate and see if he could find Sacagawea's true burial site.

From January through March 1925, Charles immersed himself in written materials about Sacagawea. He traveled across Wyoming, North Dakota, and Oklahoma, interviewing members of three different tribal groups who might have had some knowledge of her life and death. He corresponded with Grace

Hebard and spoke with several of the historians who disputed her contentions. In 1925 he submitted a report to his superiors in Washington that aligned with Hebard's theory: he believed Sacagawea died in 1884 and was buried near Fort Washakie in Wyoming. His report was reprinted years later in *The Annals of Wyoming* but never generated much publicity. In the first paragraph he noted, "I fully realized the importance and delicacy of this investigation."[12] However, the "delicacy" of his investigation did not end when the investigation did.

Grace Hebard was writing a book about Sacagawea's life. She asked Charles to write an introduction, but he never responded to her request. Wilson speculates Charles "also planned to write an account of her life"; historian David Miller postulates that due to his near-constant travel, it's possible Charles never received her request.[13] (Copies of her letters to Charles Eastman she kept shows she sent them to addresses in Munsonville and Northampton, places Charles no longer resided but Elaine did.) Charles wrote to Grace Hebard in October 1925, after he submitted his report, stating, "I am now preparing a true story of Sacajawea's life. I think the whole course of her life bears out the spirit and heroism in her." (In an earlier letter to Hebard, Charles referred to Sacagawea as "the Ben Hur of the Indian.")[14]

Hebard wrote to Charles again in 1926, asking what he intended to publish about Sacajawea because she didn't want to "run amuck with you" or have competing publications.[15] He also never responded to this query. In 1927 she wrote to Charles, "I am wondering if you have done anything in regard to a possible publication of Sacajawea," to deafening silence. And then again in 1928, she reached out to him: "May I ask you as one author to another, if you have found anything in your investigations that would make you reverse your opinion which you gave to the Indian Department in 1925. . . . I am not asking about any one additional fact that you may have found, it is merely that in my interest in Sacajawea, it would be humiliating if I send my MS to a publisher and had it published, and should state that there was not one Sacajawea and so forth, and then you should find some material that would make you reverse the decision previously given to the Indian Department." Finally, in 1929, Charles responded to her: "I have been migrating like my ancestors the Sioux, every year," he wrote. "The spirit of nomadic life has never gone out of me; therefore many important letters have been left unanswered."[16] It wasn't only the letters he left unanswered; he never answered her questions.

Charles *was* busily trying to publish something about Sacagawea. His article "Sacajawea, Her Lost 70 Years" didn't get published until 1949, when Elaine edited and published it as part of a retrospective, posthumous series of Charles's works in the *New Bedford Standard Times*, a series picked up and reprinted in several other papers. It's impossible to know whether sentences such as "At every stage of her life, up to the very last, her remarkable courage and vitality were observed by all who knew her. The hardships of this journey were met with the buoyant spirt of the old days" emanated directly from Charles's pen or from Elaine's typewriter.[17]

* * *

Charles resigned from his position as Indian inspector in March 1925. Sixty-seven years old and ill with bronchitis, he sought respite from his near-constant travel. From approximately the end of March through the beginning of October, he took up residence near Stone Lake, Wisconsin. Of his 1910 journey in the northern woods with the Ojibwe, Charles had written, "Every day it became harder for me to leave the woods."[18] During the time he spent near Stone Lake, he undoubtedly began to think there might come a time when he would not have to leave his beloved woods at all. But that time wasn't yet.

In fall 1925 Charles traveled to New York and Washington. In New York he met with members of the board of directors of the Brooks-Bryce Foundation. This foundation, dedicated to promoting better American-British relations, sought to send Charles on a two-month lecture tour of Great Britain, speaking about Indian-white relations. "This will involve a portrayal of the aims, ideals, and philosophy of the Indian prior to his contact with the white man. One of his most important lectures about the Jesuits and the Indians is designed to show the peaceful and friendly feeling of one people toward another when both seek universal peace rather than materialistic gain," described the public relations blurb about his talks.[19] Charles would not commence on this tour for another couple of years.

In November 1925 he moved temporarily to Chicago, apparently for proximity to the Newberry Library, where Charles spent time looking at documents relating to his family history. In 1911, Edward E. Ayer, a trustee of the Newberry Library and first president of the Field Museum of Chicago, a wealthy businessman who had amassed an astounding collection of books and maps about Indigenous people, as well as hundreds of artifacts, donated a large part of his collection to the Newberry.

Ayer's niece, Clara Smith, was a librarian at the Newberry. In April 1925 she wrote her uncle, telling him of an extraordinary encounter she'd had two days prior. She had been helping another patron when a distinctive-looking person walked into the room. "I saw at once that the man was Dr. Charles Eastman," she wrote. Charles shook her hand and told her he had long wanted to come to see the Ayer collection. "I told him that I had something that I had been wanting to show him for a long time. I brought out one of the Mayer sketchbooks and showed him a pencil sketch of Nancy Eastman, the half-breed daughter of Capt. Seth Eastman, and Dr. Eastman's mother." Clara continued emotionally, "How do you think you would feel if you were suddenly shown a picture of your mother, of whom you had no recollection, she died when he was a baby, and of whom you had no earthly reason to think that there could possibly be a picture in existence." She concluded her letter recounting that as he left, Charles "patted me on the shoulder and said, 'To think that I have seen a picture of my mother!'"[20]

Several years later Hiram Hitchcock, a businessman and historian from Minneapolis interested in Charles's family, contacted him; the two exchanged letters for several years. In one of his first responses Charles thanked Hitchcock for sending along a copy of the pencil drawing of Nancy Eastman. He said his mother had probably been "just twenty-one or approaching it" when the picture was drawn. "The entire Mde wakan towan tribe mourn [*sic*] for her loss because she was generous and kind and a friend to every body, young and old," he recounted. "Mother's beautiful face, body, soul was easy [*sic*] explained when one knows the line of her forebear, humblest line is her Puritan father, but again he was unusually gifted."[21]

In 1927 Charles traveled to Hanover, New Hampshire, to attend his Dartmouth reunion. He was once again asked to play the part of Samson

Occom in a tableau, once again photographed in his Sioux regalia alongside classmates in suits. He also sat for a portrait commissioned by his classmates. This portrait by artist Julius D. Katzieff depicts Charles not as an average Dartmouth student (or alumnus) of the day, but standing with a large, feathered headdress, embroidered buckskin and moccasins, holding what appears to be some kind of sacred stick.

Historian Kiara Vigil points out the many ways in which the college used Charles's appearances at the Hanover campus to claim him as "Dartmouth's Indian" but suggests that in his own mind, he was likely considering himself as "a modern exemplar of Dartmouth's continuing mission, which for Eastman rested not in civilizing indigenous peoples through the process of education, but rather in educating Americans about Indian civilization."[22]

Charles was also sincere in his efforts to educate white people in Great Britain about Indian civilizations. In January 1928 he set off for his two-month speaking tour. His schedule in England included twenty lectures on Indian culture at Oxford University, as well as talks at the prestigious Eton School, the Royal Colonial Institute, and other schools. He met with numerous people including the seventh Earl of Dartmouth and David Lloyd George, the former British prime minister, and he participated in many public events, including a radio broadcast entitled "An Interview with Dr. Charles Eastman Chief of the Sioux Indians." Unfortunately, neither a recording nor a transcript of this talk exists.

The press assiduously covered his travels around Britain. An extraordinary photo in the *Liverpool Courier* shows Charles in an enormous feathered headdress trailing almost to his feet, surrounded by white British schoolboys in their uniforms; the caption reads "Ohiyesa the Conqueror: a full-blooded Sioux chief, who also bears the less romantic name of Dr. Charles Eastman, of Dartmouth College, USA, at Balfour Institute, Liverpool, yesterday." There's an article from the *Irish Times* stating Ohiyesa "laments the popularity of Fenimore Cooper's tales as conveying a false impression of the old Indian life. Cooper, he says, represents the Indians as they were when their life had been corrupted. The white man had placed a bounty on scalps, and a people normally peaceful was reduced to savagery." An article in the *Bristol Times* called

Charles "one of the most cultured Indians that ever lived, that is from our point of view, Indian culture having, no doubt, something still to teach the white man in the direction of bravery, stoicism, and philosophy." And there's a hilarious description of a fox hunt Charles went on in Wales: "Probably for the first time in the history of the Tanatside Harriers, Dr. Charles Alexander Eastman (Ohiyesa the Conqueror)—a Chief of the warlike Sioux Indians of North America—took part in a special meet held at Llanfechain." This article describes Charles's pursuit of the foxes on horseback at "great pace," as well as some of the usual newspaper misinformation about his medical degree from Harvard, his role as an "official attorney of the Indian cause at Washington," and his turn to literature and medicine once "it was evident that the fighting days of the Red Indian were over."[23]

But the days of Ohíye' S'a were not quite over.

* * *

While Charles generated a paper trail in the first seven decades of his life between letters he wrote, stories, books, and papers he delivered and the enormous cache of newspaper articles about him, there's little to go on in his final decade. He traveled, but only a little compared to his earlier days; he gave a few lectures, but the schedule was not nearly as grueling—or as remunerative—as it once had been. He tried to write, but the only publications from this period were reprints of pieces he had previously published or international versions of his previously published books. He received a few honors, but his fame faded. He evinced greater interest in his ancestral history as his nuclear family's immediate history experienced dramatic shifts. And as his years mounted and his health diminished, Charles Eastman increasingly turned to the roots and the ways of his life as Ohíye' S'a.

When he returned from his Great Britain tour in 1928, he began looking for some land upon which he could build a cabin in the north woods of Sault Ste. Marie, an area straddling Michigan's Upper Peninsula and Ontario on Lake Huron. Home to the Ojibwe before any Euro-Americans arrived, the heavily forested area is filled with lakes, canals, and locks. When French settlers came along in the seventeenth century, they named the area for the cascading rapids. In the eighteenth century the region became an important outpost of the fur trading industry; by the time Charles arrived in the early twentieth century there were still large areas of relatively untouched wilderness. He had been through this area in 1910 on his travels with the Ojibwe during the University of Pennsylvania–sponsored artifacts expedition, finding it among the last places in North American where Indians could "hold civilization at bay." Being about 350 miles from Detroit, where Ohi lived and where Charles could spend the coldest part of the winters, was a bonus. In April 1928 he purchased land on the north shore of Wilson Channel, about three miles away from Desbarats, Ontario. According to historian David Miller, who in the 1970s corresponded with people who lived across the channel, Charles hired two Ojibwe to help build his cabin. "The 'lodge' was a one room cabin furnished with a wind-up phonograph, oil lamps, and presumably a chair or two and a bed. All the plumbing was out-of-doors. The cabin was forty feet above the water and could only be reached by a stair and a steep path."[24] Charles referred to his dwelling as Matotee Lodge.

The relative isolation of the cabin enabled Charles to fish, hunt, and take the morning swim he loved preceded by his "moose call," which, according to someone who had a nearby cabin, echoed off the rocks of a nearby island. He decorated the walls with portraits of famous Indians, whose stories Charles told to any visitors, regaling them with anecdotes and informing them about how reservation life and the incursions of the white man with his diseases and vices had ruined the Indian. Occasionally Charles returned to medicine to treat Indian patients in the Sault Ste. Marie region, and he reportedly gathered with others to play cards or listen to baseball games on the radio. But for the most part he lived a life of isolation, going out on his boat, walking through the woods, or swimming by himself.

During some of the time he was not living at Matotee Lodge, Charles stayed with his son in Detroit. This proved a difficult arrangement. Ohi moved there sometime after graduating from the College of Idaho in 1924. He became an appliance salesman, working on and off for the Kelvinator Corporation, a refrigeration pioneer based in Detroit. At one time he apparently attempted to get a job with the Indian Service. For a number of years, he worked at part-time jobs;

Elaine wrote to Rose in the middle of 1933, "Ohi has found nothing to do and is getting very hard up and restless, I judge. It's a real misfortune." He also had a series of unfortunate relationships with women, also marked by his mother in letters to his aunt. But in 1936 he married Marion Nutting, a woman who had a daughter from a previous marriage. Elaine did not approve of this relationship either. She later wrote to Rose, "His twelve years in Detroit were anything but happy ones—city life indoors uncongenial, the work monotonous, his relations with Marion and with his father a great strain."[25]

Apart from whatever strain Charles's presence for weeks on end put on the marriage between his son and daughter-in-law, there were also apparently a few times when Charles asked his son for money. He also asked Elaine. She reported that Ohi (and probably Marion) started to feel resentment toward Charles, as did she. "I would not give him the money . . . partly because I knew he would pile up several hundred dollars more in debt, and partly because I don't think he is able to take care of himself alone, he has become restless. It's a problem." She continued, "I think you can see how, although it is of course a relief in one way to have his father away, it is embarrassing to have him sponging on friends, of often borrowing of them, and running up heavy bills with tradesmen. . . . A person as irresponsible as the Doctor has become should really have no money at all at command and no credit. Whether he likes it or not, he SHOULD be restrained for the sake of others."[26]

The life of the itinerant lecturer became more difficult for Charles as he aged, plagued by chronic bronchitis. Occasionally isolated snippets from one of his talks would be published in a newspaper demonstrating the more obvious anti-Euro-American, pro-Indian stance he was taking; for instance, the *Lancaster News* in Pennsylvania highlighted "Charles A. Eastman, Sioux Indian physician," saying, "The average American businessman is a pile of human junk. He needs closer communion with nature." What talk this came from or the context in which it was said was lost; the paper's editors were only interested in the sensational quote. His few talks generated far less media coverage than in the past.

In 1930 Charles went back East to give talks in Philadelphia and New York and also traveled to Minnesota to speak at a celebration marking the

250th anniversary of the "discovery" of the Falls of St. Anthony by Belgian missionary and priest Father Louis Hennepin. This may have been the last major public address Charles ever gave.

In 1680 some Dakota captured Father Hennepin and two of his companions on the Mississippi River. Hennepin ended up living with the Dakota, his writings documenting his perspectives on the tribe. Contemporary Dakhóta perspectives on Hennepin's time, including commentary by Syd Beane, a descendant of John Eastman's, suggest Father Hennepin did not "discover" the falls—a sacred place to Dakhóta—but was brought there by the Dakhóta as a guest. Charles Eastman quite possibly had a similar perspective. Unfortunately, there is no record of what he said; the recap from the Minnesota Historical Society and newspaper reports from the time only mentions that Charles, a "descendant of Cloud Man, who befriended Father Hennepin," spoke as part of an afternoon program, his talk overshadowed by remarks from Prince Albert de Lige of Belgium and a telegram from President Herbert Hoover.[27]

* * *

For someone who had long been heralded as "the most educated Indian" or "a great Sioux chief" or "the finest specimen of Indian . . . an example of what education can do" by Euro-Americans, the award Charles Eastman received in 1933 "for the most distinguished achievement by an American Indian" probably wasn't surprising to him. But this award was probably also the most meaningful praise he'd ever received.

Founded in Chicago in 1923, the Grand Council Fire of American Indians (later the Indian Council Fire, ICF), was an organization involved with a range of educational, legislative, and social service activities for Indians locally and nationally. Dedicated to validating and celebrating Native American achievements and cultures, it became the first large Indian organization in Chicago. On its tenth anniversary, coinciding with the World's Fair, the Indian Council Fire selected Charles from among fifty possible nominees to receive its first-ever Indian Achievement Award. According to a newspaper article printed in many papers across the country, the medal was to be awarded "to the Indian of today whose achievement in the field of the fine arts, religion, medicine, law, science, politics, education, social service, agriculture or service to the federal or state government has been most outstanding." The wide swath of fields was matched by the numerous award nominees, who included Luther Standing Bear, Gertrude Bonnin, Arthur Parker, and Jim Thorpe, as well as prominent Native artists, dancers, tribal leaders, attorneys, physicians, and educators. The article named those on the selection committee, who included a few Native historians, authors, and chiefs, but ironically, many more prominent Euro-Americans, including Ernest Thompson Seton, John Collier—the current commissioner of Indian Affairs—and Mrs. Harold Ickes, wife of the current secretary of the interior "and an authority on Indian subjects." Scott Peters, a Chippewa serving as president of the ICF stated, "Few people know that the Indian has made any progress in view of the conditions with which he has had to cope, but there are Indians in every walk of life who are making good."[28]

Charles was selected from among this illustrious group. In this selection, note Rosalyn LaPier and David Beck, the committee went with an Indian who signified to white America the "savage savage" who, through his education, became "civilized" and an emblem of what Native Americans could do.[29]

Charles received the medal on American Indian Day in September 1933. Some ten thousand guests witnessed the event.[30] Unfortunately there is no record of any remarks he made upon receiving this award, so we can only surmise his appreciation for the irony of receiving it at the "Century of Progress Exhibition," depicting how Indians only "progressed" if they departed from traditional ways. But there are images from this time. Almost certainly not part of the event organized by the Indian Council Fire and much more likely part of the "Birth of Chicago Pageant" at the World's Fair, the series of photos could not possibly provide a starker contrast to a Dakhóta being honored for "Indian achievement."

A studio shot depicts Charles wearing his feathered headdress, a fringed, beaded shirt, and leggings with moccasins. He's holding a tomahawk and looks amused. Another shot bizarrely depicts him in Sioux regalia posing in front of birch-covered wigwams constructed for the fair alongside "Miss Fort Dearborn," a white woman with a 1920s-style bob and a short white dress. She is holding a tomahawk. Another photo shows Charles with two white men in

FIGURE 10.2. Charles with "Miss Fort Dearborn," 1933. National Museum of the American Indian/Smithsonian.

suits in front of Chicago's Soldier Field; he's holding a bow and arrow he "playfully" aims at one of them. Another shot has Charles posed outdoors; arms raised, he appears to be making an offering to some unknown great spirit; the next one has Charles dressed in Sioux regalia, sitting on the ground with two white men who are dressed as Indians (who was actually "playing Indian" there is certainly in the eye of the beholder!). And in the final photo of the series, he is sitting in an auditorium at the Marshall Field's department store, surrounded by white Boy Scouts in uniform. These photos, now held by the Smithsonian/National Museum of the American Indian, dramatically illustrate the contrasts of Charles Eastman's life: the man who'd gained the tools to succeed in a Euro-American world but fervently desired to return to his Dakhóta past; the man who knew when to "play Indian" and dress the part but did so selectively to make a point and make a buck; the man who might well have posed for these photos with an ironic smile the white photographer taking them didn't notice, and the white viewing audience simply misunderstood. Charles Eastman may once again have become Ohíye' S'a without most of the world even noticing.

* * *

In a life filled with ironies, could not have been lost on Charles Eastman that precisely at the point of his life at which he wished to delve into his family's history and reflect on and preserve the legacy of his own personal history, he seemed unable to write. Wilson suggests that after his marriage to Elaine collapsed, Charles was unable to complete any manuscripts because "he had relied too heavily on his wife's editorial revisions."[31] Elaine commented on this in a letter to Rose, quoting extensively from a letter Ohi had written her in which he delineated how Charles wanted to pay a stenographer to type up some of his notes for another book he was trying to get published. "His Mss was chaotic, in spite of having wasted hundreds of dollars on having it typed," Elaine wrote. "That was no surprise to me, of course, as I knew I had done a good half of the work on the books credited to him."[32]

In 1935, his handwriting shaky, Charles wrote to Hiram M. Hitchcock that he had been too ill to do as much as he'd hoped to; he had written something he called the "Sioux Bible," he stated, but "I have to go over it again."[33] This was probably his contribution to Ernest Thompson Seton's book *The Gospel of the Red Man: An Indian Bible*, a book compiled with contributions from numerous "Indian committee members" listed in the book's forward, though it is also possible he was working on a manuscript he hoped to publish separately. He never did. Nor did he ever manage to complete the work he planned to write on Sacagawea, nor anything from what he'd described to Hiram Hitchcock as "assembling my notes of 50 years" of American history as it related to the Sioux.

As his health became increasingly compromised, Charles sought to revisit places of personal importance. It is not entirely clear whether he returned to South Dakota when his brother John died in 1921, whether he went to New Hampshire for the wedding of his daughter Eleanor in 1928 (he does not appear in a formal photo of this event held by the Cheshire County Historical Society), or whether he returned to Massachusetts for the funeral of his daughter Florence in 1930. In the autumn of 1933 he reached out to his brother's daughter Grace Moore, the same niece who had lived with the Eastmans during a more idyllic summer at Bald Eagle Lake. Charles requested that Grace and her husband come with her mother and grandmother to meet him in Morton, Minnesota. Charles planned to visit the place of his birth. According to an interview historian David Miller conducted with Moore, the relatives met in a park built on the land where Charles had been born. Charles told the story of the Dakota War of 1862; Moore "noted that it was a magnificent afternoon and the last time she saw Charles."[34]

In 1938, it seems Charles Eastman did make one last trip to the site of Camp Oáhe. There, he visited with Earl Barrett, who years later told David Miller that Charles had come back to the site where his daughter Irene was buried under a tree.[35] We cannot know for sure what Charles was thinking as he revisited the camp that once seemed a family affair, until "family affair" took on new meaning and the Eastman family's whole world turned upside down.

In his final years of life, Charles, who for so many years espoused the importance of physical fitness and started his days with a morning swim, began to grow weaker. Sometime in 1938 a fire broke out in his Matotee Lodge; Charles was overcome by smoke inhalation and subsequently developed pneumonia. At the end of 1938 he suffered from chronic myocarditis and was admitted to a hospital in Detroit. He developed pneumonia once again and died on January 8, 1939.

Charles' eldest daughter, Dora Winona, and son Ohi were the only Eastman children to attend his funeral. Elaine did not; she wrote to Rose, bitterly, "I thought perhaps you would have seen mention of Dr. Eastman's death in the *Times*, or somewhere—he went off very easily about two weeks ago . . . and for us here who never see or hear from him there is hardly any difference."[36]

It's not surprising that the obituaries of Charles published in various newspapers across the country got some of the information about him wrong. This had been happening his entire life, the man melded into the legend and the legend melded into the man. An obituary in the *Winnipeg Tribune* mentioned that Charles, "who roamed Saskatchewan plains as Chief Ohiyesa, a full-blooded Sioux," had "won his degree in medicine from Boston College. Born in the western United States, his early years were spent migrating westward and northward, as advancing civilization made members of his tribe seek virgin territory." The *Detroit News* noted his "years of restless wandering on the plains and high plateaus of Montana, the Dakotas and Canada" before recounting the rest of his educational and professional accomplishments somewhat accurately. The *Amherst Record* had Charles dying at the home of his son instead of a hospital; the *Keene Sentinel* incorrectly listed his age and erroneously suggested "Ohiyesa" meant "the Unconquered One" while noting he was "the most learned member of his race"; and the *Detroit Free Press* unequivocally and inaccurately reported that Charles adopted his Euro-American name at the time he earned his medical degree.[37]

Charles was buried in the Evergreen Cemetery outside of Detroit. Even this was reported incorrectly by numerous newspapers. There was no tombstone to mark his burial spot—ironic, given his efforts to establish the site of Sacagawea's burial so a monument could be built. His own resting place would bear no such marker. Charles Eastman, so well known during his lifetime, seemed to vanish in his death. When members of many Native groups die, it is said they "walk on" from the journey of life to the journey beyond. Perhaps this was true of Ohíye' S'a as well, part of his return to his Dakhóta roots.

11

From Northampton to Spring Grove (1921–1953)

"It hardly seems fair after giving up so much to make a home," wrote Elaine to Rose, "that I should be a wanderer in my old age."[1] In the final three decades of her life, she led a peripatetic existence. After her marriage with Charles effectively ended (though they never officially divorced and she never publicly acknowledged their separation), Elaine moved from Amherst to nearby Northampton, where she lived with one daughter or another until almost the end of her life.

Punctuated by more sorrows than joys, the last part of Elaine's life reads like the coda to an opera—perhaps a soap opera—filled with *sturm und drang,* the personal upheaval balanced but not compensated for by the professional successes. Elaine had never been more productive in her written output. She published four books and innumerable articles; she returned to poetry and tried her hand at writing novels and plays. She continued to advocate on behalf of the Native American issues she cared about and was a frequent contributor to local, state, and national publications. But while times had changed, her views had not. Ideas once thought progressive now seemed almost reactionary, especially in the reformist spirit and optimism of the New Deal and what would become known later as the "Indian New Deal." Sadly, she demonstrated a similar inability to let go of ideas about her family and relationships with other people, retrenched in opinions rooted in childhood, limited by views formed by a time gone by.

* * *

After dropping the life-altering news about the birth of her baby daughter, Henrietta Martindale's life intersected with both Elaine and Charles's briefly, though her impact divided them permanently. The searing information about Charles's paternity and his refusal to take responsibility for it in a way Elaine considered honorable tore their long-suffering marriage apart. During the early 1920s after Elaine and Charles parted, Henrietta, still concealing her little girl's existence from her own parents, became increasingly dependent on her sister, Katharine, to help cover her tracks and her expenses. But her relationship with her sister also became increasingly strained as Katharine clearly disapproved of Henrietta's choices and Henrietta tried to limit what her sister knew of her life.

After Henrietta married Paul Wilson, friends and neighbors wrote surreptitiously to Katharine of their concern for Henrietta's safety and sanity, suggesting, among other things, that Henrietta and her daughter were being abused. Katharine urged secrecy so her sources of information about her sister would not be compromised. Henrietta later had other children with Wilson. When he was incarcerated after a shooting incident, this placed Henrietta in even more dire financial straits. She also fought to keep custody of her children since some believed her daughters would be better off in protective services, and she, better off in the care of a mental institution.[2] By the early 1930s she had fled Wisconsin and returned to California.

But her situation did not measurably improve in the Golden State. Bonno was regularly "excused" from school "because of malnutrition and nervousness," her sisters placed in a foster home, and Henrietta herself sent to a hospital. Neighbors reported Bonno had been beaten by her stepfather, who rejoined his family after his prison sentence ended. Despite her difficult circumstances, the girl seems to have excelled in school. In about 1939, when Bonno was twenty, Elaine wrote to Rose, "Ironically enough, I heard from my friend in California about Dr. Eastman's illegitimate daughter, just a few days after his death. . . . It seems she knew about her father. . . . Bonno Hyessa (as she calls herself, using part of her father's name) is in a junior college and helps support herself by serving as a model for arts. My friend was very favorably impressed by her and says she hears only good of the girl. I have written her and if she responds shall try to be of some use to her."[3]

It's not clear whether Bonno ever responded. Nor is it clear what Elaine meant by being "of some use to her" since it certainly wasn't financial help she could offer.

Theodore Sargent suggests a close reading of Elaine's novel *Hundred Maples* may provide answers to the questions of how Elaine felt about Charles's relationship with Henrietta and Bonno's birth. In the absence of documentary evidence such as a diary that might truly be a window into a writer's thoughts and feelings, it's tempting to mine her published materials for insights. And indeed, one of the main plotlines running through this 1935 novel mirrors the situation in which Elaine must have found herself.

The novel follows the intertwined lives of three friends: Ellen Strong, a New England farmgirl who aspires to be a writer but ends of marrying the boy at the nearby farm, and her two best friends from college—Marcia, an academic scientist with "steel grey eyes [that] surveyed the world keenly and a bit satirically," and Amy, a girl from Grand Forks, North Dakota, who ends up becoming a lawyer in Seattle married to Jim May, an attorney who she met when they opposed one another in court. Taken together, the three friends may present an amalgam of Elaine. But Amy's story has particular resonance.

Visiting her friend, Ellen views Amy's life as storybook perfect—a handsome husband who displays physical affection for his wife and proposed to her speaking of marriage "as a full partnership of self-respecting equals," a beautifully appointed home, a successful career. But she soon learns there's sleeplessness in Seattle. Amy's first child is stillborn after a difficult pregnancy. Jim isn't the gentleman he seems: he makes a pass at Ellen. And, as we learn later in the novel, it gets worse.

One day a young woman named Cara Hines appears, and Amy mistakenly believes she has come for legal help. Soon she learns Cara seeks help of another kind. She presents Amy with a letter from Jim, documenting that the baby she carries in her arms Jim referred to as "our love-bought little one." Shocked, Amy listens as Cara tells the story of how Jim "needed" Cara's love in the last year when Amy suffered from post-traumatic stress after losing her baby, how Cara carried her baby to term but hoped Jim would claim the boy as his own. And then, the coup de grâce: Cara suggests that with Amy's encouragement, Jim might agree to raise the baby with Amy as their own child—a replacement child for the one who died.

Amy is understandably flabbergasted. "To lose the child of her own flesh, for whom she had all but given her life, only to have another woman's bastard dropped into her lap! (No word could be too harsh, too plain for such a situation; she wanted to fling them like stones!)"[4] Amy confronts Jim, who insinuates Cara is trying to blackmail him. Only after being presented with Amy's evidence does he concede the baby might be his, though he alternatively suggests the father was someone else.

Amy confronts Jim: "'Jim, for shame!' blazed his wife. 'Are you men all alike, I wonder—to ring in that ancient, lying, cowardly excuse!" Amy logically goes through the alternatives she sees: divorce Jim so he can marry Cara, provide Cara with a financial settlement, or adopt the baby as their own. Jim refuses any of Amy's "solutions" and digs in, insisting, "Nobody on earth can *prove* it's my child!"

Dumbfounded, Amy stares "at the man she had loved and lived with—had staked her whole life upon, and never known at all." She accuses him of being cowardly; he tells her it's none of her business. In the end, "Jim had finally made up his mind to cast off the girl with her child and take whatever risks might lie in such a course. At the worst, these seemed to him preferable to open admission of wrongdoing." Amy tells him their marriage cannot continue because he will not take responsibility for his child. "And yet there are those who believe to this day that Amy parted from her husband because he took a mistress."[5]

Clearly there are parallels to Elaine's own life. Sargent concludes that *Hundred Maples* is ultimately "a self-serving document."[6] Ruth Ann Alexander understatedly suggests, "Men do not come off very well in the novel, perhaps because Eastman was speaking for herself as well as Amy. She was less troubled by her husband's sexual peccadillos, if any, than by his failure to live up to her ideal of selfless devotion to children and the family."[7] Even the title Elaine gave to the section of the novel in which she tells the sordid tale of Jim and Cara's out-of-wedlock baby, "A Hollow Shell," seems to suggest how Elaine may have felt about the parallel situation in her own life. But because there is always danger of reading too much autobiographical intent into an author's work of fiction, what do Elaine's own *nonfiction* words on the topic reveal?

In the few primary sources existing on this topic—Elaine's letters—Elaine is crystal clear it was Charles's refusal to accept responsibility for Bonno that became the source of her resolve to end the marriage. "Our final parting was on the sole issue of an honest recognition of the truth, and his assent to my wish that we do what was in our power for his illegitimate child. I was ready to make any sacrifice to that end and made that plain to him repeatedly,"[8] she wrote to Rose.

And in an extremely revealing pair of letters to Katharine Martindale, Elaine insisted she wanted what was best for Henrietta and Bonno and had made this clear to both Henrietta and Charles. Elaine explained she traveled to Chicago to meet with Henrietta, and at that time she read to her exchanges between Charles and herself (letters she clearly subsequently destroyed). Henrietta purportedly told Elaine she had seen Charles on several occasions, that "they had been repeatedly intimate"; she later told Elaine she thought her idea of divorcing Charles so he could marry Henrietta "preposterous and wonders at my presumption in 'trying to pick out a wife for another person.'"

Elaine told Katharine she'd conveyed all of this to Charles. His responses clearly became the model for what Elaine would later novelize, but the truth was even stranger than the fiction she would write. "He, on his part, called her a 'miserable blackmailer,' declared that she had come to his hotel room one night when he was ill, and had also been drinking, so that he was not in a condition to realize or recollect what occurred. He said he doubted there had been any connection and believed she had picked up an Indian baby to foist upon him as his own." After this exchange, Elaine stated Charles told her he would only continue to live with her if she accepted his story and did not listen further to Henrietta's. "I could not do this. Accordingly, he left me and our children and we have not seen him since."

Elaine concluded this lengthy letter by writing, "I have made no secret of the facts leading to the break-up of my home, after thirty years of married life." She wanted to hear from Katharine about what the family had been told of Henrietta's situation.[9]

A month later Elaine responded to a letter she had received from Katharine in which Katharine apparently suggested the situation concerned only Henrietta and Elaine. "On the contrary," Elaine insisted, "I feel that it chiefly concerns her nearest relatives. You and I, strangers to one another personally, are innocently and deeply involved in the same misfortune." Elaine felt strongly that Henrietta's family needed to be engaged, because it was clear to her Henrietta was in no state to care for Bonno herself. "That poor child is much on my mind. What is to become of her? If you can assure me that she will be provided for, and that Henrietta has enough to live on, it will be a relief."[10]

There were no further exchanges between Elaine and Katharine, and any correspondence Elaine had with Henrietta she did not preserve. But she was also unable to exorcise this chapter from her consciousness no matter how much she insisted she'd been the one taking the higher moral ground.

Elaine harbored ill feeling toward Charles for the rest of her life. In one small but revealing example, she inscribed a copy of her book *Little Brother O' Dreams* for an admirer in 1924, signing it "Elaine Goodale E."

Sometime in the late 1920s she wrote bitterly to Rose about speaking with a woman who had recently lost her husband: "I used to think to lose one's husband, by death, the most terrible thing," she lamented, "but now that I know how much worse it can be, I sometimes feel like congratulating a widow. If she can truly mourn, she is fortunate—and if not—she is fortunate to have a finis to a sad chapter."[11]

* * *

Perhaps because she did not have closure on that sad chapter, and certainly because she needed a source of income, Elaine again ramped up her writing. Her letters to Rose from the early 1920s on reveal that her motivation to pivot from focusing on Charles's career to concentrating on her own was only partially because she needed to generate money; they also reveal many of the ways in which she critiqued her own writing process and her discontent with most of her products.

In about 1933 Elaine explained to Rose that she was starting to write simple stories for popular magazines. "There are other things I should prefer to work at, but am very badly in need of an income. I simply can't afford much-needed clothes—barely manage postage and stationery" In another letter she enlarged on this: "Unless I can earn quite a bit myself by my writing, I guess I had best go on living with my children where I am very comfortable and fairly happy, and also quite useful, and really miss nothing except the fun of keeping house in my own way."[12]

Of these "pot-boiler" stories, perhaps the most remarkable was "Reward of Merit," a 1933 richly illustrated publication. The story revolves around fifteen-year-old Lois Martin, the bright daughter of freed slaves who aspires to become educated. She finds a new school for girls is to be opened by Miss Patience Cranford,[13] a Quaker who believes in equal education regardless of race. Miss Cranford sees Lois's potential and promises to teach her despite local townspeople's opposition. Though the Black characters speak in dialect and often refer to themselves disparagingly in this story in ways that would today be labeled racist ("We knows you-all means it for the best and we's grateful," says Lois's "mammy" when trying to convince Miss Patience to give up on the school amid local protest), ultimately Patience moves her school to a more congenial location so she can fulfill her promise to the girl. Lois pays it forward by becoming a teacher, going to the South and opening the People's School for Black Children. She teaches her first classes beneath a live oak—not unlike the Emancipation Oak under which Mary Peake held classes for freed Blacks on the grounds of what would become the Hampton Institute. The Editor's Note on this story states it was written and published "with the intent of indicating the contribution of different periods and sections of our country to the fuller enlightenment of the American Negro."[14] In her own way, Elaine was trying to stay relevant in a rapidly changing world.

Elaine continued to publish poetry in newspapers, even re-releasing her well-known "Ashes of Roses" in 1937 to earn additional money. She was encouraged to do this because the prior year she'd been awarded a $50 prize from the Bookfellows, a Chicago-based literary society. "The high light [sic] of my Christmas has been the letter and check from the Bookfellows—so thrillingly unexpected, and the first literary prize I ever won!"[15] she wrote.

Elaine tried her hand at writing plays, including the Indian-themed "The Earth Mother," "The Ghost Wife," and "Trail Makers," but none of them were ever sold or produced. She wrote hundreds of book reviews published in newspapers, for which she received extremely modest compensation. In the 1940s she edited and published a series of articles Charles had written over the course of his life and sold them to several papers.

Elaine also published two novels during her post-Charles writing renaissance: *The Luck of Oldacres* in 1928 and the aforementioned *Hundred Maples* in 1935. *Hundred Maples* was reviewed in the *New York Times,* reviewer Anita Moffett noting some of the book's feminist underpinnings. Elaine dedicated the novel to Ohi, writing, "To my son: for his better understanding of a woman's world." In a contemporary assessment, literary scholar Sarah Ruffing Robbins observes that *Hundred Maples* "reflects Goodale Eastman's desire to reclaim the artistic prominence she had achieved in youth" and suggests the novel rightly belongs in a "new modernist" genre of women's literature in the early part of the twentieth century.[16]

If her own life inspired some of the story in *Hundred Maples,* it may also have served as the model for elements of *The Luck of Oldacres.* Oldacres, a 125-acre homestead, is home to the five Bell children and their mother; their father was killed in an accident someplace in the West. The family suffers financially until fifteen-year-old Lorna has the idea of turning the farm into a summer camp, at which the entire family works, raising sufficient money to keep them afloat. "This is a book to stimulate the imagination of twelve to fifteen-year-olds toward healthful vacation activities," noted a reviewer in the *Reading* (PA) *Times.*[17] It was also a book in which the author's imagination turned a family-run summer camp into functional and wholesome vacation activities, envisioning a happier ending than the real-life story.

Perhaps her greatest critical success during the final three decades of her life came with her biography of Richard Henry Pratt. Entitled *Pratt, The Red Man's Moses,* this laudatory book was published in 1935, capping off a year of tremendous literary output for Elaine. In a letter to Rose, Elaine stated, "I certainly did no other book in the least like it."[18] Elaine's reflection was correct on many levels: this book *was* unlike any other she'd published. It was a

FIGURE 11.1. Elaine Goodale Eastman, undated photo, originally published in Sargent, 2005. AI Upscaler used to enhance resolution.

biography published by a university press, and perhaps more widely reviewed than any book she had written since *Apple Blossoms*.

It was also unlike any book she'd previously written because she'd known her subject and not always agreed with him. It was a suspicious General Pratt who had questioned the young Elaine Goodale about her presence when he was part of a delegation trying to procure Sioux signatures for a land deal that would further subdivide the Great Sioux Reservation. And it was a manipulative General Pratt who had brought Elaine and Charles to his Carlisle Indian School but not paid them well enough to keep them there, Pratt who believed in military-style education and boarding schools, and Pratt who espoused such a paternalistic view of Native Americans he feared having a school with both Blacks and Indians (like the Hampton Institute) would only delay successful assimilation—views with which Elaine thoroughly disagreed. But Elaine's 1935 view of Pratt significantly differed from her prior views.

As historian Gretchen Cassel Eick incisively points out, while telling the story of General Pratt's life, Elaine inserted her own views: "She did not identify when she was giving her personal views, but her voice was present throughout *Pratt*." Her sympathetic take on Pratt's life and policy views allowed Elaine to comment on decades of U.S.-Indian policy. Writes Eick, "The persistent presence of her voice makes this text an important resource for understanding how she experienced Indian policy over her lifetime."[19]

Among the many reviews of this book in newspapers across the country, views ranged from "historically correct but stodgy biography of the founder of the Carlisle Indian School" to "*Pratt* is a credit to the University of Oklahoma Press, and, in its literary excellence, and in the intense interest of the story it tells, Mrs. Eastman's historic monograph must rank as one of the most important." A reviewer in *the Kansas City* (MO) *Times* concluded his review in a way Elaine must have found most gratifying: "The life story of such a man as Richard Henry Pratt, the author says, is more than a chronicle of events—more than a portrait of an individual—more, even, than a record of achievement. Inevitably, it becomes the biography of an idea, the history of a cause."[20] And in a piece of fan mail so meaningful for Elaine she preserved it, Matilda Barker, the county superintendent of schools in Todd County, South Dakota, wrote,

"I hope to be able to get many more sales for your book. I wish everyone out here could read it."[21]

It's possible the success of using biography as a vehicle for the rearticulation of her assimilationist views about Indian education and policy—views that were falling out of favor among educators, reformers, and policymakers in the 1930s—led Elaine to pursue the idea of trying to do this again. After *Pratt*, she began researching and writing about the life of author/poet Helen Hunt Jackson. Elaine was extremely familiar with Jackson's two seminal books on Indian issues. Elaine's brief manuscript—it is just fifty-nine pages—traces Jackson's life from her girlhood through her untimely death at age fifty-five. Aspects of Jackson's life resonated with Elaine: her early career as a poet, an Amherst connection, the tremendous pain Jackson suffered after the tragic deaths of her children, her interest in Indians, and use of both nonfiction and fiction to communicate with the Euro-American reading public about the limitations and flaws of U.S.-Indian policy. But Elaine never developed this manuscript, and she never attempted to get it published. In 1938 she explained to Rose, "I wrote a good deal more fully on Helen Hunt, but was not successful in securing serial publication. . . . The biographer I told you [about] expects to have her book brought out by a New York firm in the spring, and I decided to wait and see it before making any effort to do a book on the same subject."[22]

But another extremely significant aspect of Elaine's biography of General Pratt was her use of parts of it to critique the policies of John Collier, commissioner of Indian Affairs from 1933 to 1945, and explain how Pratt's views—and her own—differed significantly from Collier's. The book was an opening salvo in the war of words Elaine would commence with the commissioner. This verbal battle was important not only for its public nature, but because it clearly illustrated Elaine's obdurate refusal to alter her thinking in changing times.

In a way, it was strange Elaine would choose to pick a fight with John Collier. Like her, Collier believed in the importance of education for Indians; moreover, he was a strong supporter of day schools and did not believe in boarding schools, something for which Elaine spent years advocating. And Collier, like Elaine, also believed elements of Indian culture were not only valid but significant. Had the two of them ever met and spoken, they probably would have found even more common ground, including the importance each placed on writing, beliefs about the role of the arts in promulgating culture, and an acceptance of interracial marriage. But rather than recognizing these fundamental similarities of belief, Elaine tended to focus on her differences with John Collier.

Collier, born in 1884 (the year after Elaine began teaching at the Hampton Institute) and educated at Columbia University, believed life in the early twentieth century had become too mechanized, too individualistic, and too anti-community. He was interested in the possibilities of applying social philosophy to government and policy. For a dozen years after graduating from college, Collier worked with an organization called the People's Institute, developing programs for immigrant communities that celebrated their cultures and helped to raise political awareness. From this work, he gained a deep appreciation for and belief in the efficacy and importance of cultural pluralism.[23]

In the early 1920s he traveled to New Mexico, where Mabel Dodge Luhan, a white artist and writer married to a Tiwa Indian, introduced him to the world of Pueblo Indians. Collier was entranced by the Native cultures he saw. The Pueblo Indians had created the kind of community this idealistic young man dreamed of, one integrating the needs of individuals with the needs of the group, managing to maintain traditional values within a march toward modernity. To Collier, this was a "Red Atlantis," an ideal and a theme to which he returned throughout his life. "It is easy at the remove of nearly a century to scoff at the image of a New York social worker falling in love with Indians in the winter chill of a Taos ceremony," stated historian Frederick Hoxie in testimony before Congress in 2011. "Few took Collier seriously. Over the next decade, both the growth of popular interest in Native American culture and the growing sense that authoritarian efforts to eradicate Indian lifeways were both unfair and doomed to fail, moved popular opinion in Collier's direction."[24]

Like Elaine, John Collier came to national prominence on issues of Indian culture and policy through his writing, publishing numerous articles in popular magazines and national papers. Collier's early publications about Native American issues brought him to the attention of the General Federation of Women's Clubs, an organization also interested in Indian affairs, and the federation appointed him as its research agent. Based on Collier's assessments, the organization took positions opposing the U.S. government's assimilation policies. Collier subsequently formed the American Indian Defense Organization in 1923, which lobbied for religious freedom for Indians and new policies regarding land ownership and stewardship.

Influenced by his own observations, conversations with some Native activists and environmentalists, and the ideas of several anthropologists, Collier became convinced U.S. Indian policy had been entirely misguided with its focus on assimilation and "Americanization" rather than cultural pluralism. He concluded that the Dawes Act with its allotment policies was the root of a dysfunctional system that enabled corrupt and inequitable land distribution, resulted in cultural destruction, and was rife with unethical individuals charged with administering bad policies to people they did not understand. Like Elaine, Collier used his facility with writing to help get his views known. By the late 1920s, his work helped to get Congress to commission a study of the overall conditions of Native Americans. Published in 1928, the massive Meriam Report—more than eight hundred pages long—issued an extensive set of recommendations for remedying many of the deficiencies the team of experts unearthed. The Meriam Report led President Herbert Hoover to allocate additional funding for Indian issues and to reorganize the offices tasked with implementing policies. By 1933, then President Franklin D. Roosevelt made the bold move of installing John Collier—seen by many career politicians as misguided and annoying but viewed by many social reformers and some Indian groups as visionary—as commissioner of Indian Affairs.

Collier immediately set out to right many of the wrongs identified in the Meriam Report. Notably, he was able to replace the Dawes Act with the Indian Reorganization Act (also called the Wheeler-Howard Act) of 1934, which formally ended the policy of land allotment; recognized tribal governments and allowed them to incorporate land trusts in a communal rather than individual manner; and gave Indians the right to manage their land and mineral rights. Collier also implemented an Indian division of the Civilian Conservation Corps, providing Native American men with jobs building schools, improving roads, and working to remedy the deforestation of Native lands.

He advocated for the "Indian New Deal," which included the Indian Reorganization Act and policies meant to strengthen tribal cultures, improve education, build economic self-sufficiency, foster local governance among tribes, and reverse the effects of years of assimilationist policies. "The new law," Hoxie concludes, "marked a brave decision to turn away from paternalism and to embrace a new federal policy based on mutual respect and faith in the future of American Indians as citizens of tribes and of the United States."[25]

Collier's philosophies and policies were, to say the least, controversial. Hoxie writes that Collier's achievements must be seen in the context of the rise of several Native activists who also worked tirelessly to create reforms. In contemporary times, as E. A. Schwartz points out, scholarship assessing the policies and impact of the Indian New Deal "has been ambivalent about John Collier," partially based on some of the contradictions within Collier's own writing, partially because of his idealistic interpretations of "Red Atlantis" and Indian culture, and partially because some of the policies he pushed through had the perhaps unintended effect of furthering bureaucracies.[26] But even in Collier's time, some tribal groups criticized a number of his ideas. Collier's plans also met resistance from Euro-American politicians, religious leaders, and erstwhile Indian reformers. One of those most opposed to many of Collier's proposals was Elaine Goodale Eastman.

Elaine's very public spat with Collier played out across the pages and letters to the editor of some of the most prestigious newspapers and periodicals in America—the *New York Times*, the *Christian Century*, and the *Atlantic Monthly*—as well as in letters to the editor she wrote to other regional publications.

Interestingly, at the beginning of Collier's ascent to the position of commissioner of Indian Affairs, Elaine seemed hopeful. In April 1933 she wrote to Rose, "I am delighted with the appointment of John Collier as Commissioner—have read his stuff with interest and even corresponded with him, for several years. A radical and a fighter!"[27] But her early optimism quickly gave way to severe disillusionment. Almost exactly a year later she was writing to Florence Bascom, referring to Collier's "Indian New Deal," "Am much disappointed in John Collier—he is developing some pretty wild theories but perhaps won't get far with them."[28] Only two months after she'd written to Rose of her optimism, she wrote a long letter to the *New York Times* blasting Collier's proposed policy shifts. Apart from disputing the numbers of Indians who lived in poverty in a report coming from the new commissioner's office, Elaine suggested Collier's belief that Indian people, regardless of their educational status or the percentage of Indian blood in their lineage, should be considered "Indian," would only perpetuate the bureaucracies of the Indian Bureau. "The commissioner's striking picture of a third of a million 'forgotten red men,' destitute, helpless and despairing, would seem, therefore, to be overdrawn," she wrote, adding that were these policies to be enacted, the Indian Bureau "now takes on a new lease of life, with command of millions annually of the taxpayers' money."[29]

Collier responded in kind. "Mrs. Elaine G. Eastman alleges, in effect, that there is no Indian problem but that, if the Indian problem should exist, the proper way to solve it would be to ignore it," he wrote. He went on disputing everything from Elaine's figures about Indian per capita income ("I do not know the source of her statistics"), to her suggestion that the Ghost Dance religion was in part responsible for what happened at Wounded Knee ("the ghost dances were as much responsible for the outbreak of that 'war' as the singing of 'The Star Spangled Banner' was responsible for our entry into the World War"). And he argued that educational policies, such as those advanced by General Pratt (whose biography Elaine was working on at the time), were "with all [their] cruelties and horrors, the system of placing with reservation superintendents' orders for certain numbers of Indian children to be delivered" to boarding schools, removed from their families, and forced to speak English, policies that were "a tragic failure."[30]

After this exchange, any gloves that might have been in their exchanges were truly off.

In 1934 Elaine published a piece in the *Christian Century* entitled, "Does Uncle Sam Foster Paganism?" In the article, she refers to Collier as the "radical new commissioner of Indian Affairs" and takes him to task for his policies aimed at allowing Native groups to practice their own religions. "Such practices . . . while not actually prohibited by the authorities, were not in my day encouraged or thought compatible with modern folkways, not to say with Christian ideals," she wrote. She suggested Collier's policies would have Indians "revert to primitive concepts," creating "bastard religions" or attacking missionaries' work.[31]

Collier's reply (published in the same issue), suggested, "Mrs. Eastman believes the earlier policy to be the only right one." He added that the educational, religious, and land policies made by the U.S. government had all been wrongly focused on assimilation to white Euro-American norms. "The government never admitted the issue of religious liberty into the debate at all. Indian religions were treated as being simply a part of the tribal and cultural complex which it was the government's business to destroy." He disputed many of Elaine's "facts," saying her "errors are important because typical" (though whether he meant typical of her, or typical of the general population, was not clear).

And importantly, he wrote that Elaine's reference to the "Ghost Dance revival" as an escapist phenomenon among the Sioux was wrong: Collier stated it was a religious movement, akin to "the origins of Christianity, with imperfect discernment. . . . I might add that the Wounded Knee massacre of 1890, which Mrs. Eastman refers to, was not a product of 'a demoralized attitude on the part of our frontier population.' It was a massacre by the army."[32] As someone who had been at Wounded Knee and witnessed the tragedy of the massacre, Elaine must have been especially stung by Collier's words here.

Her concerns about Collier's policies extended to her belief they would only increase the need for governmental oversight and intervention, not lessen it. She reached out to Gertrude Bonnin (Zitkála-Sá) and received a response that hardened her own trepidation. "While attending the House Committee Hearings, where certain members of a newly organized American Indian Federation are making complaints against Commissioner Collier . . . we have sat back silently. Their story is not new. It is the same old story of Indians suffering under the Bureau. The only startling thing perhaps . . . is the change in John Collier—once a rampant agitator condemning the atrocities of Bureaucracy; now that he is Head of the Bureau, he himself is a Bureaucrat! A man has to be an acrobat to change his coat so quickly between Acts. From Friend to Foe."[33]

The debates between Elaine and John Collier stretched out for almost a decade. In 1942, Collier published an article in the *Atlantic Monthly* entitled, "Indians Come Alive!" This lengthy article is an extraordinary attempt by Collier to encapsulate years of his thought about Indian policy and culture, providing a sweeping assessment of many tribal cultures throughout the Americas, seeking commonalities among them regarding what he termed "positive democracies." Collier explained that while different groups displayed varied "situational forms" of democracy, what bound them together was a shared belief about the connection between land and community, a belief disrupted and exploited by Euro-Americans. He concluded with a plea for Indians to be revested with their land, to have a voice in policies being crafted for them, and to work internationally so services could be coordinated and monies pooled to help Indigenous groups.[34]

Elaine had to respond. "John Collier's fellow enthusiasts for 'the magical and animistic world-view' doubtless enjoyed his eloquent panegyric," she wrote. "Thoughtful readers, however, are bound to question its relevance to present-day fact." That thoughtful reader disputed everything from Collier's assessment of the number of the American Indian population because he included "persons of mixed heredity," to his negative assessments of nineteenth-century reform policies, to his fears an assimilationist education would break up Indian heritage. Rather, Elaine stated, such an education was aimed "in all kindness, for the future that inevitably awaited them. Knowing that a natural development along strictly racial lines was forever inhibited, we gave them a more intelligent and more satisfying religion, along with the latest fruits of science. They were welcome to keep as much as they chose from the past, or as much as could be harmoniously integrated with the new." With no seeming awareness of how discordant and paternalistically infantilizing her words might have come off, she suggested, "The truth is that Mr. Collier's mystical theories are out of harmony with the deepest desires and aspirations of the contemporary young man or woman possessed of one or more aboriginal ancestors. These normal young folks are plain American citizens, and wish to be treated as such. . . . The position of an artificially protected, patronized, and isolated racial minority is hardly tolerable to their self-resect, and it is one which the developments of the past fifty years have clearly shown to be unnecessary." And significantly, she listed her name as "Mrs. Charles A. Eastman," a title she had not used for many years.[35]

In a final reply to this colloquy, Collier wrote, "Mrs. Eastman's commentary . . . is valuable because it represents a whole lapsed century of world-view—a Caucasian presumption about non-Caucasian races. . . . The successful Indian, Mrs. Eastman earnestly believes, is the de-Indianized one; the good Indian is the Indian culturally dead. A crumb of participation in Caucasian superiority is better than a whole loaf of native inferiority. And it's 'all or nothing' in Mrs. Eastman's type of thinking."[36]

Was it just policy differences driving these printed jousts between Elaine and John Collier? There were probably several ways in which these debates weren't "just" about policy, at least not for Elaine. For many years she prided herself on her knowledge of Indian policy, custom, and culture. She wanted to think of herself as she had been thought of in her younger days: an authority on a subject to which she'd dedicated her professional—and personal—life. To be called out as irrelevant and an artifact of the past must have felt hurtful and condescending. While there was some nuance to her thinking, there often wasn't a lot; that John Collier accused her of overgeneralizing and simplifying complex issues no doubt raised her hackles.

But at the heart of this debate, Elaine still firmly believed in the importance of assimilation. While she did accept the validity of many elements of Native American culture, she also thought the best ways to preserve these elements—as well as to protect Native Americans from abuses of governmental oversight—was to have Indians who were well-educated, well-integrated, and Christian. She never viewed this as taking on a paternalistic attitude, even if others increasingly did.

John Collier's insistence that mixed-race people could—and should—"count" as Indian also ran against Elaine's own beliefs. Certainly, she thought of her own children as primarily white, listed them on the U.S. Census as such, and, especially in the wake of her separation from Charles, sought to distance her children from their father as much as possible. Collier's public agenda no doubt compromised her private one.

Finally, Charles Eastman and John Collier, who had met as part of the Committee of One Hundred in December 1923, shared many philosophies and attitudes about Native American issues. Both were staunch believers in Indian citizenship, staunch advocates for better Indian health-care systems, for the revocation of the Dawes Act, and for more educational opportunities for Indians. Both saw a long history of breached treaties, promises broken, and corrupt Euro-American dealings with Native Americans. Both believed Euro-Americans had a lot to learn from Indigenous people, and that while Native people might acculturate to Euro-American ways, they would not assimilate. Perhaps on some level Elaine realized Collier's point of view was far more closely aligned with Charles's than with her own. After all she had been through with Charles, reminders of him, his beliefs, the issues he stood for, and the ways in which these differences separated them were almost always painful reminders of promises she felt gone awry.

* * *

If in the first few decades of the twentieth century Elaine's views about Native American policy were out of step with current thinking and trending more conservative, it wasn't only her attitudes on this topic that tilted ever rightward.

The 1930s are often referred to as part of the "Golden Age of Hollywood," a decade that saw advances in sound in film, the introduction of color, and many new filmic techniques. As the United States climbed out of the Great Depression era, increasing numbers of Americans spent their leisure time—and dollars—going to the movies. With greater competition between them, studios produced more varied genres (including Westerns, horror, and animated films) designed to attract moviegoers, which in turn led to concerns among political, religious, and parental groups about the content of films and their possible effects on young moviegoers. By the late 1920s, women's organizations and representatives of religious organizations began to demand more governmental control over film content. The first set of academic studies conducted to ascertain whether films had deleterious effects on children, the Payne Fund Studies, explored a range of questions ranging from how deeply films affect children emotionally to whether movies encouraged children to become juvenile delinquents. Though today the methodologies of these studies are considered subpar, when they were first published in the early 1930s they gave ammunition to those who called for change in Hollywood. Under the threat of government censorship, the movie industry created its own production code, the premise of which was that films should not "lower the moral standards of those who see them."

Elaine Eastman believed it was important to censor content she felt "indecent, unmoral and anti-social" because she also believed film had the capability of unduly affecting the emotions of younger viewers. Elaine, who had become a member of her local Daughters of the American Revolution (DAR) chapter and a member of the Northampton Motion Picture Council, typically chose to use her skill with words to try to advance this cause. "Thoughtful people have long maintained that the movies . . . are not so much immoral as untrue, possibly forgetting that this conspicuous untruth to life is in itself an insidious form of immorality," she wrote in 1933. "Even the criminals are untrue to life, appearing, as it were, ready-made, with a deceptively jaunty air. Their realism . . . is a pseudo-realism only. The true causes of crime are almost never shown."[37] Elaine wrote that because consequences of crime weren't written into movie scripts, films could contribute to "high delinquency" rates in children who viewed them (a theory later roundly debunked), and she therefore called for greater censorship of the industry. She suggested, incorrectly, that new research provided unambiguous "proof" of the ways in which films "featuring sex and crime . . . mold the manners and morals of the rising generation."[38]

The topic of film censorship was already starting to fall out of favor, at least for a time, by the mid-1930s, yet as she had with other issues she cared about, Elaine tenaciously clung to her own perspective. She wrote to Rose that although movies were improving from "an artistic and technical standpoint," she simply didn't go to see them often enough to be a good judge. But this didn't stop her from judging: "Our complaint is of the content and general atmosphere of the films,"[39] she wrote.

Elaine's conservative, somewhat prudish views extended to her attitudes about sex and birth control. In 1930s America, legal decisions made contraceptives more widely available, and the merging of two major organizations advocating for contraceptive choices (the organization later renamed Planned Parenthood) meant this once-taboo topic was more widely discussed in the popular press. Elaine Goodale Eastman felt compelled to insert herself into the public conversation. While she privately acknowledged the idea of birth control might be appealing ("having faced it personally, I ought to know!" she wrote to Rose), she believed if the use of "artificial contraceptives" were to be legalized, "the result will be not only an excess of 'race suicide' where it is least desired and desirable, but a very great increase of sexual laxity, and not only these, but a most demoralizing let-down in our whole attitude toward the marital relation."[40]

Similarly, she deplored explicit language in literature, writing of the novel *The History of Rome Hanks and Kindred Matters* by Joseph Stanley Pennell that she could not read it "for disgust at the incredible grossness—unprintable we would have said a few years ago."[41] Because she was an avid reader well into her eighties, Elaine frequently found aspects of modern literature disconcerting and let her views be known in her letters and in the many book reviews she published. Times had moved on, but Elaine Goodale Eastman had not.

* * *

After Elaine and Charles separated in 1921, Elaine had no real home of her own. She spent some time living in New Hampshire and ran Camp Oáhe until the mid-1920s. Charles's departure caused many changes at Oáhe, perhaps best exemplified by a brochure advertising the 1924 camping season. No longer were the Indian-themed activities hyped; arts and crafts no longer emphasized Indian beadwork or basketry but rather that "our teachers develop original ideas and encourage self-expression"; archery was still offered, but so were tennis, basketball, and many other sports. Charles's name did not appear anywhere on the brochure.[42] Elaine put the camp on the market in 1925 but couldn't sell it until 1928.

Apart from a few months in 1926 when she went to Seattle and lived with Ohi, thinking she might make a fresh start on the West Coast, between 1922 and 1952 Elaine lived in a series of apartments she rented in Northampton, sometimes with her oldest daughter, Dora Winona, at other times in a room in the Northampton homes of her daughters Eleanor Mensel or Virginia Whitbeck. She wrote to Rose often, about both the joys and the problems with these arrangements. Elaine bemoaned the lack of her own space: "I long for my own home and my own things around me," she sadly wrote in the late 1920s; "I still resent the fact that I never had a real home of my own and never shall have," she complained in 1936; "I hoped to keep [Lodestone] for a permanent home and still wish I could have managed it,"[43] she lamented in 1940.

Apart from pining for her own place, Elaine's final few decades were also plagued by the financial worries that had followed her throughout life. She scrimped and saved; made handmade crafts for her children, grandchildren, sisters, brother, nieces, and nephews for Christmas; and grumbled about her lack of funds to purchase necessities. She wrote as much as she could for income. She was agitated about Charles not sharing any royalties from his writing with her. "In common justice, half should have been allotted to me when we separated," she wrote Rose in 1937. "I asked for it. He agreed at first, then stalled for a long time, and finally refused."[44] Even Charles's death in 1939 didn't end her distain over how he handled royalties: "Having been always his working partner as well as wife, and especially because a large part of his living for the past 17 years had been by right mine—my own earned income in royalties—I felt and still feel that beyond question I should by rights have whatever he left."[45] But, as Elaine noted in a letter to her long-time friend Florence Bascom, Charles died intestate, and she was extremely annoyed she had to spend the money on an attorney to try to recover any royalty money that might come after his death.[46]

Living with her daughters was a mixed blessing. She enjoyed feeling useful, helping with cooking, gardening, or childcare, and she clearly enjoyed being a part of her daughters' and her grandchildren's lives, even if she did not always approve of everything they did or how they did it. She was extremely fond of her sons-in-law Ernst Mensel and Sterling Whitbeck, depended on them, and often sang their praises to Rose, sometimes contrasting the ways in which they treated their wives with how she had been treated by her husband. She frequently expressed concerns about the health of those with whom she lived; she particularly worried about Dora Winona, who never married, had a series of serious illnesses and physical maladies, and had trouble finding her true calling in life. Elaine summarized some of these concerns in a letter: "Anyone who saw with what difficulty and distress she now contrives to get through the mere mechanics of living—getting up in the morning, getting into her clothes, etc. and how she dreads and postponed indefinitely every bit of extra effort—as a telephone call or a note or a simple errand—would know it out of the question for her to fill any position calling for responsibility."[47]

Tragedy seemed never too removed from Elaine and her large family, punctuating her final decades with frightening regularity. Elaine's youngest daughter, Florence, married Earle Prentiss in 1928, another match of which Elaine did not approve. Nine months later they had a son, Robert. In 1930 Florence was pregnant again; Elaine wrote to her sister Dora of her surprise about Florence "expecting." But in the final days of December, Florence miscarried and fell ill; Elaine stayed with her youngest child around the clock. Florence died right before the new year. "We were all gathered around her bed," Elaine wrote to Rose, "in a breath of silence, rather . . . all eyes on the poor child for . . . her last painful breaths," adding, inexplicably, "Florence never meant to me all that Irene did." Elaine worried about what would become of her grandson Bobby without his mother and spent much time with the boy. She wrote to Rose, "There was not one of my six children to whom I gave more of myself—I taught her, shared a bedroom with her, went everywhere with her for years—yet—although she clung to me in a way, there was always something remote about her. And never more so than when she lay dying. She was entirely conscious, yet it was if no one was present."[48]

When Ohi married Marion Nutting in 1936, Elaine wasn't happy, and she did not attend the wedding. Suspicious of Marion, Elaine wrote to Rose in 1937, "I have been told nothing of the circumstances [of Marion's divorce from her first husband] so am letting that rest for the present. If I ever see her I shall tell her frankly about my own matrimonial experience and hope she may respond with her own confidence."[49] Though Elaine did visit Ohi and Marion in Detroit on at least one occasion, it's not known whether she ever had that conversation, and the climate of their relationship remained chilly, at best; in fact, in 1954, when Marion wrote to Rose, with whom she maintained a warm correspondence, she referred to Elaine as "Mrs. Eastman."[50] Elaine frequently reported to Rose her concerns about Ohi: he had to pick up the pieces of his father's life, he was unhappy in his job, and she just wasn't sure about Marion. At some point Elaine was surprised to learn that Ohi had a serious heart condition. He kept his condition a secret from almost everyone, working despite being told not to, and died in January 1940. Elaine was devastated. Shortly after Ohi's death she wrote to Rose, "Yes, he had some happy days in boyhood, but I feel his years in Detroit were anything but happy ones. . . . I wish he had not married and that I could have been with him up to the end." Elaine seemed to hold Ohi's death against Marion: "[She] seems trying to ignore the fact that he had been gravely ill for months, with no prospect held out for a cure (which she knew, of course . . .) but writes as if he were suddenly snatched away while well and happy." She suggested had he not married, perhaps he would not have met his fate as he did: "We will never know—but there are times when it seems too much to bear—the tie with my son was very close, in some ways nearer than with any of the girls. It seemed he understood me better than any of them, except Irene."[51]

Elaine had outlived three of her six children. To have gone through this once was tragic; twice was horrendous; three times, an almost unbearable and unimaginable grief. She wrote to George Seymour about how much she admired a poem he had written about death and how his words touched her: "A few weeks ago I lost my only son—and it is very hard to survive one's children."[52] Just how hard it was might be divined from the final verse of the final poem in Elaine's final compilation of poetry:

Still to be mindful of the dust
We spring from—the mute, patient cold
Whose speech we are—whose motion, breath,
Last hold on sense, surcease from death;

To raise up buried dreams, abate
Old longings dumbly passionate—
This be our heritage and trust![53]

* * *

Elaine's last years were also filled by revisiting issues she had never resolved. Again and again in her letters to Rose, Elaine returned to well-honed themes—never, it seemed, developing any deeper understanding of the internecine tensions between herself and her siblings, never remolding the ways in which she'd cast her relationships with her parents, never recognizing that for all she knew about child development there were many ways in which she never understood the development of her own children. She never seemed to find closure around so many of the issues that troubled her for years; she never found peace in her thoughts about Charles. And, to the last of her days, Elaine was never able to reconcile how she felt about what she considered to be the unrealized potential of her life.

Elaine's relationship with her brother Robert had never been particularly strong. She left home when he was only five years old, so no real childhood bonding occurred. Elaine knew that Robert disapproved of her marriage to Charles; Theodore Sargent writes that even when the Eastmans first moved to Amherst in 1903, Robert still harbored resentment and refused to allow Charles to visit at Lodestone where Robert was then living.[54] Elaine, in turn, thoroughly disapproved of Robert's marriage to Helen, perhaps unwittingly echoing the anti-Catholic prejudices evinced by her mother toward this marriage. She was neither surprised nor upset when Robert and Helen separated. Elaine wrote to Rose of her disappointment Robert wasn't a better uncle to her children, of her frustrations about how he handled the Lodestone property, and of her belief that their brother would be "instantly antagonized by open advice." She often noted negative attributes she thought common to Robert and Charles, especially regarding their "off-hand, rather abrupt manner . . . careless of little courtesies," though she noted her brother, at least, had "his heart in the right place."[55]

Elaine disputed Rose's contention that her relationship with their brother had been precipitated by Elaine; she insisted "there must be either some accidental misunderstanding, perhaps brought about partly by a third person, or else a total inability to understand one another, and I have always felt that I DID pretty well understand and appreciate him. . . . I could easily love him as dearly as I do you and Dora." In 1947 Robert reached out to his big sister and congratulated her on "your wonderfully interesting, varied, creative, adventurous, useful and unselfish life. I do regret—and very keenly regret—that I have had so little opportunity to know and understand it."[56] If Elaine replied to this outreach, there is no record of it.

Similarly, Elaine's long-running, if unspoken, competition with her sister Dora continued well into old age. In letters to Rose over the final three decades of her life, Elaine complained about everything from Dora's lack of reading anything Elaine considered meaningful, to Dora's suggestion to Rose—conveyed to Elaine—that she took more pleasure in the outdoors than Elaine did, to Dora's spelling the world "desert" with a capital D. Often using Rose as the intermediary to pass along an article she'd written to Dora, or to convey a thought to Dora she simply did not want to convey herself, Elaine found ways to put more than the physical distance between herself and the sister who had eschewed life in New England for life in the South. Elaine continued to make excuses for why she could not visit Rose in Redding when Dora visited from Tennessee. When Dora traveled abroad and wrote letters to her sisters, Elaine complained to Rose that she, personally, would not "work as hard at sightseeing as she [Dora] evidently does" or that "her gift of sympathy doesn't seem to extend to the south Italians, to tourists or the wealthy!"[57] Elaine contrasted her own sense of social justice with Dora's, and found her sister's lacking. Though Dora had pursued lifelong careers in both teaching and writing, Elaine continued to draw a distinction between her own writing career and Dora's, even complaining once to Rose that Dora didn't write her letters in an interesting way.

Not surprisingly, Elaine's letters to Dora did not contain any of the same types of critiques or pointed questions. They are mostly chatty, newsy, and end in warm salutations one might not have expected given the ways in which Elaine spoke of Dora to Rose. But Dora was apparently not oblivious to these inconsistencies: she shared many of Elaine's letters with Rose, and on some of them, appended her own interpretations or snide comments about Elaine. In one letter, in which Elaine had remarked her correspondence with Rose was much the same in tone as her correspondence with Dora and positioned herself as often taking a side between her two younger sisters in sisterly disputes, Dora commented to Rose, "*Utterly* unlike in tone!" In Dora's letters to Rose she sometimes wrote disparaging things of Elaine, such as one letter in which she suggested Elaine's "likeness to Mother in her mental and temperamental reactions is really startling sometimes" and, in another, "Elaine . . . harps upon what appears to me like a truism, as if it were a discovery of her own!" And following a letter Elaine wrote to her in 1930, Dora commented on the back of the letter, sent on to Rose, "Aren't E's letters provoking and depressing? I don't believe she realizes how strong her . . . reaction is!"[58]

In some of her letters to Rose, Elaine pondered what accounted for the differences between herself and Dora given their extremely close childhood. "Reared as we were, under almost exactly the same conditions and influences in all respects," she wrote, she and Dora nonetheless had a "marked difference in our way of looking at life, or attacking life's problems." She concluded this "must be due to the accidental inheritance of a different combination of traits and tendencies, mental and physical." In another letter she insisted, "Despite our intimacy and close association, I have constantly a sense of aloofness and reserve on her part, which makes her sympathy one-sided and to that extent unsatisfactory. Never does she reciprocate my frankness or return my confidences." And in a third letter she unironically suggested, "[Dora] seems to have a strong sense of frustration in her personal life, and to delight in living vicariously in the lives of others . . . yet I have never known anyone with more unbreakable personal reserve! I don't claim to be a social success, but I do object to any intimation that I am cold, or indifferent, or uninterested in other people." In one of her more oblivious letters, Elaine recalled when she came back East after her summer of traveling around the Dakotas with the Sioux, "I recall vividly thinking . . . how flat I thought your life and Dora's and mother's seemed to me in comparison with my own struggle, both before and after marriage—and the secret of the joy I found in it seemed to me then, and still seems, the exchange of a self-centered existence for one focused on the idea of others' need. I think the happiest people [are those] whose motives are more outside themselves."[59] She clearly failed to see, from the perch of old age, how such sentiments—even if more inferred than stated directly—could possibly have fostered ill-feeling with her family members.

* * *

As Elaine grew older and more infirm, her letters to Rose contained not only bulletins about her health and what she felt she was or wasn't any longer able to do and her fears about no longer being able to take care of herself, but also some more philosophical thoughts about aging. Looking back on her life, she posited, "If I had had, just a little more self-assertion, enough to tip the scale when I weighed against my perhaps unduly intense and romantic ideal of marriage, I should doubtless have made more of my life as an individual, as it seems to me now I ought to have done. However, if my husband had not failed me with such overwhelming completeness, I dare say I should have been fairly well and content." Her bitterness toward Charles never receded: "Even though he would not admit it, he could not help knowing how much of his reputation and earning power he owed to his wife. What his son had done for him the last few years was little enough compared to what I had done surely."[60]

Sadly, her reflections on her relationships with her own children continued to make comparisons among them and expressed many raw feelings. Elaine consistently cast herself as the martyr of her marriage and the only one who did anything for their children. "I would not say this to anyone else," she wrote to Rose in 1938, "but the truth is that the only one of my six who was really, devotedly attentive and thoughtful for me was the one I lost twenty years ago." In another letter she wrote she believed she would have been happier in life had her other children been more like Irene, "the only really loving and demonstrative one in the family! In fact I think that one or two of them are cold by nature and extremely self-centered."[61]

And as she looked over her long life, Elaine often felt she had made decisions that left her unfulfilled, nostalgic for a life she never realized. "Unquestionably, many of us live in the past or future rather than in the present—I do myself—when young I tended to live in the future, and now, like most old folks, largely in the past. But I don't think I am inclined to see that thro' rose-colored glasses. Up to a year or two after my marriage, I was reasonably happy and content—full of enthusiasm and large plans. The years after were sort of an endurance test—as you know, I did not complain, but no one can deny that I had a pretty tough time!" She continued, "I lived in some THIRTY different houses in the first twenty years! Moving every few months often to another city, and for months at a time with next to no money coming in from any source and a baby every two years!! My married daughters seem to me amazingly fortunate in contrast—but perhaps they do not realize it."[62]

Elaine felt the need to explain and justify not only the decisions in her personal life, but in her professional one as well. She insisted to Rose her interest on becoming a teacher for Indian children and her writing and speaking on behalf of Indian causes came out of idealism. "It seemed to me that to devote one's life to a wronged and misunderstood and suffering people was a higher aim than any other I could conceive," she wrote in a letter sometime in the 1920s. "I had no doubt then, and haven't any now, that I could have earned much more and done far better for myself in every way in some other field—there was opportunity to work up to rather important things in Washington, or in the journalistic and literary field, which appealed to me so strongly and for which I had admitted gifts." And yet, she concluded, "The altruistic spirit and life is far more desirable than the opposite."[63]

But a few years later she sent Rose a truly sad commentary on her own life. "I do think it was something to get as far as I did without any formal education at ALL or the expenditure of a dollar by my parents," she wrote, "but whether it was wise to put everything I had into a husband who, though brilliant in some ways, proved to lack moral stability, and into six children, none of whom have shown marked energy or ability except the one who died earliest, that is another question!" She concluded, "I believe my life has been largely wasted, not so much from my personal point of view but from that of the community."[64]

* * *

After she turned seventy-nine, Elaine paid one final visit to the site of her childhood home. She'd visited several times, and upon each visit noted the ways in which nature was reclaiming Sky Farm. There was less and less of the cottage and outbuildings each time she visited, more and more of the forest and fields. The lilies, long recalled from childhood, continued to bloom amid the encroaching trees and weeds.

In 1912 Elaine published a story in *Country Life in America* called, "The Hand-Made House." The story recounts the fictional journey of a young man who, taking a joyride with some friends to the Berkshires, arrives by chance at the dilapidated site of his boyhood home. The young man resolves to purchase the property that meant so much to him, build upon the site a new house made of stone, find a wife, and live a simpler farming life. Published the year after Elaine moved to Lodestone—the stone house built by hand by her own sainted father—at a time when her own troubles (with finances, being a single parent while married, and worrying about the ways in which her own writing career had faltered) were writ large, it's clear her amalgam of where she was living and where she had lived were a proxy for the life she nostalgically (and perhaps unrealistically) looked back on. Perhaps the most poignant part of this short story is the description of an old cellar hole: "I am afraid I must own that no grave ever seemed quite so sad to me as that yawning cellar hole—that rain-beaten hearth. There is a finality about graves—here there was a singular appeal, as of life arrested in full flood, awaiting only the motive to go on again. And the patient, bowed heads of the apple-trees my father had planted, and the homely dooryard lilacs dear to his mother!"[65]

After her 1942 visit to the Sky Farm site, Elaine once again returned to the affecting, tender imagery in a poem she wrote, entitled, "The Old Cellar Hole":

> Heaped in a hollow the chimney stones lie—
> No wall save the forest no roof but the sky.
> Strangled by leafy arms, lost among briars,
> Mother, your lilacs light memory's fires.
>
> Where the first apples reddened and fell,
> Where the filled bucket rose cool from the well,

Father, your dream is still living and dear—
Shrine in the wilderness, heart's home is here![66]

* * *

Elaine had been clear: she did not believe in headstones. "I can't imagine it being any satisfaction," she wrote to Rose after Ohi died, about the possibility of visiting a cemetery plot. "I never go near the graves of my children or father, except Irene's which is a bit different to me since it is in the wilds and NOT in a graveyard but a spot I loved, and she did too."[67] Accordingly, when Elaine died on December 22, 1953, after living briefly in a nursing home, her ashes were scattered in the Spring Grove Cemetery in Northampton, in a plot owned by one of her sons-in-law. Her modest obituary in the local *Daily Hampshire Gazette* identified her principally in relation to her husband, her parents, her sisters and brother, and her surviving children; her accomplishments were recorded only as "an author of note," mentioning *Apple Blossoms* along with the books "published in collaboration with her husband," and indicating she'd been the first supervisor of Indian schools in the Dakota Territory. Ironically, like Charles, this woman, so well known in her own lifetime, seemingly disappeared from view.

12

Reading the Eastmans

Biographies tell stories of lives, and biographers try to tell them with clarity, but there are often gaps in the narrative and lingering questions. Sometimes the gaps come from a lack of sources, sometimes from elisions in materials. In the case of Charles Eastman, there is little documentary information other than his books, articles, and letters he wrote, and not much of this reflects his thoughts or emotions on personal matters. And in the case of Elaine Goodale Eastman, there are plenty of published materials in many genres, an extensive archive of her papers, as well as the treasure trove of letters she wrote to her sister Rose that enable a deeper sense of some of her innermost ideas. But Elaine curated the materials she donated, and these clear excisions from her life's record are both revealing and obfuscating.

It's fortunate both Eastmans were the focus of intensive press coverage during their lifetimes. The hundreds of articles, now retrievable from long-defunct newspapers, disclose a level of detail about their lives their own papers often do not and provide a window into how others perceived this unusual interracial couple; in so doing, revealing much about changing American attitudes toward race, gender, and Indigenous-white relations, among other topics.

Both Elaine and Charles Eastman have also been the topic of many articles in academic journals, the focus of numerous book chapters, the subjects of several biographical treatments. This wealth of secondary source material represents a range of viewpoints and interpretations, many of which have been quoted and synthesized in this book.

Despite the scrutiny both Elaine and Charles received in their era and in all the years since, numerous questions about their lives and legacies remain.

Attempting to engage the issues posed by their individual and collective professional work, trying to evaluate them holistically, and endeavoring to understand their relationship dynamic is a complex, sometimes frustrating task, because there are places of clarity and places where the record of their lives obscures lucid interpretation.

Reading Ohiyesa, Charles Eastman

Charles Eastman is an enigma. Knowing how to "read" him is difficult, both because he left behind a scant paper trail and because of his shape-shifter-like qualities. Was he Ohíye' S'a or Charles, or an amalgam? And if we follow the traditional Dakhóta philosophy that people earn different names to match different points in their lives, can it be said the essence of the man followed his name, and Ohíye' S'a became Charles, who became Charles (Ohiyesa), who ultimately returned to being Ohíye' S'a? Marion Copeland concludes if you look at the sum total of Charles Eastman's life works, "one can see a strength in the developing character of Ohiyesa that he himself seems not to have seen until the late 1920s."[1] More recent scholarship suggests "Ohiyesa" was *always* a part of Charles Eastman; the possible silence of "Ohiyesa," relegating this name to parentheses, can be read as synonymous with the Dakhóta value of silence as part of the harmony of the natural order in the world.

Historians have had difficulty defining Charles Eastman and his legacies. Neither the man nor his work is easily categorized. For everything you can say about him with certainty, there is more you cannot. For everything you think you can state on one side of an argument about him, the opposite can also be said with at least as much conviction.

Raymond Wilson ultimately viewed Charles as "the foremost educated Indian," someone who'd tried to straddle two worlds, "an acculturated rather than an assimilated Indian" and "a romantic about the old Indian life, a romantic about Christianity and the white world." Wilson believes Charles developed "syncretized" beliefs about both cultures that he maintained and attempted to reconcile at different points in his life.[2] David Miller refers to Charles Eastman as "culturally confused," someone who never achieved a sense of balance and poise in his adult life, a man whose identity uneasily floated someplace between the world in which he was born and the one in which he was educated.[3]

Other scholars suggest a more nuanced interpretation. Philip Deloria lists Charles Eastman among a small group of that generation's Native Americans who is "difficult to situate culturally," and yet even in his seemingly assimilated ideas and activities—working for the Boy Scouts of America, writing for a largely white reading audience—demonstrating authentic Indian values. When he dressed for audiences in "full Sioux regalia," Deloria argues, Charles sought to "take the primitivist value attached to exterior antimodern Indian Others and reattach it to real, modern Native Americans." More recently, Deloria has suggested there is a strategic unknowability about Charles Eastman; he left us some clues about how to interpret the man and his works, but only some, perhaps intentionally.[4] Given the stereotypical ways in which Charles was consistently portrayed in the press, the descriptions of him as a "specimen" or the epitome of what assimilation could do, and the near-constant stream of misinformation about everything from the college he attended to the events of his work life to the disinformation about his marriage and children, maybe it's no surprise he chose to keep the real Ohíye' S'a unknowable.

Similarly, Kiara Vigil posits Charles Eastman never lost sight of his Indianness despite—or maybe even *because* of—his success crossing cultural boundaries. She points to the conclusion of *From the Deep Woods to Civilization*'s often-quoted passage in which Charles states he is an Indian but an American as "an ever balanced, if strategically ambivalent, image of himself that engages these challenges."[5] And David Martínez emphasizes the numerous ways we can "read" Charles Eastman's life and work as exemplifying his Dakhóta identity, even when he seemed not to. Whether it was the plethora of genres in which he wrote that can be interpreted as an embodiment of the Dakhóta outlook that does not "divide knowledge into exclusive bodies of discourse," or his work with the scouting movement trying to "get the Indian's white brothers to Indianize themselves," Martínez sees Charles Eastman's life as one that ultimately must be viewed in the context of a consistent attempt to indigenize both Native and non-Native populations because of the pressing need Charles saw in early twentieth-century America for an embrace of traditional Native values.

How to begin to reconcile and explain these diverse interpretations? Here a biographical approach is useful. Lisa Tatonetti suggests, "Eastman was, undeniably, an interstitial figure with a stake in two disparate and often conflicting cultures."[6] Several scholars believe that because Charles Eastman never actually experienced life on a reservation until *after* he'd already been through his Euro-American education and immersion into white culture, this heightened his sense of personal displacement. Drew Lopenzina argues Charles Eastman became an interstitial figure *because* of his rootlessness: "Eastman would begin to perceive himself as an Indian living in a white man's world. . . . Even after his marriage to Elaine Goodale Eastman, Eastman would live life without foundation, without roots, of wandering from one place to the next with nowhere to call home."[7] Charles's travels meant a peripatetic existence. It is ironic that despite his support of the Dawes Act enabling Native Americans to "own" property individually, the only property Charles ever "owned" himself was the cabin he purchased—in Canada. The man with the sardonic wit would no doubt appreciate this incongruity.

If it's difficult to locate Charles Eastman as someone in one world or another, or straddling both, it is equally difficult to classify his work. Charles's legacies—his medical and political work and writing—are all topics of debate and interpretation.

David Miller questions why Charles Eastman abandoned medicine after 1903, especially given the financial problems plaguing him. Wouldn't a medical career have offered more economic security? "Medicine apparently did not provide for him the satisfaction he sought," Miller writes.[8] Perhaps. Because he left no written record, we can only speculate. While the historical record does not yield definitive answers, the biographical approach offers possible explanations.

Charles's training in homeopathic medicine probably matched with his Dakhóta beliefs in the integration of mind and body, the importance of seeing a patient's medical condition in the context of culture and community.

However, by the end of the nineteenth century this approach had fallen out of favor, not gaining credence again until the 1970s. How frustrating it must have been for Charles to embrace a philosophy and method to his chosen profession commensurate with his values, only to have it no longer considered the proper approach to medicine. And how alternately vexing and disappointing it must have been for him to realize his years of preparation were of little use in trying to save the Wounded Knee victims, or subsequently, to be viewed as the "Indian doctor" utilizing "white man's medicine" from whom neither Indian nor Euro-American patients wished to receive treatment. The rampant corruption and efforts to thwart his whistleblowing in both of Charles's stints as a reservation physician surely only added to the profound sense of disenchantment and regret he must have felt about medicine.

But it's not clear Charles Eastman ever abandoned his interest and training in medicine. Many of his books contain sections about health and wellness, and his work with both the YMCA and the scouting movement emphasized outdoor activities and exercise as a key to well-being. His recognition that governmental policies often compromised the health of Native peoples was a major talking point in his writing and many of his speeches. It's clear from letters to and from his Amherst neighbors that Charles was often called upon when people fell ill. Raymond Wilson reports that toward the end of his life, Charles often treated Indian patients and in "one instance, [took] over an entire practice while the regular physician went on vacation."[9] It's also possible Charles saw his commitment to healing through the lens of his Indigenous heritage, viewing health as foundational, inextricable from social conditions, dependent on the inclusion of elders and community members, and not contingent upon the possession of an MD degree to practice throughout one's lifetime.

Placing some of Charles Eastman's other work is trickier. "Eastman can be located, by chance or by design, on what would seem the 'wrong side' of nearly every major issue he faced at the height of his prominence in the early part of the twentieth century," writes Drew Lopenzina.[10] He cites Charles's support of the Dawes Act, his employment as an "outing agent" at the Carlisle School, and his work as an agency physician. Referring to Charles's 1910 journey among the Ojibwe to collect artifacts, Neil Schmitz suggests Charles took on Euro-American roles and values in this job.[11]

And yet it is perhaps misleading and certainly simplistic to suggest Charles Eastman was somehow selling out or compromising his Indigenous values through these endeavors. As Malea Powell points out, it's important to view Charles's work through the "persistent critiques of the very characteristics of Euroamerican culture that were argued to be primary components of 'saving the Indian.'"[12] Powell reminds us Charles likely used his "doubleness" as a kind of tactical authenticity, enabling him to speak to both white and Native audiences. His support of land deals can be thought of as an effort to retain something he knew to be at the heart of Native cultural connection by linking reform efforts of pan-tribal activism with efforts of white reformers as a road map for success. His work for the U.S. government and the Carlisle School might be conceptualized as efforts to assist other Indians navigating the changing landscape and ensuring survival in an increasingly Euro-American-dominated country. David Martínez notes that Charles's work to collect Ojibwe artifacts was undertaken with a respectful mutuality and most likely with the belief this work would enable preservation rather than appropriation. Contemporary efforts by many museums to repatriate Native American artifacts, hair samples, and bones are efforts Charles Eastman would heartily have endorsed.[13]

Charles Eastman's overtly political work is in some ways as confusing and difficult to place as his work with more subtle political underpinnings. On the one hand, there is his support of and advocacy for Indian citizenship, but on the other, as Kiara Vigil acutely frames it, "How could Indian people participate in a democracy that was itself so undemocratic with particular regards to them?"[14] There is Charles's belief the Indian Bureau was an inherently corrupt organization, but also the reality of his efforts to work within its systems to try to effect change, and more than once—although he undoubtedly came to believe there was little chance of doing so. And while Charles believed in the pan-Indian movement and the need to establish the Society of American Indians, he virtually abandoned his ties with this organization.

Without explicitly using language defining it as such, Charles Eastman faulted the nature of colonialism and believed its pervasive legacies throughout U.S. history were responsible for the compromised positions in which so many Native Americans lived. Most notably in his address to the Universal Races Congress and in *The Soul of the Indian,* Charles argued that the dispossession of Indian lands directly led to dysfunctional relationships across tribal governance, and between Indians and a Euro-American government that flailed about, making ineffective policies continuing to disenfranchise Indian peoples. The long-lasting legacies of colonialism, Charles believed, could be found in the imposition of capitalistic values leading to corruption, poor health, and cultural dislocation. In the end, Charles came to believe Indian citizenship and the elimination of the Office of Indian Affairs were the best paths to dealing with colonialism's difficult legacies.[15]

But questions linger about the extent to which Charles Eastman himself was a victim of the corrupt governmental systems he hoped to work within, and whether his responses to the "harsh" governmental practices were in themselves problematic. Did his disputes with Indian agents at Pine Ridge and Crow Creek stem only from his attempts to expose their corruption, or did he, perhaps unwittingly, contribute to some of the very problems he wished to expose? Did his work on the Santee claims case emanate only from a belief he was better placed to "work the system" for reparations, or did it bleed into a belief he deserved to profit in disproportionate ways? While the historical record contains ambiguities and the biographical one is incomplete, it seems likely Charles, like so many of us, was driven to do what he did by a complicated set of beliefs and ideals that must be read in the context of the realities of his life circumstances.

Finally, how can we assess Charles Eastman's literary output? To what extent does his nonautobiographical writing reveal biographical insights? Are there ways in which the content of his writing can be read to reveal inherently Indigenous precepts or ways construction of his language divulges Indigenous strategies? And in the end, how much editorial input did Elaine have on shaping Charles's writing?

Several historians and literary critics suggest that much of Charles Eastman's literary success within his own lifetime stemmed from his ability to parlay autobiographical elements into literature that garnered a broad reading audience. Noting that as a writer Charles "frequently cast himself as a modern tribal storyteller, a figure who, like the elders in an oral society, both described the old ways and gave them a contemporary twist," Frederick Hoxie states Charles's writing sought to present Native lifeways to a general audience.[16] Adds Miyuki Jimura-Yamamoto, "Eastman's success as a writer was largely indebted to the cross-cultural skills that he gained from his early education."[17]

But it wasn't only biography Charles tried to convey through his writing. He believed—as did Elaine—that parlaying his early life and understanding of Indian cultures into materials meant for a broad reading audience furthered politics, not just literature. And it could significantly add to the family coffers. "It remains too reductive to conclude that Eastman wrote of his Indian childhood merely to celebrate the triumph of 'civilization' in his own life or to nostalgically idealize his recollections of youth," writes Tony Dykema-VanderArk. "Eastman's early autobiographical writing reflects, rather, an attempt to explore the possibility for cross-cultural understanding and identification that might exist on the common ground of childhood."[18] But Malea Powell sees his writing about childhood as something else: she believes this writing shows us Charles's "rhetoric of survivance, a use that requires persistence, intelligence and humor as it imagines a new Native subjectivity," writing about childhood stories with multiple meanings.[19]

Similarly, David Martínez implores readers to read more into Charles Eastman's writing. "Even books that were ostensibly for young readers bear the indigenous sophistication of the oral tradition, which consists of narratives that draw from a deep well of wisdom," he writes.[20] In an extensive analysis, Christopher Pexa concludes much of Charles Eastman's writing "celebrates and promulgates Dakhóta culture and practices," but often in ways that would have gone unnoticed by Euro-American readers. Talking animals aren't just animals that talk. Pointing to literary strategies employing traditional Indigenous "games of mimicry," ciphered use of Dakhóta knowledge and decolonial imagery, and use of traditional stories to articulate larger truths, Pexa interprets Charles's writing as foundationally using Indigenous techniques and tales for critique.[21]

The issue of the extent to which Charles's writing embodies Indigenous strategies is key to the question of the role Elaine Goodale played in the process and products published under Charles Eastman's name. Raymond Wilson believes that because Charles never published anything after his separation from Elaine, this reveals he had been too dependent on her editorial work.[22] Carol Lea Clark agrees, adding that the "unusual nature of their marriage" created a "mutual dependence that was fruitful for their writing but ultimately unsatisfactory."[23] Ruth Ann Alexander opines that Elaine "contributed much of the work" in Charles's books and that his success became a painful reminder to her of her own growing obscurity as time went on.[24] She believes Elaine "collected, transcribed, edited, perhaps even wrote, her husband's stories of his life and people." Citing a letter Elaine wrote to Harold Rugg in which she stated she had prepared Charles's manuscripts, "revising, omitting and re-writing as necessary," Neil Schmitz argues, "'Omitting' is the large word here. . . . [Elaine was] unquestionably there, sympathizing, obscurely challenged, polishing every trope, considering every sentence."[25]

In a 2023 book of Charles's previous unpublished essays about the Dakota creation myth, Eastman descendant Kate Beane points out, "The story and heart of the writer's words are here, with very little polishing—this book does not include the 'flowery' poetic flow of the previously published works that were edited by Ohiyesa's wife, Elaine Goodale Eastman." Eastman descendant Gail Johnsen notes it is "extremely doubtful" Elaine had much hand in this manuscript, "particularly given the minor punctuation problems, very occasional typographical errors, indefinite pronoun references, and other small problems that editors correct automatically."[26] These assessments also seem to suggest that at least on some of Charles's earlier published writings, Elaine did play a more significant role.

But there are at least two alternative theories.

First, as Neil Schmitz suggests, both Elaine and Charles had transcultural experiences, and while these experiences profoundly affected their writing, giving each an understanding of the other's culture, ultimately the cultures they could not leave behind were their own. Elaine "went native," he writes, during her time among the Sioux, dressing and experiencing life in a way so different from her upbringing, and Charles had years of attending Euro-American schools, living primarily among white people. To Schmitz, Charles's writing is a by-product of both their experiences and Elaine's heavy hand in editing them. She knew enough to leave in some of the Dakhóta voice and perspective he intended, but still intensively edited—he believes her presence and voice is evident in the published works: "Goodale Eastman would remain faithful to her biased understanding of transcultural cross-allegiance."[27] Martha Viehmann agrees, writing that to the extent there is an "assimilationist" perspective expressed in Charles Eastman's writing, it's probably not fair to attribute this to Elaine's imposition and reworking of his texts: "This makes the art of collaboration and the psychology of these individuals too simplistic. . . . Elaine had extensive knowledge of her husband's people and could write sympathetically of their lives. Charles had every reason to support assimilation, for his very life was built on it. The Eastmans shared a desire to inform white readers about the values they found in Native cultures. . . . Their differences lay in their emphases and in the emotional value each attached to traditional Dakota culture."[28] We need to understand the large issues of race—how Elaine embraced an assimilationist perspective and Charles came to abandon it—and of gender—how and why Elaine would have interpreted her own role in her husband's writing and what it meant for her own—to truly understand the complex push-and-pull of editorial voice that ultimately occurred when these books went to press.

The other theory posits there is so much subtle Dakhóta presence in Charles Eastman's writing that it is unlikely Elaine played a major role in shaping it, though surely, she shepherded it to publication. Ruth Heflin points to the circularity of some of Charles's arguments and the nonlinear storytelling in many of his stories as in concert with Native storytelling traditions; she stresses his use of "more anthropological" descriptions in his writing is not necessarily proof of Elaine's voice but, rather, evidence he understood such descriptions help to make for a story with depth. "Scholars do more disservice to Eastman as a writer to assert that his writings were not wholly his own," she argues.[29] Kiara Vigil unpacks how the "accomodationism" in some of Charles's texts reflects both the shift in his ideology and an Indigenous perspective;

Erik Peterson suggests that for all of the "assimilationist" content of *From the Deep Woods to Civilization,* the text actually has a structure paralleling traditional Lakota narratives; Christopher Pexa insists you cannot ascribe simple motives to Charles Eastman's writing because, in Dakhóta tradition, he "deconstructs even as it repeats . . . constitutive terms."[30]

The biographical truth probably lies somewhere between these positions. Because no publicly available drafts of Charles's manuscripts or Elaine's markups of them exist, the true extent of Elaine's editorial input may never be known. "Dr. Eastman's books left his hand as a rough draft in pencil, on scratch paper," Elaine wrote to Harold Rugg at Dartmouth in 1939 when he'd requested copies of Charles's manuscripts. "From this I made two or three typed copies, . . . All imperfect copies were destroyed."[31] Of course, she didn't say *why* they were destroyed, and her lack of pronouns in the last sentence doesn't explain *who* destroyed them.

In some ways, what is of greater interest than the extent of her revisions or her stewardship of his writing is the biographical fact Elaine alternately told Rose that Charles authored pieces bearing his name and that she'd only assisted him editorially, but also that she had done more than simply clean and type his manuscripts and perhaps should have appended her name to more books than she did. She had written to one of Charles's Dartmouth classmates that she collaborated on ALL his books. Elaine also wrote to Rose that, looking back on the matter of whether she did not get the credit she deserved for collaboration on Charles's books, "I did enough to feel that I fairly earned a half of the money proceeds."[32] The bitterness Elaine felt over this "unfair" compensation never ended and perhaps continued to cloud evidence about authorship. Her flip-flop suggests her ambivalence, perhaps her profound frustration, that his success came, at least in part, to the detriment of her own. Early on she viewed his literary victories as shared; later, she came to see them differently.

In some ways, perhaps, Charles Eastman ultimately represented the shapeshifter, the mythical figure found across cultures who changes appearance to alter its meaning. In many Native American traditions, the shapeshifter takes an animal form, sometimes associated with negative traits but often with very positive ones. In Lakota folktales, Iktomi the spider is a shapeshifter, his morality lessons responsible for passing along Lakota culture. Through his writings, his appearance, his many lectures, and his political work, this, too, was part of Ohíye' S'a's mission—even if many of those who read him, heard him, and even knew him intimately were not fully aware of this legacy at the time.

Reading Elaine Goodale Eastman

In the end, it's also difficult to know how best to read Elaine. Were her ideas about education, women's roles, and Native American policy progressive at one time? Why did someone who prided herself on her knowledge of forward-looking initiatives, read widely, and carried on lively correspondence about ideas refuse to shift her perspective? Because she so heavily curated anything having to do with her marriage and her feelings about Charles, how much autobiographical intent can be read into her fiction or poetry that focuses on relationships? How can we best situate some of her views about her own family within the context of her life? And how does her self-assessment of her work hold up more than seventy years after her death?

Like many bright women of her era, Elaine Goodale had few career options. Her choices further circumscribed by a family that could not afford to support her, and through her unwillingness to marry for economic security, Elaine chose what countless other nineteenth-century women selected—a teaching career. But Elaine's choice of a school differed from many of her peers: going to the Hampton Institute, she allied herself with white women reformers who, as Tamara Berg writes, "turned to the Native American Other to envision and articulate a host of new possibilities for white female agency and identity."[33] As a teacher and later as a writer, Elaine Goodale's interest in Native American cultures enabled her to contravene conventions of the time within professions seen as acceptable for women.

Since she was a neophyte teacher with no formal training and a person whose own education had taken place entirely outside of classroom settings, Elaine Goodale had to rely on her pedagogical instincts. That she quickly realized the importance of experiential education and understood—despite the

English-only instructional decree—how a bilingual approach would enhance education for her students and her own understanding of them demonstrated Elaine's inherently progressive approach. When she and Laura Tileston opened their school at White River, they had few directives about curriculum and utilized an interdisciplinary approach that would come into favor decades later. As a teacher, school administrator, and someone who wrote frequently about educational policy for Indians, Elaine firmly championed the validity of day schools over boarding schools, an unusually progressive attitude for the era. In Elaine's opinion, day schools also mattered because they could involve their surrounding communities. That said, Elaine's belief that Euro-American–run day schools would impact Native communities by "lifting them up gradually," while progressive in some ways, was also consistent with the prevailing assimilationist philosophy of the time.[34]

And though we cannot know for sure, it seems likely that twenty-first-century revelations about how dangerous boarding schools would prove for the physical and mental well-being of their Native students would only have hardened Elaine's opposition to them. Information about how many children died and were buried at places like the Carlisle Indian Industrial School would have horrified Elaine and reinforced her beliefs about why day schools were preferable. Most likely she would have lauded President Joseph Biden's 2024 formal apology on behalf of the U.S. government for the mistreatment of generations of Native children taken from their homes and forced into boarding schools.[35]

Two generals, Armstrong and Pratt, influenced Elaine's overall philosophy about Indian education. Both believed assimilation key for Indians' survival. Elaine Goodale absorbed this attitude, filtering it through her belief that it was important to "figure out which characteristics of Native life were innocuous," as Tsiania Lamawiama points out.[36] Berg posits that despite her relative obscurity today, "Elaine Goodale Eastman is an important figure. . . . Through her work and writing (particularly during the period 1885–1891), she offered the American public a viewpoint on assimilationist practices as in service to the Indian, she gave voice to Indian experience and perspectives challenging the popular notion that barbarism reigned whenever one left the boundaries of white society, and she advocated the value and humanity to be found in Indian life and culture."[37] Elaine used her platforms as teacher and writer to demonstrate that elements of Native culture were valid and significant, but she never abandoned her belief in the primacy of Euro-American cultural practices. By the 1930s, when she engaged in her public debates with John Collier, these views were on full display, no longer seen as the least bit progressive. Neil Schmitz identifies limits to reading Elaine's approach to Indian policy sympathetically: "The language of her recollection is resolutely acculturist, missionary, Unionist." He suggests her writing is an "often cruel imperialist voice describing her experience, imposing her judgment, and yet also describing, reporting an inside tribal story."[38]

Her poetry, like her prose, also revealed her unyielding attitude. The collection of poems in her 1930 compendium are divided into three sections, one focusing on topics of motherhood and love; one on "cosmic" issues including religion, odes to some of her departed mentors, and even Halley's Comet; and one called "Songs of Nature and the Red Man." The combination of topics in this section embraced the prevailing Euro-American linkage of Native Americans and a "back to Nature" approach, emphasizing white takeovers of Native lands. One of the poems in this section is "Song of the Oregon Trail," a paean to Lewis and Clark, the "westward-facing captains, your fame is safely kept," who "first with seeing eyes our glorious land possessed." Even the poems focusing on Native American characters reveal something of Elaine's assimilationist stance: "The End of the Hunt," for example, which tells of "A race of hunters, a proud nation once who, dwindled to this petty, roving band" have their "charmed circle," but "there are few left like him, And when these few are gone, there'll be no more; none to succeed them, for their children bear the mark, world-famous, of our conquering race."[39]

Ultimately, despite her own personal experiences teaching Native Americans, living among the Sioux, and marrying a Dakhóta, Elaine Goodale Eastman's position never changed. It arguably hardened in her later years.

Similarly, we cannot neatly categorize Elaine's ideas about gender. Aspects of her attitudes and behaviors both challenged and reinforced gender norms of her time. Citing her mother as the "feminist" model on whom she based her own ideas about women's rights, Elaine broke with convention many times in her teens and twenties—by not marrying but by leaving home, and by writing under her own byline. She traveled around the Great Sioux Reservation unchaperoned. She eschewed any interest in fashion for what was practical and comfortable. She leveraged her relationships with powerful men to attain positions of authority, and her public voice and opinions on a range of issues gave her agency throughout her long life. Though she mostly wrote fiction and poetry—genres within the conventional nineteenth- and early twentieth-century woman's sphere—her journalistic writing offered social commentary, highly unusual for women of the late nineteenth century.

And yet Elaine Goodale Eastman cannot, ultimately, be thought of as a feminist by standards of the early twentieth century, let alone by today's benchmarks. She married, for many years gave up her own writing career to promote her husband's, and traded in the mentoring and care of her students for that of her own children. "Every woman who has surrendered a congenial task and financial independence will understand," she insisted in *The Voice at Eve* as she looked back and tried to justify her choices, while admitting, "Whether or not this was wise, is perhaps an open question."[40] Elaine's views about contraception, sexuality in films, and the division of labor within a family were all extremely conservative and remained so, not at all aligned with more progressive ideas about women's roles, even in her own time.

It is impossible to fully disentangle Elaine's attitudes toward either Native American policy or gender from her attitudes toward Charles. She fell in love with Dakhóta culture and with a Dakhóta man, and yet her staunch assimilationist beliefs remained a contradiction throughout her life, challenging her work with Native Americans and complicating her relationship with Charles. Apart from the comments she made in letters to Rose, Elaine left us very little to go on in trying to understand how she reconciled these beliefs. It's tempting to see her listing of her children's race as "white" on the 1910 census or read her question of "have we not seen the individual freed from tribal claims carry with him into the larger world the eternal best of the ancient soul?" in one of her retorts to John Collier as evidence that she, at least at one time, viewed her own husband as the epitome of what assimilation could make possible. Perhaps this is how she squared her genuine love of at least aspects of Indian culture with her belief that much of it simply needed to go if Indians were to survive in late nineteenth- and early twentieth-century America.

It is tempting to read into Elaine's fiction, such as *Hundred Maples*, some of the feelings she must have harbored toward Charles when Henrietta Martindale entered their lives, the intensely private emotions made public in a widely reviewed book. Or conversely, to read into some of her late poetry—for example, "The Woman's Challenge"—a fierce justification of a marriage so many had questioned and that, by that point in time, had all but dissolved:

> I have chosen a mate from the people, I have chosen with open eyes,
> For who would love for a lifetime must either be mad or wise.
> Subtle am I as the serpent and fond as the nesting dove—
> Not for an hour of passion; for a sane and steadfast love.[41]

And yet, because she did not leave behind any notations about this, we cannot be sure. It problematizes the biographer's task.

Elaine's letters to Rose Goodale Dayton are perhaps the purest, least curated source available about Elaine's inner thoughts. This is especially true because while Elaine destroyed Rose's letters to her, she did not know one day Rose would turn over her sister's letters as part of the public record. It is in these letters that so many of the contradictions of Elaine Goodale Eastman's life become clear: her early belief in Charles's "brilliance" and the importance of publishing his writing, which later yielded to her claims of just how much her own editorial voice was inserted into his; her suggestion that she was expert on so many issues of child development and parenthood, which clashed with her inability to see the ways in which she pigeon-holed her own children and seemed not to recognize or acknowledge their existence as biracial individuals, compared one against another, and so clearly evinced preferences for one child over others. Even her insistence to Rose that "no doubt but that our emotional life is of greatest importance and I am far from believing that it should be kept hidden as far as possible. As a writer, especially of poetry and fiction, I know that its expression is essential to human interest"[42] seems contradicted by her expunging of almost any expression of emotion from the record of her life.

FIGURE 12.1. Rose Sterling Goodale Dayton, 1889. Eastman-Goodale-Dayton Papers, Smith College Special Collections, Northampton, MA.

Elaine's late-in-life letters to her sister disparaging "the Doctor" must also be read through the lens of her great bitterness and the disappointments of decades. Few among us can live up to our ideals consistently; Elaine's acrimony in these letters reflects an indignant unwillingness to accept this.

For someone who prided herself on introspection, Elaine Goodale Eastman was seemingly unable to see some obvious parallels within her own life and family. She criticized her mother for being a "disappointed woman," for being someone whose "temperament was her greatest enemy," for having forsaken her marriage, and for not fulfilling her own potential as a writer. Elaine failed to see these were all things that could be said of herself. Like her mother, Elaine was highly critical of other people's relationships, and yet she saw no irony in this. She was also quick to call out her sister Dora for traits she, too, possessed—aloofness, dogmatism, inability to engage emotionally. But rather than bond the two sisters closer together, these similarities in their personalities and outlooks drove a wedge further between them.

Today, to the extent she is recalled at all, Elaine Goodale Eastman is not remembered in the way she would most want to be known: as a writer. In *The Voice at Eve*, Elaine spoke of "deserting literature for life" and her son's insistence his mother was forever a poet, whether she put words to paper or not. Yet Elaine was acutely aware of what might have been. "As a romantic child of fifteen, I promised myself to 'sing along the way,'" she wrote. "And I have kept my word after a fashion, for the scattered verses now at last bound between covers have appeared in magazines over a stretch of more than half a century. How broken-winged they flutter and fall, beside the soaring dreams of youth!"[43]

Literary critic Sarah Ruffing Robbins argues that during her own era, Elaine Goodale Eastman "still held greater celebrity author status, based on her years of poetry-publishing and her journalism recounting experiences as a white woman educator of, and expert on, Dakota people. Though Charles later claimed a highly visible role as interlocutor on Native experience, in the first years of their marriage, Elaine remained the more prolific writer addressing Indian issues in a range of periodicals." Elaine later downplayed the role of her journalism, dismissed her "pot-boilers," and bemoaned the lack of critical success her more serious works of writing achieved. But as Ruffing Robbins posits, Elaine's "vexedly hybrid" writing should be seen both in the context of her efforts to revisit issues of the gendered challenges women faced and as part of "a modernist experiment blurring lines across several life-writing forms: memoir, life-based poetry, and autobiography-inflected novel."[44]

Though "Ashes of Roses" can still be easily found on poetry websites, all of Elaine's other verse has long since fallen out of favor and out of print. Her hundreds of articles in over twenty national magazines and newspapers, as well as dozens of regional outlets, can be retrieved electronically, at least many of them, and yet most lists of "significant American women journalists" do not contain her name. Her novels are no longer in circulation. "Elaine Goodale Eastman was everywhere in the 1890s," writes Neil Schmitz, "in New England and New York City newspapers and magazines, in the liberal Christian press, in missionary periodicals and newsletters. She was a force."[45] Elaine acknowledged, "My songs of Indian life exhibit a pardonable coloring of romance. However, I continued to write mainly in prose and with serious educational purpose—in other words, to turn out propaganda rather than literature"[46]—quite an admission from someone who had been told she could have been one of America's greatest poets. It must have been enormously disappointing for her to look back and realize her poetry and fiction would not stand out in the future, and to see that her writing of "serious educational purpose" was no longer being taken seriously. The woman who was once labeled "the shyest woman in the United States" cherished her public platform; her writing enabled her to have a voice that her own proclivities did not allow. Though Elaine wished for her literary production to be her greatest legacy, it was, perhaps, not her most lasting one.

Reading and Situating the Eastmans

The stories of Elaine Goodale and Charles Eastman are in many ways stories about the changes in thought about race and about gender in late nineteenth- and early twentieth-century America. The vision they shared early in their marriage of presenting Native American culture to white America as a form of cultural mediation and Indigenous preservation diverged when Elaine clung desperately to her vision of the assimilated Indian as the only one who could thrive in an ever-changing society, and Charles ultimately reclaimed his beliefs in the primacy of his Dakhóta roots. He'd probably never forsaken them.

By the time Elaine and Charles met in the waning days of 1890, what most white Americans knew of Native Americans came from Buffalo Bill's Wild West shows, serialized novels, or museum displays. For Elaine, the wide-open prairies she first encountered, along with the Sioux whom she taught, represented a foreclosing of the frontier and a potential vanquishment of the people who held a particular—if limited—position in the Euro-Americans' vision of the West. Her beliefs in the importance of service and sense of social justice melded with her appreciation for aspects of Lakota culture and created in her an unyielding sense of what must be done: assimilation, with heavy-handed help from sympathetic white allies like herself. For Charles, the foreclosing of Indian lands and his family's tragic displacement, along with the collective displacement of so many Native Americans, meant a new imperative to preserve the culture and values he knew within the context of a modernizing and mechanizing world. The first seemingly viable solution—formal Euro-American education and Christianization—ultimately left him believing only the ideal of Indian citizenship while quietly retaining Native values and trying to subtly impart them more broadly, could bridge the gap between traditional cultures and new American culture. The disparities between Elaine and Charles's visions set up a relationship that was bound to be fraught; ultimately, their disparate views proved irreconcilable differences.

As Sherry Smith has written, by the late 1890s, the Euro-American optimism about "total assimilation" for Native Americans had already begun to fade, as new ideas about racial determinism and cultural relativity became more widespread and gained popularity.[47] Along with fears about an increasingly industrialized society, the "back to nature" nostalgia and antimodernist quest for a "simpler life" led many white Americans to embrace some idealized version of Native Americans and Native Americana. Charles Eastman was able to tap into this through his writings, his work with the YMCA and the scouting movement, his work with summer camps, and his many public talks dressed in his "Sioux regalia." Without doubt, this served as a way of generating income as much as it also had true educational purpose. Philip Deloria and others have noted the many ways in which this "playing Indian" might have been for Charles a wink and a nod, showing non-natives what they believed Natives should look like but, in fact, demonstrating how his orientation in Native culture had shifted from one that belonged only to a romanticized past to one that was a valuable resource for the present—and for the future. His audiences may not have gotten it, but he did. For Elaine, these public performances may have meant something quite different. Though she was no doubt supportive of Charles's efforts to generate income, she disapproved of anything she viewed as the commercialization of Indianness; "Eastman's use of a costume may have been a source of increasing tensions in Elaine and Charles' marriage," writes Martha Viehmann.[48] If so, this was only another indicator that Elaine probably did not truly understand what Charles's traditional dress meant to him.

These were not the only sources of tension in their marriage. Economic pressures, Charles's near-constant travel, evolving differences in their beliefs about gendered identity, and their differences in thought about family and responsibility simmered below the surface for years until the pairing of Irene's tragic death and Bonno's tumultuous birth brought all the frictions to the surface. Elaine's sense of betrayal emanated as much from the ways in which she believed Charles abandoned a shared belief in the efficacy and importance of assimilation as from the sense he committed adultery—perhaps not for the first time—and more importantly, abandoned a child he'd helped to bring into the world.

And more deeply, many indications in Elaine's writings, both the public record she left behind in her books and articles and poems, and the more private record in her letters to her sister, suggest in a fundamental sense that she never understood the ways in which Charles was Ohíye' S'a. Though we cannot know for sure, the way in which Charles chose to live his final years seems both a reclamation of his essential identity and a statement that the years of his marriage were a flawed attempt to put this aside.

Given all the ways the Eastmans' marriage was set up from the beginning for failure by a country demeaning Native Americans and a society frowning upon interracial relationships, and all of the financial and familial pressures, career changes, and personal tragedies they experienced, it is actually remarkable their marriage lasted as long as it did.

* * *

In a way, the story of Elaine Goodale and Charles Eastman ends where it began: at Wounded Knee.

According to the American Psychiatric Association, an estimated one in eleven people will be diagnosed with post-traumatic stress disorder (PTSD) every year. PTSD affects about 3.5 percent of American adults each year; women are two times as likely as men to be affected, and Latine, African American, and Native American people are all disproportionately affected and have higher rates of diagnosed PTSD than non-Latine whites.[49] That's only the reported and diagnosed cases, and this comes in contemporary times when medical practices recognize, acknowledge, and treat such ailments; it is probably even more widespread. Because PTSD is known to occur most frequently among people who have experienced or witnessed a traumatic disaster and given the profiles of those most affected by PTSD, it seems likely the effects of what the Eastmans witnessed at Wounded Knee had long-lasting impact for them both.

They didn't save any personal writings about this time, so if there were nightmares, times when the sadness was crushing, or when anything sounding like the "distant thunder" of the Hotchkiss guns they'd heard set off difficult associations and a cold sweat, we don't know about it. We don't know if there were times during their marriage when a dream fragment caused one of them to wake up and hold onto the other. We don't know if there were triggers that sent one or the other or both right back to that time of profound uncertainty, that time of indelible sorrow.

We do know that what they experienced at Wounded Knee affected their writing for years to come. Writes Martha Viehmann, Wounded Knee provides a useful lens through which to see Charles Eastman and his life: "Eastman's elegiac evocations in his writing of the Native American past coupled with his assertions that the old ways are gone and that the new way includes the embrace of life among whites bears this out."[50] But Charles Eastman would not advocate for policies or practices that were only assimilationist in nature. "If Wounded Knee has often been regarded as the last gasp of Native resistance in the 19th century," states Drew Lopenzina, "through Eastman it became the seminal event ushering him into continued advocacy for American Indians . . . the shape of a new century of American Indian activity."[51] Lopenzina and other scholars note that while Charles's writing about Wounded Knee maintains a more neutral tone, it is actually a "galvanizing moment" for him, as he begins to assign responsibility for the tragedy squarely on the policies of U.S. government officials. Charles viewed the Ghost Dancers not as agitators but as people with a right to practice their religious rituals. From this time forward Charles would cast his arguments in a progressivist stance that Euro-American policies toward Native Americans needed to be reformed. If the United States could adopt models from Native America, the country could more consistently live up to its own stated ideals.

If the events of Wounded Knee began an articulation of Charles's thought that Native America could be preserved by teaching white America some of its principles, for Elaine, Wounded Knee came to mean the opposite. As was perhaps most clear in her public arguments with John Collier, Elaine Goodale Eastman suggested, "The ghost dance religion . . . initiated a fair-sized war." Indians needed to assimilate, and the tragedy at Wounded Knee—which Elaine did view as a tragedy for which the Seventh Cavalry was squarely to blame—would not have occurred had a more amiable accommodation been made.

Life is never as clear as a causational model; relationships never as simple. One event—even one as horrific as Wounded Knee—cannot be said to cast the die for an entire marriage of three decades' standing. What they experienced together at Wounded Knee drew Elaine and Charles together in compelling ways. They both experienced a renewed sense of commitment to the concept of service for Native Americans, Elaine writing of having "embraced with a new and deeper zeal the conception of life-long service to my husband's people." And yet, she added, "How simple it all seemed to me then—how far from simple has been the event!"[52] It wasn't simple. What happened at Wounded Knee affected Elaine and Charles's relationship in ways they could not have known at the time, because the events, the place, and all that it came to symbolize, crystallized the differences in perspective that would ultimately drive them apart. As David Treuer has written more recently, Wounded Knee "was a cruel, slow, painful point—maybe even the lowest point since Europeans arrived in the New World—but a low point from which much of modern Indian and American life has emerged."[53] Adds Jerome Greene, Wounded Knee "perhaps, not unfittingly . . . also has come to symbolize the worst elements in America's long and tragic history of relations with its Native people. For the Lakota today, Wounded Knee is omnipresent. . . . They have not forgotten the human trauma that event caused."[54] Although Charles and Elaine came to see the meaning of their experience at Wounded Knee differently, there is no doubt this experience deeply affected each of them, and their relationship. From their time at Wounded Knee forward, Elaine and Charles's crossings in and out of Indian Country were as hopeful as a new day's dawning, as ineffably sad as the sunset's end. Their stories tell a tale of American change and progress, yet simultaneously, of just how elusive progress can be.

Afterword

The challenges of archival work are many. Sometimes you're dealing with systems of categorization that don't seem systematic. You can contend with paper so fragile it almost disintegrates. At times you are confronted with handwriting from another century that is difficult, if not impossible, to decipher. Occasionally there is an intriguing lead guiding you to an unexpected discovery, but sometimes you pursue an archival rabbit hole going nowhere. You can be blessed with an enormous amount of documentary evidence making you struggle to figure out what is important, or you can find you don't have enough evidence, at all.

In the case of Elaine Goodale Eastman there was also the challenge of knowing she significantly curated the written record of her life and, with Charles Eastman, the challenge he simply didn't leave much apart from his published writings. I was extremely fortunate to have returned to the story of Elaine and Charles at a time when it became easier to locate materials germane to their story everywhere; indeed, I drew from archives in fifteen states and Washington, DC, two Canadian provinces, the BBC and newspaper archives in Great Britain, and one Native American library on the Pine Ridge Reservation. To trace the lives of two people who crossed in and out of Indian Country as much as the Eastmans did, the ability to find materials in so many places was incredibly useful. All of this helped to mitigate Elaine's archival elisions and Charles's archival paucities.

In an odd way, doing a lot of this research during the pandemic proved more of a boon than a bust. Although archives across the country were closed, archivists were still working remotely. They were only too happy to help with locating and digitizing materials that would have taken many more hours to unearth had I been able to visit. Archivists are always the unsung heroes for biographers; for me, they were among the most important frontline workers during the COVID-19 pandemic.

Another significant challenge I faced was writing about race during a time of increased racial reckoning. Strangely, in May 2020 as I tried to piece together the story of Charles Eastman's difficulties working as an Indian physician in St. Paul in 1893 and the racial prejudice he faced, only eight miles from the site of Charles's original office a police officer murdered a Black man named George Floyd. In the weeks and months following, millions in the United States and around the world were inspired to start or to continue confronting issues of systemic racism in its many forms. Work on issues of diversity, inclusion, equity, and social justice can be painfully slow and frequently attacked, but the contemporary incident of George Floyd's tragic death, and the historical incidents of Charles Eastman's unwarranted difficulties earning a living as a doctor, demonstrate how critical this work was, is, and will continue to be.

As I researched and wrote this book, I was also influenced by contemporary Indigenous scholarship recasting the way I learned and interpreted American history. It is a profoundly different experience to think about the lives of Elaine and Charles Eastman through a lens suggesting, as Ned Blackhawk and others posit, that Native American history cannot—and should not—be thought of as separate from American history. I've tried to incorporate this perspective in my interpretations, as well as to be as cognizant as I can be of my own positionality and how that inevitably affected both my methods in investigating the Eastman's lives, and my interpretations in writing about them.

Before I began working on this book, much of what I knew about Charles Eastman I knew from reading secondary sources. I began to immerse myself in his writings. And yet as a white woman I knew I needed to do more to try to understand him. I have attempted to read everything I could written by Indigenous scholars about Charles/Ohíye' S'a and about Dakhóta culture and lifeways. I've been very fortunate to engage in lengthy conversations with several Indigenous historians who have been gracious and patient in sharing their thoughts and knowledge, and what I've absorbed I have tried to apply in my quest to "know" Charles. I am also aware that while I may have a pretty good handle on Charles, I'm humbled by the knowledge there is still much I don't know about Ohíye' S'a. I also realize that understanding him is an iterative process. It's much like the traditional Lakota legend of how people learned to fish, modeling themselves after the Small Bear, Mahto, whose mother taught him to drink in the cold stream to make him alert and to catch fish in the river by being patient. Awareness is the first step toward understanding, but true knowledge only comes slowly for those who wait.

* * *

An important part of trying to understand one's biographical subjects is foot-stepping—literally walking where those about whom you're writing walked, seeing the places they lived and worked, experiencing their environments in some small visceral way. For me, going to the places of note in the Eastmans' lives has not only been informative, but it's also been emotional.

Sky Farm, Elaine's birthplace and childhood home, is today part of the Mount Washington State Forest in westernmost Massachusetts. It's very isolated. The only sounds you hear in the summer are the chants of grasshoppers rising from the tall grasses overtaking the ruins of the barn where the Goodales once housed their cows, or the melodies of birds flitting across meadows where once Henry Goodale grew his legendary crops of potatoes. The occasional vehicle goes down East Street, but there's no other sign of humanity. Nothing remains of the cottage in which Elaine was born and raised except for some stones of the house's foundation. The cellar hole, discernible, is exactly as Elaine described it in a nostalgic 1942 poem following her final visit to Sky Farm: "Heaped in a hollow the chimney stones lie—No wall save the forest, no floor but the sky." Descendants of the orange daylilies planted by Dora Hill Read Goodale grow in front of the homesite, a cheerful reminder of the bucolic childhood Elaine and her sister Dora captured in their verse. Other than a placard about the Goodale sisters placed on the side of the road by the Mount Washington Historical Society overlooking the fields and barn skeleton I saw on my most recent pilgrimage, there is nothing alerting the visitor that once upon a time, the elegiac Sky Farm was a well-known spot in this corner of the Berkshires.

The precise place of Ohíye' S'a's birth is not known; multiple sources state he was "born in a tipi near Redwood Falls, Minnesota." Today Redwood Falls is a town with a population of almost five thousand. In the summer of 2021 when I traveled there, it had been economically devastated by the pandemic—many of the stores were closed, and in the middle of the day, no one was out on the town's main streets. Dusty parked pickup trucks and Trump political signs dotted the roads. The structures marked "historic building" referenced the early twentieth century, overtaken by different businesses over the years. One lone sign contained the Dakhóta place name, but otherwise there was nothing, anywhere, suggesting the presence of what had once been a thriving Sioux village before the Native people had to flee for their lives and the area was recolonized by Euro-Americans.

Most of the places the Eastmans lived and worked show two things: they clearly illustrate some of what's been lost in the name of "American progress," and they graphically demonstrate some of the ways in which Native American culture has been marginalized—often to the point of becoming all but invisible for those who don't know to look for it or don't know what to look for. With few exceptions, most sites labeled sites of historic importance are those related to Euro-American history; most of the sites of natural wonder retain names of white people who "discovered" them rather than the traditional names ascribed by Native people who considered these places of incredible natural beauty sacred. The erasure of Indigenous names no doubt continues to serve a painful reminder of the relative invisibility of Native Americans in America. Language becomes a bitter illustration of this in places like Fort Snelling in Minnesota, which has some guides who speak about the U.S. government's "acculturation" policies toward Indians rather than its "forced assimilation" policies, or how the Sioux were "exiled" from their homes in Minnesota rather than stating they had to flee from their dwellings when hunted down and pursued by U.S. soldiers. I found myself struck not only by what was said, but also by what was not.

Some of the places they lived would be unrecognizable to the Eastmans today. Oglala Lakota, South Dakota, is the poorest county in the United States, and the Pine Ridge Indian Reservation has the highest poverty rate of any reservation, clocking in at over 50 percent; in 2024 Oglala Lakota, in which Pine Ridge is situated, had a poverty rate of 55.8 percent. Unemployment affects very large numbers of people here. In the summer of 2021 when I visited, there were many boarded-up, vacant stores; many trailers and broken-down cars, their wheels, motors, and other parts splayed out in the hot sun like herds of decaying, eviscerated beasts. It's depressed and depressing. I wondered whether Elaine and Charles would be surprised by the extreme poverty here or whether they would see this as proof positive of the ways in which the U.S. government's treatment of the Sioux imperiled their way of life more than a century ago and set the stage for what exists today. I also thought they might have stated they'd tried to send up flares in their writings; seeing Pine Ridge today, they would know their warnings had gone unheeded.

The vast landscape of the Pine Ridge Indian Reservation, almost eleven thousand square miles, probably looks somewhat the same as it did in 1890, with enormous tracts of open land. There are grassy plains, sparse prairies, and, in the northernmost region, pine-covered hills and about 160,000 acres of the Badlands National Park. The raw and powerful beauty of the Black Hills amply demonstrates why Native groups considered them sacred, and why their sense of loss when Euro-Americans discovered gold and claimed the land was so profound. The enormous distances and remoteness of the reservation made me realize that Charles Eastman's determination to make house calls on horseback was both a medical necessity for ill patients who could not travel to his office, and a truly selfless—even heroic—decision.

The St. Paul, Minnesota, neighborhoods where Elaine and Charles lived have changed and turned over in the years since the Eastmans resided there. One of their street addresses no longer exists as a single-family dwelling, replaced by a multistory apartment building. The Falls of St. Anthony that Charles lectured about in his 1930 address to the Minnesota Historical Society look very different than they did when he spoke about them: today they feature water forcefully cascading over a concrete barrier built by the Army Corps of Engineers in 1937, the water no longer gracefully tumbling over rocks in a way the Dakhóta referred to as *mnirara* (curling waters). Bald Eagle Lake, where the Eastmans sought refuge from city life in the summers and to which they withdrew after the disastrous stint at Crow Creek Agency, is no longer just a summer retreat; year-round homes with satellite dishes on their roofs have replaced summer cottages, surrounding the entire thousand-acre lake along more than nine miles of shoreline.

In Amherst, Massachusetts, one of the three houses in which the Eastmans lived no longer stands, razed in 1940 and rebuilt as a fraternity, now a dormitory. The second house in which they lived on College Street was taken over by Amherst College. When I walked past it in 2023, I thought perhaps the large old copper beech tree off to the side of what is now the Keefe Health Center was a tree Elaine and Charles gazed at, as well, or read books under its ample canopy, or that their children may have joyfully climbed upon its many branches. Lodestone, the home Henry Goodale built by hand, was sold by the Dayton family in 2015, ending the decades-long ownership of this property by the Goodale family and their descendants.

Camp Oáhe in Munsonville, New Hampshire, ceased operation as a summer camp decades ago. When Camp Oáhe was running there were only three or four houses around Granite Lake; today there are probably ten times as many. The house in which the Eastmans lived that also served as camp headquarters is privately owned, and its present owners graciously gave me a tour in 2021. Walking along the same slanting floorboards the Eastmans walked, and seeing the sloped ceilings and walls covered with old photos, made me wonder about conversations they'd had within these walls, conversations that must have been excruciating after Irene's death, and even more difficult after Henrietta Martindale alerted them to the birth of her daughter. And when I saw the orange daylilies blooming in front of the house by the lake, I was certain it was Elaine who had planted their forebears; they are the same as those in front of her childhood home at Sky Farm.

In the early 2000s, AT&T proposed to erect a cell tower on Melville Hill, behind the Camp Oáhe site. This was the same hill Charles called "the hill of vision," the same hill upon which they buried Irene. Many residents protested the cell tower proposal, citing conservation and aesthetic concerns. Some of Charles Eastman's descendants traveled from South Dakota and Wisconsin to join the protests, pleading with the local zoning board to "respect the land." The cell tower was ultimately defeated. As I glanced up at the hill behind the house, covered by the trees that have grown up there, knowing Irene's body lies under one of the older ones, I felt the activists' victory was also a victory for her.

As for Wounded Knee—the location that perhaps more than any other would have multifold and intense meanings for Elaine and Charles—I, too, found it an incredibly moving place. It's a place of almost mystical solemnity, where the earth and sky meet upon vast horizons, and the knowledge of what happened there hangs heavily in the air.

The Episcopal Church of the Holy Cross where the Eastmans met, declared their commitment to one another, and worked side by side in the church-turned-hospital to save the victims of the Wounded Knee Massacre was moved from its original location to Oglala, also on the Pine Ridge Reservation, in 1924. It has been rebuilt twice. The building's relative anonymity contrasts sharply with the jaggedly painful events that connect it to its past.

In 1956 a large sign was erected overlooking the battlefield, describing some of what occurred in 1890 and referring to it as "The Battle of Wounded Knee." Sometime later, someone covered the world "battle" with the more apt word, "massacre"; the replacement patch is a clear and visible symbol of why this word change mattered. The sign has been vandalized, defaced with graffiti, even shot at on numerous occasions. In 1973 the marker site became the setting for the American Indian Movement's occupation and protest; Sherry Smith suggested the protest at Wounded Knee was one of the most potent reminders of the U.S. government's broken promises to Native peoples.[1] In 1965 the entire battlefield site was declared a U.S. National Historic Landmark; it was listed on the National Register of Historic Places the following year. The Wounded Knee Survivors Association, founded in the early years of the twentieth century, continues to be engaged in many activities, including the repatriation of objects removed from the massacre site, the return of clothing stolen from

FIGURE A.1. Its patch visible, this sign marks the Wounded Knee Massacre site. Photo: Larry Vale.

the victims that landed in museums in many localities in the United States and overseas, and protection of the Wounded Knee environment. The organization's social media documents and promotes activism around this place, which serves not only as a memorial to the dead from more than a century ago but also as an engagement for the living to prevent future centuries of dishonor. As Jeffrey Ostler writes, "Wounded Knee was the single most devastating event in Plains Sioux history, but it did not destroy the Sioux nation."[2]

Across the street, high on a hill above the stark landscape, is a small cemetery with an engraved monument marking the mass grave of the Wounded Knee victims. The monument was erected in 1903 by descendants of those who had died. Tall brick pillars joined by a simple metal arch with a cross on it leads up to the fenced cemetery; traditional prayer ties of different hues have been placed on some of the chain links. It's a lonely, desolate place suffused with ineffable sorrow, a bleak reminder of the horror that occurred there. You can't help but think of the phrase popularized by Dee Brown's best-selling 1970 book, *Bury My Heart at Wounded Knee.*: Many hearts are buried there.

On an extremely hot day in July 2021 when the car thermometer read 107 degrees, I ascended the hill to the cemetery. I stood silently for a while before paying my own tribute to the victims by placing a small rock on a piece of the fencing, a nod to the traditional Jewish practice honoring the dead. There was no breeze to break the sweltering temperature, no sound to break the silence enveloping me as completely and as searingly as the heat. I thought of how this place must have looked, blanketed with snow in the blizzards of 1890 after the massacre, and how the snow would have made the Wounded Knee valley as eerily silent then as it was on this scorching day.

Tawa Ducheneaux, archivist at Woksape Tipi at the Oglala Lakota College, kindly connected me to Guss Yellowhair, an artist, activist, and director of Tatanka Rez Tours. Guss and his daughter Tianna met my family and me in front of the Wounded Knee memorial sign and took us to a plateau overlooking the valley. They retold the story of the Wounded Knee Massacre, unspooled some of the complex collective memories of this place, sang songs of healing, and urged us to join with those seeking to revoke the Congressional Medal of Honor from the twenty U.S. Army officers of the Seventh Cavalry awarded it for their "genuine acts of courage" at Wounded Knee. The anguish this place continues to bring to the Lakota—and more widely to many Native Americans—was so clear, so poignant. Wounded Knee, perhaps more than any other site in America, embodies all the policies and practices that killed more than 250 Sioux that bitterly cold and wrenchingly bitter day in December 1890, and all the policies and practices that continue to marginalize Native peoples in all the years since. The pain of the past is clearly still so present. Because of this, Wounded Knee was not just a moment in time; it's a moment in which time seems to stand as still as the buttes that surround the valley.

Toward the end of our time together, Guss lit some sacred silver-leaf sage in a carved wooden bowl and waved the smoke toward the valley below. "What happened there will stay there," he said, "but you can go forth and help to tell its story." This is what I've tried to do.

ACKNOWLEDGMENTS

Biographers are often indebted to archivists; I am no different. This book would not have been possible without the considerable assistance of many archivists—assistance more considerable than usual because of the pandemic's constraints. As I sat on my screened porch in Massachusetts doing the bulk of the research in summer 2019, I was amazed and gratified by the quick, thorough responses from archivists. Though working remotely, they were only too happy to field my queries and digitize materials I was unable to dig up myself. For this I will always be grateful, and I give most sincere thanks to Daisy Allen, National Scouting Museum, Cimarron, New Mexico; Julie Bartlett-Nelson, Elise Bernier-Feeley, and Benjamin Kalish, Forbes Library, Northampton, Massachusetts; Alex Bentley, YMCA Archives, University of Minnesota; Rose Buchanan and Rebecca Sharpe, National Archives, Washington, DC; Fred Burwell, Beloit College; Lori Cox-Paul and Wayne Popp, National Archives/Kansas City; Kristie Couser, Hood Museum, Dartmouth College; Cara Curtis and Blair Williams, Cumberland County Historical Society; Dorothy DeSimone, Dana Hall School Archives; A'Llyn Ettien, Boston University Medical School Archives; Maria Galban and Nathan Sowry, National Museum of the American Indian/Smithsonian; Jim Gerencser, Carlisle Indian School Digital Resource Center, Dickinson College; Lee Grady and Teri Holford, Wisconsin Historical Society; Laurie Langland, Dakota Wesleyan University Archives; Meg Lloyd, Ruth Lilly Special Collections and Archives, Indiana University/Purdue University; Maryjo McAndrew, Special Collections and Archives, Knox College; Jeff Monseau, Springfield College, Massachusetts; Kate O'Brien, BBC Written

Archives Centre, Reading, U.K.; Andreese Scott, Hampton University Archives; Lisa Schoblasky, Newberry Library; Wayne Shoaf, USC Archives; Kimberly Smith, South Dakota Historical Society; Valerie Stenner, Special Collections, University of Delaware; Anne Thayer and Jenny McElroy, Gale Family Library, Minnesota Historical Society; Morgan Walsh, University of Wyoming Archives; and Julia Wiggin, Moody Center, Northfield, Massachusetts.

I'm also grateful to the librarians I got to interact with in person. Thanks to so many at my home library at Tufts University: Quetzalli Barrientos, Susan Brady, Elliott Brandow, Dianne Brown, and Micah Saxton, who helped me navigate databases, fielded my many requests, and got me copies from long-defunct publications with remarkable alacrity. Amy Hague, Kate Long, Elizabeth Myers, and Bena Williams at the Smith College Special Collections deserve and have my very special thanks; this is where I first learned about Elaine Goodale Eastman, and it was a joy to return and complete the work. Miranda Fuentes and Scout Noffke at the Rauner Library at Dartmouth College were incredibly helpful, both on email and in person. Analú María Lopez at the Newberry Library in Chicago helped me find materials when I visited and subsequently on email. I was delighted to be able to spend a day at the Berkshire County Historical Society, where Erin Hunt and Eileen Myers took great interest in my project. Alan Rumrill at the Cheshire County Historical Society deserves a special shout-out; not only did he guide me through the archival holdings, but also took me on a tour of Granite Lake, where he grew up, and introduced me to CeCe Frechette, who graciously let me tour her home, once headquarters of Camp Oáhe. In summer 2020 I also had the opportunity to use archives at Woksape Tipi at Oglala Lakota College in South Dakota; I thank archivist Tawa Ducheneaux for opening this up for me.

Cyndi Harbeson and Katherine Whitcomb from the Jones Library Special Collections in Amherst, Massachusetts, and Mimi Dakin, from Amherst College's Archives and Special Collections, became valued collaborators and good friends during the research for my previous book. I was grateful for their assistance and friendship with this one, too.

The late Jeremy Johnston, curator of the Buffalo Bill Museum in Wyoming, had astounding encyclopedic knowledge of the West. My conversation with him helped point me in several directions I might not otherwise have gone. Stuart Reeve, an archaeologist and genealogist who worked on the Read family, was instrumental in helping me find the ruins of Sky Farm; Ellen Berkland of the Massachusetts Department of Conservation also assisted me in this regard. I'm grateful to Mary-King Austin, who shared her research and clippings on the Goodale sisters. Hans and Harriet Bergmann have been consistently valuable in opening resources and connecting me to people telling the stories of Mount Washington. Jeff Green in Arizona, bibliophile extraordinaire, assisted me in locating first editions of the Eastmans' books.

I was informed and sometimes redirected by correspondence and discussions with several scholars whose own work focused or touched on aspects of the Eastmans' lives. Tamara Berg and Martha Viehmann both wrote dissertations that examined the Eastmans; their excellent insights in our conversations helped to shape my work. Margaret Jacobs, Neil Schmitz, Sherry Smith, and Ruth Spack each wrote important books quoted within this one; I'm also grateful to each of them for answering my questions.

David Martínez was particularly helpful in my understanding of Charles Eastman's work collecting Ojibwe artifacts and how to contextualize this. Kiara Vigil's work on Charles and Elaine Eastman helped to ground mine; our conversations more recently helped me understand better what I don't know. I'm also grateful to Kiara for kindly and patiently guiding me to Indigenous scholarship and perspectives. Philámayaye!

Five colleagues who became friends during my work on this book deserve special thanks. First I have to credit and thank the late Neal Salisbury. Neal, who was one of my professors at Smith College, was the first person who taught me to think about Native American history in new ways. Neal supervised my college work on Elaine Eastman, and when I decided to return to the Eastmans in more recent years, he was encouraging and supportive.

Ronnie Coleman, who wrote about Charles Eastman years ago but never lost her interest, helped shape and cultivate my interest. Ronnie always believed my book needed to be written, and for her unshaken faith and inspiration I'll be forever grateful. Ray Wilson, whose seminal book on Charles Eastman was for so long the north star, became a source of information and support throughout my work. I feel honored to have coauthored articles with Ray, and I'm so pleased to count him as a friend.

Fred Hoxie, whose many important works on Native American history were foundational for my work, offered to read an early draft of this book. Fred's amazingly careful reading and many suggestions made it a much better—and more accurate—book. What a gift his collegiality has been!

I met Philip Deloria through other work I was doing at the Massachusetts Historical Society, but soon afterward we commenced what's been an ongoing conversation about the Eastmans and their worlds. Phil's magnificent foreword to this book brilliantly encapsulates much of what drew me to the enigma of the Eastmans in the first place and locates their importance within Native scholarship and within American history. I will be eternally grateful for Phil's suggestions and interpretations; I'm even more grateful for his friendship.

Some of my biographer friends provided ongoing support and important perspective. I thank Natalie Dykstra, Megan Marshall, and Lucy Wilson for their advice and for telling me to hang in there when I most needed to hear that.

On a trip tracing some of the Eastmans' crossings in and out of Indian Country, I was very lucky to have Ginny and Craig Allen in St. Paul to help me scope out places to visit and take me there; I'm even luckier to have them as family. I also thank Tianna and Guss Yellowhair in Pine Ridge for their moving and inspirational explanations of Wounded Knee.

Colleague/sister Jennifer Burton always provides support, cheerleading, and warmth. I'm grateful for our Half the History work and our friendship.

Other colleagues listened and encouraged, Martha Pott and Tracy Geary most of all. My agent, Stephanie Cabot, always believed in this book. And my college roommate and dear friend, Beth Henderson Norton, has probably listened to me talk about the Eastmans more than almost anyone else over many, many years.

The New York University Press and Westchester Publishing Services teams are amazing, and I thank them all for their thoughtful and professional assistance at every turn, including Michelle Asakawa, Abigail Michaud, Jenny Rossberg, and Valerie Zaborski. Brianna Jean was always responsive, thorough, and one step ahead of me. And my wonderful editor, Clara Platter, not only shared my vision of this book but helped to sharpen it in important ways.

It might take a family to write a book; it certainly takes one to support the writer. My brothers, Marty and Joe, are endless sources of inspiration as they pursue their own important projects, modeling creative research and even more creative writing. My children and their partners—Mira and Nick, Aaron and Ying, Jeremy, and Jonathan—deserve special thanks. They probably can't realize all the ways they've helped me throughout this process, but I hope someday they will. Jeremy's facility with AI photo enhancement of old photos, Nick's wonderful mapwork, and Mira's thoughtful ideas about how to simplify a complicated timeline, all grace this book. My husband, Larry, editor and love for life, has always been there for me—and for this book—in more ways than I can count.

My parents laid the foundation for my interests in history, the West, reading, and writing. My mother passed away before this book was completed, and I wish she could have known. My dad's love of Western history originally helped drive me to this topic, and his support and interest in my work on the Eastmans—ever since I started it in college—never flagged. Sadly, he died before seeing this book published, but I'll be forever grateful he knew it would be.

NOTES

FOREWORD

1 "Thomas Jefferson to Benjamin Hawkins," February 18, 1803, *Founders Online*, National Archives, https://founders.archives.gov. Original source: *The Papers of Thomas Jefferson, vol. 39, 13 November 1802–3 March 1803*, ed. Barbara B. Oberg (Princeton, NJ: Princeton University Press, 2012), 546–549.

PREFACE

1 "Poetry Wedded to Science," *New York Herald*, June 22, 1891; "Elaine Goodale's Indian Lover," *Boston Herald*, January 14, 1891.

2 Ned Blackhawk, *The Rediscovery of America* (New Haven, CT: Yale University Press, 2023), 3–10.

AUTHOR'S NOTE

1 Claudio Saunt, *Unworthy Republic* (New York, NY: W. W. Norton, 2000).

INTRODUCTION

1 EGE, *Sister*, 152.

2 Ibid., 153.

3 CAE, "Selections from *From the Deep Woods to Civilization*," in Michael Oren Fitzgerald, ed., *The Essential Charles Eastman (Ohiyesa)* (Bloomington, IN: World Wisdom, 2007), 182.

4 EGE, *Sister*, 169.

5 CAE, in Fitzgerald, *The Essential Charles Eastman*, 183.

6 EG, "Incidents of the Indian War," *The Independent*, January 22, 1891.

7 EG, "Christmas Morning," in *All Round the Year: Verses from Sky Farm* (New York, NY: G. P. Putnam's Sons, 1881).

8 David Martínez, *Dakota Philosopher: Charles Eastman and American Indian Thought* (St. Paul, MN: Minnesota Historical Society Press, 2009), 7.

1. FROM SKY FARM TO "LITTLE SCOTLAND" (1863–1883)

1 EG, "Land and Home," in *All Round the Year* (New York, NY: G. P. Putnam's Sons, 1881).

2 Sky Farm guest book, Smith.

3 EGE, "Letter to the editor," *Berkshire Eagle*, June 24, 1946, 12.
4 EGE, *Sister*, 1–2.
5 *Berkshire Courier*, cited in Gerard Chapman, "Henry Sterling Goodale," *Berkshire Eagle*, November 1, 1994.
6 "Obituary of Henry S. Goodale," *Springfield Republican*, July 21, 1906.
7 Otis E. Lamson, "Historical Sketch of Mount Washington" (Mt. Washington, MA: Mt. Washington Historical Society, 1908).
8 Stuart Reeve, *A Path from England to Lonetown: History of the Hill and Read Families of Redding, Connecticut* (Danbury, CT: Joseph Merritt, 2013).
9 EGE, *Sister*, 2.
10 C. W. Balestier, *The Cornell Era*, 1878, article clipping, Smith.
11 Ibid., 7.
12 EGE to RSG, February 15, 1931, Smith.
13 EGE to RSG, April 14, 1940, ibid.
14 EGE, *Voice*, 17.
15 Herbert F. Keith, *History of Taconic and Mount Washington* (Pittsfield, MA: Berkshire Historical Society, 1912).
16 EGE, *Sister*, 5.
17 EGE, *Voice*, 13.
18 Ibid., 14, 21.
19 EG, *Journal of a Farmer's Daughter* (New York, NY: G. P. Putnam's Sons, 1881), 1–2.
20 Mrs. D. H. R. Goodale, "How I Became a Teacher: A Non-Professional Confession" n.d., Smith.
21 EGE, *Voice*, 18.
22 EGE, *Sister*, 4.
23 Mary Mapes Dodge, "Poems by Two Little American Girls," *St. Nicholas Magazine*, December 1877, Vol. 5 (2), 109.
24 Longfellow also wrote a letter to William Stuart Appleton stating he read some of Elaine and Dora's poems and thought them "very remarkable. . . . The versification also is wonderfully good and gives promise of future excellence." Henry Wadsworth Longfellow to William Stuart Appleton, February 11, 1877. In *The Letters of Henry Wadsworth Longfellow*, ed. Andrew Hillen, (Cambridge, MA: Harvard University Press, 1982),vol. 6, 244.
25 Cited in Eastman, *Sister*, 10.
26 Thomas Wentworth Higginson to HSG, 25 February 1877, Smith.
27 Thomas Wentworth Higginson to Dora Hill Read Goodale, March 7, 1877, Smith.
28 Sargent, *Life*, 8.
29 "Review of *Apple Blossoms*," *The Watchman*, December 19, 1878; "Review of *Apple Blossoms*," *New York Post*, 1878; *Berkshire Eagle*, 1878, article clippings, Smith.
30 EG and DRG, "Papa's Birthday," "Two Sonnets: Mother," and "Jewels," in *Apple Blossoms: Verses of Two Children* (New York, NY: G. P. Putnam's Sons, 1878), 65, 141, 81.
31 EGE, *Sister*, 13.

32 *Washington Evening Post*, August 5, 1878; "Sky Farm and Its Poets/A Glimpse of Two Wonderful Children," *Boston Post*, 1878; *Berkshire Courier*, 1878, article clippings, Smith.
33 "Review of *In Berkshire with the Wild-Flowers*," *National Journal of Education* 10 (20), December 1879, 326.
34 "Review of *All Round the Year*," *Sacramento Daily Record-Union*, March 19, 1881.
35 "Review of *Apple Blossoms*," *Chicago Daily Tribune*, December 7, 1878, 9; Professor E. G. Giddings, *Berkshire Courier*, n.d.; George McKnight, December 25, 1878; "Recent Poetry," *New York Times*, 3.
36 Mary Mapes Dodge to Dora Hill Read Goodale, November 6, 1878, Smith.
37 "A Resemblance, Certainly," *Charlotte Observer*, November 1, 1878.
38 Mary Mapes Dodge to HSG, November 20, 1878, Smith; G. P. Putnam to HSG, November 28, 1878, ibid.
39 "Explanation alluded to in the above letter," *Louisville Courier-Journal*, December 14, 1878; F. W. Bourdillon to HSG, December 3, 1878, Smith.
40 EG, "A Disputed Question Settled!," *Louisville Courier-Journal*, 1878.
41 EGE, *Sister*, 13–14.
42 EGE, *Voice*, 18; EGE to RGD, November 22, 1927, Smith.
43 EGE, *Sister*, 14.
44 Ibid., 13–14.
45 Ibid., 13.
46 Ibid., 14; EGE, *Voice*, 18.
47 EGE to RGD, April 15, 1940, Smith.
48 Lyman Abbott, "Snap-Shots of My Contemporaries," *American Periodicals*, August 17, 1921.
49 Edith Armstrong Talbot, *Samuel Chapman Armstrong: A Biographical Study* (New York, NY: Doubleday, 1904).
50 EGE, *Sister*, 15–16.
51 Samuel Chapman Armstrong to HSG, January 6, 1880, Smith.
52 "A Philosopher's Attic," *New York Times*, June 23, 1895.
53 Ibid., 17; EGE, *Voice*, 22.
54 Hampton University Archives, "Notes about Mansion House," n.d., Hampton University Archives, Hampton, VA.

2. FROM HAMPTON INSTITUTE TO WHITE RIVER CAMP (1883–1890)

1 In a biography of her father, Edith Armstrong Talbot noted throughout his constant pleas for funds; General Armstrong realized that "people are best reached through their emotions," and so he began taking small groups of Black and Indian students with him to tell their personal stories and entertain potential funders with song. Edith Armstrong Talbot, *Samuel Chapman Armstrong* (New York, NY: Doubleday, Page & Company, 1904), 233.
2 Eli T. Winkler, "Traveling the White Man's Road: The Quest for Identity in Hampton's Indian Newspaper, 1886–1907" (MA thesis, College of William and Mary, 1998).

3 Donal F. Lindsey, *Indians at Hampton Institute 1877–1923* (Urbana, IL: University of Illinois Press, 1995), 44.
4 EG, "Hampton's Work for Two Races," *The Chautauquan* 8 (3), December 1887, 153.
5 Paulette Fairbanks Molin, "Training the Hand, the Head and the Heart: Indian Education in Hampton Institute," *Minnesota History* 92 (Fall 1988).
6 This would prove particularly true for Native American students; out of a total of 1,230 Native students who attended Hampton between 1878 and 1912, only 158 graduated. Ruth Spack, *America's Second Tongue: American Indian Education and the Ownership of English, 1860–1900* (Lincoln, NE: University of Nebraska Press, 2002), 73.
7 See, for example, Hoxie, *Final Promise*, 205–206.
8 Richard H. Pratt, "The Advantages of Mingling Indians with Whites," in *Americanizing the American Indians: Writings by the "Friends of the Indian" 1880–1900* (Cambridge, MA: Harvard University Press, 1973), 260–271.
9 Paulette Fairbanks Molin, "Training the Hand, the Head and the Heart: Indian Education in Hampton Institute, *Minnesota History* 92 (Fall 1988), 82–98.
10 Samuel Chapman Armstrong, "Report of the Principal," *Southern Workman*, December 1, 1878.
11 Alan Trachtenberg, *Shades of Hiawatha: Staging Indians, Making Americans 1880–1930* (New York, NY: Farrar, Strauss, Giroux, 2005), 42.
12 Jeffrey Ostler, *The Plains Indians and U.S. Colonialism from Lewis and Clark to Wounded Knee* (New York, NY: Cambridge University Press, 2004), 150.
13 Katherine Ellinghaus, "Assimilation by Marriage," *Virginia Magazine of History and Biography* 108 (3), 2000, 279–303.
14 EGE, *Sister*, 19. Historian Donal Lindsey disputes Elaine's assertion, suggesting Armstrong tried to mix students from both races as much as possible. See Lindsey, *Indians at Hampton Institute*, 118.
15 Armstrong Talbot, *Samuel Chapman Armstrong*, 275.
16 Ibid.
17 EG, "The Indian School," *Southern Workman*, June 1, 1886, 69.
18 Spack, *America's Second Tongue*, 63.
19 EG, *Southern Workman*, June 1, 1885.
20 EGE, *Sister*, 18.
21 Ruth Ann Alexander, "Finding Oneself through a Cause: Elaine Goodale Eastman and Indian Reform in the 1880s," *South Dakota History*, 1992, 5–6.
22 Ibid., 2.
23 Frederick Hoxie points out that Helen Hunt Jackson's engagement with Indian causes after hearing Ponca Chief Standing Bear, the formation of the Boston Indian Citizenship Committee, and the beginnings of the Women's National Indian Association all began around the same time in the early 1880s. Hoxie, *Final Promise*.
24 Valerie Sherer Mathes, *Amelia Stone Quinton and the Women's National Indian Association* (Norman, OK: University of Oklahoma Press, 2022), 6.
25 EGE, *Voice*, 22.

26 Fairbanks Molin, 86.
27 EGE, *Voice*, 22.
28 EGE, *Sister*, 18.
29 Sargent, *Life*, 21, 31.
30 Armstrong Talbot, *Samuel Chapman Armstrong*, 204.
31 EGE, *Sister*, 21.
32 EG, "Impressions of Indian Education at Hampton," *The Independent*, June 5, 1884, 1.
33 EGE, *Voice*, 23.
34 EG, "A Missionary Journey," *Harford Courant*, October 10, 1885.
35 EGE, *Sister*, 25.
36 Hoxie, *Final Promise*, 43.
37 Ibid.
38 Definitions of which groups are considered "Lakota" and which "Dakota" are sometimes dependent on linguistic distinctions, sometimes geographic ones, and sometimes distinctions of social organization. Author personal communication with Philip J. Deloria, February 17, 2021.
39 Hämaläinen, *Lakota America*, 274.
40 EG, "Indian Farms and Indian Homes," *Hartford Courant*, April 1, 1885.
41 Margaret D. Jacobs, *After One Hundred Winters* (Princeton, NJ: Princeton University Press, 2021), 149.
42 Blackhawk, *The Rediscovery of America*, 353.
43 Spack, *America's Second Tongue*, 17.
44 Herbert Welsh, "Letter from Mr. Herbert Welsh," *Southern Workman*, September 12, 1885.
45 EG, "With the Indians," *Boston Weekly Advertiser*, September 29, 1885.
46 EGE, *Sister*, 28.
47 EG, "Indian Farms and Indian Homes."
48 Tamara Berg, "White Women Writing for Their Lives" (PhD diss. Indiana University, 2002), 93.
49 EG, "An Indian Love Story," *Southern Workman*, February 1, 1885. In an interesting irony, years before, Helen Hunt Jackson, widely known as one of America's premiere poets, critiqued young Elaine and Dora's poetry, writing, "There has never before been a time in literature when a young thrush and a bobolink have printed a book!"
50 EGE, *Sister*, 29.
51 EGE, *Voice*, 23.
52 "Miss Elaine Goodale's Life Work," *Hartford Courant*, January 1887.
53 Reeve, *Path*, 116.
54 "Elaine Goodale Eastman," *Leslie's Weekly*, May 23, 1897.
55 EGE, *Sister*, 30; EGE, *Voice*, 24.
56 EGE, *Sister*, 31.
57 Ibid.
58 *Southern Workman*, August 1, 1886.

59 Laura Tileston to Ruth Tileston, September 13, 1886, Gregg-Tileston Family Papers, Massachusetts Historical Society.
60 Laura Tileston, "How to Do It," *Southern Workman*, December 1, 1886.
61 EG, "Preparing for School at White River Camp," *The Independent*, April 14, 1887, 39.
62 Ibid.
63 EGE, *Sister*, 32–33.
64 EG, "The Opening of White River School," *The Independent*, May 19, 1887, 39.
65 Haircuts Native American students received at boarding schools became a part of their indoctrination into Euro-American culture and sometimes were used as propaganda. Peter Hayes Mauro writes that Richard Henry Pratt staged "before and after" photos of some of his Carlisle Indian School students as a way of "persuading the public that not only were such schools viable for congressional funding, but that the assimilation project was moral and just." Peter Hayes Mauro, *The Art of Americanization at the Carlisle Indian School* (Albuquerque, NM: University of New Mexico Press, 2011), 82.
66 Ibid.
67 Ibid.
68 EGE, *Voice*, 25.
69 EGE, *Sister*, 42.
70 Ibid., 41.
71 Spack, *America's Second Tongue*, 14.
72 EGE, *Sister*, 35.
73 Ibid., 43.
74 EGE, "The Indian—A Woman among the Indians," in Frances A. Goodale, ed., *The Literature of Philanthropy* (New York, NY: Harper & Bros., 1893), 132–133.
75 Ibid., 45.
76 EGE, *Voice*, 23–24.
77 EGE, *Sister*, 48.
78 Treuer, *Heartbreak*, 150.
79 Indian Rights Association, "The Herbert Welsh Years, 1882–1904" (Philadelphia, PA: Indian Rights Association, 1985), 55.
80 EG, "After Mohonk—What?," *The Independent*, November 4, 1886, 38.
81 Hoxie, *Final Promise*, 77.
82 Ostler, *Plains Indians*, 217; Roxanne Dunbar-Ortiz, *An Indigenous Peoples' History of the United States* (Boston, MA: Beacon Press, 2014), 158.
83 Hoxie, *Final Promise*, 24.
84 Hämaläinen, *Lakota America*, 380.
85 EG, "The Senator and the School-House," *The Independent*, March 4, 1886, 1.
86 EGE, *Sister*, 65.
87 EG, "Among the Sand-Hills of Nebraska," *Christian Union*, November 21, 1889, 21.
88 EG, "Will the Indians Sign?" *The Independent*, August 16, 1888, 6.
89 EG, "With the Indians," *Southern Workman*, November 1, 1885.
90 EGE, *Sister*, 88.

91 Ibid., 91–92.
92 EG, "The Sioux in Council," *The Independent*, October 18, 1888, 4.
93 EGE, *Voice*, 25.
94 EGE, *Voice*, 26.
95 EGE, *Sister*, 95.
96 EG, "Among the Sand-Hills of Nebraska," *Christian Union*, November 21, 1889, 21.
97 Bishop William Hare to Indian Commissioner, November 9, 1899; General Samuel Armstrong to Indian Commissioner, 1899; W. W. Anderson to Indian Commissioner, November 11, 1899; all in Smith.
98 Department of the Interior, Office of Indian Affairs, March 14, 1890, Smith.
99 EGE, *Sister*, 120.
100 EG, "The Model Indian Day School," *Christian Union*, August 21, 1980, 232.
101 EGE, *Sister*, 126.
102 Ibid., 121.
103 EG, "Attacks upon Indian Education," *Christian Union*, January 30, 1890, 152.
104 EG, "The Health Question on the Reservations," *The Independent*, June 5, 1890. 5.
105 EGE, *Sister*, 152.

3. FROM INDIAN COUNTRY TO DARTMOUTH AND BACK (1858–1890)

1 Hämaläinen, *Lakota America*, 6.
2 Ibid., 220.
3 Seth Eastman would go on to become a major Euro-American illustrator of Native American life. His second wife, Mary Henderson Eastman, gained fame recording Indian cultures.
4 Wilson, *Ohiyesa*, 13.
5 CAE, *Indian Boyhood*, 5.
6 Ibid., 7.
7 Ibid., 11.
8 Hämaläinen, *Lakota America*, 253.
9 Miller, "Journey," 27.
10 This war's name is another example of how words themselves expose differing worldviews.
11 For detailed information, see Gary C. Anderson, *Massacre in Minnesota* (Norman, OK: University of Oklahoma Press, 2019).
12 CAE, *Indian Boyhood*, 16.
13 Ibid., 19.
14 Drew Lopenzina, "Good Indian: Charles Eastman and the Warrior as Civil Servant," *American Indian Quarterly* 27 (3&4), Summer/Fall 2003, 740.
15 Martínez, *Philosopher*, 29.
16 Yvonne Wynde, "Remembering Relatives," in Charles A. Eastman, *In the Beginning, The Sun*, ed. Gail Johnsen and Sydney D. Beane (St. Paul, MN: Minnesota Historical Society Press, 2023), 160.
17 CAE, *Indian Boyhood*, 107.

18 Jennifer Bess, "'Kill the Indian and Save the Man!' Charles Eastman Surveys His Past," *Wicazo Sa Review* 15 (1), Spring 2000, 15.
19 Katherine Beane, Woyakapi Kin Ahdipi, "Bringing the Story Home: A History within the Wakpa Ipaksan Dakota Oyate" (PhD diss. University of Minnesota, 2014).
20 CAE, *Indian Boyhood*, 45.
21 CAE, *Deep Woods*, 7.
22 CAE, *Indian Boyhood*, 289.
23 Dakota Iapi Teunhindapi (Morton, MN: Dakota Wicohan, 2013).
24 CAE, *Deep Woods*, 7.
25 Ernst Mensel, "John, Charles and Elaine Goodale Eastman: Their Story—a Contribution to the American Indian" (BA thesis, Dartmouth College, 1954), 19.
26 CAE, *Deep Woods*, 29.
27 Ibid., 30.
28 John Eastman was the Presbyterian minister in Flandreau, 1876–1906.
29 Lopenzina, "Good Indian," 741.
30 Alfred L. Riggs to President A. L. Chapin, September 26, 1876, Beloit.
31 Annual Catalogue of Beloit College, 171–72, Beloit.
32 CAE, *Deep Woods*, 50.
33 Martínez, *Philosopher*, ix. Beane, "Bringing the Story Home," suggests that while many people have written about Ohiyesa as caught between two worlds, this serves as a binary separating Indigenous and non-Indigenous ways of thinking.
34 CAE, *Deep Woods*, 53.
35 Vigil, *Indigenous Intellectuals*, 64.
36 CAE, *Deep Woods*, 54.
37 Knox College Catalog 1880–1881, Special Collections and Archives, Henry M. Seymour Library, Galesburg, IL.
38 Wilson, *Ohiyesa*, 25.
39 CAE, *Deep Woods*, 60.
40 Wilson, *Ohiyesa*, 32.
41 Charles Eastman, "Recollections," cited in Mensel, "John, Charles and Elaine Goodale Eastman," 24.
42 Colin Calloway, *The Indian History of an American Institution: Native Americans and Dartmouth* (Hanover, NH: Dartmouth College Press, 2010), 116.
43 CAE, *Deep Woods*, 70.
44 Ibid., 69.
45 Roy Harvey Pearce, *Savagism and Civilization* (Baltimore, MD: Johns Hopkins University Press, 1967), 135.
46 Kate Beane, "This Is Our Truth," and Gail Johnsen, "A Journey through Time and Family," in CAE, *In the Beginning, The Sun*, 184, 7.
47 32 Newsletter, n.d., Dartmouth; Frances Karttunen, "Three Civil Servants," in *Between Worlds: Interpreters, Guides and Survivors* (New Brunswick, NJ: Rutgers University Press, 1994), 143.

48 Fred E. Winn, "Ohiyesa, Dr. Charles A. Eastman," n.d., Dartmouth.
49 CAE, *Deep Woods*, 69.
50 "Dr. Charles A. Eastman," *Housekeeper's Weekly*, July 18, 1891.
51 Winn, "Ohiyesa, Dr. Charles A. Eastman."
52 Calloway, *The Indian History of an American Institution*, 113.
53 "Dr. Charles A. Eastman," *Housekeeper's Weekly*, July 18, 1891.
54 "The Sioux Who Went to Dartmouth College," *New York Sun*, October 15, 1916, 2.
55 Stanley E. Johnson, "The Indian Ohiyesa," *Dartmouth Alumni Magazine*, June 1929, 521, Dartmouth.
56 Cited in Mensel, "John, Charles and Elaine Goodale Eastman," 25.
57 Johnson, "The Indian Ohiyesa."
58 Ibid., 43.
59 Deloria, *Playing Indian*, 123.

4. FROM BOSTON UNIVERSITY TO PINE RIDGE AGENCY (1887–1890)

1 Boston University School of Medicine Catalogue, Boston University Alumni Medical Library Archives, 1887, 10.
2 Miller, "Journey," 85.
3 CAE, *Deep Woods*, 71.
4 Boston University School of Medicine Catalogue, Boston University Alumni Medical Library Archives, 1887, 10.
5 CAE, *Deep Woods*, 71.
6 Ibid., 73.
7 CAE, *Deep Woods*, 74.
8 Author correspondence with A'Llyn Ettien, BU Medical School Archives, June 29, 2020.
9 "He's a Winner," *Boston Daily Globe*, June 5, 1890, 4.
10 CAE, *Deep Woods*, 186.
11 Frank Wood to Thomas J. Morgan, May 19, 1890, National Archives, RG 75, document #15646.
12 Margaret Jacobs, *After One Hundred Winters*, (Princeton, NJ: Princeton University Press, 2021), 126.
13 Larry E. Burgess, "We'll Discuss It at Mohonk," *Quaker History* 60 (1), Spring 1971, 20.
14 Dr. Charles A. Eastman, "Reports from the Field," *Proceedings of the 8th Annual Lake Mohonk Indian Conference*, October 8, 1890, 46.
15 Frank Wood to Thomas J. Morgan, May 19, 1890, National Archives, RG 75, document #15646.
16 Frank Wood to Frank Dorchester, July 18, 1890, National Archives, RG 75, document #24038.
17 Miller, "Journey," 92.
18 Charles Eastman to Thomas Morgan, August 20, 1890, National Archives, RG 75, document #25761.

19 Frederick Hoxie, *Talking Back to Civilization* (Boston, MA: Bedford/St. Martin, 2001), 2.
20 Thomas J. Morgan to John Willock Noble, November 23, 1892, National Archives, RG 75.
21 Martínez, *Philosopher*, 4.
22 CAE, *Deep Woods*, 76.

5. THE WOUNDED KNEE MASSACRE (1890)

1 Hämaläinen, *Lakota America*, 51.
2 Mario Gonzalez and Elizabeth Cook-Lynn, *The Politics of Hallowed Ground: Wounded Knee and the Struggle for Indian Sovereignty* (Urbana, IL: University of Illinois Press, 1999).
3 Gretchen Cassel Eick, "U.S. Indian Policy, 1865–1890 as Illuminated through the Lives of Charles A. Eastman and Elaine Goodale Eastman," *Great Plains Quarterly* 28 (1), Winter 2008, 35.
4 Ostler, *Plains Indians*, 221.
5 Heather Cox Richardson, *Wounded Knee: Party Politics and the Road to an American Massacre* (New York, NY: Basic Books, 2010), 169.
6 James Mooney, *The Ghost Dance Religion and Wounded Knee* (New York, NY: Dover Publications, 1896, 1973), 771–772.
7 Ibid., 262. Also see Robert M. Utley, *The Last Days of the Sioux Nation* (New Haven, CT: Yale University Press, 1963).
8 Richard E. Jensen, Eli R. Paul, and John F. Carter, *Eyewitness at Wounded Knee* (Lincoln, NE: University of Nebraska Press, 1991), 73.
9 "Latest Indian News: Gov. Mellette Issues a Proclamation," *Wessington Springs Herald*, December 5, 1890, 2.
10 Ostler, *Plains Indians*, 288.
11 CAE, *Deep Woods*, 82–84.
12 EGE, *Voice*, 28.
13 EGE, *Sister*, 148.
14 EG, "After the Ghost Feast," *The Independent*, March 6, 1890, 4.
15 EGE, *Voice*, 28.
16 CAE, *Deep Woods*, 78.
17 Ibid., 81.
18 EGE, *Sister*, 169.
19 CAE, *Deep Woods*, 86.
20 EGE, *Sister*, 169.
21 Robert Utley, *The Indian Frontier of the American West 1846–1890* (Albuquerque, NM: University of New Mexico Press, 1984), 253.
22 By the end of his life, Royer, retired in California, lost his medical license due to self-dealing and misusing prescriptions. He lost his livelihood and his health from drug use and alcoholism.
23 "Hon D. F. Royer's Record," *Wessington Springs Herald*, April 5, 1889, 8.
24 Daniel F. Royer, November 19, 1890. Cited in John Koster, "Sioux Agent Daniel F. Royer Saw Dancing and Panicked," *Indian Life*, December 2010, 24.

25 Richardson, *Wounded Knee*, 220.
26 Utley. (1984), 254.
27 Richardson, *Wounded Knee*, 170, 175.
28 EGE, *Sister*, 146.
29 CAE, *Deep Woods*, 99.
30 Ibid.
31 EGE, *Sister*, 141.
32 Ibid., 157.
33 CAE, *Deep Woods*, 105–106.
34 EGE, *Sister*, 169.
35 Ibid., 170–171.
36 CAE, *Deep Woods*, 86–87.
37 EGE, *Sister*, 172.
38 CAE to RG, January 20, 1890, Smith.
39 CAE, *Deep Woods*, 107.
40 EGE, *Sister*, 160.
41 CAE, *Deep Woods*, 108.
42 Ibid., 109; EGE, *Sister*, 160.
43 Ibid., 161–162.
44 CAE, *Deep Woods*, 112.
45 Doug Hughes, "Standing Room Only Crowd Learns of BUSM Alum, First Native American Graduate of U.S. Medical School," Boston University School of Medicine, March 19, 2014.
46 Joe Dobrow points out that John Burke may or may not have played other roles at Wounded Knee, including whether he was on the battleground. For more information about this, see Joe Dobrow, *The Pioneers of Promotion* (Norman, OK: University of Oklahoma Press, 2018), 189–191.
47 Renée Sansom Flood, *Lost Bird of Wounded Knee* (New York, NY: Scribner's, 1995). The baby, originally called Zintkála Nuni or Lost Bird, later christened Margaret Elizabeth Colby, led a tragic life that probably included sexual abuse by her adoptive father, prostitution, and syphilis. Years after she died in California, her remains were reinterred at the cemetery of the victims of the Wounded Knee Massacre.
48 Jensen, Paul, and Carter, *Eyewitness at Wounded Knee*, 20.
49 "The Situation Is Serious," *Madison Daily Leader*, January 7, 1891, 1.
50 "A Sioux Defense," *Pittsburgh Dispatch*, January 10, 1891, 10.
51 "A Step toward Healing: Barre Museum Returns Looted Wounded Knew Artifacts to the Lakota," *Boston Globe*, November 5, 2022.
52 Ibid., 39.
53 Treuer, *Heartbreak*, 1.
54 "Conflict at Last," *Washburn Leader*, January 3, 1891, 4.
55 L. Frank Baum, "The Wounded Knee Editorial," *Aberdeen Saturday Pioneer*, January 3, 1891.
56 EGE, *Voice*, 28.

57 “The Wounded Knee Fight: Elaine Goodale Says the Indians Were Not Much to Blame,” *Los Angeles Herald*, January 17, 1891, 1.
58 “‘Had an Old Grudge to Repay’: Miss Elaine Goodale’s Version of the Wounded Knee Battle,” *Boston Post*, January 17, 1891, 2.
59 Berg, “White Women Writing for Their Lives,” 165.
60 EG, “Incidents of the Indian War,” *The Independent*, January 22, 1891, 6.
61 EG, “Why Should Not the Indians Enlist?,” *The Independent*, June 4, 1891, 1.
62 George W. Baird, “Are Soldiers Murderers?,” *The Independent*, June 25, 1891, 3.
63 “The Wounded Knee Affair,” *Watertown* (NY) *Times*, January 17, 1891, 4. Note: it is tempting to think that Elaine Goodale Eastman’s contemporaneous writings about the role of the Seventh Cavalry at Wounded Knee have played some small role in modern-day efforts to review the awarding of Medals of Honor to soldiers who participated in the massacre. See, for example, “Defense Department to review Medals of Honor awarded for Wounded Knee Massacre,” *Washington Post*, July 25, 2024.
64 Charles A. Eastman, “The Dakota Indians,” *Boston Journal*, January 8, 1891, Newberry.
65 CAE, *Deep Woods*, 117.
66 See Martha Viehmann, “Writing across the Cultural Divide: Images of Indians in the Lives and Works of Native and European Americans, 1890–1935” (PhD diss., Yale University, 1994).
67 EGE to RGD, February 15, 1932, Smith. Elaine was probably referring to *Black Elk Speaks*, the “autobiography” of Sioux medicine man Black Elk written by John G. Neihardt, published in 1932. Even at the time, the book was criticized for exaggerating parts of Black Elk’s life to make it marketable; in more recent years it has been criticized as an inaccurate representation of Lakota beliefs.
68 EG, Letter to the editor, *The World*, January 10, 1891.
69 EGE, *Sister*, 167.
70 Martínez, *Philosopher*, xii, 14.
71 Gerald Vizenor, *Manifest Manners: Narratives of Post Indian Survivance* (Lincoln, NE: University of Nebraska Press, 1994), 48.
72 CAE, *Deep Woods*, 135.
73 EGE, *Sister*, 169.
74 Treuer, *Heartbreak*, 1.

6. FROM ST. PAUL TO WASHINGTON (1891–1899)

1 EGE, *Voice*, 29.
2 RSG to Redington M. Dayton, January 1, 12, 1891, Collection of Deborah Read (Dayton) Scoblick, cited in Sargent, *Life*, 46.
3 DRG to RGD, circa 1930, Smith.
4 Cited in Sargent, *Life*, 47.
5 CAE to RG, January 20, 1891, Smith.
6 *Buffalo Evening News*, January 12, 1891.
7 “The New Idyl of Elaine,” *The World*, January 18, 1891.

8 "Miss Goodale's Betrothal: The News Confirmed—Some Account of the Man of Her Choice," *Poughkeepsie Daily Eagle,* January 12, 1891.
9 *The Indian Helper,* January 16, 1891, Carlisle.
10 "Elaine Goodale's Indian Lover," *Boston Herald,* January 14, 1891.
11 "A Scatterbrained Correspondent," *Buffalo Courier,* January 31, 1891, 4.
12 Margaret D. Jacobs, "The Eastmans and the Luhans: Interracial Marriage between White Women and Native American Men, 1875–1935," Department of History at DigitalCommons@University of Nebraska-Lincoln, October 2002, 31.
13 Anne F. Hyde, *Born of Lakes and Plains* (New York, NY: W. W. Norton, 2022).
14 C. Joseph Genetin-Pilawa, "All Intent on Seeing the White Woman Married to the Red Man," *Journal of Women's History* 20 (2), 2008, 75.
15 Cathleen D. Cahill, "You Think It Strange That I Can Love an Indian," *Frontiers* 29 (2–3), 2008, 118.
16 Sargent, *Life,* 51.
17 "Married a Sioux," *Madison Daily Leader,* June 19, 1891; "An Indian Princess," *Boston Daily Globe,* June 19, 1891, 4. This headline emphasized a stereotype many consider derogatory.
18 "An Indian Princess," *Boston Daily Globe,* June 19, 1891, 4.
19 "A Poetess Weds a Big Injun," *Watertown Times,* June 18, 1891, 1; "An Indian Princess," *Boston Daily Globe.*
20 "Wedded a High-Born Sioux," *The World,* June 18, 1891, 1.
21 "Wedded to a Sioux/The Child Poet of Sky Farm Becomes Mrs. Eastman," *New York Sun,* June 19, 1891.
22 "Address: The New Education," *Wellesley Prelude,* June 27, 1891.
23 Jean Kincaid, "Greeted by Friends, Dr. Eastman and His Wife Given a Reception," *Boston Daily Globe,* June 26, 1891.
24 CAE, *Deep Woods,* 126.
25 EGE, *Voice,* 29.
26 CAE, *Deep Woods,* 126–127.
27 Miller, "Journey," 154.
28 EGE, *Sister,* 173.
29 EGE, "A Day with an Agency Physician," *The Independent,* April 14, 1892, 9.
30 CAE, *Deep Woods,* 127.
31 EGE, "A Day with an Agency Physician."
32 EGE to RGD, March 1, 1933, Smith.
33 Eick points out this wasn't a trivial sum of money. In 2020 dollars, this would be about $2.8 million. Gretchen Cassel Eick, *They Met at Wounded Knee* (Reno, NV: University of Nevada Press, 2020), 11.
34 David Reed Miller, "Charles Alexander Eastman: One Man's Journey in Two Worlds" (MA thesis, University of North Dakota/Grand Forks, 1975), 135.
35 James A. Cooper to Thomas J. Morgan, July 22, 1892, National Archives, RG 76, #26737.
36 Wilson, *Ohiyesa,* 72.

37 "Both Cannot Rule: The Agent at Pine Ridge Is Sustained and Dr. Eastman Is Removed," *Boston Post*, February 14, 1893, 4.
38 Frank Wood to Thomas J. Morgan, December 3, 1892, National Archives, RG 76; Thomas J. Morgan to John W. Noble, November 23, 1892, ibid.
39 "Elaine Is Discharged," *St. Paul Daily Globe*, December 25, 1892.
40 "McGillicuddy's Indian Scare: Elaine Goodale Eastman Tells about the Coming 'Outbreak at Pine Ridge,'" *Sioux City Journal*, November 25, 1892, 2.
41 "Pine Ridge Agency Controversy Is Settled by Secretary Noble," n.d., Dartmouth.
42 "Pine Ridge Rottenness," *Sioux City Journal*, January 8, 1893, 5.
43 "Elaine Is a Tartar: An Indian Agent Talks about the Grown-Up 'Child Poetess,'" *St. Louis Post-Dispatch*, June 4, 1893, 3.
44 CAE to Thomas J. Morgan, December 18, 1892, National Archives, RG 75.
45 Miller, "Journey," 150.
46 "Indian Agency Dispute," *New York Times*, January 25, 1892.
47 "General Domestic News," *Herald-Advance*, August 26, 1892; *Cortland Standard*, September 16, 1892; "An Interesting Baby," *Berkshire Eagle*, June 20, 1892, 3.
48 CAE, *Deep Woods*, 135.
49 EGE to RGD, March 1, 1933, Smith.
50 "Fear Indian War; Dr. Eastman of Pine Ridge Looks for a General Uprising," *St. Paul Daily Globe*, February 9, 1893, 2.
51 Eick, *They Met*, 111.
52 Teresa Swanson, Sydney Beane, and William Beane, "Charles and Elaine Eastman: Their Years in St. Paul, 1893–1898," *Ramsey County History* 53 (1), Spring 2018, 8.
53 Ad in the *St. Paul Globe*, February 1891.
54 CAE, *Deep Woods*, 137–138.
55 EGE, *Voice*, 30.
56 CAE, *Deep Woods*, 139.
57 CAE, "Recollection of the Wild Life: Hakada, 'the Pitiful Last,'" *St. Nicholas Magazine*, December 1893, 129.
58 Swanson, Beane, and Beane, "Charles and Elaine Eastman," 9–10.
59 Christopher Pexa, *Translated Nation: Rewriting the Dakhóta Oyáte* (Minneapolis, MN: University of Minnesota Press, 2019), 102.
60 Charles A. Eastman, "Sioux Mythology," address to the International Folk-Lore Congress of the World's Columbian Exposition, Chicago, IL, 1893.
61 David Murray, *Matter, Magic and Spirit: Representing Indian and African American Belief* (Philadelphia, PA: University of Pennsylvania Press, 2013), 44.
62 EGE to RG, March 1894, Smith.
63 CAE, *Deep Woods*, 140.
64 Rob Eshman, "Stranger in the Land," *Dartmouth Alumni Magazine*, January 1981, 22.
65 EGE to RG, September 12, 1894, Smith.
66 YMCA Year Books of North America, "Charles A. Eastman's Work among American Indians," Kautz Family YMCA Archives, University of Minnesota Libraries.

67 "Work among the Indians," *World Herald*, September 22, 1894, ibid.
68 "Evangelizing the Indians," *Omaha Daily Bee*, September 9, 1894, 8.
69 EGE, "Religious Intelligence: A New Opportunity for the Indian," *The Independent*, January 16, 1896, 13.
70 "Wedded to a Sioux and Finds that Marriage Is a Success," *Cook County Herald*, April 20, 1895.
71 "Back from the West; Elaine Goodale Eastman Revisits New York," *St. Louis Post-Dispatch*, October 7, 1895; "Work for the Indian," Dartmouth.
72 *Proceedings of the Thirteenth Annual Lake Mohonk Indian Conference*, 1895, 66, 92. Available at the Digital Public Library of America, https://dp.la/item/588dd4d25c366caa195f525eace9d71a.
73 Sargent, *Life*, 61.
74 Martínez, *Philosopher*, 22.
75 "Dr. C. A. Eastman Makes an Eloquent Address," *Boston Globe*, October 23, 1895, 7.
76 EGE, *Voice*, 30.
77 EGE to RGD April 14, 1940, Smith.
78 EGE, *Voice*, 30.
79 EGE, "Papa's Kisses," *The Independent*, October 4, 1894, 27.
80 Raymond Wilson, "Forty Years to Judgment: The Santee Sioux Claims Case," *Minnesota History*, Fall 1981, 285.
81 As Hoxie points out, the Santee claims case became part of a larger movement for Native Americans to become an "independent and self-sustaining minority community." Hoxie, *This Indian Country*, 212.
82 CAE, *Deep Woods*, 152.
83 "He Is an Educated Sioux," *Black Hills Union*, February 17, 1899.
84 "Indian a Physical Degenerate," *Washington Post*, June 20, 1898, 10.
85 CAE, *Deep Woods*, 155.
86 "Renew Allegiance; Songs of Praise from Dartmouth College Graduates," *Washington Evening Star*, February 8, 1899, 10.
87 Miller, "Journey," 183.

7. FROM CARLISLE TO AMHERST (1899–1903)

1 EGE, *Pratt, The Red Man's Moses* (Norman, OK: University of Oklahoma Press, 1935), 13.
2 Alan Trachtenberg, *Shades of Hiawatha: Staging Indians, Making Americans 1880–1930* (New York, NY: Farrar, Strauss, Giroux, 2005), 42.
3 Peter Hayes Mauro, *The Art of Americanization at the Carlisle Indian School* (Albuquerque, NM: University of New Mexico Press, 2011), 77, 85.
4 *The Indian Helper*, July 1, 1899.
5 Letter from Richard Henry Pratt to Commissioner of Indian Affairs, November 9, 1899, Carlisle.
6 *The Indian Helper*, July 21, 1899; November 2, 1899; August 26, 1899.
7 EGE, "Comrades All," *The Indian Helper*, October 13, 1899.

8 EGE, "Song of the Carlisle Indians," *The Independent*, November 1, 1899.
9 EGE, "A New Method of Indian Education," *The Outlook*, January 1900, 222.
10 CAE, "The Story of the Little Big Horn," *The Chautauquan*, July 1900, 358.
11 Angela Calcaterra, *Literary Indians* (Chapel Hill, NC: University of North Carolina Press, 2018), 167–173.
12 CAE, *Indian Today*, 71.
13 Richard A. Pratt to William A. Jones, January 1, 1900, Carlisle.
14 *The Indian Helper*, January 26, 1900.
15 Ibid., March 2, 1900.
16 EGE to RGD, February 9, 1938, Smith.
17 Wilson, *Ohiyesa*, 106.
18 EGE to DRG, November 7, 1901, Smith.
19 It's possible Charles Eastman's early work trying to counter vaccine hesitancy among Native populations helped to pay this forward. During the COVID-19 pandemic, non-Hispanic American Indian and Alaska Native populations had the highest first-dose and full vaccination rates of any racial or ethnic groups, according to an article in the *New England Journal of Medicine*. Raymond Foxworth et al., "Covid-19 Vaccination in American Indians and Alaska Natives—Lessons from Effective Community Responses," *New England Journal of Medicine*, December 23, 2021.
20 CAE, *Indian Today*, 141.
21 Eick, *They Met*, 111.
22 CAE, *Deep Woods*, 185.
23 Dartmouth.
24 *New York Sun*, "A book of very great interest," September 20, 1902, 10; *Washington Evening Star*, "Review of *Indian Boyhood*," September 20, 1902, 22; *Brooklyn Daily Eagle*, "Dr. Charles A. Eastman, a full blooded Dakotah, describes his childhood and youth," October 2, 1902, 8.
25 See, for example, David J. Carlson, "Indian for a While: Charles Eastman's Indian Boyhood and the Discourse of Allotment," *American Indian Quarterly* 25 (4), Fall 2001, 619; Calcaterra, *Literary Indians*, 153; Gale P. Coksan-Johnson, "What Writer Would Not Be an Indian for a While? Charles Alexander Eastman, Critical Memory, and Audience," *Studies in American Indian Literature* 18 (2), Summer 2006, 106.
26 "Romance Worthy of Cooper," *St. Paul Globe*, December 29, 1902, 8.
27 "Wed an Indian and Is Happy," *Portsmouth Herald*, December 16, 1902, 1.
28 EGE, *Red Man and Helper*, September 27, 1901, Carlisle.
29 William Least Heat-Moon, "A Stark Reminder of How the U.S. Forced American Indians into a New Way of Life," *Smithsonian Magazine*, November 2013.
30 CAE, *Indian Today*, 44.
31 Wilson, *Ohiyesa*, 110.
32 "Interior Department's Action in Case of Indian Agent Chamberlain," *New York Tribune*, February 11, 1903, 3.
33 Ibid., 115.

34 *Courier Democrat,* "Resume of the news," January 15, 1903, 2.
35 *New York Tribune,* "Books and Authors," January 17, 1903, 10.
36 EGE to RGD, March 1, 1933, Smith.
37 Sarah Pripas-Kapit, "We Lived on Broken Promises: Charles A. Eastman, Susan La Flesche Picotte, and the Politics of American Indian Assimilation during the Progressive Era," *Great Plains Quarterly* 35 (1), Winter 2015, 51.
38 Miller, "Journey," 203.
39 Sargent, *Life,* 69.
40 EGE to RGD, March 1, 1933, Smith.
41 "Former Neighbor of Indian Author Writes Recollections," *New Bedford Standard Times,* January 30, 1949.
42 EGE to RGD, July 24, 1931, Smith.
43 Ibid., circa 1932.
44 EGE, *Buffalo Enquirer,* April 29, 1903, 2.
45 Francis Paul Prucha, *The Great Father: The United States Government and the American Indian,* vol. 1 (Lincoln, NE: University of Nebraska Press, 1984), 674.
46 For a fuller discussion of Hamlin Garland's views and work, see Hoxie, *Final Promise.*
47 Charles Eastman to Hamlin Garland, November 17, 1902, USC.
48 Ethan A. Hitchcock to Hamlin Garland, February 27, 1903, USC.
49 Ibid., December 3, 1902.
50 CAE, *Deep Woods,* 184.
51 "Indian Names: Complete Revision Now Going on under the Government," *Washington Evening Star,* March 24, 1903.
52 Ibid., 183.
53 CAE to William Jones, November 20, 1903, USC.

8. FROM AMHERST TO LONDON (1903–1911)

1 Amherst Indian Association Ten Year Report, 1900, Jones.
2 "Lecture by Dr. Eastman Addresses an Amherst Audience on 'A School of Savagery,'" *Springfield Daily Republican,* December 3, 1903, 4.
3 Mabel Loomis Todd, "Diary," December 2, 1903, Yale.
4 CAE to J. B. Pond, February 14, 1903, James B. Pond Papers, Special Collections, University of Delaware Library, Newark, DE; ibid., April 19, 1903.
5 Southern Lyceum Bureau, 1904–1905, "Dr. Charles A. Eastman (Ohiyesa)," Historical Society of Cheshire County, Keene, NH.
6 *Springfield Daily Republican,* December 31, 1903.
7 EGE, "The Life of Little Yellow Star," *Iowa County Democrat,* February 18, 1904, 7.
8 Wilson, *Ohiyesa,* 126.
9 "Naming Sioux Indians: Dr. Eastman of Amherst Has Nearly Completed Big Task Assigned by Government," *Daily Hampshire Gazette,* November 27, 1907.
10 "Renaming the Indian: Interesting Work by Dr. Charles Alexander Eastman; the Unpronounceable Red Man's Name to Go," *Boston Globe,* n.d.

11 CAE, *The Soul of the Indian* (Boston, MA: Houghton Mifflin, 1911), 44.
12 See, for example, Eick, *They Met*, 150.
13 Richard K. Popp, "Information, Industrialization, and the Business of Press Clippings, 1880–1925, *Journal of American History* 101 (2), 2014, 438.
14 "Review of *Red Hunters and the Animal People*," *Brooklyn Daily Eagle*, November 26, 1904, 8; *New York Tribune*, November 11, 1904.
15 Christopher J. Pexa, "More than Talking Animals: Charles Alexander Eastman's Animal Peoples and Their Kinship Critiques of United States Colonialism," *PLMA* 131 (2), 2016, 653.
16 EGE to RGD, circa 1936, Smith; EGE to Mr. Winn, April 7, 1939, Dartmouth.
17 Sargent, *Life*, 73.
18 Hyde, *Born of Lakes and Plains*, 311.
19 EGE to RGD, late 1920s, Smith.
20 Deloria, *Playing Indian*, 4.
21 Vigil, *Indigenous Intellectuals*, 45.
22 "Ohiyesa Came in Real Sioux Costume and Told Story of Genuine Heart Interest," *Lewiston Sun*, December 7, 1912.
23 Lucy Maddox, *Citizen Indians: Native American Intellectuals, Race and Reform* (Ithaca, NY: Cornell University Press, 2005), 128.
24 "Remarkably Clear and Instructive Lecture by Dr. Charles A. Eastman," *Barre Daily Times*, November 1, 1911, 1.
25 Tony Dykema-VanderArk, "Playing Indian in Print: Charles Alexander Eastman's Autobiographical Writing for Children," MELUS 27 (2), March 2002, 9–30.
26 See, for example, Hoxie, *This Indian Country*; Ian Harvey, "Photos of Native Americans Who Performed in 'Buffalo Bill's Wild West,'" 2016, https://www.thevintagenews.com; Gilbert King, "Edward Curtis' Epic Project to Photograph Native Americans," *Smithsonian Magazine*, 2012, https://www.smithsonianmag.com.
27 EGE to RGD, March 1, 1933, Smith; ibid., February 3, 1937.
28 Ibid., April 28, 1939.
29 James W. Dayton to RGD, 1910, Smith.
30 "Sacred to the New Woman: An Apartment House Where She Devotes Herself to Art and Light Housekeeping," *New York Times*, April 10, 1898, 14.
31 EGE to RGD, September 17, 1926, Smith.
32 "Obituary of Henry S. Goodale," *Springfield Republican*, July 21, 1906.
33 EGE to RGD, February 15, 1932, Smith.
34 Ibid., August 13, 1940.
35 EGE, *Voice*, 121.
36 EGE to RGD, February 15, 1931, Smith.
37 Sargent, *Life*, 93–94.
38 "Review of *Yellow Star*," *San Francisco Call*, November 12, 1911.
39 Sansom Flood, *Lost Bird*.
40 EGE, *Voice*, 31.

41 Sarah Ruffing Robbins, "Elaine Goodale Eastman Modernist Author? Re-visiting a Border-Crossing Woman Writer's Place in Literary History," 2019, 1. https://journals.openedition.org/erea/7121.
42 "Indians Not a Dying Race," *Caney Chronicle*, September 13, 1910, 2.
43 CAE, *Deep Woods*, 173.
44 Martínez, *Philosopher*, 75.
45 David Reed Miller, "Charles Alexander Eastman, Santee Sioux, 1858–1939," in Margot Liberty, ed., *American Indian Intellectuals of the Nineteenth and Early Twentieth Centuries* (Norman, OK: University of Oklahoma Press, 1978), 72.
46 Neil Schmitz, *White Robe's Dilemma: Tribal History in American Literature* (Amherst, MA: University of Massachusetts Press, 2001), 110.
47 Martínez, *Philosopher*, 75.
48 David Martínez, "Out of the Woods and into the Museum: Charles A. Eastman's 1910 Collecting Expedition across Ojibwe Country," *American Indian Culture and Research Journal* 32 (4), 2008, 81.
49 "Review, *Little Brother O' Dreams*," *Topeka State Journal*, February 26, 1910. 16; *New York Sun*, February 26, 1910.
50 DRG to EGE, June 13, 1910, Smith.
51 Reeve, *Path*, 120.
52 EGE, "Halley's Comet," *The Independent*, April 21, 1910, 865.
53 Kyle Mays, "Transnational Progressivism: African Americans, Native Americans, and the Universal Races Congress of 1911," *Studies in American Indian Literatures* 25 (2), Summer 2013, 243–261.
54 CAE, "The North American Indian," in Gustave Spiller, *Papers on Inter-racial Problems, Communicated to the First Universal Races Congress* (London: P. S. King and Son, 1911), 367–377.
55 CAE, *Deep Woods*, 190.
56 EGE, *Voice*, 98.

9. FROM CAMP OÁHE TO NORTHAMPTON AND DETROIT (1912–1921)

1 EGE to RGD, December 18, 1914, Smith.
2 Vigil, *Indigenous Intellectuals*, 47, 58.
3 Cristina Stanciu, "Americanization on Native Terms: The Society of American Indians, Citizenship Debates, and Tropes of 'Racial Difference,'" *Native American and Indigenous Studies* 6 (1), 2019, 124.
4 For a fuller discussion, see Hoxie, *This Indian Country*, 225–276.
5 "Review of *The Indian Today*," *Evening Public Ledger*, August 20, 1915, 5.
6 Miller, "Journey," 243.
7 CAE, *Deep Woods*, 195.
8 Malea Powell, "Imagining a New Indian: Listening to the Rhetoric of Survivance in Charles Eastman's Deep Woods," *Paradoxa* 15 (2001), 223. See also David Brumble, ed.,

An Annotated Biography of American Indian And Eskimo Autobiographies (Lincoln, NE: University of Nebraska Press, 1981).

9 Lisa Tatonetti, "Disrupting a Story of Loss: Charles Eastman and Nicholas Black Elk Narrative Survivance," *Western American Literature* 39 (3), Fall 2004, 286.

10 Lopenzina, "Good Indian," 729.

11 "Review of *From the Deep Woods to Civilization*," *Boston Globe*, October 28, 1916, 3; *New York Times*, December 24, 1916, 66.

12 *Springfield Union*, July 17, 1912, 12.

13 *Christian Science Monitor*, n.d., 1917.

14 Lucy Maddox, "Politics, Performance and Indian Identity," *American Studies International* 40 (2), 2002, 17.

15 "Indian Says Pale Face Is Incubator Hatched," *Boston Herald*, n.d., Dartmouth.

16 "Daughter of Poet Sings Tribal Songs," *South Bend News-Times*, March 21, 1914, 1.

17 Hamlin Garland, *My Friendly Contemporaries: A Literary Log* (New York, NY: MacMillan, 1932), 59.

18 Michelle Wick Patterson, "'Real' Indian Songs: The Society of American Indians and the Use of Native American Culture as a Means of Reform," *American Indian Quarterly* 26 (1), 2002, 44.

19 EGE, May 13, 1912, Smith.

20 Wilson, *Ohiyesa*, 100.

21 Ernest Thompson Seton to William Howard Taft, October 18, 1912, Seton Memorial Library, National Scouting Museum-Philmont Scout Ranch, Cimarron, NM.

22 Abigail Van Slyck, *A Manufactured Wilderness: Summer Camps and the Shaping of American Youth, 1890–1960* (Minneapolis, MN: University of Minnesota Press, 2006), 170.

23 Deloria, *Playing Indian*, 106.

24 Kiara Vigil, "Charles Eastman's 'School of the Woods': Re-creation Related to Childhood, Race, Gender, and Nation at Camp Oahe," *American Quarterly* 70 (1), 2018, 35.

25 Miyuki Jimura-Yamamoto, "Truly Indian . . . Truly American. Native American Activism and Identity at the Turn of the Twentieth Century" (PhD diss., Doshisha University, 2015), 34.

26 Livia Gershon, "Summer Camp Has Always Been about Escaping Modern Life," *JSTOR Daily*, April 26, 2016.

27 Vigil, "Charles Eastman's 'School of the Woods,'" 32.

28 "Boy Scouts Open Season at Camp Archibald Butt," *Washington Evening Star*, June 30, 1914, 11.

29 Jeanette Atwood, "America's Only Indian Camp for Pale-Face Girls," n.d., Smith.

30 "School of the Woods," 1915, promotional brochure, Special Collections, Forbes Library, Northampton, MA.

31 "Training American Girls in Indian Woodcraft," *New York Sun*, June 13, 1915, 40.

32 Sargent's Handbooks, *A Handbook of American Private Schools* (Boston, MA: Porter Sargent, 1920), 419.

33 U.S. Department of Education, *120 Years of American Education: A Statistical Portrait* (Washington, DC: Center for Educational Statistics, 1993).

34 "Training American Girls as Indians: Dr. Eastman, College-Bred Brave, to Teach Pretty Palefaces from Big Cities Primitive Ways in New Hampshire Nook," *Boston Sunday Post*, June 20, 1915.

35 Vigil, "Charles Eastman's 'School of the Woods,'" 45.

36 Ibid., 30.

37 Penelope Myrtle Kelsey, "A 'Real Indian' to the Boy Scouts: Charles Eastman as a Resistance Writer," *Western American Literature* 38 (1), Spring 2003, 37.

38 Camp Oáhe brochure, 1915, Jones.

39 EGE to RGD, June 3, 1945, Smith.

40 Evan Andrews, "Why Was It Called the "Spanish Flu?," *History*, January 12, 2016. www.history.com; CDC, "History of the 1918 Flu Pandemic," CDC, www.cdc.gov. See John M. Barry, *The Great Influenza: The Story of the Deadliest Pandemic in History* (New York, NY: Penguin, 2005), and Alfred W. Crosby, *America's Forgotten Pandemic: The Influenza of 1918* (New York, NY: Cambridge University Press, 2003) for information on the pandemic.

41 John Clayton, "The Epidemic of Death: 1918 Spanish Flu in Manchester," *New Hampshire Union Leader*, March 15, 2020, www.unionleader.com/.

42 Prucha, *The Great Father*, vol. 2, 855.

43 John Clayton, "The Epidemic of Death: 1918 Spanish Flu in Manchester," *New Hampshire Union Leader*, March 14, 2020.

44 Lois Corcoran, "Great Influenza Epidemic Swept through Keene a Century Ago," *Keene Sentinel*, September 10, 2018.

45 Sargent, *Life*, 104.

46 EGE to DRG, January 16, 1931, Smith.

47 "Obituary of Irene Taluta Eastman," *New York Times*, October 25, 1918; "Obituary of Irene Taluta Eastman," *Musical America*, November 9, 1918, 55.

48 *American Indian Magazine* 6 (3), 1918, 151–152.

49 HM to Mother, Dad and Katharine, August 15, 1918, Wisconsin.

50 HM to Sophie, Stephen and Katharine Martindale, August 12, 1918; August 15, 1918; and August 30, 1918, Wisconsin; HM to Sophie and Stephen Martindale, August 15, 1918; ibid.

51 HM to Mr. and Mrs. Stephen Martindale, November 9, 1918, Western Union Telegram, ibid.

52 Ibid.

53 EGE to Redington Dayton, April 4, 1919, Smith.

54 Miller, "Journey," 266.

55 Julie Dobrow and Raymond Wilson, "Good Night, Irene: The 1918 Influenza Pandemic and Irene Taluta Eastman," *South Dakota History* 52 (1), 2022.

56 HM to KM, 21 October 1921, Wisconsin.

57 See Theodore D. Sargent and Raymond Wilson, "The Estrangement of Charles Eastman and Elaine Goodale Eastman," *South Dakota History* 40 (3), Fall 2020.

58 EGE to RGD, ca. 1932, Smith; ibid., ca. February 9, 1938; Sargent, *Life*, 110.

59 EGE to RGD, ca. 1932, Smith; HM to KM, July 10, 1921, Wisconsin.

60 Sargent and Wilson, "The Estrangement of Charles Eastman," 239.
61 Paul Wilson to KM, March 12, 1939, Wisconsin.
62 Ibid.; EGE to KM, January 8, 1926, ibid.
63 Sargent and Wilson, "The Estrangement of Charles Eastman," 233; Eick, *They Met*, 235; HM to KM, December 13, 1923, Wisconsin; Sargent, *Life*, 112; EGE to KM, March 2, 1939, Wisconsin.
64 EGE to RGD, November 3, 1933, Smith; ibid, circa 1938.
65 Ibid. June 24, n.y.

10. FROM DETROIT TO LAKE HURON (1921–1939)

1 CAE, *Indian Heroes and Great Chieftains* (Boston, MA: Little, Brown, 1918), 1.
2 Miller, "Journey," 269; Wilson, *Ohiyesa*, 165; Eick, *They Met*, 236.
3 For a detailed discussion of this issue, see Hazel Herzberg, *The Search for an American Indian Identity* (Syracuse, NY: University of Syracuse Press, 1971).
4 "Citizenship for Indians," *Wilkes-Barre Record*, January 27, 1919, 15.
5 Zitkála Sá, "Editorial Comment: Hope in the Returned Indian Soldier, an Indian Citizenship Campaign," *American Indian Magazine*, 1919.
6 "Charges Indians Fleeced," *The Tomahawk*, May 29, 1919, 1.
7 *The Red Man*, July 1899, Carlisle.
8 Wilson, *Ohiyesa*, 162; EGE to RGE, circa 1936, Smith.
9 Maddox, "Politics, Performance and Identity," (2002), 32.
10 Raymond Wilson, "Forty Years to Judgment," *Minnesota History*, Fall 1981, 291.
11 Wilson, *Ohiyesa*, 176.
12 CAE, "Report," *Annals of Wyoming* 13, March 2, 1925 (reprinted July 1941), 194.
13 Ibid., 179; Miller, "Journey," 312.
14 CAE to Grace Hebard, October 21, 1925, Wyoming; ibid., March 2, 1925.
15 Grace Hebard to CAE, July 14, 1926, Wyoming.
16 Grace Hebard to CAE, September 7, 1927, and May 14, 1928, Wyoming; CAE to Grace Hebard, May 17, 1929, ibid.
17 CAE, "Sacajawea, Her Lost 70 Years," New Bedford *Standard Times*, April 3, 1949.
18 CAE, *Deep Woods*, 172.
19 "American Indian Chief Lectures in England: Dr. Charles Alexander Eastman Goes to Address English School Children," *The Collegian*, University of Richmond, February 3, 1928.
20 Clara Smith to Edward Ayer, April 8, 1925, Newberry.
21 CAE to H. M. Hitchcock, September 8, 1927, Newberry.
22 Vigil, *Indigenous Intellectuals*, 81.
23 "Ohiyesa the Conqueror," *Liverpool Courier*, February 21, 1928; "The Red Indian," *Irish Times*, February 27, 1928; "Visit of a Sioux Chief," *Bristol Times*, March 14, 1928; "Visit of Indian Chief to Llanfechain," *Llanfechain Counties Advertizer*, April 11, 1928.
24 Miller, "Journey," 319.
25 EGE to RGD, July 16, 1933, Smith; ibid., January 1940.

26 EGE to RGD, February 3, 1937, Smith.
27 While the Minnesota Historical Society has remarks of some of the other speakers from this event, it does not have any record of Charles Eastman's.
28 "Who Is the Greatest Indian of Today?," *Birmingham Reporter*, September 2, 1933, 2.
29 Rosalyn R. LaPier and David R. M. Beck, *City Indian: Native American Activism in Chicago, 1893–1934* (Lincoln, NE: University of Nebraska Press, 2015), 144.
30 Janusz Mucha, "From Prairie to the City: Transformation of Chicago's American Indian Community," *Urban Anthropology* 12 (3/4), Winter 1983, 345.
31 Wilson, *Ohiyesa*, 191.
32 EGE to RGD, February 3, c. 1937, Smith.
33 CAE to H. M. Hitchcock, January 14, 1935, Newberry.
34 Miller, "Journey," 324.
35 Ibid., 328.
36 EGE to RGD, 1939, Smith.
37 *Winnipeg Tribune*, January 10, 1939, 3; *Detroit News*, January 9, 1939; *Amherst Record*, January 11, 1939; *Keene Sentinel*, January 9, 1939; *Detroit Free Press*, January 10, 1939, 19.

11. FROM NORTHAMPTON TO SPRING GROVE (1921–1953)

1 EGE to RGD, October 2, 1929, Smith.
2 For a fuller discussion about Henrietta Martindale and Bonna Hyessa, see Sargent and Wilson, "The Estrangement of Charles Eastman."
3 EGE to RGD, circa 1919, Smith.
4 Elaine Goodale Eastman, *Hundred Maples* (Brattleboro, VT: Stephen Daye Press, 1935). 200.
5 Ibid., 204–222.
6 Sargent, *Life*, 114.
7 Ruth Ann Alexander, "Elaine Goodale Eastman and the Failure of the Feminist Protestant Ethic," (1988), 90.
8 EGE to RGD, November 3, 1933, Smith.
9 EGE to KM, January 8, 1926, Wisconsin.
10 Ibid., February 21, 1926.
11 Ibid., late 1920s.
12 EGE to RGD, November 22, circa 1933, Smith; Ibid., n.d.
13 Elaine modeled this character on Prudence Crandall, an abolitionist who ran a school for Black girls in 1833 Connecticut, faced retaliation, but continued to fight for integrated education and women's suffrage.
14 EGE, "Reward of Merit," *The Classmate*, October 14, 1933, C41–44.
15 EGE to the Bookfellows, December 25, 1936, Special Collections and Archives, Henry M. Seymour Library, Knox College, Galesburg, IL.
16 Sarah Ruffing Robbins, "Elaine Goodale Eastman Modernist Author?," 1.
17 "Review of *The Luck of Oldacres*," *Reading Times*, November 15, 1928, 12.

18 EGE to RGD, October 15, 1942, Smith.

19 Eick, *They Met*, 265, 274.

20 "Review of *Pratt, The Red Man's Moses*," *Honolulu Advertiser*, December 8, 1935, 2; *Hartford Daily Courant*, March 8, 1936; *Kansas City Times*, March 23, 1936.

21 Matilda Barker to EGE, May 11, 1936, Smith.

22 EGE to RGD, circa 1939, ibid. Elaine was referring to Ruth Odell's biography of Jackson, published in March 1939.

23 For more information on Collier, see Kenneth R. Philp, *John Collier's Crusade for Indian Reform* (Tucson, AZ: University of Arizona Press, 1977).

24 Frederick E. Hoxie, "The Goals of the Indian Reorganization Act," Testimony before the Committee on Indian Affairs, U.S. Senate, first session, June 23, 2011, 11.

25 Ibid., 20.

26 E. A. Schwartz, "Red Atlantis Revisited: Community and Culture in the Writings of John Collier," *American Indian Quarterly* 18 (4), Autumn 1994, 524.

27 EGE to RGD, April 15, 1933, Smith.

28 EGE to Florence Bascom, May 26, 1934, Florence Bascom papers, SSC-MS 00012, Smith.

29 EGE, "Collier Indian Plan Held Backward Step," *New York Times*, June 3, 1934, E5.

30 John D. Collier, "Our Indian Policy Has Definite Aims," *New York Times*, June 10, 1934, E5.

31 EGE, "Does Uncle Sam Foster Paganism?," *Christian Century*, August 8, 1934, 1017.

32 John Collier, "A Reply to Mrs. Eastman," ibid, 1019.

33 Gertrude Bonnin to EGE, March 8, 1935, Smith.

34 John Collier, "Indians Come Alive!," *Atlantic Monthly*, September 1942, 75–81.

35 Mrs. Charles A. Eastman, "Response to Indians Come Alive," *Atlantic Monthly*, November 1942, 165–168.

36 John Collier, "John Collier Replies," *Atlantic Monthly*, January 1943.

37 EGE, "Movies and Crime," Scrapbook, May 11, 1933, Smith.

38 EGE, "Community Responsibility for Motion Pictures," *Junior Home*, 1933.

39 EGE to RGD, July 16, 1933, Smith.

40 EGE to RGD, June 24, no year, ibid.

41 Ibid., September 7, 1939.

42 Camp Oáhe brochure, 1924, Historical Society of Cheshire County Archives, Keene, NH.

43 EGE to RGD, November 3, 1920; February 26, 1936; November 13, 1940; Smith.

44 Ibid., February 3, 1937.

45 Ibid., October 8, 1940.

46 EGE to Florence Bascom, March 10, 1940, Florence Bascom Papers, Smith.

47 EGE to RGD, June 3, 1945, Smith.

48 EGE to DRG, December 26, 1930, ibid.; EGE to RGD, January 2, 1931; August 11, 1931; ibid.

49 EGE to RGD, circa 1937, ibid.

50 Marion Nutting to RGD, December 22, 1954, ibid.

51 EGE to RGD, February 9, 1940, ibid.

52 EGE to George Seymour, March 8, 1940, Special Collections and Archives, Henry M. Seymour Library, Knox College, Galesburg, IL.
53 EGE, *Voice*, 121–122.
54 Sargent, *Life*.
55 EGE to RGD, June 21, late 1920s, Smith; n.d., Smith.
56 EGE to RGD, May 31, 1938, ibid.; Robert Chester Goodale to EGE, October 9, 1947,ibid.
57 EGE to RGD, November 15, 1927; November 10, 1927; ibid.
58 EGE to DRG, February 26, 1931; March 29, 1930; ibid; DRG to RGD, n.d., ibid.
59 EGE to RGD, November 10, 1927; November 22, 1927; December 1, 1927; March 4, n.y.; ibid.
60 Ibid., April 10, 1927; October 8, 1940.
61 Ibid., May 31, 1938; November 6, 1945.
62 Ibid., April 15, 1940.
63 Ibid., March 14, n.y.
64 Ibid., November 24, 1945.
65 EGE, "The Hand-Made House," *Country Life in America*, October 13, 1912, 33.
66 EGE, "The Old Cellar Hole," *Washington Post*, 1943.
67 EGE to RGD, June 15, 1940, Smith.

12. READING THE EASTMANS

1 Marion W. Copeland, *Charles Alexander Eastman (Ohiyesa)* (Boise, ID: Boise State University Western Writers Series, No. 33, 1978), 38.
2 Wilson, *Ohiyesa*, 189, 192.
3 Miller, "Journey," 322.
4 Deloria, *Playing Indian*, 123; Deloria, conversation with author, July 2021.
5 Vigil, *Indigenous Intellectuals*, 84.
6 Lisa Tatonetti, "Disrupting a Story of Loss," 290.
7 Lopenzina, "Good Indian," 740.
8 Miller, "Journey," 334.
9 Wilson, *Ohiyesa*, 185.
10 Lopenzina, "Good Indian," 727.
11 Schmitz, *White Robe*, 110.
12 Powell, "Imagining a New Indian," 220.
13 See, for example, Christina Chung, "Harvard Museum Will Return Hundreds of Native American Hair Samples," *New York Times*, November 10, 2022.
14 Vigil, *Indigenous Intellectuals*, 50.
15 Ibid., 51.
16 Frederick E. Hoxie, "Exploring a Cultural Borderland: Native American Journeys of Discovery in the Early Twentieth Century," *Journal of American History* 79 (3), December 1992, 977.

17 Miyuki Jimura-Yamamoto, "Truly Indian . . . Truly American. Native American Activism and Identity at the Turn of the Twentieth Century." (PhD diss., Doshisha University, 2015), 20.
18 Dykema-VanderArk, "Playing Indian in Print," 27.
19 Powell, "Imagining a New Indian," 225.
20 Martinez, *Philosopher,* xv.
21 Pexa, "More than Talking Animals," 102.
22 Wilson, *Ohiyesa,* 191.
23 Carol Lea Clark, "Charles A. Eastman (Ohiyesa) and Elaine Goodale Eastman: A Cross-Cultural Collaboration," *Tulsa Studies in Women's Literature* 13 (2), 1994, 272.
24 Alexander, "Finding Oneself through a Cause," 1992, 37.
25 Ruth Ann Alexander, "Elaine Goodale Eastman and the Failure of the Feminist Protestant Ethic," *Great Plains Quarterly,* 1988, 93; Schmitz, *White Robe,* 101.
26 Kate Beane and Gail Johnsen, "This Is Our Truth" and "A Journey through Time and Family," in CAE, *In the Beginning, The Sun,* 187, 7.
27 Schmitz, *White Robe,* 101.
28 Viehmann, "Cultural Divide," 62.
29 Ruth J. Heflin, "Examples for the World: Four Transitional Sioux Writers and the Sioux Literary Renaissance" (PhD diss., Oklahoma State University, 1997), 66.
30 Kiara Vigil, "From Ohiyesa's 'Deep Woods' to the 'Civilization' of Charles: Critiquing and Articulating Native American Manhood in Eastman's Autobiography" (MA thesis, Dartmouth College, 2006), 122; Erik Peterson, "An Indian, an American: Ethnicity, Assimilation and Balance in Charles Eastman's *From the Deep Woods to Civilization.,* *Studies in American Indian Literatures* , 4 (2), Summer/Fall 1992, 153; Pexa, "More than Talking Animals," 665.
31 EGE to Harold G. Rugg, April 19, 1939, Smith.
32 EGE to RGD, c. 1936, ibid.
33 Berg, "White Women Writing for their Lives," 5.
34 "Only a Teacher," Episode 3: "Educating to End Inequality." Films for the Humanities and Sciences, PBS, 2000.
35 See, for example, "Biden Apologizes for U.S. Abuse of Indian Children, Calling it 'a Sin on Our Soul'," *New York Times,* October 25, 2024.
36 Ibid.
37 Berg, "White Women Writing for their Lives," 82.
38 Schmitz, *White Robe,* 104.
39 EGE, *Voice,* 62–64, 58–59.
40 Ibid., 30.
41 Ibid., 96–97.
42 EGE to RGD, November 6, 1945, Smith.
43 EGE, *Voice,* 32.
44 Ruffing Robbins, "Elaine Goodale Eastman Modernist Author?"
45 Schmitz, *White Robe,* 99.

46 EGE, *Voice*, 25.
47 Sherry Smith, *Reimagining Indians* (New York, NY: Oxford University Press, 2000).
48 Viehmann, "Cultural Divide," 69.
49 American Psychiatric Association, "What Is Post-Traumatic Stress Disorder?," https://www.psychiatry.org/patients-families/ptsd/what-is-ptsd.
50 Viehmann, "Cultural Divide," 58.
51 Lopenzina, "Good Indian," 750.
52 EGE, *Voice*, 29.
53 Treuer, *Heartbreak*, 15.
54 Jerome A. Greene, *American Carnage: Wounded Knee, 1890* (Norman, OK: University of Oklahoma Press 2014), xii–xiv.

AFTERWORD

1 Sherry Smith, *Hippies, Indians and the Fight for Red Power* (New York, NY: Oxford University Press, 2014), 184.
2 Ostler, *Plains Indians*, 9.

INDEX

Page numbers in italics indicate images.

ABOUT THE AUTHOR

Julie Dobrow is Distinguished Senior Lecturer in the Department of Child Study and Human Development, and on the faculties of the Film and Media Studies Program and the Tisch College of Civic Life at Tufts University. She serves as director of the Center for Interdisciplinary Studies, and is co-Principal Investigator of the Half of History Project, which uses short-form biography, film and podcast to tell the untold and under-told stories of women's lives. Her previous biography, *After Emily: Two Remarkable Women and the Legacy of America's Greatest Poet*, was long-listed for a Penn/Bograd biography prize and finalist for the Plutarch and New England Society Book Award. Her writing has appeared in the *Boston Globe Magazine* and the *Huffington Post*, among other venues. She lives outside of Boston.